Economic History of Puerto Rico

Economic History of Puerto Rico:

Institutional Change and Capitalist Development

JAMES L. DIETZ

Princeton University Press

Princeton, New Jersey

Copyright © 1986 by Princeton University Press
Published by Princeton University Press, 41 William Street,
Princeton, New Jersey 08540
In the United Kingdom: Princeton University Press,
Guildford, Surrey

All Rights Reserved
Library of Congress Cataloging in Publication Data will be
found on the last printed page of this book

ISBN 0-691-07716-9 (cloth)
      0-691-02248-8 (pbk.)

Publication of this book has been aided by a grant from
the Whitney Darrow Fund of Princeton University Press

This book has been composed in Linotron Times Roman

Clothbound editions of Princeton University Press books are
printed on acid-free paper, and binding materials are chosen
for strength and durability. Paperbacks, although satisfactory
for personal collections, are not usually suitable for library
rebinding

Printed in the United States of America
by Princeton University Press
Princeton, New Jersey

Para Jaimito

*que un día conocerá bien
la historia de la tierra
de su mamá*

Contents

Illustrations

All photos by Jack Delano, except as noted.

Figures

Tables

Preface

The writing of this book has been a long journey, not just in time but in what I have learned. Though trained as a mathematical economist, I was fortunate to have studied with E. Kay Hunt, now at the University of Utah, who deepened my understanding of heterodox economics from the Ricardians and Sraffa, to Veblen and the American institutionalists, to Marx. His courses were always very special, and the demands on his time were intense, but for those of us fortunate enough to have shared those heady and intellectually exciting days in Riverside from 1969 to 1972, the lasting influence of Kay's probing intellect is evident in our efforts to emulate him.

Still, the jump from mathematical economics to the political economic history of Puerto Rico was not easy. Beginning with a paper prepared for the Latin American Studies Association meetings at Houston in 1977, which compared the modern development experience of Puerto Rico and Jamaica, I have read volumes and volumes of history—and not just Puerto Rican history, but histories of Latin America in general—to form the necessary background. My admiration for the work of Puerto Rican historians, old and new, is nearly unbounded. Without either the traditional histories of authors like Lidio Cruz Monclova or of the "new" historians like Francisco Scarano, Angel Quintero Rivera, Laird Bergad, Fernando Picó, and others, the writing of this book would have suffered immensely and immeasurably. Most of this historical work has focused on the nineteenth century; much remains to be done on twentieth-century themes. Though no author is likely to be totally satisfied with what I have written, I hope that those whose research I have drawn upon so heavily will feel pleased with the use I have made of their work.

The modest purpose of this book is to contribute to the rewriting and reinterpretation of Puerto Rico's political economic history. There are, in fact, no scholarly works that cover the entire period analyzed here, nor are there any that give the attention to the fundamental thread of economic forces underlying the process of economic and social transformation in Puerto Rico that is the focus of this book. Its goal is to uncover and explain the thrust of economic and social evolution that makes the island's history an unfolding, connected, and comprehensible ensemble of processes, rather than just discrete events. This history can be under-

stood only by examining Puerto Rico's role within the developing capitalist world and market economy that emerged in the seventeenth century
and left its imprint nearly everywhere on the globe. It is this imprint
which gives to this book its organizing focus.

   To those who read the following pages: I hope you will gain a fuller
understanding of the complexity of Puerto Rico's economic development
since the eighteenth century and, if you do not already have it, a deep
and wondrous appreciation of what Puerto Rico is.

Acknowledgments

Many people have made the task of writing this book if not easier at least more pleasant. John and Marcia (Pousie) Hellman helped me on a number of trips to Puerto Rico. They found me places to live, put me up in their home, and shared with me their understanding of the island in conversations over many dinners and during trips that crisscrossed Puerto Rico. I not only enjoyed their company; I needed it. Their boys, Christopher and Keith, made the long distance from home and family more tolerable.

The staff at the Colección Puertorriqueña of the library at the University of Puerto Rico processed many requests for materials, some more than once. This collection is an unsurpassed reference source, and I have fond, even sentimental, memories of many weeks spent there. Closer to home, Karen Swindell, acquisitions librarian at California State University, Fullerton, efficiently worked to obtain all the materials on Puerto Rico that I found in catalogs and other sources; her efforts not only helped me but have also greatly strengthened the library's Caribbean collection.

Many people read the manuscript or parts of it in various stages. For their comments and feedback I thank Laird Bergad, Pedro Cabán, Alberto Fournier, Ivan Gutiérrez, María Merrill-Ramírez, Sidney Mintz, Emilio Pantojas-García, Plácido Rodríguez, Victor Rodríguez, Lydia Vélez, and David Wong. I was fortunate to have been associated for more than a decade as an editor with *Latin American Perspectives*. To all of the internal collective at that journal, including some no longer with it, I owe a great debt of gratitude for the experience I had, the knowledge I gained, and the friendships I made. Without the influence of the journal, I doubt if this book would now exist.

There are others who have always had an interest in my work and were constantly encouraging me: Teresa Myrwang, who grew up in Puerto Rico and longs to return; and Paula Tuchman and Beto Darszón, who helped me spend a productive month writing in Mexico City in 1980. Princeton University Press editor Sandy Thatcher has earned my special thanks for his gentle prodding and his ample understanding of what it is to write a book; I found him to be an ideal editor. Thanks, too, to Sue Domínguez and Heather McGuigan, who put most of the first draft on a word processor, where it was reworked many times.

I am especially pleased to be able to thank Jack Delano for making available to me the photos included on the dust jacket and in the body of the book. Since his arrival in Puerto Rico in 1941 under the auspices of the Farm Security Administration, Mr. Delano has been one of the island's most important chroniclers of daily life, and his photos are elegant testimonies to the changes and contrasts in Puerto Rico's modern history.

To Robert A. Feldmesser, I owe a debt impossible to repay. Bob performed the too-often-thankless task of editing the manuscript. He saved me from embarrassing errors, needless wordiness, unnecessary repetition, and rhetorical flourishes. I am deeply grateful for his efforts, and I exonerate him from responsibility for any weaknesses which remain, while hoping he will share in any accolades the book may receive.

It is impossible to know Puerto Rico just from reading. Some of my deepest understanding has come from people who probably have never realized how much they helped me. I can never adequately thank them for enriching my perspective. Francisco (Paco) Valpais worked in the building where I lived. He spent many hours sharing his unpretentious views, took me as a friend to Llorréns Torres, a housing project avoided by most, and taught me the pleasures of Don Q. In Quebradillas, Antonio Vélez, Gregoria Román, Hermes Vélez, Anacely Ayra, Aníbal Vélez, Celida Rodríguez, all part of my extended family, have deepened my feel for Puerto Rico and its past beyond anything I might have imagined. Don Antonio and Doña Gregoria have lived through the modern transformations described in this book, and conversations with them, often when they did not suspect I was investigating their past, have helped me immensely.

I wish to acknowledge the financial assistance of California State University, Fullerton, for a sabbatical leave in 1981, spent in Puerto Rico, and to the Department of Economics and the School of Business Administration and Economics for typing, photocopying, and other expenses as well as for generous released time which permitted me to complete my research.

My parents, James Senior and Edna, and my sisters, Debbie and Melissa, always have given me support and have shown interest and pride in my work, even when it was not always clear what I was doing or why I had to do it so far away from them. I hope they can share in the pleasure I feel in having completed this book.

The most important support I have had has been the constant encouragement of my wife and friend, Lydia Vélez. She always believed in me and helped me, but never did she let me forget my other responsibilities. She has given me the balance necessary for a sane existence. For too many hours away from home, and late nights, I hope she, my son, Jaimito, to whom the book is dedicated, and Ilia Rolón, my stepdaughter, will be able to look back and say, "Well, I guess it was worth it."

Abbreviations and Spanish Terms

AAA	Agricultural Adjustment Act
Administración de Fomento Económico	Economic Development Administration
AID	Aid to Industrial Development
agregado	squatter on privately owned land
arrendatario	renter
arrimado	same as agregado
bacalao	dried codfish
Cédula de Gracias	Decree of Pardon (1815)
CENEP	Centro de Estudios Puertorriqueños
central	sugar-processing complex, including mill and land
CEREP	Centro de Estudios de la Realidad Puertorriqueña
CGT	Confederación General de Trabajadores
colmado	small store
colono	independent sugar producer
Confederación General de Trabajadores	General Confederation of Workers
Cortes	Spanish parliament
criollo	Spaniard born in Puerto Rico or other colonial area
cuerda	measure of land area (= .9712 acre)
cupón	food stamp
esclavo	slave

Estado Libre Asociado	Free Associated State (official designation of Puerto Rico in Spanish)
Federación Libre de Trabajadores	Free Federation of Workers
FERA	Federal Emergency Relief Administration
finca	farm
finca de beneficio proporcional	proportional-profit (profit-sharing) farm
FLT	Federación Libre de Trabajadores
GDB	Government Development Bank
hacendado	landowner
independentista	supporter of independence
ingenio	small, technologically rudimentary mill for grinding sugar cane
jornalero	laborer paid by the hour or day
liberto	freed slave
libreta	workbook required of jornaleros (1849–1873)
mayordomo	overseer
medianero	sharecropper
municipio	municipality
Operación Manos a la Obra	Operation Bootstrap
parcela	small plot of land
Partido Nacionalista	Nationalist party
Partido Nuevo Progresista	New Progressive party
Partido Popular Democrático	Popular Democratic party

peninsular	derogatory term for Spaniard (19th century)
PN	Partido Nacionalista
PNP	Partido Nuevo Progresista
PPD	Partido Popular Democrático
PRERA	Puerto Rico Emergency Relief Administration
PRIDCO	Puerto Rico Industrial Development Company
Programa de Asistencia Nutricional	Nutritional Assistance Program
PRPB	Puerto Rico Planning Board
PRPC	Puerto Rico Policy Commission, or Chardón Commission
PRRA	Puerto Rico Reconstruction Administration
público	privately owned car licensed to operate on a regular route
quintal	measure of weight (= 100 lbs.)
real	unit of currency (= .125 pesos)
riles	hacienda or merchant chit used to pay workers
situado	subsidy from Mexico to colonial government of Puerto Rico
tenducho	small store
tienda	store
trapiche	rudimentary sugar-grinding machine
vales	same as riles

Economic History of Puerto Rico

I

The Period of Spanish Colonialism

INTRODUCTION

Before the island that is now called Puerto Rico was "discovered" by Christopher Columbus on Tuesday, November 19, 1493, during his second voyage, it was already inhabited by Taino Indians, who, having themselves previously discovered the island, called it Boriquén.[1] As was his duty, Columbus claimed the island for the Spanish empire, renaming it San Juan Bautista de Puerto Rico. Neither Spain nor the adventuresome Spanish conquistadors showed much interest in this new acquisition, however, which was but one among many and not particularly promising of easy wealth by comparison with the others. The Spanish crown tried to initiate colonization in 1505 by granting to a Spaniard Vicente Yáñez Pinzón, the right to oversee the settlement of the island, but this grant was never fulfilled.[2] Only in August 1508, nearly fifteen years after Columbus had touched shore, did Juan Ponce de León and a group of fifty men arrive from Santo Domingo to colonize the island and begin the search for gold that so frenetically drove the Spanish westward.[3] Thus began a period, which has now lasted nearly half a millennium, in which Puerto Rico has been the colonial possession of one metropolitan empire or another: initially the Spanish and, since 1898, the United States.

Foreign influence in Puerto Rico has been pervasive (although so has the resistance to it, even when the struggle has been passive and hence, to many, seemingly absent). Foreign domination and colonial control have given direction to Puerto Rico's socioeconomic development, have largely

---

[1] In the Taino language, Boriquén meant "Land of the Proud Lord." It is common today to hear "Boríquen," "boricua," and "borinqueño" used to refer to the island or its inhabitants, reflecting the residual influence of the indigenous culture, as do many place and food names.

[2] *Boletín Histórico de Puerto Rico* 1:214–21 (hereafter cited as *BHPR*). Yáñez had been captain of the *Niña* on the first voyage of Columbus.

[3] The number of persons given as accompanying Ponce de León is the figure he himself reported: Brau, *La colonización*, p. 97, n. 31. Ponce de León became governor in 1509. In an unexplained reversal of names in the sixteenth century, the island became known as Puerto Rico, while the main port took the former name of the island, San Juan.

delimited its possibilities, and have conditioned and evoked the responses to it. The history Puerto Ricans have made is thus not solely of their own choosing; the colonial experience has shaped the boundaries of action and has contributed to the "rules of the game," and always and ominously the colonial power has been ready to back up its material interests with force to defend them. As Marx has written:

> Men make their own history, but they do not make it just as they please; they do not make it under circumstances chosen by themselves, but under circumstances directly encountered, given and transmitted from the past. The tradition of all the dead generations weighs like a nightmare on the brain of the living.[4]

Nevertheless, the metropolitan ruling class, its power mediated through the colonial apparatus, has never been so omnipotent that the colonial relationship could be said to have been the determinant factor in Puerto Rico's development. The effects of external domination are abundantly apparent and cannot be ignored, but it is not necessary to elevate this domination to a level of theoretical priority. It is equally imperative to take account of the productive structure and its functioning, the social relations, and the nature of the social and class struggle *within* the island's social formation. These internal forces have been affected by colonial dominance, of course, but they also have reciprocally and complexly had an essential impact on the colonizers' influence and policies and are equally important to an understanding of the overall development of the socioeconomic system. It is this double expression of dominance and resistance, the external and the internal, that will occupy our attention.

It also needs to be said at the outset, though it should be axiomatic, that foreign dominance has been neither entirely deleterious nor wholly beneficial in its effects on Puerto Rico. Colonial control has had contradictory impacts, and the burden of any complete analysis must be to assess both sides of such domination. This study identifies the results, both positive and negative, of foreign domination on Puerto Rico's development while also considering the internal evolution of classes and class fractions that have emerged alongside the economic, political, judicial, ideological, and cultural structures of society, and often in opposition to them.

COLONIAL PUERTO RICO FROM 1508 TO 1800

Spain's early interest in Puerto Rico was spurred primarily by the lust for gold, a mercantilist obsession that Spain retained long after that doc-

[4]Marx, *Eighteenth Brumaire*, p. 15.

Map:
Municipalities in Puerto Rico (modern)

◉ Places of 100,000 or More Inhabitants

• Places of 50,000 to 100,000 Inhabitants

○ Places of 25,000 to 50,000 Inhabitants Outside SMSA's

trine had become discredited in the rest of Europe. Puerto Rico did have gold, but only in relatively small amounts that could be easily mined, and these were depleted rapidly (by the mid-1530s, according to most accounts).[5] Native labor was used in the mines, including many so-called Caribs captured on neighboring islands, brought to Puerto Rico, enslaved, and branded with hot irons (the *carimbo*) to distinguish them from indigenous Tainos already granted to Spaniards via *repartimientos* (distributions) and *encomiendas* (royal grants), as in the rest of the New World.[6] All slave laborers, whether indigenous or imported, were forced to work the mines and tend herds, as well as to produce crops for their own consumption. This native population, however, was soon decimated by illness, overwork, maltreatment, suicide, and the slaughters that followed Indian rebellions (the first in 1510, giving rise to the legend of Urayoán) against the better-armed Spanish. Others, perhaps as many as a third of the native peoples, fled to nearby islands or the mountainous interior of Puerto Rico itself, where they founded settlements the Spaniards did not easily find.[7] And many indigenous people intermarried with the Spanish, leading to the common, but erroneous, assumption that the native population had disappeared almost totally, when what actually had transpired was a complex process of social and cultural assimilation.

When the placer deposits of gold had been exhausted, and as native labor became increasingly difficult to find, Spain, and especially the Spanish colonizers who were interested in getting rich quickly and with the least effort, began to lose interest in Puerto Rico. Not even the importation of African slaves in the second half of the sixteenth century to supplement and eventually replace native labor did much to stimulate the growth of the colonial economy. Many Spanish left Puerto Rico in search of the greater and more easily obtained riches promised in South America (especially Peru) and New Spain (Mexico), and "Dios me lleve al Perú"

[5] Brau estimated that between 1509 and 1537 some three million pesos of gold were extracted: "Las clases jornaleras," p. 16. Cayetano Coll y Toste suggested that the figure was closer to four million: "La propriedad territorial de Puerto Rico," *BHPR* 1:241. The total value of gold *and* silver extracted from all of Latin America between 1503 and 1660 has been estimated to have been more than 500 million pesos. Puerto Rico's contribution was thus small, though hardly insignificant, compared to the riches of other colonies, like Peru and Mexico: Hamilton, *American Treasure*.

[6] Slavery was made legal in the colonies in 1501 by an order of the Spanish crown, and the use of slave labor (Indian, African, and in some cases white) became increasingly important. Two black slaves, perhaps the first, were brought to San Juan in 1510: *BHPR* 8:277 and 2:89–92 (for the royal *cédula*, or warrant, permitting Indian slaves in 1511), and Fernández Méndez, *Historia cultural*, pp. 78–79, 108–9.

[7] Fernández Méndez, *Historia cultural*, chaps. 4 and 7, and Moscoso, "Chiefdom and Encomienda." For a more impressionistic perspective, see Steiner, *The Islands*, chaps. 1 and 3.

(May God bring me to Peru) was on the lips of many others who wished to leave. The declining attractiveness of the island as a source of wealth and hence as a colonial settlement resulted in a substantial population exodus beginning in the 1530s, an outflow of such magnitude that at one point the colonial governor invoked stringent measures—including death by hanging—in an attempt to slow the movement; to show his determination, he cut off the feet of two Spaniards who did try to flee.[8] Nevertheless, the population remained virtually constant well into the late eighteenth century. In 1530, total population, according to a census by the governor, was 3,040 (369 whites, 1,148 Indians, and 1,523 black slaves). In 1556, the "city" of San Juan had only 130 *vecinos* (residents) and San Germán but 20. Population had increased to just 3,600 by the close of the sixteenth century, according to a royal census. By 1776, it had reached 80,246, but that represented a growth rate of only about 1.3 percent per year over nearly two and one-half centuries, hardly a dynamic rate of expansion.[9]

Spain's interest in Puerto Rico after the gold had been extracted and exported was primarily tactical and military. The crown did grant loans in 1546 and again in 1552 for the construction of sugar mills, the output of which was to be exported to Spain, but in the main, Puerto Rico, like Cuba, was more important as a strategic location for protecting ships en route to and from Mexico and Central and South America and for guarding the entrance of the Caribbean Sea from incursions by filibusters, privateers, and European-financed invaders. Control of Puerto Rico and Cuba gave Spain an important commercial and military edge over the other European powers through the domination of the sea lanes to the New World. In recognition of this, French ships attacked Puerto Rico numerous times, beginning in 1528 and continuing to the end of the century; they sometimes succeeded in penetrating the island's defenses, but they failed to achieve dominion.[10] The repeated attacks by the French contributed to the decision to begin construction, in 1539, on the imposing El Morro fortress, overlooking the mouth of San Juan Harbor, a type of defense common in the insular Caribbean and one which was to hold firm

[8] Morales Carrión, *Puerto Rico and the Non-Hispanic Caribbean*, p. 7, and Fernández Méndez, *Historia cultural*, p. 115. Brau tells of one "energetic governor" who whipped some and cut open the soles of the feet of others who tried to flee: *Historia*, pp. 55–56.

[9] Silén, *Historia*, pp. 55, 57, and Brau, "Las clases jornaleras," p. 18. If the figure of 44,883 reported for 1765 (see text, below) is correct, then the rate of population growth from 1530 to 1765 was a little more than 1.1 percent per year and from 1765 to 1776 was about 5.4 percent per year (compound rates), showing that, as will be commented on later, the rate of growth accelerated rapidly in the last third of the eighteenth century.

[10] *BHPR* 11:63–71, includes a fine essay by the historian Cayetano Coll y Toste, the founder and editor of *BHPR*, on French invaders.

against later attempts. There was little doubt that the country that controlled Puerto Rico was in a better position to protect the goods sent to, and produced in, the colonies and to extract a surplus from them, wealth which contributed to the growth of the new bourgeoisie in the metropolitan countries and to Western Europe's rapid economic development.

Other efforts to capture the island were made: Francis Drake's failed British expedition of 1595; the Count of Cumberland's more successful British invasion by land in 1598, in which the city of San Juan was held for nearly three months; an attack by the Dutch in 1625, in which part of the city again was occupied for nearly thirty days and then the most important buildings were burned as the troops fled. This last occupation led to the construction, financed by revenues from the state tobacco monopoly, of the massive wall with its guard towers that still surrounds much of the city of Old San Juan.[11] There were to be later attacks, too, but none (until the U.S. invasion in 1898) was able to reap the ultimate prize: control of the island and easier access to the sea route to the colonies of the New World.[12] Puerto Rico was exceedingly important to protecting the Spanish empire, and she served well.

During their long rule, the Spanish introduced plants and animals not indigenous to the island: ginger, sugar cane (in 1515), coffee, bananas, date and coconut palms, rice, and other grains, nuts, and seeds, and cows, horses, pigs, chickens, and other animals.[13] During the seventeenth century and the early part of the eighteenth, cattle-raising for the export of hides was a key agricultural pursuit, and many black slaves tended the herds and prepared the skins for sale. In 1620, an estimated 100,000 head of cattle were being raised for their meat and hides for export.[14] For some time, ginger was a leading, perhaps the most important, export crop (though Spanish policy essentially made the ginger trade illegal). It was so important that the production and export of sugar, which were being officially promoted by Spain, went into a precipitous decline between the late sixteenth and the early seventeenth centuries, at least partly due to the lack of transport to Spain. The colonial government ultimately took steps, mostly unsuccessful, to try to revitalize sugar production by ordering the end of ginger plantings.[15] In 1564, sugar output

[11] Ortiz, *Eighteenth-Century Reforms*, p. 48.

[12] Fernández Méndez, *Historia cultural*, pp. 139–41, and Golding, *Short History*, chaps. 4–7.

[13] Silén, *Historia*, p. 73; López, "Beginnings of Colonization," p. 17; and *BHPR* 1:256–57.

[14] By comparison, during the 1800s, the average number of cattle was between 4,000 and 6,000: Gómez Acevedo, *Organización y reglamentación*, p. 460.

[15] *BHPR* 1:245.

had been 250 tons; in 1582, with 11 *ingenios* (small sugar grinders) in operation, output had fallen to 188 tons; and by 1602, it was but 38 tons, as land formerly devoted to sugar cane was turned over to ginger cultivation. By 1647, the number of ingenios had declined to seven. Besides sugar, coffee, oranges, hardwood (*guayacán*), cotton, and of course hides also were exported, often as contraband.[16]

Puerto Rico, like all of Spain's colonies, was restricted to trading exclusively first with Seville (until 1715) and then with Cádiz, using Spanish ships and merchants, though a series of decrees between 1776 and 1804 permitted temporary trade with friendly countries during wars, and more Spanish ports were opened to Caribbean trade in 1765.[17] However, there was substantial, and often officially tolerated, illegal trade with other nations and, increasingly, with North America, transacted through Ponce, Fajardo, Humacao, and other Puerto Rican ports distant from the colonial seat of government and the one official port in San Juan. In 1804, these other ports were opened to legal trade (except Humacao, which was not opened until 1815), as were Cabo Rojo, Mayagüez, and Aguadilla, in the hope of capturing the trade revenues that were being lost to contraband.[18] Exports were determined to a great extent by the demand of the contraband trade as well as by the products Spain desired and was prepared to buy, primarily sugar and, to a lesser extent, tobacco, but even for the production of these commodities, Spain never attempted to turn the island, or any of its colonies, into the kind of agricultural-export, plantation-type economy characteristic of the British West Indies. This absence of attention to production highlights a fundamental failing, commented on in detail below, which permeated the economy of Spain itself and was reflected in its policies toward its colonial possessions. In any case, despite unauthorized trade with the English, North Americans, French, Dutch, and others, and the legal commerce with Spain, the Puerto Rican economy cannot be said to have been particularly dynamic before the late

---

[16] Smith and Requa, *Puerto Rico Sugar Facts*, p. 115, table I. The first small ingenio was introduced in 1510 and the first substantial mill sometime after 1523 in what is now Añasco: Brau, *Ensayos*, pp. 279, 225–27, 280, 282–84, and *BHPR* 1:87, 163, 243–44.

[17] *BHPR* 1:163; Cruz Monclova, *Historia* 1:12; and Ortiz, *Eighteenth-Century Reforms*, p. 91.

[18] The actual opening of Ponce's port did not take place until 1812 because of delays in setting up a customs house: Sanchez Tarniella, *La economía*, p. 51; López, "Beginnings of Colonization," p. 37; and *BHPR* 1:169. The same ports were closed to legal trade again in 1839 and were not reopened until 1848, though contraband trade continued: Cruz Monclova, *Historia* 1:285. Brau, *Ensayos*, pp. 284–85, suggests that Spain's leaders feared the free flow of liberal ideas as much as, if not more than, the free flow of goods, but this policy, so characteristic of Spain's mercantilist mentality, was a reflection, at root, of the backwardness of the Spanish socioeconomic structure in all its dimensions.

1700s. Small-scale, self-sufficient, peasant-type production predominated, and what hacienda production there was remained on an extremely
small scale by Caribbean or any other standards. Spain's policy toward
Puerto Rico until the late eighteenth century can best be described as one
of neglect born of its own internal economic backwardness and incomplete productive structure.

The first three centuries of Spanish rule thus resulted in slow, uneven
growth and in minimal progress for the great majority of the inhabitants
of the island. This is not to imply that there were no important transformations. The colonization process itself and the forces of change which
accompanied it were anything but insignificant: the indigenous population
was reduced, dispersed, or assimilated, and the beginnings of a new nation and people definitely took root. Yet Alejandro O'Reilly, a special
envoy of the Spanish King, discovered on his inspection tour in 1765 that
the overall situation in Puerto Rico had only slightly improved and perhaps even had deteriorated by that date. His *"Memoria"* or official report
declared the people of Puerto Rico to be ''the poorest that there are in
America''; for example, there were no roads after more than 250 years
of Spanish rule.[19] Sugar production had increased to only 137 tons by
1776, hardly more than half the level of production attained more than
two centuries before. O'Reilly also reported that smuggling and contraband trade had been of greater importance to the island's development—
its value has been estimated at some ten times that of legal trade in the
eighteenth century[20]—than were official trade relations with Spain, a surprise, perhaps, to the Spanish, though likely not to the island's export
traders. Agricultural production utilized backward methods and production was low, due primarily, O'Reilly believed, to the small population
of 44,883, many of whom were military deserters, criminals, and soldiers
without knowledge of agriculture, and which also included 5,037 slaves.[21]
Nor had the Spanish colonial administrators who had succeeded in buying
their positions in Puerto Rico been of particularly high caliber, a reflection of the island's low priority as a colonial post.

[19] *BHPR* 8:115 (the complete text of O'Reilly's "Memoria" of June 20, 1765, and others
of his documents can be found in ibid., pp. 108–24), and López, "Beginnings of Colonization," p. 34.

[20] Morales Carrión, *Puerto Rico and the Non-Hispanic Caribbean*, p. 84. Morales Carrión also comments: "In the course of time, contraband was generalized until it developed
into a kind of free trade, forbidden by law but sanctioned by the pressure of daily needs":
ibid., p. 70. Spain's relative indifference to Puerto Rico during this early period is amply
illustrated by the fact that, as one governor complained, for a period of eleven years before
1660 not one officially registered Spanish ship arrived at an island port: Brau, *Ensayos*, pp.
228, 285–86, and *BHPR* 1:245, 258.

[21] "Memoria" of O'Reilly, *BHPR* 8:108–9, and Flinter, *Account of the Present State*,
chap. 1.

The extent of the island's poverty is shown by the dependence of the colonial government on the *situado*, a subsidy from Mexico begun in 1582, for the bulk of the funds to carry out its official functions, particularly the building of fortifications and the payment of official, including church, salaries. Colonial administrators were unable to raise sufficient revenues in the form of land taxes, head taxes on slaves, a sales tax (2 percent), the state's share of tithes, and trade revenues to pay all of its expenses. For example, in 1789, while government revenues were 186,391 pesos, the situado amounted to 384,260 pesos; in 1790, revenues rose to 215,967 pesos but the situado also rose, to 642,817 pesos; in 1794, the comparable figures were 518,344 pesos of income and 299,979 pesos from the situado.[22]

Complicating matters, the situado did not always arrive as needed or scheduled, and this meant that colonial employees, including the military, often went for months without pay. Such delays contributed to periodic economic downturns, as the money supply available for exchange shrunk and export and import trade suffered. During some of the periods when the situado was delayed, paper notes were issued, redeemable when the situado arrived, to compensate for the empty treasury.[23]

Besides making recommendations on how to fortify the island militarily, including the construction of the fortification of San Cristóbal in San Juan, O'Reilly's "Memoria" made suggestions for improving economic conditions and expanding the colony's wealth by liberalizing trade relations and improving internal communication and transportation. He suggested that population could be increased by granting incentives to white Catholic immigrants, particularly those with agricultural skills and capital. He especially urged expansion of sugar cultivation, including a proposal for royal financing to build a sugar mill as one means to give agriculture a much-needed push.[24]

O'Reilly's sobering report and other observations on the problems in Puerto Rico were taken seriously by the crown. Military strength and the morale of soldiers—who often were even without uniforms—was improved. As well, measures were taken which contributed to a spectacular growth of population, which was reported to stand at 155,426 in 1800 (see below). If this figure can be accepted as accurate, it means that population increased more rapidly in both absolute and percentage terms between 1765 and 1800 than in the previous two and one-half centuries. Puerto Rico thus began in the late eighteenth century to become something more than just a military outpost and a neglected way station be-

[22] Cuba also received a similar subsidy: *BHPR* 1:163, 2:239, 5:301; and Cruz Monclova, *Historia* 1:15.

[23] Ortiz, *Eighteenth-Century Reforms*, pp. 54–55, 159.

[24] Morales Carrión, *Puerto Rico and the Non-Hispanic Caribbean*, p. 87.

tween Spain and the rest of its colonies in the Americas, and this transition continued at a quickened pace throughout the nineteenth century. In Sánchez Tarniella's classification, Puerto Rico left its period of "colonial economy in the strict sense" and entered "the beginnings of a national economy."[25] Immigration increased, population grew, and the foundation of a thriving sugar industry was laid.

The Decline of the Spanish Empire

Although production increased during the last third of the eighteenth century and throughout the nineteenth century, living conditions were to improve only slightly if at all, for most Puerto Ricans. The bulk of the population—perhaps as much as 90 percent—remained illiterate. Colonial control over the dissemination of information, and thus ideological control over the population, remained very strong. Almost all written materials, including newspapers, came from outside Puerto Rico until well into the nineteenth century. There was no printing press on the island until 1806, and it was used at first to print only official and, later, commercial information.[26] Sugar output, however, began to grow in the early decades of the century, quickly becoming the most important export cash crop, as Spain moved to further liberalize its trade policies to permit local producers and merchants to seek, now legally and openly, customers other than those in Spain. It was primarily the United States, because of its proximity, purchasing power, and growing economy, which gained most from such reforms. By the end of the nineteenth century, the United States was one of Puerto Rico's largest trading partners, importing rum, tobacco, sugar, and molasses and supplying wheat and manufactured goods, though imports from the United States were of considerably less importance to the island's economy than were its exports to the United States.[27]

The nineteenth century witnessed the end of the long reign of the Span-

---

[25] Sánchez Tarniella, *La economía*, p. 37.

[26] The first newspaper/periodical was *La gaceta*, which began publishing in 1806 and was the official publication of the government. The *Diario económico de Puerto Rico*, published from 1814 to early 1815, was the second periodical. It published articles on business; information on taxes collected, prices, and foreign trade; and, under the editorship of Intendente Alejandro Ramírez, a series of articles on classical political economy and the advantages of international trade. The *Diario económico* might be likened to an early-day *Wall Street Journal*.

[27] By 1830, nearly half (49 percent) of Puerto Rico's exports (by value) were bought by the U.S. and 6.8 percent by Spain, while 27.2 percent of the imports came from the U.S. and 12.1 percent from Spain; the West Indies, including other Spanish colonies, supplied 53.5 percent of Puerto Rican imports and brought 25.7 percent of exports: Steward et al., *People of Puerto Rico*, p. 52.

ish empire in the Americas; by midcentury, Spain was no longer a leading world power. Spain deteriorated economically and militarily and lagged
further and further behind the rest of Europe, primarily because it had
had no bourgeois, capitalist revolution like those that had shaken England, France, and Germany and that had created the essential political
base for the industrial revolutions in those countries. Spain's decline as
an empire was virtually inevitable.[28] A backward, predominately feudal
economic order with a stifling state monopoly of trade, such as Spain
had, was sooner or later destined to be surpassed by the emerging, expansionary, more dynamic and productive capitalist nations of Western
Europe and the United States.[29] To make matters worse, the scramble for
control of Spain's wealthy colonies—their resources, labor, internal markets, and strategic locations—provoked costly wars with England and
France during the early 1800s and then with the United States, fatally for
the Spanish empire, in 1898.

The wars with England and France, fought in Europe and on the seas,
had direct and almost immediate repercussions in Spain's colonies. With
Spain literally fighting for survival as an entity on the continent, Madrid's
control over its colonies relaxed, of necessity, during this period. Less
direct colonial control provided the latitude the creole elite in the colonies
required to begin the transformations that would extend its power and
control beyond the economic sphere and into the political superstructure.[30] The creole elites in Latin America and, to a lesser extent, the
Caribbean had gained a measure of economic power via their control over
the productive structures, but political power resided in the colonial apparatus dominated by Spaniards, many of whom were appointed, served,

[28] For an overview of the historical process of the bourgeois revolutions, see Hobsbawm,
Age of Revolution. For an engaging historical picture of the progressively weakened Spanish
empire in another corner of the Caribbean (Trinidad), see Naipaul, *The Loss of El Dorado.*
An interesting though brief consideration of Spanish backwardness can be found in Fernández Méndez, *Desarrollo histórico.*

[29] Even much of Spain's earlier dominance had been illusory. In the sixteenth and seventeenth centuries, perhaps two-thirds of the silver destined for Spain had to be turned over
to foreigners to pay debts incurred by the importation of manufactured products: Elliott,
Imperial Spain, p. 174.

[30] Creoles (*criollos*) were persons of Spanish descent born in the colony, i.e., the gener-
ations deriving from settlers, the military, and so on. The creole elites were relatively
privileged groups, just below Spaniards in the hierarchy, and were involved in key economic activities as professionals, landowners, and sometimes members of the bureaucracy.
Their position depended, to an extent, on their relation with dominant Spain. On the other
hand, creoles were blocked from political control in their own countries; they were often
denied commercial contracts which, since they were granted by the Spanish crown, tended
to favor Spaniards. In effect, their aspirations were thwarted by the control that Spain
exercised while at the same time their favorable position derived from Spanish dominance.

and then left their posts, usually much wealthier, to return to Europe. This lack of political power resulted in restrictions on the creole-dominated economic structure which frustrated the expanding economic and political aspirations of the local elites. What emerged was an open, festering colonial contradiction, a conflict between a foreign superstructure of laws and administration imposed on an emerging and developing national economic base. Ultimately, the creoles were to rebel at Spain's vulnerable back door in the Americas at the same time that Spain was attempting to defend its front door in Europe. Throughout Latin America, the colonies took advantage of the relative autonomy they had gained vis-à-vis Spain. National revolutions spread as demands for and actions directed toward attaining greater local control turned into full-blown independence movements, with the active participation and backing of creoles, who hoped to enlarge their economic powers, to be able to engage in less restricted trade, and to govern in their own interests.[31]

The Wars of Independence which spread throughout Latin America were economic and political revolutions directed against Spain in the interests of creole elites, who formed the social base from which would emerge an embryonic national, agrarian bourgeoisie.[32] From Mexico in the north to Chile in the south, successful independence movements and revolutions unseated Spanish colonial governments, drove the Spanish army out, and split the Spanish empire. Weakened by challenges on the European continent, Spain was not able to resist the tide pressing for economic and political liberation which swept over the New World. By the mid-1820s, only Cuba and Puerto Rico, where revolutions did not take place, remained as colonies of the Spanish empire in the Americas; all the others—Chile, Ecuador, Peru, Mexico, Argentina, Paraguay, Uruguay, Venezuela, Colombia, Bolivia, and the nations of Central America—had achieved formal political independence, although fragmented into nation-states that mirrored the divided colonial viceroyalties they had struggled against.

The fact that there was no independence movement in Puerto Rico did not mean that the national independence movements and revolutions elsewhere in Latin America had no impact on the island. On the contrary, their effects reverberated throughout the society. Puerto Rico became a haven for Spanish loyalists fleeing the rebellious colonies, as well as a location to which Spanish soldiers who had been defeated in battle were reassigned in an effort to fortify one of the last remaining Spanish possessions against the possibility of revolt and from which they embarked to strike against the armies of Bolívar on the mainland. Spanish loyalists

---

[31] See Stein and Stein, *Colonial Heritage*, pp. 106–19.
[32] Cueva, *El desarrollo del capitalismo*.

brought with them not only exaggerated tales of terror and carnage but all-too-true reports of the decline of Spanish fortunes that accompanied the revolutions in the New World. This sounded a warning signal for the colonial government in Puerto Rico that it could neither ignore the activities of its creole reformers nor permit them to go on unfettered. Rather, it was necessary to meet the demands for greater participation head-on, with force if necessary, lest this island, too, became embroiled in revolution.

It was thus precisely those most opposed to independence for the colonies, those most uncompromising in their views on economic liberalism, democracy, and abolition of slavery and on an expanded role for the local elite, and those most subservient to Spain and most willing to defend Spanish claims to dominance who found their way to Puerto Rico during and after the Latin American revolutions.[33] The impact of this influx of immigrants is not difficult to imagine. Often forced to escape with only their lives, these privileged refugees brought an extremely conservative impetus to island political life as they actively sought to thwart not only revolutionary change but also legitimate and needed reforms. Emigration of the most reactionary sectors of the Spanish elite, the colonial administration, and the routed military from the other colonies of the Americas to Puerto Rico exerted an extremely pro-Spanish, anti-independence, and anti-autonomy force within the island, with long-lasting effects. The absence of a comparable independence movement in Puerto Rico during the period when the other colonies were openly taking up arms against Spain was at least partly the result of the intransigently conservative influence of the Spanish and other refugees.[34]

There is no doubt that Puerto Rico's creole elite suffered from contradictions and pressures similar to those suffered by the creole elites in the other American colonies. It was restricted by the same economic sanctions mandated by Spain curtailing its economic activity and preventing it from controlling its own economic and political life, particularly in the development of new trade partners, expansion of certain types of production, and adoption of new means of production. Puerto Rico briefly tasted some of the fruits of greater autonomy and expanded rights when the Cádiz constitution of 1812 was extended to the colonies, only to have

[33] The slave rebellion led by Toussaint l'Ouverture in St. Domingue (Haiti), and which resulted in 1804 in the first black republic in the Caribbean, had contributed to the immigration of many French planters into Puerto Rico; they were just as conservative a force as the Spanish loyalists were to be soon after.

[34] Lewis, *Puerto Rico*, p. 49. González, *El país de cuatro pisos*, pp. 13–18, argues that the material base for such an independence movement did not exist at that time in Puerto Rico, anyway, so that regardless of the conservative influence of the immigrants, an independence movement was not objectively possible.

this taken away in 1814 with the return of the absolutist government in Spain. The constitution was applied again in 1820, and then revoked once more in 1823 upon the restoration of the Spanish monarchy (and applied again only briefly in 1836–37). Rescission of Puerto Rico's provincial status and Spanish citizenship and other constitutional rights, once they had been granted, was not accepted by the elites with great enthusiasm. Tension within the creole elite and between this elite and new Spanish immigrants intensified and began to be manifested as an increasing national identity and pride and a growing nationalist sentiment. Still, in spite of comparable forces at work in Puerto Rico, a widespread and popular movement for independence did not emerge, though separatist activity, particularly in the western end of the island, caused the colonial governors grave concern.[35]

CHANGES IN THE ECONOMIC STRUCTURE

The nineteenth century was a period of relative economic and social progress, certainly by comparison with the nearly three hundred years of colonial rule which preceded it. Population increased more than sixfold, reaching nearly one million by the time of the U. S. occupation in 1898. Though Spain attempted to block the development of manufacturing and to slow industrialization—for example, by forbidding the importation of industrial machinery and by placing restrictions on banking and credit— the manufacturing stage of sugar, rum, and cigar production, as well as other small, mostly home, production, nonetheless made advances, albeit on a small scale. Spain's lingering allegiance to a mercantilist policy which equated a nation's wealth with a positive trade balance, resulted in measures designed to prevent its colonies from producing manufactured goods for their own consumption, since that might have reduced their need for imports. Instead, manufactured goods continued to be transshipped to the colonies from Western Europe through Spanish ports, while agricultural products flowed back the other way, all in the mistaken belief that this trade was the source of and key to Spanish progress, wealth, and dominance. The capitalist revolutions in Europe, and Spain's own lack of development amidst its material wealth, surely demonstrated that a nation's prosperity derived from production, not simply from trade. But Spain did not make the transition to expanded capitalist production and probably could not have made it, given the easy source of wealth which flowed to it from its colonies. As a consequence, primitive agricultural production remained the basis of Puerto Rico's economy, as technologi-

[35]Cruz Monclova, *Historia* 1:120–2, 126, and 178–82, for example, though the theme of separatism and the Spanish response is constant throughout the six volumes of this work.

cal development and manufacturing were blocked from above and from without by Spain's own lack of progress and its failure to fully enter the capitalist age.

The island's economic structure had evolved only slowly during the latter part of the eighteenth century. In 1775, there were 5,581 *fincas* or *estancias* (farms) of all sizes (only 87 were classified as large), producing sugar cane, coffee, cotton, bananas, plantains, rice, and corn. Sugar, coffee, tobacco, and manioc were important cash crops. There were 234 *hatos* (ranches), on which cattle were raised (there were more than 77,000 head), as were pigs and other animals for export—a continuing source of concern to Spain, since other crops were neglected and overall agricultural growth lagged as a result.[36] Plantains, sweet potatoes, other vegetables, sugar, bananas, beans, rice, and manioc also were produced for domestic consumption. In 1783, agricultural production included 137 tons of sugar, more than 1,000 tons of rice, 111,875 pounds of cotton, 1,550,600 pounds of corn, 563 tons of coffee, and 701,775 pounds of tobacco. Plantains, a basic subsistence crop, were planted on 8,315 *cuerdas*.[37]

In the nineteenth century, however, a number of dramatic changes took place. In 1812, coffee and sugar, the two important export crops, were produced in amounts of roughly equal value (512,261 pesos for coffee and 508,375 for sugar). In that year, 838 tons of sugar were produced on 5,765 cuerdas and 3,905 tons of coffee on 9,493 cuerdas, representing substantial growth in both outputs over 1783. In 1817, production of sugar reached 2,340 tons and that of coffee, 2,423 tons, on fewer cuerdas in both cases.[38] After the 1820s and until midcentury, growth was concentrated in sugar production (including rum and molasses, made as by-products of sugar processing), cattle-raising and hides, and, to a lesser extent, tobacco, though subsistence crops remained as important as export crops in terms of cultivated area.[39] In 1830, well over half of all cultivated land was still planted in subsistence crops like starchy vegetables (*viandas*), rice, plantains, and corn. Export agriculture, however, had begun an unmistakably rapid expansion. By 1830, the number of cuerdas devoted to sugar cane had increased to 11,103 (a 93 percent increase over 1812) and production of sugar had risen to 14,126 tons (or

[36] Fernández Méndez, *Desarrollo histórico*, p. 31; Ortiz, *Eighteenth-Century Reforms*, pp. 177–78, 185; and *BHPR* 1:252.

[37] "Memoria" of Dario de Ormaechea, *BHPR* 2:229. A *cuerda* is slightly less than one acre.

[38] Bergad, *Coffee and the Growth of Agrarian Capitalism*, p. 16; and Scarano, "Azúcar y esclavitud," p. 15, table 1.

[39] The number of cuerdas devoted to rice (15,290) was about the same as that used for sugar cane (15,242) and only slightly less than the amount of land in coffee production (17,247 cuerdas): Perloff, *Puerto Rico's Economic Future*, p. 14.

TABLE 1.1
Value of Puerto Rican Foreign Trade, 1814 to 1883
(in pesos)

	Exports	Imports	Total	Per Capita Value
1814	—	—	484,684	2.65
1819	1,098,083	1,131,594	2,229,677	—
1824	1,114,438	1,290,837	2,405,275	9.19
1834	4,682,785	3,209,381	7,891,166	21.99
1844	6,204,704	5,257,288	11,461,992	28.65
1854	—	—	10,598,698	21.54
1865	5,959,392	8,359,860	14,319,252	20[a]
1874	6,882,790	12,931,568	19,814,358	31[b]
1878	13,070,020	14,787,873	27,857,893	
1880	8,572,545	14,054,024	22,626,569	}28[c]
1883	11,807,720	13,785,843	25,593,563	

SOURCE: *BHPR* 2:229–33, 4:215–16, and 5:299–300.
[a] Average for the decade of the 1860s.
[b] Average for the decade of the 1870s.
[c] Average for the decade of the 1880s.

282,521 quintals, an increase of more than 1,500 percent over 1812 and more than 500 percent over 1817). Coffee production was 131,372 quintales or 6,569 tons.[40] Table 1.1 shows the subsequent growth in the value of exports as a whole and table 1.2 the growth in exports of the leading crops.

It can be seen in table 1.1 that until about the middle of the century, exports were equal to or greater than imports; on the whole, that is, there was a positive trade balance. In the second half of the century, however, imports grew more rapidly than exports, and trade deficits appeared. To some extent, the growth in imports resulted from the need for more food imports, as will be discussed later. But imports also increased because of rising demand for manufactured inputs, particularly capital goods. The total value of trade more or less kept pace with population growth during the last two-thirds of the century.[41]

Table 1.2 shows how exports of coffee and sugar responded to world market and internal forces (tobacco exports fluctuated around 43,000 quintals throughout the period). Exports of sugar grew rapidly in the early decades of the century, then leveled off, but showed another spurt of growth between the mid-1860s and the mid-1870s. The expansion of

[40] Scarano, "Azúcar y esclavitud," p. 15, table 1.
[41] See also V. Clark et al., *Porto Rico and Its Future*, p. 605.

TABLE 1.2
Volume of Exports of the Three Leading Crops, 1828–32 to 1879–83

	Sugar		Coffee		Tobacco	
Period	Volume of Exports[a]	Percent Change	Volume of Exports[a]	Percent Change	Volume of Exports[a]	Percent Change
1828–32	291,892	—	125,176	—	33,634	—
1833–37	415,144	+42.2	97,802	−21.9	43,646	+29.8
1838–42	793,283	+91.1	104,687	+ 7.0	46,070	+ 5.6
1843–47	874,046	+10.2	101,188	− 3.3	55,071	+19.5
1848–52	1,052,437	+20.4	106,990	+ 5.7	40,210	−30.0
1853–57	1,046,446	− 0.6	116,381	+ 8.8	35,268	−12.3
1858–62	1,075,680	+ 2.8	129,801	+11.5	50,656	+43.6
1866–70	1,383,251	+28.6	186,723	+43.9	34,632	−31.6
1874–78	1,510,767	+ 9.2	195,307	+ 4.6	46,949	+35.6
1879–83	1,570,667	+ 4.0	331,244	+69.6	44,553	− 5.1

SOURCES: Koenig, *Comprehensive Agricultural Program*, p. 28, table 8, and *BHPR* 5:300. See Brau, *Ensayos*, p. 291, for yearly figures on sugar, molasses, and rum. Cotton was also an important export crop in the first half of the nineteenth century.

NOTE: 1 quintal = 100 lbs.

[a] Annual average, in quintals.

coffee exports began in the middle 1850s and accelerated into the early 1880s, by which time the coffee economy of the interior overtook the sugar economy of the coast and became the most dynamic sector. Sugar exports, however, remained at their previously attained level even as coffee exports expanded. This indicates the responsiveness of sugar producers to lower world market prices, and it will be commented on further below.

Between 1814 and 1854, foreign trade increased nearly 2,100 percent in total value, and from 1854 to 1883, another 141 percent. These figures strongly suggest that external trade was a much more visible part of the economic process by midcentury than it had been at the beginning. Without corresponding data on total national production, however, it cannot firmly be asserted that this expansion of trade indicated a stronger external orientation for the economy. However, table 1.3 provides evidence that during the nineteenth century an increasing proportion of cultivated land area was being devoted to export crops and, hence, that the economic structure was moving toward an external orientation. Whereas more than 70 percent of cultivated land had been devoted to subsistence crops in 1830, less than half was so utilized in 1862 and only about a third by 1899. Given that imports grew throughout this period—including, and

TABLE 1.3

Proportion of Land Devoted to Sugar, Coffee, and All Export
Crops, 1830, 1862,
and 1899

	Percentage of Cultivated Land Devoted to:		
	Sugar	Coffee	All Export Crops
1830	12.4	14.0	28.9
1862	30.2	18.5	51.3
1899	17.8	48.9	68.4

SOURCES: Bergad, "Agrarian History," p. 63, and Perloff, *Puerto Rico's Economic Future*, p. 83. For other years, see Quintero Rivera, "Background to the Emergence of Imperialist Capitalism," p. 94.

importantly, basic foods like rice and flour, which accounted for 40 percent of the value of all imports near the end of the Spanish regime—this seems sufficient to demonstrate a developing level of dependence of the economy on trade and foreign markets and a shift away from the subsistence economy characteristic of the period prior to 1830.[42]

Some significant advances in production technique were taking place in the sugar industry already in the early decades of the nineteenth century and production was becoming more efficient either in the field or, more likely, at the processing stage in the mills.[43] However, the expansion of sugar production and exports became more difficult after midcentury as sugar prices on the world market continued to decline, prime

[42] The main agricultural imports at this time were rice, flour, and pork products; agricultural products constituted 95 percent of exports: Perloff, *Puerto Rico's Economic Future*, pp. 15, 18. Not only were imports of food important, but the bulk of government receipts—from 60 to 75 percent—was obtained from taxes on basic food imports, which obviously fell most heavily on the mass of poor consumers who were forced to buy an increasing proportion of their food needs. Díaz Hernández, *Castañer*, p. 15, explains how the extension of coffee production not only reduced the amount of land devoted to rice, beans, sweet potatoes, and other subsistence crops, but also forced the former producers of these crops to buy goods in the hacienda store, a source of further enrichment to the owner's family and a process that occurred everywhere on the island.

[43] Scarano, "Sugar and Slavery," chap. 2, includes a description of the improvements made by some of the larger hacienda owners in Ponce, and most were in the mills. Scarano also includes cost and tentative income data based on hacienda accounting books. "Rates of return to capital" increased with production size, varying from 7.8 percent for the smallest units to 26.5 percent for the largest (producing 601 to 700 tons of sugar annually), and output per worker also was positively related to hacienda size: ibid., p. 177, table 3.4. The largest Ponce haciendas, though of smaller scale than the Cuban plantations, were more productive than any of the largest of the latter in 1860: ibid., p. 182.

sugar land became more difficult and costly to obtain, and the supply of slaves decreased and their cost rose. The growth in land use, output, and exports in sugar during the second quarter of the nineteenth century indicates that the steps taken by the metropolitan government to improve economic conditions in Puerto Rico had been successful either in themselves or in unleashing latent productive forces within the island economy. It is worth considering these initiatives made by Spain in somewhat more detail.

The recommendation to initiate policies to increase population growth, which O'Reilly had made in 1765, was implemented in more than one decree. Restrictions against the immigration of foreign capitalists and skilled laborers were eased. By a royal decree of January 14, 1778, following years of demands by landowners, Spain granted the right to own land privately (with the obligation of tax payments ranging from 0.75 to 1.25 reals per cuerda). Until then, land had been "owned" by the crown and held in use without title.[44] The creation of the right to private property was a fundamental change, though the application of the decree was not uniform or rapid. It provided a measure of security for landholders and creditors and facilitated the consolidation of large estates. The creation of property rights also would provide a legal basis for the dispossession of those who could not show title to the land upon which they lived and worked, and the granting of legal title became increasingly important in the nineteenth century. However, even with the creation of private property in land, at the end of the eighteenth century most land remained under the control of the crown.[45]

In August 1815, another stimulative measure, the famous *Cédula de Gracias* (roughly, Decree of Pardon), was promulgated. This act was designed to promote population growth by encouraging immigration (although Spaniards fleeing the Wars of Independence, especially from Venezuela, would have come, anyway). It provided for about six acres of land to be granted to every free, white immigrant and an additional three acres for each slave. Free black immigrants were to receive the same allotment as slaves.[46] Immigrants attracted by these land grants—from

---

[44] *BHPR* 1:164, 13:60–63 (for the royal decree), and 14:104–8; Scarano, "Sugar and Slavery," pp. 58–59; and Bergad, *Coffee and the Growth of Agrarian Capitalism*, p. 7. Land grants and quasi-titles actually predated this regulation (from 1754), but land tenure remained a thorny issue and a basis for conflict between the colonial administration and hacendados throughout the eighteenth century: Ortiz, *Eighteenth-Century Reforms*, pp. 69–70, 76–78.

[45] Villar Roces, *Puerto Rico y su reforma agraria*, p. 27, and Steward et al., *People of Puerto Rico*, p. 47.

[46] Each white settler, male or female, was to receive 4 2/7 *fanegas*, and blacks were to receive one half that amount (a fanega is approximately 1.5 acres): Cruz Monclova, *Historia* 1:79.

Spain, France, other parts of Europe, the West Indies, and the United States[47]—brought with them not only slaves and other means of production; they came laden with the ideas, experiences, skills, and emphasis on production and profits of the capitalist revolutions sweeping Europe and North America. In this way, through the infusion of a new ideology, the Cédula de Gracias contributed to an expansion of the economy far beyond the simple number of immigrants who took advantage of the land grants. The cédula also contained other measures designed to encourage greater economic activity: It provided for unrestricted trade between Puerto Rico and Spain for fifteen years and set reduced tariffs of 2 percent on goods traded between Puerto Rico and other Spanish colonies and 6 percent on trade with friendly nations carried in Spanish ships (tariffs were higher on goods carried in foreign ships).[48] In a major break with colonial restrictions of the past, agricultural equipment imported from Spain was permitted to enter the island without being subjected to tariffs, a factor that very likely contributed to improvements in sugar productivity.[49] The impact of these liberalizing measures on exports after 1815 is quite clear from the figures in table 1.1.

The Cédula de Gracias also exempted new colonists from taxes for ten years, though this was reduced to five by the local administration. Significantly, foreigners (that is, all non-Spanish immigrants) were prohibited from engaging in trade or commerce for a period of five years, a provision which enhanced the ability of Spanish immigrants and residents to accumulate capital outside of and/or in conjunction with their agricultural pursuits. Other limitations and further local colonial tampering with the cédula's provisions, however, probably weakened this as well as other effects.[50]

[47] Between the proclamation of the Cédula de Gracias and May 21, 1816, 324 foreign Catholics and 83 persons from Louisiana with their slaves arrived: Brau, "Las clases jornaleras," p. 24.

[48] *BHPR* 1:299–302, and Cruz Monclova, *Historia* 1:81. Free trade put an end to much of the raison d'être for smuggling, while permitting the collection of taxes on more goods by the colonial administration.

[49] Sánchez Tarniella, *La economía*, pp. 55–56. It has also been argued that the measures of the Cédula de Gracias were designed to forestall revolution by opening the economy to the benefit of landowners, thus reducing their dissatisfaction with colonial restrictions: Cruz Monclova, *Historia* 1:246; Silén, *Historia*, pp. 83–84; and Figueroa, *Breve historia* 2:42.

[50] Cruz Monclova, *Historia* 1:84, and Scarano, "Sugar and Slavery," pp. 59–61, 227–29. Scarano's position is that it was not the cédula, especially in its somewhat diluted state, but the international sugar market's need for new production as the result of the loss of Haiti's output and of the growth in demand in the U.S., and the connection between St. Thomas merchants and Puerto Rican growers, which were fundamental, in stimulating production and exports. Many of the local alterations in the application of the cédula were made at the recommendation of the liberal intendente (similar to the secretary of the treasury

One consequence of the Cédula de Gracias and of land grants in general, whether to new immigrants or to privileged creoles, was that many small peasant producers found that the land they had worked now belonged to someone else by decree. They thus often found themselves burdened with labor or rent obligations owed to a landowner, a fundamental transformation which was speeded up during the first half of the nineteenth century.

The necessity of making Puerto Rico into a more lucrative and more nearly self-financing colony became especially pressing for Spain in the early nineteenth century. As a result of the Wars of Independence, the Mexican situado ended in 1810, and Puerto Rico's colonial administration was forced to try to finance its own expenditures by taxing production, trade, land, slaves, and the people. In 1812, it resorted to printing paper money, Puerto Rico's first domestically produced money supply. The value of this currency rapidly declined, however, to a level where ten paper pesos were equal to only one silver peso, because of a general uncertainty about the use of paper money, and so it began to be removed from circulation in 1815.[51]

The importance of the Cédula de Gracias in increasing the productive wealth of the economy is undeniable, though it is not the entire, and perhaps not even the primary, explanation for the expansion that followed its promulgation.[52] Another institutional and legal mechanism that was propitious for the expansion of commercial operations was the Spanish *Código de Comercio* (Code of Commerce) of 1829, which was extended to Puerto Rico in February of 1832 and remained in effect until superseded by new legislation in 1885. This enactment continued the prohibition on foreigners engaging in commerce within Puerto Rico. It also clarified the legal status of different categories of business organization: the *regular colectiva*, the equivalent of an individual proprietorship or partnership; the *sociedad en comandita*, a limited-liability form of commercial organization similar to a family-run corporation; and the *sociedad anónima*, another limited-liability unit operated not by its owners but by hired ad-

---

today) Alejandro Ramírez, who had taken this post on February 13, 1813. Ramírez also founded and edited the *Diario económico de Puerto Rico*, in which many of the more progressive economic ideas he held were shared with the literate community: *Diario económico* 1:16 and 18.

[51] U.S. Department of War, *Census of Porto Rico, 1899*, pp. 16–17 (hereafter cited as USDW, *1899 Census*); Sánchez Tarniella, *La economía*, pp. 52–53; and *BHPR* 1:172.

[52] Scarano, "Sugar and Slavery," pp. 58–61, cogently explains why the measures, though perhaps necessary, were not sufficient to explain the growth process that followed. The cédula granted what the historical and economic conditions demanded; it did not generate those conditions (see n. 50 above).

ministrators.[53] With these and other changes, which helped to remove the more onerous mercantilist restrictions that Spain had imposed on commerce and production and which modernized the legal structure to facilitate the development of corporate-type units, the colonial apparatus provided an opening for the merchant and agricultural elite. This liberalization occurred at a particularly favorable moment, for it coincided with the rapid expansion of world trade and capitalist markets. Opportunities for commerce with countries other than Spain grew, and, with the addition of more local producers, particularly immigrants, the per capita value of trade expanded more than eight times between 1814 and 1854. Many immigrants brought with them not only new skills and knowledge of new methods of production, but also a predisposition toward entrepreneurial risk-taking, as well as the tools, machinery, and financing necessary for production on an expanded scale. Immigrants tended to be more market- and profit-oriented than creoles, and they very often were more forward-looking and cosmopolitan in their thinking, imbued with the capitalist spirit of Western Europe and the United States.

Prior to 1815, few production units in sugar were deserving of the designation "hacienda." The average area under cultivation was from ten to fifteen cuerdas, and half of all farms had less than five cuerdas in production. Grinding equipment (*trapiche*), made of wood, was of a form "whose prototype was first used in Europe in the late Middle Ages and had been amply superseded by the seventeenth century in all the main sugar producing regions."[54] Perhaps but one farm in the main sugar-producing region of Ponce, the Quemado hacienda owned by José Gutiérrez del Arroyo, could legitimately have been described as a hacienda.[55] Following the sugar boom that began in the 1820s, the number of haciendas around Ponce rose to forty-nine in the official record-keeping. By 1828, five of them were utilizing modern, steam-driven mills to grind cane, making them as productive as any in the Caribbean. By 1845, there were eighty-six haciendas around Ponce, forty-eight of which had twenty-five or more slaves.[56] Some of this change must be attributed to the Cédula de Gracias. Besides encouraging population growth, expanded trade, and agricultural development, it provided those who had acquired bourgeois ideology and tendencies with a partial opening which permitted

[53] Cubano Iguina, "Economía y sociedad en Arecibo," pp. 84–88.
[54] Scarano, "Sugar and Slavery," p. 110.
[55] The Quemado hacienda was the second-largest slaveholder in the region, with 110 slaves in 1827. There were two animal-powered mills, sugar houses, a hospital, and slave quarters, but less than 100 cuerdas were cultivated in cane. In general, Puerto Rican haciendas were of a much smaller scale than the plantations on other islands of the West Indies: ibid., pp. 109–11, 127–32.
[56] Scarano, "Sugar and Slavery," pp. 113–15.

them to more easily satisfy their drive to emulate and participate in the revolutions of production transforming Europe and the United States, though the effects were more evident in the agricultural sector than in industry for most of the century. Ominously, however, the de facto break with Spanish markets which the cédula accelerated by its limited free-market provisions was followed by the growth of greater dependence on U. S. markets. As the creole elite and the new immigrant producers attempted, if not to totally untie themselves from Spain, to at least loosen the knots, the changes unleashed by Spanish liberalization and the subsequent growth in the forces of production brought Puerto Rico and the United States ever closer.

Changes in production affected not only the economic base of society but also the evolution of its associated class structure. Though Puerto Rico often has been presumed to have been primarily a sugar exporter throughout the nineteenth century, this was so generally only for the first half of the century, when the industry was undisturbed by international competition because of a rapid growth in demand that made even Puerto Rico's inferior sugar desired. In the second half of the century, particularly in the last three decades, coffee production began to gain, while the sugar industry experienced a serious crisis. Plagued by a lack of finance capital to expand production and now beset by increased competition from beet-sugar production in Europe and hence ever lower market prices, Puerto Rican sugar production stagnated and sugar exports were displaced in importance by coffee exports in the last quarter of the century.[57] Because of the European competition, island producers could only watch helplessly as prices fell from a high of about 15 cents a pound at the time of the Cédula de Gracias to 2–4 cents at the end of the century.

The lack of finance capital was also an internal restraint on the island's social formation. It made it difficult for producers to change their production methods in ways that would have permitted them to meet the competition of a rapidly changing world market increasingly subject to and guided by the tendencies of capitalist development. This condition was a legacy of the past, the price paid for being the poorest colony, in which savings, profits, and agricultural surplus had not accumulated to any significant degree. As well, Spain's colonial policy had restricted the

[57]For a useful summary of the rise of the coffee industry and its impact on Puerto Rico and its class structure, see Bergad, "Agrarian History." Mintz, *Caribbean Transformations*, p. 101, notes the problem of the lack of finance capital which had troubled Puerto Rico since the beginning of colonization. In the absence of an adequate infrastructure (banks, a supply of generally accepted currency, etc.), the sugar industry had made advances from its inception only with aid from Spain in the forms of laws (e.g., on debt), financing, and acceptance and promotion of the slave trade.

process of capital accumulation directly,[58] what surpluses there were had been drawn off, and credit facilities that might have permitted the institutionalized organization of financing were prohibited from being founded.

The lack of financing manifested itself in two distinct ways, both of which adversely affected the production process. First, larger sugar growers found it difficult to upgrade their machinery or introduce new production technologies. Second, it was not possible for *hacendados* (hacienda owners) to purchase sufficient slaves to provide the labor needed in the fields and mills. This second factor was of particular importance, for there was a very severe shortage of free, or wage, labor throughout the nineteenth century, and large-scale agricultural production, such as characterized the production of sugar for export, relied on slave labor to an important, though not exclusive, extent. The increasing difficulty in obtaining labor contributed to the deterioration of the sugar industry in the last quarter of the nineteenth century.

Puerto Rican sugar producers found themselves facing a crisis as the nineteenth century came to a close. The number of sugar *centrales*, or large processing factories that ground cane into raw sugar from the land of many small, neighboring producers, had declined, a result of the decline of the sugar industry itself rather than of greater centralization and monopolization of capital, as some authors have argued. The smaller number of centrals in operation at the end of the century is a concrete sign of the failure of the Puerto Rican sugar industry to adapt to the rapidly changing conditions of the capitalist world market. The vitality of the sugar economy was destroyed not only by external competition, however, but equally by internal productive limitations—the lack of capital, credit, and surpluses and the resultant primitive production methods still in use at this time. Sugar producers were unable to transform their production processes so as to compete with foreign, and increasingly capitalist, sugar producers. Table 1.4 records the decline in the relative monetary value of sugar exports. Whereas sugar had accounted for more than two-thirds of the value of all exports in 1871, by 1896 its share had fallen to one-fifth, while the importance of coffee exports dramatically increased.[59]

After 1876, new markets for Puerto Rican coffee opened in Europe. The United States had made it easier for Brazilian coffee to enter its

---

[58]This was accomplished, for example, by high taxes on machinery imports and raw materials: Perloff, *Puerto Rico's Economic Future*, p. 15.

[59]The *volume* of sugar production did not show such a decline. Export values are of course dependent not only on the volume exported but also on the price, and it was particularly the decreasing price of sugar relative to the rising price of coffee that accounts for the declining relative value of sugar exports.

TABLE 1.4
Value of Coffee and Sugar Exports as
Percentage of Total Value of Exports,
Selected Years, 1871 to 1896

Year	Coffee	Sugar
1871	—	68.5
1876	17.6	62.5
1881	54.5	28.9
1886	49.4	43.6
1896	76.9	20.7

SOURCES: Bergad, "Agrarian History," pp. 65, 69; Bergad, *Coffee and the Growth of Agrarian Capitalism*, p. 145; and Perloff, *Puerto Rico's Economic Future*, pp. 18–19.

market, and this resulted in a shortage of coffee on the continent. Puerto Rican exports rapidly expanded to fill the gap. Coffee quickly became the island's leading export crop. (Tobacco, while important, was much less significant than sugar and coffee in terms of export values.) Thus, while both sugar and coffee were export-oriented crops (with an important home market), they were produced for two very different external markets: sugar increasingly was destined for sale in the United States; coffee, on the other hand, found its markets primarily in Europe and Cuba. This separation of markets was to have significant effects on Puerto Rico's future development and its class structure, particularly after the U.S. occupation in 1898.

The increase in export production over the course of the nineteenth century came at the expense of reduced production for the domestic market. Both newly opened land and land originally devoted to subsistence crops were put into export-crop production. For example, in Utuado in 1851, there had been 6,543 cuerdas planted in plantains, rice, corn, sweet potatoes, beans, yams, and other crops intended for local consumption; 1,491 cuerdas were devoted to coffee, the primary export crop in the region. In 1897, by which time the population in Utuado had doubled, only 4,874 cuerdas were devoted to local food crops, while 15,883 were in coffee.[60] Grazing land also was reduced, with a further adverse effect on local diets. Rice, a basic item in the diet, had been an important crop in the southwest of the island, but coffee trees took over more and more of this land, too. As a result, Puerto Rico was forced to import an in-

[60] F. Picó, "Deshumanización del trabajo," p. 192.

creasing proportion of its foodstuffs, a process that accelerated especially in the last third of the nineteenth century.[61]

Throughout the second half of the nineteenth century, exports continued to grow, and the economy moved even further toward external orientation and dependence for markets, commodities, and income. In the period from 1828–1832, external trade had averaged 5.5 million pesos per year; in 1865–69, this had increased to about 14 million pesos, and in 1874–78 trade expanded to an average of 22.5 million pesos per year.[62]

The shift in the last third of the nineteenth century toward coffee production was reflected not only in the change in the structure of exports, but also in a change in land use. Table 1.5 shows the great importance agricultural production for export had attained by 1897, just prior to the

TABLE 1.5
Agricultural Land Use in 1897

Use	Area (cuerdas)
Coffee	122,358
Sugar cane	61,556
Tobacco	4,227
Grains	93,508
Other cultivation	17,176
Pasture land	1,127,086
Woodland, swamps, barren land	664,270
Total	2,090,181

SOURCE: USDW, *1899 Census*, p. 146.

U.S. occupation. At the same time, however, it should be noted that only about 15 percent of the total land area was under cultivation; the greatest share of land was used for grazing horses, cattle, and other animals.

DEVELOPMENT OF THE INFRASTRUCTURE

The infrastructure of transportation and banking facilities, generally recognized as a precondition for economic development, was almost nonexistent in Puerto Rico. At the time the of U.S. occupation, there were only 159 miles of railroad, and they were in disconnected pieces, most of them along the coast; none extended into the interior. The rails had been built by sugar producers to enable them to move cane from the fields

[61] V. Clark et al., *Porto Rico and Its Problems*, p. 34, and Díaz Hernández, *Castañer*, p. 39.

[62] Sánchez Tarniella, *La economía*, p. 67.

to the grinding mills. Most other kinds of roads, except for 285 miles of military roads, were extremely poor, unpaved, and virtually useless after heavy rains.[63] Thus, the internal movement of goods was time-consuming and expensive, leading to higher prices and reinforcing the island's external orientation. Sánchez Tarniella believes that the lack of roads and other infrastructure was a major factor in Puerto Rico's economic problems throughout the nineteenth century.[64] Without accepting a position of technological determinism,[65] it is certain that the absence of adequate transportation and communication was a significant hindrance. The colonial government's lack of attention to roads, postal service, and other infrastructural "public goods" was but another aspect and indication of the underlying resistance to economic development in the colony.

Perhaps the most debilitating weakness in the infrastructure, as noted earlier, was the lack of an adequate institutional framework for financing expanded production of sugar, coffee, and other crops. The shortage of savings or surplus for productive investment was real enough, but the absence of banks or other lending institutions which might have mobilized such funds as were available exacerbated the problem. Agricultural producers, large and small were forced to borrow from merchants or larger landowners at often usurious interest rates (as high as 1.5 to 2 percent a month). When a loan could not be repaid, land often was taken as payment, which, as Díaz Hernández's study of Hacienda Castañer demonstrates, contributed greatly to the process of land concentration, particularly among immigrant hacendados.[66] The first attempt to establish a bank—actually, a branch of the Colonial Bank of London—was made in 1836, but it was not successful.[67] Sometime between 1850 and 1853, a limited-function bank did open, but its operations were minor. In 1866, the Caja de Ahorros de San Juan de Puerto Rico, the first savings bank, began operations. Throughout this period, however, local merchants and Spanish merchant houses maintained their dominance and continued to ac-

[63] USDW, *1899 Census*, p. 12.

[64] Sánchez Tarniella, *La economía*, pp. 62–63, 68.

[65] It must be asked *why* roads and other infrastructure did not develop, and that requires an understanding of Puerto Rico's colonial social formation and class relations.

[66] Díaz Hernández, *Castañer*, p. 45, comments on the tendency for landholding to shift toward more recent immigrants.

[67] The branch bank was established, but its operations were quickly suppressed. This was not the first recognition of the need for a bank, though it was the first real effort to found one. In 1812, in 1814, and again in 1828, the establishment of a bank had been recommended to Spain by its colonial representatives in Puerto Rico. Several more efforts to found a bank were made between 1847 and 1872, but all met with opposition from Spain in the interest of protecting the position of the merchant lenders: Gómez Acevedo, *Organización y reglamentación*, p. 44, n. 39, and pp. 44–45, and Cruz Monclova, *Historia* 1:68, 99, 250.

tively oppose banks and lending institutions that might have cut into their very lucrative lending activities. However, in the 1870s the first bank to provide loans finally appeared: the Sociedad Anónima de Crédito Mercantil. Then followed the Banco Español in 1888; the Banco Territorial Agrícola in 1894; Banco Popular, also in 1894; and Banco de Crédito y Ahorro Ponceño in 1895.[68]

Besides the absence until late in the nineteenth century of an institutional structure for mobilizing financial resources, there existed a further barrier to capital development: There was no generally accepted and widely circulating currency until very late in the century, and even then it was not sufficient to create a predominately monetized economy. Puerto Rico's first experience with its own money had failed when the paper currency issued in 1812 to attempt to compensate for the loss of the situado in 1810 rapidly declined in value because of apprehension over its use.[69] In 1813, coins from Venezuela, *macuquinas*, were permitted to circulate, not only to replace the discredited paper currency but also because it was convenient to do so, since many Venezuelan immigrants, fleeing Bolívar's armies, were arriving with substantial sums of potentially liquid capital. The macuquina remained in circulation until 1857—all gold and silver foreign coins had been permitted to circulate in 1848—when it was replaced primarily by the Mexican silver peso, which circulated until 1895. Besides the variety of foreign coins, which must have greatly complicated exchange, many haciendas and commercial houses also issued their own coins and some paper money, reflecting the constant shortage of money.[70] It was not until the decree of August 17, 1895, authorizing Puerto Rico's own coins, minted in Spain, that the island was able to maintain the value and acceptability of its own money, which was quoted on international money-market exchanges just before the end of the century at 1 P.R. peso = U.S. $0.75.[71]

Lastly, while not strictly an economic factor, population growth certainly affected the possibilities for economic development. Table 1.6 shows that the population of Puerto Rico almost doubled between the middle of the nineteenth century and 1899, when the first U.S. census was taken.

[68] Sánchez Tarniella, *La economía*, p. 62.

[69] The *Diario económico* ran a series of articles attempting to convince the public of the usefulness of paper money as a means of exchange and to reassure them of its value as backed by the colonial government. This was to no avail, however. Coins remained the desired medium of exchange.

[70] Gould and Higgie, *Money of Puerto Rico*, includes photos of all known money up to the early twentieth century. *BHPR* 1:168, 2:113, 115, and 3:225–30, provides information on the introduction of paper money on August 12, 1812, to replace the loss of the situado. See also Cruz Monclova, *Historia* 1:263.

[71] Gould and Higgie, *Money of Puerto Rico*, p. 11, and Sánchez and Tarniella, *La economía*, pp. 62–63, 79.

TABLE 1.6
Population of Puerto Rico,
Selected Years, 1765 to 1899

Year	Population
1765	44,883
1776	80,246
1783	87,994
1797	138,758
1800	155,426
1802	163,192
1812	183,014
1815	220,892
1820	230,622
1824	261,661
1827	302,672
1830	323,838
1832	330,051
1834	358,836
1846	447,914
1854	492,452
1860	583,308
1872	617,328
1877	731,648
1887	798,565
1899	953,243

SOURCES: USDW, *1899 Census*, p. 40; *BHPR* 1:169, 2:228; Díaz Soler, *Historia de la esclavitud negra*, pp. 117, 122; Silén, *Historia*, p. 57; CENEP, *Labor Migration*, p. 82, table 3.4.

PERSPECTIVES ON THE SOCIAL FORMATION

There is little serious disagreement among scholars over the nature of Puerto Rico's economic and class structure prior to the nineteenth century: precapitalist class relations and production methods prevailed within a precapitalist social formation, all circumscribed by the colonial context. Most producers were involved in small-scale, individual, subsistence production and had but limited contact with the market as either buyers or sellers. Technology and tools on these small units of production were very unsophisticated, and production growth tended to follow population growth rather than being the result of improvements in technology or in the productivity of other means of production.[72] Exports of sugar and its by-products, as well as of coffee, cotton, ginger, and hides were, of course, important, but even for these commodities, relatively primitive tools, machinery, and methods of organization predominated. On the larger sugar haciendas, a significant part of the work was done by slave labor beginning in the late eighteenth century.

Despite Puerto Rico's integration into the world market via trade relations, legal and illegal, during its prenineteenth-century history, an external orientation did not greatly affect the *internal* organization of production or the social formation. Spanish colonial policy, and the internal structure of the Puerto Rican economy itself—with its surplus of land, shortage of labor, lack of finance capital and money, and small internal market—worked to reinforce and reproduce precapitalist relations of production and low-level technological production methods. The result, of course, was the conspicuous lack of progress noted by O'Reilly in his official report to Spain 1765, and which ultimately led Spain to introduce modernizing policy changes like the Cédula de Gracias of 1815.

If the first three centuries of Spanish rule saw little fundamental change in the social formation and the organization of production, during its last century of control Spain presided over rapid and revolutionary changes in the economy and in the associated class structure and class relations, many of which were not of its design. It is in the analysis of the nature of the economic and production relations and the class structure of Puerto Rico in the nineteenth century that scholars part ways. Three contending hypotheses have been used to characterize them. These positions can briefly be stated as:

1. Puerto Rico's production methods and relations, as exemplified by the hacienda, were *capitalistic*.

2. Puerto Rico's production methods and relations on haciendas and on peasant lands were *precapitalist* (or certainly *noncapitalist*).

3. Puerto Rico had elements of *both* capitalist and noncapitalist production and social relations within the same social formation.

The fundamentals of these three arguments will be examined before turning to the specifics of the organization and evolution of the production process and social relations in the nineteenth century.

1. Production and class relations were capitalistic. This position has

---

[72] See the photo facing p. 146 of USDW *1899 Census*, showing the most common tools in use as late as the American occupation. Even at that time they were very simple: machetes, hoes, and other hand tools.

deep intellectual roots in Latin America and the third world and is generally associated with so-called dependency analysis.[73] According to this thesis, a world capitalist system had emerged by the sixteenth century which encompassed not only the core (metropolitan) countries of Western Europe but also, via conquest, the peripheral (satellite) areas of Asia, Africa, and the Americas. Within this system, the periphery provided cheap argicultural products and mineral resources for the development of the core countries. As well, the periphery offered a limited market for manufactured goods produced in the metropolitan countries. As primary products and surplus (profit) flowed from the periphery to the core countries, there was development in the latter and the "development of underdevelopment" in the former. Thus, the impoverishment of the periphery and the enrichment of the core countries were two aspects of the same process within the world capitalist system. Underdeveloped countries, in this view, are not now, and have not been since the conquest, precapitalist or feudal in their production methods or relations. Rather, they are and have been capitalist and an integral part of the world capitalist economy. The agricultural sector in the periphery was capitalist just as certainly as was the industrial production of the core, despite the different forms of labor in use.

   2. *Puerto Rico had precapitalist/noncapitalist relations of production.* This hypothesis has been the dominant view among most scholars, including Marxist writers. In this view, market relations, even extensive export production, are not by themselves sufficient to establish the presence of capitalism, since they indicate nothing about the way the production process is organized internally or about the class structure and class relations, particularly how surplus production is appropriated. Commodity production, though necessary and fundamental to capitalism, is not sufficient to define it. Capitalism requires in addition the presence of a relatively large and mobile wage-labor force; in fact, the logic of capitalist growth demands such a free (i.e., propertyless) proletariat if capital is to expand and if expanded accumulation, the sine qua non of capitalism, is to occur. A system of production cannot be capitalist, in this perspec-

---

[73] See, for example, Frank, "Development of Underdevelopment" or almost any other of his works; Amin, *Accumulation on a World Scale*; and Wallerstein, *Modern World System*. For a critique and history of Frank's ideas, see David Booth, "André Gunder Frank." *Latin American Perspectives*, Summer 1981, contains a useful collection of articles, some critical and others supportive, on dependency analysis. For dependency perspectives applied to Puerto Rico, see Fernández Méndez, *Historia cultural*, p. 208; Wessman, "Demographic Structure of Slavery," "Is There a Plantation Mode of Reproduction?," "Sugar Cane Hacienda," "Theory of Value," and "Towards a Marxist Demography"; and Mintz, *Caribbean Transformations*, chap. 2 and 3, and "Labor and Sugar" and "The So-Called World System."

tive, if it depends upon forced labor and if tendencies toward capital accumulation, technological progress, and expansion of commodity production are absent. This has led scholars in this tradition to describe the island economy as feudal, semifeudal, or certainly noncapitalist, because of the absence of a functioning labor market and the continued importance of coercive labor forms.[74] The general impression in most cases is that the nineteenth-century economy was feudal, becoming capitalist only in the twentieth century, following the U.S. invasion and the infusion of U.S. capital into the economy.

3. Puerto Rican production and social relations were both capitalist and noncapitalist. The third theoretical perspective argues that economic systems must be seen as complex structures at the same time as they are viewed as totalities. It is not necessary, desirable, or historically accurate to force all types of production into a single mode—whether capitalist, feudal, or some other category—at either the world or the national level. The recognition that real-world economies may be better represented and understood as complex and dynamic social formations, rather than as simple, static modes of production, permits a richer analysis of economic processes and social relations, including those in Puerto Rico in the nineteenth century.

To anticipate our conclusions, of the three theoretical approaches, the historical facts would seem to be encompassed best by the third perspective. However, we will also argue that the noncapitalist forces in the economy were stronger than and hence dominated the capitalist forces during the period in question, though this dominance was severely challenged at the end of the century. To give substance to what is at this point little more than an assertion, it is necessary to look in some detail at the relations of production both on the haciendas and off, to consider in detail the class structure and the ways in which production and commerce were organized, and to look closely at the internal and external changes which affected production and class relations.

VARIETIES OF LABOR USE

During the course of the nineteenth century, production was carried out with several different forms of labor.

[74] For the most sophisticated view, see Quintero Rivera, "El desarrollo de clases sociales," pp. 59–61, n. 4. Subsequently, in *Conflictos de clase*, p. 139, n. 4, Quintero revised his view, writing that his original perspective was "suppressed" because his later work approached the question of the nature of nineteenth-century Puerto Rico with "more precision."

SLAVERY

Slaves had been utilized as field workers, in sugar mills and other small manufacturing, and as domestics since the early 1500s. The African slave trade had provided a much-needed labor force in Puerto Rico, as in the rest of the Caribbean, where land was relatively abundant and labor scarce. Though Spain agreed, in a decree issued in 1817 at England's urging, to end its involvement in the slave trade by 1820 (in a two-step process), slaves were still being brought to the island long after that date.[75] Slavery itself was not abolished until March 22, 1873, and even then freed slaves, or *libertos*, were required to serve a three-year "apprenticeship" with their former owners, another landowner, or the government, and they had to have their former owner's permission to leave the area.[76]

Despite this long history, slaves did not form a very large proportion of the Puerto Rican population in the eighteenth and nineteenth centuries. In 1776, at the beginning of Puerto Rico's growth process, the number of slaves was far exceeded by the number of *agregados*, or peasant squatters (who will be discussed below).[77] Table 1.7 gives information on the number of black slaves for various years. From 1765 to 1802, the slave population grew by more than 2.6 times, and in the period from 1766 to 1770, more than 13,300 African slaves were brought to the island.[78] This is an indication of the growth in production, particularly of sugar, that already had begun prior to the turn of the century, even before the impetus to economic growth provided by the Cédula de Gracias. The slave

[75] Other countries of Western Europe had ended their involvement in the slave trade earlier: Denmark, 1802; England, 1808; Sweden, 1813; Holland and France, 1814. See Mintz, "The So-Called World System," p. 264 and Díaz Soler, *Historia de la esclavitud negra*, pp. 109ff. Because of the obvious failure of Spain's 1817 agreement, England persuaded Spain to agree again to halt the slave trade in 1835 and 1845: Díaz Soler, *Historia de la esclavitud negra*, pp. 117, 133; Brau, *Historia*, p. 219; and *BHPR* 4:90–93.

[76] *BHPR* 4:381–82. According to USDW, *1899 Census*, p. 32, these conditions were applied so as to avoid damaging sugar-cane production. Because of their former oppression, it was believed that emancipated slaves, especially field slaves, were likely to flee the work that had bound them to their owner: Gómez Acevedo, *Organización y reglamentación*, pp. 53–54. This "apprentice" period was instituted to prevent recently freed slaves from associating with other freed slaves and thus to reduce the likelihood of acts of revenge by the former slaves. A "partial abolition" decree had been published in July 1870. It granted freedom to all children born to slaves after that date, though they had to remain with their former owners until the age of twenty-two; to those who had served in the military; to slaves over the age of sixty (without compensation to their owners); and to slaves of the state. It also provided conditions for manumission by the state of children born after September 1868: *BHPR* 10:15–17.

[77] Steward et al., *People of Puerto Rico*, p. 48.

[78] Bergad, *Coffee and the Growth of Agrarian Capitalism*, pp. 6–7.

TABLE 1.7
Black Slave Population, Selected Years, 1765 to 1873

Year	Number of Black Slaves	Percentage of Total Population
1765	5,037	11.2
1776	6,537	8.1
1802	13,333	8.2
1812	17,536	9.6
1815	18,621	8.4
1820	21,730	9.4
1827	31,874	10.5
1830	34,240	10.6
1834	41,818	11.7
1846	51,265	11.4
1854	46,918	9.5
1860	41,736	7.2
1872	31,635	5.1
1873	29,229	a

SOURCES: Díaz Soler, *Historia de la esclavitud negra*, pp. 117, 121, 122; USDW, *1899 Census*, p. 31; Silén, *Historia*, p. 58; Bergad, *Coffee and the Growth of Agrarian Capitalism*, p. 14; and *BHPR* 2:228, 4:95–96.

a No population figure available.

population continued to increase in the first half of the nineteenth century, but at its maximum, it formed only a little more than 11 percent of the total population. In the second half of the century, even the absolute number of slaves declined, and it represented barely 5 percent of the population in the year before emancipation.[79] In no other colony in the Caribbean did slaves constitute such a small proportion of the population during the nineteenth century. In Cuba in 1842, for example, out of a population of slightly more than one million, there were 436,459 slaves, more than 43 percent of the total.[80]

These figures have led to the too-hasty conclusion that slaves were

[79] Díaz Soler, *Historia de la esclavitud negra*, p. 123, points out that between 1846 and 1860, between 9,300 and 9,600 slaves were lost to the island because of "death, emigration or flight." There was a cholera epidemic in 1855 which particularly affected blacks. Of the total of 26,820 who died, 5,469 were slaves and 21,079 Puerto Ricans of "color": ibid. Hence, it appears that between 1846 and 1860, very few slaves either won or bought their freedom.

[80] Foner, *Spanish-Cuban-American War*, 1:xvi.

relatively unimportant to the Puerto Rican economy. Slaves were extremely important in one crucial sector of the economy, the production
of sugar cane. In those *municipios* (municipalities) producing sugar, particularly the largest ones, slaves constituted a much larger share of the
population. In 1828, in the three municipios with the highest level of
sugar production (more than 1,000 tons a year)—Mayagüez, Ponce, and
Guayama—slaves were 21.1 percent, 21.5 percent, and 29.8 percent of
the respective local populations. In these same regions between 1812 and
1828, the slave population had grown by 288 percent, 202 percent, and
623 percent, respectively, a rate that was four to six times greater than
that of the free population. In those municipalities producing from 201 to
1,000 tons of sugar in 1828, all—Bayamón (where slaves where 14.4
percent of the population), Loiza (17.7 percent), Trujillo (12.9 percent),
Río Piedras (32.0 percent), and Toa Baja (11.9 percent)—had proportions
of slaves larger than the percentage in the island population as a whole,
though in none of these areas had the slave population been growing very
rapidly.[81]

It is also important to note that the above figures relate slaves to the
total population, which is not, of course, the same as relating slaves to
the labor force. In Ponce in 1845, for example, out of a total labor force
of 4,216 on eighty-six haciendas, 3,460 were slaves—i.e., 82.1 percent,
though this proportion had declined to about 50 percent by 1859. On
smaller sugar-producing farms, the ratio of slave to total labor was about
the same, though the total number of slaves used on these smaller units
of production was only abut 13 percent of those in use on the haciendas.[82] In the sugar-growing municipios in 1864, slaves outnumbered wage
workers by 1.5–2.5 to 1; in coffee-growing areas, on the other hand,
wage workers outnumbered slaves by 2.4–10.6 to 1. In municipios with
mixed production (sugar and coffee), the use of slave and wage labor
showed no discernible pattern, though in absolute numbers wage labor
was much greater overall.[83] In short, slavery was important to the early
development of the sugar economy.

[81] Scarano, "Sugar and Slavery," p. 78, table 1.6.

[82] Ibid., p. 160, table 3.1; Curet, *De la esclavitud a la abolición*, p. 2; Bergad, *Coffee
and the Growth of Agrarian Capitalism*, p. 57. Bergad found a correlation coefficient (R^2)
of .9 when the number of slaves was regressed on cultivated area in the principal crop—
that is, the larger the area, the greater was the number of slaves.

[83] Bergad, *Coffee and the Growth of Agrarian Capitalism*, p. 126, table 3.23. The coffee
municipios (with the number of slaves and wage workers) in 1864 were: Adjuntas (61 and
572); Ciales (84 and 198); Lares (125 and 1,324); and Utuado (242 and 1,461). The sugar
municipios were Arroyo (1,023 and 417); Guayama (2,063 and 811); and Juana Díaz (1,243
and 830). Municipios producing both sugar and coffee were: Ponce (4,721 and 3,226);
Mayagüez (3,842 and 4,118); San Germán (2,918 and 5,546); and Yauco (490 and 1,519).

Though slaves were also to be found in the interior regions, where coffee became the major export crop, slavery was never important to production there. In part this was probably due to the fact that the first spurt in coffee production (in the 1840s) began when slavery was already on the decline, following the end of the legal slave trade. Additionally, new colonial regulations on the flow of labor contributed to the creation of a labor force that made slavery less of a necessity. Lastly, and perhaps most important, slaves were less necessary after the middle of the century because land concentration in the highlands, accompanied by dispossession of former peasants and agregados, created an expanding class of wage workers for the coffee fincas. The peak number of slaves in Utuado, for example, the coffee capital in the second half of the century, was only 267, reached in 1839, and most of these were domestics, not field workers. In 1842, Lares registered just 83 slaves.[84]

Many observers have pointed to the small proportion of slaves as evidence of the benign nature of slavery in Puerto Rico and the minor role of slaves in the economy. However, the relatively small number of slaves in comparison to Cuba or the other dependencies in the West Indies owed more to Puerto Rico's backwardness and the lack of finance capital for the purchase of slaves than to any generalized progressive tendencies within Puerto Rico's elite, landed class. Furthermore, the argument that slave labor was relatively unimportant neglects the role of slavery in the sugar economy, as described above. The decrease in the number of slaves shown in table 1.7 paralleled the declining fortunes of sugar production. In any case, slavery could hardly be called benign; to give but one example, the barbarous practice of branding slaves with the carimbo to identify those legally brought to the island was permitted until 1784.[85] Finally, as will be evident from the discussion below of the labor laws, landowners were not reluctant to place restrictions on the freedom and actions of their laborers, black or white, slave or free.[86] The appearance of strict labor

[84] F. Picó, "Deshumanización del trabajo," p. 202, and Bergad, *Coffee and the Growth of Agrarian Capitalism*, p. 43, table 2.9. Bergad notes, however, that in 1846, Hacienda La Esperanza in Lares used 33 slaves on the 69 cuerdas devoted to coffee and that in Moca, where coffee also was the major cash crop in the 1840s, there were 363 slaves and 130 wage workers: *Coffee and the Growth of Agrarian Capitalism*, pp. 57–58, and "Coffee and Rural Proletarianization," p. 88.

[85] After 1784, with the end of branding, only the 6 percent per slave head tax was required. This, too, was abolished in 1789: *BHPR* 1:167. For a view of slavery from the nineteenth-century perspective, see Alejandro Tapia y Rivera, "African Slavery," in Závala and Rodríguez, *Intellectual Roots*, pp. 54–61.

[86] At times these efforts to control behavior reached what today seem absurd proportions, such as the banning of mustaches by Governor Méndez Vigo and Governor Pezuela's restrictions on holding dances without government approval: Cruz Monclova, *Historia* 1:257, 291, and Miranda Quintero, *Development*, p. 31. Many of these measures were designed to control slave behavior and to prevent planning for rebellions by separatist elements.

laws (1849) at the very time that the number of slaves was declining is no mere historical coincidence.

It is thus difficult to avoid the conclusion that it was the lack of finance capital, together with the declining fortunes of the sugar industry, that explains Puerto Rico's "uniqueness" in the relative number of slaves, rather than any diffusion or acceptance of liberal ideas about slaveholding, abolition, or the inherent rights of human beings.[87] A shortage of labor was perhaps the major problem of landowners for most of the nineteenth century, and there is little doubt that if slaves could have been purchased they would have been.

There were three categories of slaves: *esclavos domésticos*, or domestic workers; *esclavos de tala*, or field workers; and *jornaleros*, or rented slaves (literally, "day laborers"). Domestic workers were responsible for the slave owner's house, including caring for the children. Their living conditions were superior to those of the other two categories. Field slaves did the main work of the hacienda, including planting, weeding, cutting cane, gathering firewood for the sugar mill, tending the mill, and so on. There is some evidence that slaves did not work as hard or produce as much as hired wage laborers. For example, Darío de Ormaechea reported that slaves harvested an average of about 105 quintals (1 quintal = 100 pounds) of cane per day while hired "white" workers harvested 157.5 quintals.[88] This is hardly surprising, however, since the condition of slavery is not a notable incentive for high productivity.

The third category of slaves, jornaleros, is a particularly interesting one. These were slaves who were hired out or "rented" on a temporary basis, their "wages" being paid directly to their owner. Such slave workers often performed skilled labor. For example, in 1849, two slave carpenters were rented by their owner, Rosa Dronet of Mayagüez, for fifteen pesos a month. Rented field slaves, on the other hand, brought less to their owners, in one case six pesos a month.[89] It seems that the lives of these slaves were the most difficult. Their owners often sent or brought them to the cities to look for work when they were not occupied on the hacienda or when it was otherwise economically advantageous for the owners, and sometimes the jornaleros were then abandoned or discharged by those who had hired them, a situation from which the slaves, without

[87] Díaz Soler, *Historia de la esclavitud negra*, p. 118, refers to the writings of David Turnbull, an English traveler to Puerto Rico in the late 1830s, who believed that "the fundamental reason for the ending of the African trade in Puerto Rico [was] the scarce economic resources of the hacendados." See also Wessman, "Demographic Structure of Slavery," pp. 284–87.

[88] *BHPR* 2:253.

[89] Bergad, *Coffee and the Growth of Agrarian Capitalism*, p. 59.

housing, money, or legally defined rights, suffered greatly until alternative employment could be found.[90]

AGREGADO LABOR

Agregados (sometimes called *arrimados*) lived as squatters on someone
else's land. Work arrangements and other obligations between agregados
and landowners varied greatly. At times, there was no rent paid or labor
services provided to the landowner; what the landowner received in these
cases was protection from having his land overrun by other squatters.
More often, the landowner received some labor services or a part of the
agregado's crop in return for letting the agregado and his family remain
on the land. Interestingly, Bergad found that, in Lares, nearly all of the
agregados with access to land also received wages, as an additional incentive, for work done on the hacienda, and it was not uncommon for a
landowner to require agregados, as Picó found in Utuado, to pay a portion or all of the taxes assessed on the land.[91] In some areas, agregado
families were permitted to use an area entirely for their own production,
though the area was not always large enough to meet all their subsistence
needs and so outside work for cash or for payment in kind sometimes
had to be done to supplement what they raised. Díaz found in his study
of Hacienda Castañer, however, that agregados were not permitted to
grow any crops or to tend animals, so as to not reduce the area devoted
to coffee on the hacienda.[92] In nearby Lares in 1846, on the other hand,
of 450 agregado families, 379 had access to land for their own use, though
about half of them had less than two cuerdas and nearly all less than five.
About 65 percent of the land used by agregados was dedicated to subsistence crops, particularly beans and tubers.[93]

The condition of the agregados, and the frustration often expressed by
landowners and others with them, vividly illustrate one of nineteenth-
century Puerto Rico's most enduring problems: a shortage of laborers *for
hire*.[94] Land was relatively abundant (population density was less than

[90] Diaz Soler, *Historia de la esclavitud negra*, p. 160.

[91] Bergad, *Coffee and the Growth of Agrarian Capitalism*, p. 66, and F. Picó, "Deshumanización del trabajo," pp. 197–98.

[92] Díaz Hernández, *Castañer*, p. 11, and Bergad, *Coffee and the Growth of the Agrarian
Capitalism*, p. 123.

[93] Bergad, *Coffee and the Growth of Agrarian Capitalism*, pp. 65–66, table 2.16 and
2.17.

[94] For example, see the view of the mayor of San Juan in 1809 quoted in Mintz, *Caribbean Transformations*, pp. 88–90. He saw the agregados and the lack of sufficient labor
the ruin of agriculture, unless the situation changed. One of the twenty-one requests presented (of twenty-two) by Puerto Rico's first representative to the Spanish Cortes, Ramón
Power y Giralt, was that the landless be controlled and their labor organized. However,

100 persons per square mile for most of the first half of the century[95]), so for sometime it was relatively easy for agregados (as well as for independent peasants) to gain access to land and correspondingly difficult for large landowners to obtain sufficient labor willing and needing to work on their haciendas. As Mintz has written, "The history of newly discovered and newly occupied areas has demonstrated again and again that free men will not work as employed agricultural laborers if they have access to land which they can cultivate for themselves."[96] Thus, as long as land was available, hacendados found it difficult to obtain labor with which to expand the scale of their production or produce on more of the land for which they already held title. Slavery, of course, was one means by which to get labor, but as already noted, not enough finance capital was available for the purchase of slaves, and the end of the slave trade greatly reduced the supply of slaves. Free peasants (those who worked unowned or crown land) lived primarily by subsistence farming, though many also grew some cash crops as well, particularly on small coffee fincas in the interior highlands. They were a potential source of labor, especially if they became agregados rather than remaining as independent producers, since landowners could extract at least some work or crop payments in exchange for the "right" to a plot of land for a house and perhaps a garden.

In 1776, there had been somewhat less than 8,000 agregados, and the number of free peasants was larger still.[97] The agregado population exceeded the number of slaves by 20 percent. It is little wonder, then, that Puerto Rico's landowning class, with the backing of the colonial apparatus, moved toward the "legalized coercion of free fellow citizens, whose only real sin was their landlessness."[98] Actually, their "sin" was not literally landlessness, since many did have access to land, but their inability to show *title* to the land they farmed (or their ownership of a quantity of land insufficient to meet their needs). In 1824, restrictions were placed on those who did not have legal title to the land they worked, including free peasants cultivating crown land, many of whom were then forced from the interior to the coastal areas to work on sugar haciendas where labor was in short supply. Private landowners also expanded their

---

though the growth of agricultural production was rapid in the nineteenth century, the growth of population was *potentially* sufficient to meet the need for labor: Gómez Acevedo, *Organización y reglamentación*, p. 52.

[95] Wessman, "Is There a Plantation Mode of Reproduction?," p. 27, table 1.

[96] Mintz, "Foreword," p. xiv.

[97] Silén, *Historia*, p. 58.

[98] Mintz, *Caribbean Transformations*, p. 91.

holdings by seizing peasant land for which there was no title, actions later sanctioned by the legal system.

As a result of such "legal" as well as more dubious actions, the agregado population increased from 14,327 in 1824 to 38,906 in 1827, as formerly independent peasants found themselves occupying privately owned land.[99] Given the large quantity of uncultivated land that many hacendados controlled, the presence of agregados was often preferable to the alternative of less production. In effect, land concentration helped to mitigate the labor shortage, since the landowner obtained not only the land but also its residents, in a manner reminiscent of the encomiendas of the colonial period. Often, indeed, the land was accumulated not to be put into production but precisely to gain control of the peasant labor living on it. As a result, land underutilization was often quite remarkable. In 1839, on a farm of 1,000 cuerdas in Barrio Río Prieto in Lares, the heart of the coffee-producing region, only nine cuerdas were in production— and only one of these was in coffee! By 1846, this farm had grown to 2,294 cuerdas, but only 16 were in coffee production. The largest coffee-producing hacienda in Lares in 1846 was La Esperanza, with 33 slaves, no wage workers, and only 69 of the 420 cuerdas in production.[100] It was not unusual to find hacendados granting the use of animals as well as land to attract more agregados to their haciendas, a practice which was condemned as ruinous to large-scale export agriculture.

By 1832, nearly one-third of the population was classified as agregados (an increase of almost 300 percent over the figure for 1824, though this may have been as much a statistical artifact as a reflection of reality). Still, 44.7 percent of the population remained as small independent and semi-independent producers, though they may have done some temporary work on neighboring haciendas.[101] There were, of course, wage workers or jornaleros who either were without any land or had insufficient land to support their families, but continued easy access to uncultivated land in the first third of the nineteenth century prevented the emergence of a labor market that could meet the labor shortage. A short-term and partial solution to the shortage, however, was found in the creation of what might be termed a "quasi-labor market."

THE LIBRETA SYSTEM

In 1837, by an order of the crown, it was decreed that the Spanish constitution was not applicable to overseas provinces like Puerto Rico.

---

[99] López, "Socio-Politico Developments," pp. 62–63; Mintz, *Caribbean Transformations*, p. 91; and Mintz, "Note on the Definition of Peasantries," p. 100.

[100] Bergad, *Coffee and the Growth of Agrarian Capitalism*, pp. 49–50.

[101] Quintero Rivera, "Background to the Emergence of Imperialistic Capitalism," p. 96.

They were to be governed by special laws appropriate to the specific conditions in those areas. Accordingly, in 1838 Governor Miguel López de Baños issued his *Bando de Policía y Buen Gobierno*, legislation which was partly aimed at solving Puerto Rico's labor problems by direct, extraeconomic coercion of the large free peasant and agregado population.[102] Purportedly a measure necessary to combat the "laziness" of both the landless and the peasant population, the bando required all persons, slaves excepted, not having sufficient property for their subsistence needs—persons who were to be legally classified as jornaleros—to find work on the land of another. Each municipio was required to maintain a registry of the jornaleros in its jurisdiction.[103] Those so classified were not required to work every day, but if they did not work during any given month, they would be declared vagrants, the penalty for which (after two warnings) was forced labor in public-works projects of the municipio. Repeated vagrancy could be punished by imprisonment. This legislation, however, was overturned by the Spanish overseas ministry in 1839 as being inappropriate and oppressive.[104] Then, in 1847, Governor Juan de la Pezuela promulgated another, more inclusive law, which defined as vagrants all those who had "no trade, profession, income, salary, occupation, or lawful means of livelihood and those who, having some trade, did not practice it, or those who received an income insufficient for their necessities."[105] The potential for abuse from such an open-ended definition is obvious, and the new legislation did indeed frequently allow municipal governments to mistreat persons regarded as undesirables.

The intent of these regulations was to enforce more work on otherwise unwilling workers. In 1845, according to one estimate, there were some 80,000 free laborers, about 18 percent of the population (though it is not clear whether this figure included only landless laborers).[106] The reason for the so-called labor shortage, and the source of the conflict that resulted from it, was that it did not take daily and arduous labor for a jornalero, a peasant-jornalero, or a semi-peasant to obtain the necessities

---

[102] *BHPR* 2:29; Gómez Acevedo, *Organización y reglamentación*, pp. 89, 105–6. With the restriction of the slave trade, which exacerbated the "labor shortage," the colonial government was both forced and ready to find other remedies to ensure a laboring population: F. Picó, *Libertad y servidumbre*, p. 108.

[103] Brau, "Las clases jornaleras," p. 26, points out that before 1837 official records did not make the distinction between owners and workers but solely between free persons and slaves. This, of course, does not imply there were no jornaleros before this date, but it does indicate that the importance of nonslave, jornalero labor was rising.

[104] Gómez Acevedo, *Organización y reglamentación*, pp. 89–92, and Cruz Monclova, *Historia* 1:233–34.

[105] Gómez Acevedo, *Organización y reglamentación*, p. 92.

[106] Ramos Mattei, "La importación de trabajadores contratados," p. 127.

of life. In his "Memoria" of 1765, O'Reilly wrote: "With five days of work a family has plantains for the entire year. With these, milk from their cows, some manioc, sweet potatoes, and wild fruits, they are fully contented."[107] As economic anthropologists have found in other situations, the level of needs of those in precapitalist societies or of persons with a noncapitalist vision of the world, even of those who perform some wage labor, is typically low relative to the means to satisfy them. As a result, such people labor only long enough to meet these limited needs and then spend a major part of their time at leisure or other activities.[108]

In Puerto Rico, the unwillingness of many jornaleros and peasants to work more than was required to meet their simple needs was a source of increasing irritation to hacendados, who perceived it as "laziness." *El Ponceño* complained, in its edition of March 5, 1853, that jornaleros regularly left work at noontime and often even failed to appear at all, because they found two or three days of work to be sufficient. A similar complaint had been registered by a government functionary in Mayagüez, in a letter to the governor in 1838, in which he wrote: "Hacendados refuse to employ [jornaleros] because as free men they don't appear for work and it is impossible to subject them to the strict discipline and difficult labor conditions they subject their slaves to."[109]

The purpose of the "antivagrancy" laws was to coerce more labor out of those who would otherwise not work. Bergad notes that it is not surprising that this legislation appeared in a period of falling sugar prices and difficult economic conditions, which increased the pressure to reduce costs of production. In his view, slave labor was relatively expensive, and it was therefore not merely the lack of labor that motivated the promulgation of such legislation but the *cost* of obtaining labor as well.[110]

There can be little doubt that the antivagrancy laws did nothing to raise

[107] *BHPR* 8:109.

[108] For example, see Dalton, *Primitive, Archaic, and Modern Economies*, and Sahlins, *Stone Age Economics*. Sahlins refers to the "affluence" of premodern peoples (e.g., peasants or even recently alienated peasants), whose needs are "scarce" and the means to satisfy them abundant. Thus, such people do not, and do not need to, labor very long or with much difficulty to meet their needs. That appears to have been the situation of peasants in Puerto Rico: Gómez Acevedo, *Organización y reglamentación*, pp. 87–88.

[109] Ramos Mattei, "La importación de trabajadores contratados," pp. 127–28, and Bergad, *Coffee and the Growth of Agrarian Capitalism*, p. 35, n. 59.

[110] Bergad, *Coffee and the Growth of Agrarian Capitalism*, p. 92. Prices for slaves varied with their sex and age. Peak prices for male field slaves in Ponce—nearly 700 pesos—were reached around 1860. Normally, prices were in the range of 200 to 350 pesos. Slaves commanded high prices until just before abolition. In October 1872, Hacienda Mercedita acquired a female slave for 300 pesos: Curet, *De la esclavitud a la abolición*, p. 14, chart 2; Scarano, "Sugar and Slavery," p. 345, table 6.1; and Ramos Mattei, *La hacienda azucarera*, p. 96.

the standard of living of those forced to work more, especially for those peasants whose own plots of land were neglected when they were required to labor elsewhere. Hacendados, on the other hand, were able to extract more surplus labor, and hence produce more output, than would have been possible without the legislation, and they, of course, were the moving force behind it. However, the antivagrancy acts resulted in less of an increase in the labor supply than was desired, partly because of the ambiguities in defining precisely who was a vagrant. Jornaleros and small landholders were quite ingenious in their efforts to resist being classified as vagrants. And, of course, the legislation left "nonvagrants" free from increased labor requirements.

Thus, on June 11, 1849, Governor de la Pezuela took a further step and published the *Reglamento Especial de Jornaleros*.[111] This law defined as jornaleros all males age 16 or over who, because of a lack of capital or a skill, had to work for another, regardless of the nature of the work (e.g., whether as a domestic, an agricultural worker, an artisan, or in transportation) or the length of time spent at such work. The definition included even those who owned land, or had access to the land of someone else as agregados, but who could not provide for all their necessities from that land and who thus found it necessary to work elsewhere in return for wages or goods at least part of the year. This went far beyond the previous antivagrancy laws by bringing under the legislation anyone who did any labor for others, regardless of the length of time spent working for outside income relative to home production. All jornaleros thus defined were required to register in their municipio and were to receive a *libreta*, or workbook, with a registration number. Being found without a libreta was punishable by eight days of public labor at half pay. The libreta was to show not only labor contracts and the location where work was performed and for whom, but also the jornalero's behavior at work and the debts incurred while employed. A responsible official in each municipality was charged with the duty of seeing to it that "the jornaleros of their territory are constantly employed"; when a worker with a good record (as shown in the libreta) could not find a position, employment in public works at full pay was to be provided.

The reglamento authorized prizes for workers "to develop the love for work," and it provided for the care of (Article 17) orphaned or abandoned children of jornaleros. Like the previous laws, it prohibited jornal-

---

[111] Gómez Acevedo, *Organización y reglamentación*, pp. 449–53. Gómez writes that in the reglamento there was a "laudable desire" to mobilize labor for Puerto Rico's development. That he is able to say this, despite the powers aligned against jornaleros, peasants, and agregados to increase their labor for the gain of others, evidences a certain lapse of perspective.

eros from participating in cockfighting, gambling, drinking, or engaging in other diversions on workdays. Penalties for employers who abused the libreta system or their jornaleros were specified, but there was more appearance than substance to these protections against the capriciousness of landowners.[112]

The libreta system also went beyond previous regulations in its provisions concerning agregados. The purpose of these specific articles, and of a clarification issued in December 1849, was to eliminate agregados altogether—and thus further expand the supply of jornaleros—by prohibiting landowners from maintaining agregados on their land after June 11, 1850. Agregados were required to move to the nearest town, unless they were paying rent or were personal servants, in which cases the landowner was responsible for their behavior. This not only was designed to prevent agregados from using privately owned land without incurring any obligations to its owner; it also provided landowners with a legal basis for dispossessing unwanted and recalcitrant agregados, and it was intended to concentrate jornaleros and former agregados in the towns, where they could be more easily controlled and their labor regularized and increased.[113] As a consequence of these provisions, many semi-jornaleros and agregados were dispossessed of what little land they had cultivated, a dispossession which took place without any compensation to them for the crops and structures they were forced to leave behind. The reglamento can thus be seen as a complement to the process of primitive accumula-

[112] Brau, "Las clases jornaleras," pp. 51–52, and Gómez Acevedo, *Organización y reglamentación*, p. 104. The study of F. Picó, *Libertad y servidumbre*, is an invaluable micro-study of jornalero and other types of labor in Utuado, the largest coffee-producing municipio and the second-largest population center, after Ponce, at the end of the nineteenth century. It is worth noting that Puerto Rico's libreta system was not entirely unique as a means of regulating labor. In Guatemala, Indians were required to carry similar workbooks; contract workers in the West Indies carried passes; and in Cuba, workers had a similar libreta system, imposed in 1851. Vagrancy laws were quite commonplace in the Americas, as was debt peonage. Still, the *general* application of the libreta regulations to jornaleros does appear to be unique to Puerto Rico. It may have emerged to compensate for the scarcity of a generally accepted currency, which necessitated another instrument, the workbook, to mediate between hacendados and workers. Given Puerto Rico's labor/land ratio— 131 persons per square mile in 1846 and 214 in 1877, compared to 33 in Cuba in the latter year—it would appear that labor was relatively plentiful. See Duncan and Rutledge, *Land and Labour*, esp. the introduction; McCreery, "Debt Servitude," pp. 745–46; and Stubbs, *Tobacco*, p. 73. Kloosterboer, *Involuntary Labour*, provides a survey of forced labor around the world.

[113] F. Picó, *Libertad y servidumbre*, pp. 40, 164, and Gómez Acevedo, *Organización y reglamentación*, pp. 107–11. Gómez, however, does not see this as anything other than desirable; he seems to believe that it was the scattered living arrangements of rural dwellers that made them "lazy," poorly educated, and sickly, and that town living would reverse that.

tion via dispossession which has been repeated time and again in agriculture wherever capitalist methods have begun to take root.

Unfortunately for the hacendados, the regulations on agregados did not result in the desired influx into the towns. In January 1850, de la Pezuela's colonial government issued another directive aimed at clarifying the terms under which nonlandowners and those without a skill or profession were exempted from registering as jornaleros. Renters of land (*arrendatarios*) with a notarized rent contract and at least four cuerdas of land under cultivation, for example, were not required to register. This provision proved to be a gaping loophole; at least in Picó's study of Utuado and Bergad's of Lares and Yauco, many family members "rented" land to relatives to permit them to avoid having to register as jornaleros, carry a libreta, and work for someone else. Bergad found a dramatic increase in small farms in Yauco between 1846 and 1857 as a result of such maneuvers (though most small holders were unable to retain their land once the coffee boom began and land concentration accelerated); in Lares, of 728 heads of agregado families, 70 percent had been classified as arrendatarios by September 1850.[114]

In many cases, agregados simply formalized their status by becoming arrendatarios, but this ultimately redounded to the advantage of the landowner and to the disadvantage of the agregado, who often was then prohibited from raising certain products and was forced to pay at least a portion of the landowner's taxes.[115] Still, some potential jornaleros avoided becoming subject to the scrutiny of the overseers of the libreta regulations and to their social stigma as they were exempted by landowners (usually larger ones) who wished to keep their agregados tied to the land. Landowners could use the rent-contract provision as leverage over former agregados to impose payments or work on them. Rent contracts often specified that new land be cleared and crops planted, thus extending the area under cultivation. At times, as an incentive for higher productivity, a portion of the crop would continue to be received by the arrendatario even if the rent contract was not renewed. Very often, rent contracts prohibited the renter from working for anyone else, and rents, in Lares at least, were not paid in cash but in labor at the rate of five pesos monthly, both of which were measures which bound labor to the land.[116]

Nevertheless, if it had been an effectively applied measure, the libreta system might have had the effect of creating a labor force working under

[114] Bergad, *Coffee and the Growth of Agrarian Capitalism*, pp. 109–10, 110 (table 3.16), 117.

[115] F. Picó, *Libertad y servidumbre*, pp. 39–40, 80–81, 84–88, 153.

[116] F. Picó, "Deshumanización del trabajo," pp. 199–201, and Bergad, *Coffee and the Growth of Agrarian Capitalism*, pp. 116–21.

labor-market conditions. But for a number of reasons, that is not what happened. First, in practice, the libreta system was often used by landowners to keep jornaleros on their land by requiring them to pay back debts accumulated either through direct borrowing or, more typically, from purchases on credit at the hacienda store. Indeed, since most jornaleros were illiterate, it was quite possible for landlords or their employees to falsify a debt record, though debt usually accumulated rapidly enough without such deception because of the low level of wages and the inflated prices the hacienda stores were able to charge by virtue of their monopoly position. Hence, many hacendados were able to maintain a bound labor force as long as they wished, with the force of the law to back them.[117] For example, a judge in Manatí in 1863 ordered Clemente Matos to work six months on a hacienda to pay off a debt of twenty-five pesos that he owed to the owner, and it was no coincidence that the sentence was set to begin in January—the start of the sugar harvest, when hands were badly needed.[118] Since it was not unusual for a hacendado to hold a jornalero's libreta until any debt was liquidated, the effect of the legislation was to severely restrict labor mobility.[119] At times it appeared as if there was a form of semiforced, servile labor working at the landowner's convenience, rather than a mobile supply of free laborers that the libreta seemed to have been designed to create. At best, what resulted was a quasi-labor market, with workers only partially mobile and not particularly responsive to wage differentials.

Second, a labor market could not easily emerge at this time because of the prevailing institutional structure. Very important was the scarcity of money with which to pay workers, as a result of which jornaleros were paid in script, known as *riles* or *vales*, redeemable at the company store of the hacendado who issued them or at nearby stores which agreed to honor them.[120] The denomination of some of this script was in *almudes*, a measure of quantity used for coffee, and some in *jornaldiarios* (a day's labor), while other script was denominated in more conventional *centavos* and *reales*. Hacienda tokens were accepted on the island generally, but merchant tokens, issued by town stores, were more typically valid only in a limited local area.[121]

[117] Many of the hacendados and the more liberal thinkers understood that this situation of virtual debt peonage blocked the development of free labor and the increase of productivity; Gómez Acevedo, *Organización y reglamentación*, pp. 124, 125, 157, 166–67, 182.

[118] Ramos Mattei, "La importación de trabajadores contratados," p. 131. In 1866, in a judgment brought against Rosa Vega for a debt of forty-eight pesos, her son was required to work for sixty-four weeks on the land of José del Río at a wage of 0.75 pesos per week!

[119] F. Picó, "Deshumanización del trabajo," p. 201.

[120] This of course enhanced the efficacy of debt as a tool in the landowners' hands.

[121] Gould and Higgie, *Money of Puerto Rico*, pp. 16–17.

Third, as mentioned above, those threatened with having to register as jornaleros were often able to avoid doing so by becoming, or by simply being classified as, arrendatarios or household laborers. As long as land remained available and relatively cheap, as it was during the first half or so of the nineteenth century in many regions, particularly the interior, the attempt to regulate the flow of labor was met with many forms of subtle evasion and opposition.[122]

Finally, the libreta regulations often were only weakly and sporadically enforced, because of a lack of funds to finance boards of enquiry, because of a shortage of persons to oversee the regulations, and because the distances between municipios and the administrative center in San Juan gave the localities a degree of freedom in deciding how vigorously to enforce them.[123]

The libreta system was officially ended in June 1873, three months after slavery was abolished. Even before this, the libreta's usefulness had been questioned officially as early as 1866, and the libreta regime as a means of regulating labor had fallen into disuse—and disrepute—to a great extent by 1868. Spain was dissatisfied with the labor regulations for a number of reasons, but most important was the belief that they interfered with the free movement of labor and enabled landowners to obtain labor at less than the market wage.[124]

The end of the libreta regime did not mean that the hacendados had relinquished their desire for a captive, cheap, and servile labor force. In fact, the end of slavery led some landowners, especially in sugar-cane regions, to advocate a revised libreta scheme.[125] They argued that the regulations were needed to deal with the continued scarcity of labor, and perhaps there was some validity in that position. Slaveowners had received payment for their freed slaves only in the form of numbered certificates with a value of 100 pesos for each slave. Many landowners, short of funds, sold these notes at a discount to obtain money with which

[122]F. Picó, *Libertad y servidumbre*, p. 146, and F. Picó, *Amargo café*, p. 52. Once the coffee economy boomed, the demand for land increased, land prices rose, and this avenue for escape from the classification of a jornalero was closed off. The average price for a cuerda of land in Lares, for example, rose from about 5 pesos in 1835–40 to 7.3 in 1841–50, to 12.4 in 1885, and 37.6 in 1868. The growth in the number of those classified as jornaleros and the decline in the number of arrendatarios paralleled this increase. In 1850, the ratio of arrendatarios to jornaleros was 2:1; by 1870, it was at most 1:2: Bergad, "Grito de Lares," pp. 625, 627, 630, 634–35.

[123]Gómez Acevedo, *Organización y reglamentación*, pp. 37–38.

[124]Ibid., 132–33, 252; Brau, "Las clases jornaleras," pp. 52–53; and *BHPR* 3:141–42. In Utuado, Picó found that the regulations had been abandoned in practice beginning in the 1860s; the authorities seemed to be more concerned with harassing unmarried persons living together than with regulating workers: *Libertad y servidumbre*, pp. 114–15.

[125]Gómez Acevedo, *Organización y reglamentación*, chaps. 15–17.

to hire jornaleros. For them, a captive labor force would have been quite attractive. Anticipation of abolition and the compensation that was expected to accompany it also probably accounts for the large number of orders—around 300—for steam-driven sugar-grinding machines between 1870 and 1880, though not all of them were put into place when it became apparent that immediate compensation was not forthcoming.[126]

In April 1874, Governor José Laureano Sanz did publish a new decree on vagrancy, but it was only a temporary measure, and in practice, at the municipio level, it served more as a means of harassing political opponents than of regulating the flow of labor.[127] As late as 1877, the Sociedad de Agricultura de Ponce, which represented sugar hacendados, was still asking for new labor regulations, complaining that a free labor market was ruinous to agriculture and that forced labor was necessary since jornaleros would not work sufficiently otherwise.[128] Spain, however, denied this and later requests to regulate the movement of labor by extra-economic means, at least partly because of a perceived threat of labor disturbances and of the increased class conflict that such regulations were believed likely to engender.[129]

There is no doubt, though, that the ending of slavery and of the libreta system in the same year exacerbated the labor shortage. The lack of means of exchange for financing and facilitating commodity transactions, including the hiring of labor, became more critical and the shortage more onerous with the greater demand for money that accompanied the shift away from the coercion of a labor supply. Interestingly, many hacendados returned to an earlier system of labor supply: they granted small plots of land to resident workers, both to limit their mobility and to win their loyalty. In effect, agregados were reconstituted as a labor source, in consequence of the shortage of money and the tenaciousness of precapitalist attitudes toward work.[130]

[126]Ramos Mattei, "La importación de trabajadores contratados," p. 132. Spain did not have the funds for redeeming the certificates issued as compensation for emancipating the slaves and so resorted to annual lotteries (until 1890) to choose which of them would be honored. The financing for the lotteries came from an additional tax levied on sugar exports. Hence, former slaveowners helped to furnish their own compensation: Ramos Mattei, "El liberto," pp. 116, 120.

[127]Gómez Acevedo, *Organización y reglamentación*, pp. 283–89, and *BHPR* 6:227, n. 1, and 228, n. 2. Governor Sanz was of the opinion that many labor problems, including the inadequate supply, were the result of the fact that workers, including and perhaps especially newly freed slaves, had freedoms for which they were unprepared, and thus regulations were necessary. The Spanish authorities did not see it that way and severely chastised this effort to reintroduce labor regulations: *BHPR* 12:233–36.

[128]Gómez Acevedo, *Organización y reglamentación*, pp. 297–99. Of course, the owners meant that workers were not going to work as much as *they* wanted them to.

[129]Brau, "Las clases jornaleras," pp. 55–56.

[130]Ramos Mattei, "El liberto," pp. 121–22.

JORNALERO LABOR

As discussed above, a jornalero was a person who worked for someone else on a contractual basis in return for wages or some form of compensation in kind. Some jornaleros may have had small land holdings, though these were insufficient to meet the needs of their families. An increasing number of persons—agregados, arrendatarios, *medianeros* (sharecroppers), or free peasants—needed monetary income to pay taxes, buy imported goods, reduce debt, or pay rent on the land they worked. The founding of hacienda tiendas, particularly in the interior, led to debt for many peasants as they bought merchandise on credit. Many of them lost all or a part of their land as a result, and in this way hacendados gained not only more area to cultivate but also more jornaleros needing work.

Increased commodity exchange and monetization thus helped to forge the class of jornaleros and created a need for work and for cash income that otherwise would not have been so pressing.[131] These subtle and evolutionary changes—land concentration, rising debts and taxes, greater dependence on food imports—had a stronger and more lasting impact on the supply of labor than the combined effect of all the state's regulations. The relationship of jornalero to employer was mediated by cash or goods payment, which was disruptive of the more personal, even if clearly hierarchical, relations that had characterized the associations among agregados, landowners, and peasants, all of whom long had been bound together by tradition, custom, and ceremony. The growing institutionalized importance of money and the market, in short, weakened the old class structure as capitalist relations penetrated into these areas.

Three distinct categories of jornaleros may be identified: (1) A town-dwelling fraction, with no land ownership other than, possibly, a house and small garden—in effect, an urban proletariat. Such jornaleros worked in the cigar, furniture, pastry, match, soap, ice, rum, or other small-scale, mostly artisan, industries, or they labored on nearby farms as agricultural day workers or as *mozos de labor* (house servants). (2) A rural proletariat of landless, rural-living agricultural workers. Such workers often were concealed among the semi-independent peasantry, agregados, medianeros, and arrendatarios.[132] (3) A rural semiproletariat or semipeasantry, who worked for wages or payment in kind but who also owned or

---

[131] F. Picó, *Libertad y servidumbre*, pp. 81–83. "The credit system meant restricted consumption for many, wage labor for others": Steward et al., *People of Puerto Rico*, pp. 192–93. The credit system and the resulting debt were fundamental forces in the breakdown of the semisubsistence life style of peasants and semipeasants. See also Díaz Hernández, *Castañer*, p. 35.

[132] Mintz, "Rural Proletariat."

had access to land (as agregados or arrendatarios) on which they produced at least a portion of their subsistence.[133]

It was the third category of jornaleros that predominated in the middle
of the nineteenth century. Their connection to the land was a source of
some independence, but it was also a basis for paying them lower wages
when they did work elsewhere. Not only they themselves but also members of their family performed labor for hire as well as working on their
land. During harvest periods, particularly in coffee regions, this labor by
women and children helped to relieve temporary labor shortages while
contributing (usually in pitifully small amounts) to family income.[134]

It is clear that jornaleros did not form a homogeneous class whose
members had similar origins or real cohesiveness; as Picó writes, it was
more "a class in formation" than one whose boundaries were well defined.[135] And, at least judging from the libretas of some jornaleros, their
employment was very unstable and discontinuous, further evidence of the
incomplete nature of labor markets late in the nineteenth century.[136]

THE PEASANTRY

Defining who is a peasant is notoriously difficult, given the variety of
arrangements cultivators have employed in the control and use of land.[137]
Eric Wolf's distinction seems to be most pertinent: "The peasant . . .
does not operate an enterprise in the economic sense; he runs a household, not a business concern."[138] That is, the peasant's motive is reproduction of a way of life rather than the production of commodities or
profit per se. Peasants in Puerto Rico were not isolated in an economic
sense; they were connected to the larger society of haciendas and trade
in many ways, including temporary work arrangements. They often sold
a part of their output, especially coffee, to merchants in order to be able
to pay their taxes or to pay off a debt, as well as to buy some consumption goods. This market nexus, however, did not cause them to lose their
basic characteristics as a peasantry.

Like jornaleros, the peasants did not form a homogeneous class. Some
worked for hacendados or even for other peasants; that is, they were
actually semipeasant or semi-jornalero. Richer peasants, like the bigger

---

[133] F. Picó, *Libertad y servidumbre*, p. 35, points out that, at least in Utuado in some
years, only those living in the town were classified as jornaleros; "farmers," on the other
hand, covered many different labor forms, including slaves, so a respectful suspicion for
the usefulness of the categories is called for.

[134] Díaz Hernández, *Castañer*, p. 35.

[135] F. Picó, *Libertad y servidumbre*, p. 164.

[136] Ibid., p. 92.

[137] See Mintz, "Note on the Definition of Peasantries."

[138] Eric Wolf, *Peasants*, p. 2, quoted in ibid., p. 93.

hacendados, often exploited poorer peasants through these labor arrangements or through loans extended at high interest rates. Poorer peasants worked for wages on land other than their own to protect and preserve their peasant existence, for they considered themselves peasants first and foremost and jornaleros only temporarily and out of a necessity enforced upon them by the evolving nature of the social formation and the institutional structure.

Agregados and arrendatarios were peasant adaptations to Puerto Rico's specific conditions. Though for analytical purposes agregados were considered separately above, they too were part of the peasant population. Agregados had some of the characteristics of peasants (e.g., relatively independent production), of feudal serfs (provision of labor services to a landowner in return for use of land for their own production), and of semi-proletarians (receipt of income in wages or kind). Thus, the agregados occupied an inconsistent position within the late nineteenth-century class structure; like the jornaleros, they also were a class in transition. They were a bridge between the independent peasant and small-farmer production of the highlands and the future wage-labor relations that would come to dominate social relations on the coast and, later, in the interior. However, even though changes in the economic structure of the social formation clearly pointed in the direction of more wage labor, the continued existence and resilience of agregado and other peasant production hindered the full development of capitalist relations and forces of production, as did the other institutional barriers and infrastructural weaknesses already noted.

The Role of Immigrants

It is impossible to read any of the recent studies of Puerto Rico's economic history without being impressed with the importance of immigrants in the emergence of hacienda production and the shift toward capitalist methods of production during the nineteenth century. Scarano found, for example, that 77.5 percent (38 out of 49) of the hacendados in the Ponce region in 1827 were immigrants; in 1845, 74.4 percent (64 out of 86) were immigrants.[139] In the latter year, German, French, and British immigrants owned seven of the eight largest haciendas (those with a capital value in excess of 65,000 pesos); the other was Spanish owned. Of the ten "medium-large" haciendas (40,000–65,000 pesos), three were owned by creole Puerto Ricans and five by Spaniards (but none by other Europeans). Over the period from 1827 to 1845, the position of creoles in the

[139] Scarano, "Sugar and Slavery," p. 203, table 4.1.

productive structure declined in Ponce, while that of Spanish immigrants improved appreciably, at the expense of other European immigrants.[140] Deterioration in the economic position of the creoles seems to have been quite general in the areas of major export production; Díaz noted the loss of land among landowners in Barrio Bartolo in Lares to Hacienda Castañer, a major coffee hacienda, usually as the result of excess debt.[141]

Scarano's work provides valuable insight into the differences that divided immigrant and creole growers, and a consideration of these can help to explain the changes that began after the turn of the century. Seven of the ten non-Hispanic sugar hacendados in Ponce had been involved in the sugar business in the eastern Caribbean (five in St. Thomas) before coming to Puerto Rico. They brought to Puerto Rico skills, knowledge, contacts with world markets, and, in many cases, substantial initial capital resources. It appears that in the areas they left, they had been relatively small-scale entrepreneurs compared to other planters or merchants in the same areas, but they loomed large in their new location, given the relative backwardness of Ponce in the early decades of the century. The liquid and material wealth these immigrants brought with them permitted them to purchase the best and most productive sugar land while it was still relatively inexpensive and while there still was unsettled land available, a situation that did not last beyond midcentury.[142] They also were able to purchase a sufficiently large slave-labor force to be able to expand their production without going immediately into debt. These early immigrants were thus able to complete a process of land consolidation well before the sugar boom increased the demand for both land and slave labor, raising their prices and making it more difficult for later planters, immigrant and creole, to duplicate these early successes.

Later Spanish immigrants often became hacendados only after first operating tiendas or being otherwise involved in commerce, a route to enrichment reserved especially for Spanish citizens. Others had been employed as skilled workers or overseers, both well-paying positions (a manager of a large hacienda could earn up to 1,000 pesos per year plus expenses). From these positions, many immigrants were able to accumulate not only the capital but also the knowledge about land, production methods, and financial accounting techniques increasingly required for success as exporters to world markets. Primitive accumulation through commerce also characterized the emergence of coffee hacendados in the second half of the century. For example, Juan Castañer came to Puerto Rico from Mallorca in 1861 and worked for seven years on a coffee

[140] Ibid., pp. 204–9.
[141] Díaz Hernández, *Castañer*, pp. 13–14.
[142] Scarano, "Sugar and Slavery," pp. 211–15.

hacienda in Lares, which enabled him to buy a piece of land and open a *tenducho* (a small store). By 1870, he had amassed enough wealth and land to establish Hacienda Castañer, and the Castañer family became large landowners and important merchants and lenders in the region between Lares in the mountains and Yauco in the southwest near Ponce, as their hacienda acted as a growth pole for their own extensive operations.[143]

Because of legal restrictions, Spanish immigrants predominated in commerce; in many locations, they were the sole merchants. Interestingly, however, both Cubano's study of Arecibo and Bergad's of Lares suggest that there was a substantial turnover among immigrants, as newcomers replaced not only creoles but earlier immigrants as well. This was true among commercial establishments in Arecibo and among hacendados in Lares, where only seven of the twenty-eight largest landowners in 1848 were still there in 1867. However, it should be noted that the earlier migrants, who returned to Spain or Mallorca, were succeeded by newer *peninsulares*. The turnover thus did not reflect a failure of Spanish immigrants within the insular social structure.[144]

Immigrants also contributed to the technological advance of the industrial phase of sugar production. The first steam-driven sugar-grinding mill, for example, was introduced about 1823 by two Irish brothers, Robert and Josiah Archbald, who had come to Puerto Rico in 1818 and who owned the largest hacienda in Ponce by the 1840s.[145]

Bergad's study of Lares, Yauco, San Germán, and Mayagüez underscores the importance of immigrants to the expansion of commerce and hacienda production. In Yauco, Corsicans dominated commerce by mid-century and controlled four of the six sugar haciendas. In Lares, Mallorcans controlled commerce during the last half of the century, and they also led the expansion of the coffee economy in the interior. Even in 1848, before the coffee boom began, immigrants controlled three-quarters of all merchant capital in Lares.[146] They almost never employed creoles; rather, if an assistant was required, they sent for relatives or the son of a friend, an attitude which did nothing to improve relations between peninsulares and creoles.[147]

The provision of credit was an important means by which merchants gained control over the coffee crop for export to Europe. The need for simple, daily articles of consumption led small and medium farmers into

[143] Ibid., pp. 215–18, 221–23, 225–27, and Díaz Hernández, *Castañer*, pp. 6–7.
[144] Cubano Iguina, "Economía y sociedad en Arecibo," p. 118; Bergad, *Coffee and the Growth of Agrarian Capitalism*, p. 97; and Bergad, "Grito de Lares," p. 623.
[145] Scarano, "Sugar and Slavery," pp. 215–16.
[146] Bergad, *Coffee and the Growth of Agrarian Capitalism*, p. 26.
[147] Ibid., pp. 31–32.

debt, which they liquidated, or attempted to liquidate, by turning over their harvest to the merchant who had advanced funds to them. Some merchants took land from those who could not repay a debt in full, but most realized it was more advantageous to carry a part of the debt, keep the land in production, and receive the crop than it was to accumulate small properties that would have to be worked by someone, anyway. Very often, this debt carryover resulted in accounting balances that would be hard to understand if one did not appreciate the importance of debt as a mechanism for binding landowners to merchants. For example, one store in Arecibo, Roses y Companía, had assets of 579,367 pesos in 1889, a very large sum for the time, and of these assets, 307,634 pesos (53.1 percent) were in the form of current debt owed by the store's customers. Such a situation, in which half of a company's assets were in accounts receivable, was not at all unusual, at least among merchants in Arecibo.[148]

The possibility for earning profits by the extension of credit was immense, and it is understandable why merchants did not rush to claim the land used as collateral when one of their clients failed to fully repay a debt (though later in the century commerce and hacendado ownership came to be concentrated in the same hands). Profits were earned, first, on the value of the goods advanced, and then through the interest (1-2 percent a month) on the credit balance; and finally, there was a potential for additional, sometimes substantial, profit to be gained by speculation, as on coffee prices, for example.

Three different coffee prices existed at any one time. First, there was the *credit price*, which was the amount to be paid when the crop was delivered after the harvest to liquidate, or reduce, the debt incurred in the merchant's store prior to the harvest. This price for future delivery was set at the time credit was extended. Second was the *market price*, the actual spot price of coffee as quoted on the world market. To the extent that the market price—the price at which the merchant could sell the coffee obtained from his customers—exceeded the credit price (which the merchant determined), additional profits from the indebtedness of the coffee growers were earned. The third price, the *farm price*, was what merchants paid to those growers who were not in debt to them. This was an intermediate price, below the market price but above the current credit price. Bergad gives an example of a Lares merchant who in 1867 set a credit price of 6 pesos per fanega of coffee and a farm price of 7.5 pesos, and who in 1868 received a market price of 14.5 pesos per fanega.[149]

[148] Cubano Iguina, "Economía y sociedad en Arecibo," pp. 104–5.
[149] Bergad, *Coffee and the Growth of Agrarian Capitalism*, pp. 79–80, 85, 86. As a measure of weight, the fanega was equal to about one quintal or one hundred pounds.

There is no doubt, though, that immigrants to Puerto Rico provided a
dynamic impetus to the economy from outside that would have been slower
to develop internally. As embryonic capitalists, immigrants contributed
to the transformations in technology, production, and class relations that
were to result in the emergence of limited capitalist production within the
predominately noncapitalist nineteenth-century economy.

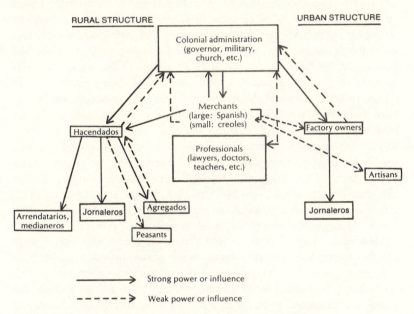

Figure 1.1 Class Structure in Nineteenth-Century Puerto Rico

THE CLASS STRUCTURE

A complete picture of the nineteenth-century class structure and class
relations must also of course consider the hacendados and small factory
owners, the merchants, those involved in the colonial apparatus (including the military and the clergy), and the emerging professional strata
composed mainly of creoles educated abroad as lawyers, teachers, and
doctors, and who often were the descendants of displaced creole hacendados. Figure 1.1 is a schematic representation of the overall class structure.[150] The arrows indicate the nature of the relations between classes.
Hacendados, professionals, and factory owners are shown on the same

[150] Quintero Rivera independently has developed a similar representation to show the class
base of political parties at the end of the nineteenth century: "La base social," p. 39,
fig. 1.

level because they occupied similar positions of dominance, power, and influence within the overall social formation, though not necessarily the same class interests. In fact, the differences among these elite classes were quite significant, as will be seen in the discussion below of their political positions.

Jornaleros in the rural areas were dominated by hacendados, in sugar and coffee production especially, and their relations were characterized by the provision of labor services in return for income (in money, in script, or in kind). Agregados, medianeros, and arrendatarios were also in a subordinate position relative to hacendados, especially after the imposition of the 1849 reglamento; they paid rents to and gave labor services to or shared output with their landowners. Some peasants were relatively independent of the hacendado class; others needed to supplement their production with labor, and that was typically done for a larger landowner, but even such peasants had a degree of security, however fragile, not shared by jornaleros. Urban artisans operated in a more or less independent manner within a mode of small production (cigars, bread and pastries, furniture, ice, etc.), though, of course, their output was sold on the market. In urban areas like San Juan, Ponce, and Mayagüez, factory owners—small and medium capitalists—were the dominant economic class; jornaleros, a classical urban proletariat, provided the labor.

Merchants operated in both rural and urban areas. The largest were Spanish immigrants, or peninsulares, while creoles operated smaller general stores (*pulperías*), which depended upon the larger commercial firms for goods and credit. The merchants not only imported products to the island and purchased crops for export; they were also the main source of loans for agricultural producers, as was seen above. They preserved their profitable and powerful position for a long time, earning a reputation for ruthlessness in collecting on loans through crop deliveries or by taking land.

The professional stratum of doctors, lawyers, and teachers occupied a relatively privileged and influential position within the class structure. Their ability to advance economically was not matched by their political power, however. As was the case for most creole hacendados and emerging capitalists, their path was blocked by the colonial administration, which held a monopoly of power in the state, the church, the military, and the courts (though at the local level, in the municipios, it was possible for creoles to exercise some political leverage and to share in political power and patronage). The power of the colonial apparatus was manifested in laws and regulations, taxes, the special rights granted to Spanish merchants, restrictions on trade, and so on. However, the colonial administration was not omnipotent, as the arrows from below are meant to indicate. The economic base, in which hacendados, including creoles, were the most powerful force, and the intellectual base of professionals, were able to influence colonial policy, especially in its implementation, which very often could be bent to local purposes. Furthermore, local participation by the creole elite increased as the nineteenth century came to a close. Though the power of the colonial administration was never seriously challenged, the growing influence of the creole elite did narrow its boundaries of operation.

CHANGES IN PRODUCTION AND THE CLASS STRUCTURE

The nineteenth century was a period of dynamic change in Puerto Rico. Immigrants came from Haiti, Louisiana, the Caribbean, the Americas, and Europe, attracted by the land grants of the Cédula de Gracias or the promise of riches in an expanding colony, or in flight from Bolívar's armies or other uprisings. They gave a great stimulus to production through the introduction of capital, new technology, and capitalist ideas about the organization of production. The ensuing transformation was facilitated by the opening of the island to legal trade with countries other than Spain. In the first half of the century, there was a rapid growth of sugar-cane production, where slaves provided an important part of the labor. As more land was devoted to sugar cane, however, neither the number of slaves nor the funds available to purchase them were sufficient to meet the growing labor requirements. The growth process was not self-sustaining, either, since the internal market was nearly negligible. Raw sugar and molasses were produced primarily for an external market, which was outside the control of local forces. It was through this external dependence that the hacendados developed a market orientation.[151]

Though many slaveowning hacendados may have wished to organize their production differently, the absence of a substantial pool of jornaleros prevented a change. Slaves were an economic drain; it was necessary to feed, clothe, and maintain them even when there was little work to do, as during the periods between harvests. Because slaves were an important and expensive asset of the landowner, it was not possible, or not desirable, to acquire physical means of production to augment the productivity of their labor; in this context, it was the slave who was the capital. Hence, extensive rather than more intensive and efficient production methods were encouraged.[152]

---

[151] Though sugar haciendas around Ponce were export-oriented, they were also nearly self-sufficient. About one-fourth of the land was devoted to sugar cane and the remainder to minor crops for subsistence consumption and grazing: Curet, *De la esclavitud a la abolición*, p. 3.

[152] Curet calculates the internal rate of return to slave capital in 1845 as greater than 17 percent (ibid., pp. 11–12), but the meaning which should be attached to this calculation is unclear. See Dietz, "Puerto Rico's New History," p. 218, for further comments.

Accumulation of capital and growth are fundamental characteristics of capitalism, be it industrial or agrarian. The initial outlay and the maintenance cost of slaves interfered with and slowed this process of capital accumulation. The potential surplus was used to maintain slaves, thus reducing the funds available for purchasing the new production machinery becoming available and increasingly in use in Europe and the United States. The decline in sugar-cane acreage and in the number of grinding mills during the last decades of the nineteenth century, and the signs of crisis increasingly evident during that time, are evidence of the failure of capitalist adaptation in this sector.[153]

The 345 sugar mills in Puerto Rico in 1899 had but one-tenth the total capacity of the 207 Cuban mills then in operation.[154] Only a few Puerto Rican producers were able to modernize, usually because of their connections with the main merchant nationalities, who often made credit available to their compatriots but not to others, or because they had their own sources of capital.[155]

Sugar exports did increase until the mid-1870s, but only because of a strong sellers' market, which protected local producers from competition—not because of the aggressiveness, technical efficiency, or capital accumulation of the cane producers. Mintz described the typical hacienda as follows:

Steam or cattle provided the power for the crude grinding mills, which consisted of vertical iron rollers. Sugar processing was also crude, and the *moscovado* [unrefined] sugar "logs" or "heads" or "cones," produced by successive boiling, evaporation, and draining, were typical of much earlier developments in the sugar-making industry. Fertilizing was limited to the use of animal manure, and manuring was not always practiced; rudimentary hook-type plows were employed in field operations. Potential profits were lost in badly ground cane, poorly manured land, low-quality sugar, and high interest rates. The plantations were usually owned by individual families, with agents or single

[153] "What might have been interpreted as a reluctance to invest in increasing the size and efficiency of plantations in the 1840s and 1850s had by 1870 become sheer inability to do so": Mintz, *Caribbean Transformations*, p. 100. In Ponce, at least 80 percent of the milling facilities were of seventeenth-century design, though this may be related more to the level of production (i.e., the absence of economies of scale) than to gross inefficiency: Scarano, "Sugar and Slavery," pp. 191–97.

[154] Bergad, "Agrarian History," p. 65, and USDW, *1899 Census*, p. 155. A similar comparison can be made with Trinidad; though it had half the land area and one-sixth the population of Puerto Rico, it exported roughly the same value of goods: José Julián Acosta, "El sistema prohibitivo y la libertad de comercio en America" (1879), *BHPR* 7:284.

[155] Scarano, "Sugar and Slavery," pp. 178–180, and Ramos Mattei, "La importación de trabajadores contratados," p. 131.

members of the family supervising the operations . . . [A] constant
profit could be assured without additional investment in irrigation, improved technology, or enlarged operations.[156]

Given this low level of technology, it was easy for new producers to
enter the market during the sugar boom. However, when the technology
of sugar production led to the creation of large-scale centrals in other
countries and more efficient and inexpensive extraction methods like the
Jamaica train method and centrifugal processing, competition from beet-
sugar producers intensified, prices dropped, and the sellers' market disappeared. To make matters worse, Puerto Rico produced a low-quality
sugar, and the outdated technology in use extracted from the cane only
about half the sugar content as the new methods did. Attempts by producers to get Spain to reduce or eliminate its tariff on sugar so as to open
that market met with failure.[157] When the United States raised its tariff
in 1894 and again in 1897, to protect its own sugar producers in the
South, the situation deteriorated further.

As noted above, some sugar-cane producers did succeed in modernizing. Hacienda Mercedita installed advanced machinery and was a "fully
modernized mill" by 1890.[158] The first mill, San Vicente in Vega Baja,
had begun operations as early as 1873.[159] Haciendas Las Claras and Mon-
tegrande, around Arecibo—an area which seems to have retained its dynamic during the sugar-export crisis—became centrales, as did others,
like Luisa in Maunabo, San Luis in Carolina, and Josefina in Río Piedras,
though most, including San Vicente, were bankrupt by the 1880s.[160] As
Bergad observed, "pockets of modernization existed while the industry
as a whole stagnated."[161] Clearly, these were "pockets" of nascent capitalist organization, but the sugar industry as a whole was unable to transform itself in this way. Its revitalization came only after the U.S. intervention, when North American capital flowed into the sugar industry,
permitting it to introduce modern techniques of production on a wide
scale.

[156] Mintz, *Caribbean Transformations*, p. 99.

[157] In 1876, each quintal of sugar paid a tax of 8.741 pesetas. The cost of production was
20 pesetas, so this represented an effective tariff of 44 percent: *BHPR* 13:346.

[158] Ramos Mattei, *La hacienda azucarera*, pp. 28 and 43ff., gives detailed information
on Mercedita's operations: technology, land use, irrigation, and so on.

[159] Sánchez Derga, "La industria azucarera," p. 26.

[160] Cubano Iguina, "Economía y sociedad en Arecibo," pp. 77, 80, and passim. Sugar
exports from Arecibo expanded until the late 1840s and then leveled off. However, in the
late 1860s, exports again grew rapidly and had increased more than 50 percent over the
previous twenty-year average by the mid-1870s. Crisis set in again during the 1880s.

[161] Bergad, "Agrarian History," p. 66.

IMPACT OF THE LIBRETA SYSTEM

The purpose of the libreta system was to increase the supply of labor available to hacendados, not only from full-time jornaleros but also from small peasants, agregados, and others who did not have an adequate independent source of livelihood. The libreta regulations were integral to the process of primitive capitalist accumulation, in which free access to the means of production—in this instance, land—for one's own production was legally denied to ever greater numbers of persons.[162] Time spent by peasants and agregados who had to work for others as jornaleros meant time away from their own land and crops. Production of so-called minor crops for local consumption declined as a result.[163] Thus, the libreta system created not only a "love" for work, which was its stated goal; it created the *need* for work in order to earn wages with which to buy products no longer produced at home, or produced only in smaller quantities.[164]

Money income, however, was never large enough for most jornaleros to cover their necessary purchases at the hacienda or town store. Agricultural workers in the early 1870s received about 1 to 1.25 pesos a week, or about 25 centavos a day.[165] A family of five would use two to three pounds of rice daily, at a cost of 8 to 12 centavos. A pound of bacon cost 32 centavos; potatoes, 18; *bacalao* (dried codfish), 32; bread, 10 centavos. A pair of work shoes cost 2.5 pesos, about two weeks' wages. Díaz estimated that a family of five had about 35 centavos in daily expenditures, which makes it quite easy to see how debt at hacienda stores piled up quickly and why it was rarely liquidated completely.[166]

[162] Quintero Rivera has referred to the system as "white slavery," since it was imposed primarily on free, white citizens: "Background to the Emergence of Imperialist Capitalism," p. 95. See also Mattos Cintrón, *La política y lo político*, pp. 28, 33–34. Land scarcity due to concentration, and the accompanying rise in land values, did affect social organization. For example, marriages were delayed and/or took place among relatives to reduce the breakup of farms into small units through inheritance: F. Picó, *Amargo café*, pp. 53–56, 92–94, 97–98.

[163] Gómez Acevedo, *Organización y reglamentación*, p. 56.

[164] Still, until the mid-1860s, the volume of production of minor crops exceeded that of agricultural exports: Steward et al., *People of Puerto Rico*, p. 40.

[165] By comparison, in 1814, weeding had paid three pesos per month; cleaning coffee, eight pesos: Cruz Monclova, *Historia* 1:71.

[166] Díaz Hernández, *Castañer*, p. 40. Immediately after emancipation and the end of the libreta system in 1873, wages rose slightly, reflecting the demand for labor and the need to attract workers. In Carolina, wages were 37½ centavos a day for men aged twenty to forty-five but only 17 centavos for men over forty-five. Women earned 25 centavos per day. In other locations, wages for men rose to 50 centavos: Ramos Mattei, "El liberto," pp. 109–10. Bergad notes that these higher wage rates indicate the increasing importance of the labor market as a regulator of labor flows: "Coffee and Rural Proletarianization," pp. 93–94.

Increased expenditures on imported products also meant that an ever larger volume of exports was required to finance the imports and, in a vicious cycle, more land was needed for export crops, requiring more imported food, and so on. In the process, more and more of those who worked became jornaleros, proletarianized by the advances of capitalist production.

The increase in imported consumption goods represented a substantial change from the early 1830s, when George D. Flinter, an Irish adventurer and proslavery writer who resided for a time in Puerto Rico, reported on conditions on the island. Though incensed even then over what he regarded as an excessive volume of imported food, Flinter noted that Puerto Rico produced sufficient rice to be able to export small quantities. Pedro Tomás de Córdova, a secretary in the colonial government, determined that, of the 85,076 cuerdas under cultivation in 1830, more than a quarter (28.8 percent) were devoted to the main export crops: sugar cane (11,103 cuerdas), coffee (9,135), tobacco (2,199), and cotton (2,080). On the other hand, the remainder of the cultivated area was in subsistence production; 11,855 cuerdas in rice, 21,761 in plantains, 8,224 in sweet potatoes, and 12,194 in Indian corn, among other domestically consumed crops.[167] This was a situation that was to rapidly change as the nineteenth century progressed and labor and land tenure relations were transformed.

For some hacendados, especially in cane-producing areas like Ponce, the libreta system never did provide the desired supply of workers; they wanted a more complete regulation of labor and the imposition of truly servile labor relations, as already noted. However, the intellectual currents of the time and the changing needs and tendencies within the productive base moved in the direction of a landless and hence mobile labor force. The libreta system had contributed to the process that alienated peasants from their means of production and created a growing pool of workers obliged to sell their labor on the market as a commodity, even if by itself it was not the leading force for the creation of wage laborers.[168]

[167] Flinter, *Account of the Present State*, pp. 133–36, 159, 193; Córdova, *Memorias* 2:406–8. Rice production grew from 57,621 quintales in 1824 to 77,338 in 1832, a 34.2 percent increase. Production of sugar over the same period, however, grew 103 percent, and of coffee, 49.5 percent. Interestingly, production of oranges for the export market grew 244 percent: Córdova, *Memorias* 6:432–35. In Lares, the amount of land devoted to food crops declined from 1,961 cuerdas to 1,390 between 1846 and 1865. Given the nearly threefold increase in population over the same period, the per capita amount of land in subsistence crops fell dramatically: Bergad, "Grito de Lares," p. 629.

[168] After 1865, hacendados were prevented from holding a jornalero on a hacienda to pay accumulated debt through uncompensated labor services. By the conversion of tienda debt into common debt to be paid in coin and not labor services, the mobility of labor was furthered, the power of any individual hacendado was reduced, and laborers were "freed"

EFFECTS OF EXPANDED COFFEE CULTIVATION

The cultivation of coffee, which had begun in 1736, began to expand in the last third of the nineteenth century, and this growth exerted a partial counterforce to the emergence of capitalist production.[169] Coffee typically was grown in conjunction with other crops, like plantains and bananas, which provided shade and protection to the coffee plants, and the plants themselves were interspersed with other subsistence crops. It was therefore an ideal commodity for peasant and small-scale production.[170] In Arecibo, for example, of the 283 cuerdas devoted to coffee, 72 percent were on farms of less than 30 cuerdas (50 percent on farms of 8 cuerdas or less), and there was but one coffee hacienda, though this was an exceptional case.[171] Furthermore, the preparation of coffee for the market required very little capital investment. Peasants thus were able to combine subsistence production with a cash crop, and the improved market for Puerto Rico coffee in Europe after 1876 helped to slow the decline of the independent peasant population that was set into motion by increased land concentration, the imposition of the libreta system, greater monetization of the economy, and the spread of market relations in general. A related result of the growth of coffee production can be seen in the fact that the most rapid population growth between 1887 and 1889 occurred in the inland and mountainous regions—the areas of coffee production— rather than in the low-lying coastal regions, where most of the sugar cane was produced.[172]

Small coffee producers were able to survive, then, because they were

---

to sell their ability to work to whomever they could rather than being bound to a particular hacendado until any debt was liquidated. This definitely contributed to the development of the labor market.

[169] It was the rise in coffee prices on the world market—from 8–10 pesos per quintal in the 1850s and 1860s to 14–20 in the 1870s—that led to increased plantings of coffee: Bergad, "Coffee and Rural Proletarianization," p. 87.

[170] In 1830, nearly five times as much coffee was produced by small family farms as by the 148 coffee haciendas on the island: Flinter, *Account of the Present State*, p. 187.

[171] This was a sharp contrast with the pattern in sugar-cane cultivation. For example, in Arecibo in 1845, there were fifteen sugar haciendas, and they controlled 97 percent of the sugar land (and produced 68 percent of the total agricultural output of the region): Cubano Iguina, "Economía y sociedad en Arecibo," pp. 68–69, 72.

[172] USDW, *1899 Census*, pp. 41–42. Population in the interior municipios increased 22.2 percent, and in the coastal regions, 17.6 percent. If growth in the coastal cities of San Juan, Ponce, and Mayagüez is excluded, the difference is even larger. The rate of population growth on the island as a whole was 19.4 percent, indicating a relative shift to the interior. In certain areas, the population increase was more dramatic; for example, in the coffee area studied by Eric Wolf, population more than doubled between 1871 and 1897: Wolf, "San José," p. 193.

not wholly dependent on crop sales for their existence. (In Utuado, some 60 percent of coffee production came from small and medium-sized land-owners.)[173] On the other hand, coffee provided cash or collateral with which to buy food, clothes, and other items that could not be produced, or were difficult to produce, within the peasant household, and to pay taxes and repay loans. For peasant producers, coffee was a sideline activity, important but not the sole focus of attention. In 1865 in Yauco, for example, while some 1,811 cuerdas were planted in coffee, 3,480 still were being used for minor crops.[174]

Nevertheless, despite this countertendency, labor relations continued to change in the direction of more wage labor overall. Even in a coffee area studied by Wolf, municipal records showed 1,660 landowners in 1871 but only 555 by 1892, a period during which the population had doubled. It is thus apparent that many former owners had become wage workers, agregados, or sharecroppers on someone else's land.[175] In Lares, only 17.2 percent of all families owned land in 1870, down from about half in 1846. Whereas over 80 percent of agregados had had the right to land use in 1846, by 1870 less than one-third did. As early as the 1860s, jornalero labor predominated on the larger coffee fincas in Lares.[176]

Coffee haciendas, though typically of smaller scale than sugar-cane haciendas, were important in the highlands even as early as the middle of the nineteenth century, when in Lares, for example, the twenty-nine haciendas larger than 200 cuerdas (7.4 percent of all farms) occupied 48 percent of the land.[177] Buitrago Ortiz's study of southeast Puerto Rico clearly shows the dominance of hacienda over individual production in the cultivation of coffee.[178] This and other studies affirm that immigrants, particularly Spaniards, were more likely to found haciendas than were native Puerto Ricans, an indication of the transforming effect of the flow of liberal ideas and new methods of production, as well as the greater capital, which immigrants brought to the island.[179] The immigrants organized large-scale production and hired wage workers; Puerto Ricans, many of whom were being forced from their land, increasingly provided

---

[173] F. Picó, *Amargo café*, p. 29.

[174] Bergad, *Coffee and the Growth of the Agrarian Capitalism*, p. 112.

[175] Wolf, "San José," p. 192. In the leading coffee region, the living conditions of the majority of the population were worse at the beginnings of the twentieth century than at the start of the nineteenth; the diet of workers worsened, and the difficult living conditions led to more crime and alcoholism: F. Picó, *Libertad y servidumbre*, chap. 4.

[176] Bergad, *Coffee and the Growth of Agrarian Capitalism*, pp. 64–65, 193 (n. 107).

[177] Ibid., pp. 47, table 2.12.

[178] Buitrago Oritz, *Los orígenes históricos*.

[179] Ibid., pp. 12–13, 19.

the labor.[180] In such a situation, the emergence of resentment toward Spaniards among creoles is hardly surprising.

The movement toward capitalism in the largest units of production in the coffee-growing regions, as in the sugar regions, was particularly marked after 1885, as new machinery for drying and processing coffee beans came into greater use, credit became more readily available, and transportation and marketing facilities improved.[181] Buitrago Ortiz, though noting the complexity and diversity of labor forms in use in the coffee region he studied, nevertheless argues that the class structure retained feudal, precapitalist forms and methods of production throughout the nineteenth century. Picó's study of Utuado leads him to a similar conclusion: small and medium-sized farms relied on unpaid family labor with but a minimal specialization of tasks.[182] The growth of the coffee industry, unlike that of the sugar industry, was thus two-edged: it furthered the process of separating labor from the means of production, creating a landless working class, while at the same time it provided opportunities for the continuation of small-scale production and peasant and small-farmer adaptation.

A consideration of land-use patterns at the end of the century will help to round out the picture. In 1899, 41 percent of cultivated land was in coffee production; 56 percent of all farms were involved in some coffee production, and the average size of those that were involved was 9 cuerdas. Only 15 percent of cultivated land was in sugar-cane production, and only 6 percent of all units of production were involved in sugar-cane production. The average size of sugar-cane farms, however, was slightly more than 31 cuerdas, three and one-half times the average size of coffee fincas. In the municipalities producing the most coffee, average farm size ranged from 4 to 11 cuerdas; in the sugar regions, on the other hand, average farm size ranged from 6 to 115 cuerdas.[183] Thus, even though the sugar-cane sector was in crisis—in particular, export sales lagged far behind those of coffee throughout the last quarter of the nineteenth century—sugar-cane production remained on a larger scale.

Land ownership in all crops, however, became more concentrated during the last half of the century. Landholdings of less than ten cuerdas constituted more than three-quarters (76.2 percent) of all production units in 1899, but they occupied only 20.7 percent of the cultivated land (see table 1.8). By comparison, the 851 largest farms (2.2 percent of the total

[180] Wolf, "San José," pp. 190–93. In the coffee region of Utuado, a shift of political and economic power toward Spanish immigrants also was quite evident: F. Picó, *Libertad y servidumbre*, pp. 16–17, 76–77.

[181] Buitrago Ortiz, *Los orígenes históricos*, pp. 35, 37, 45–46, 109.

[182] Ibid., pp. 81, 92, 109; F. Picó, *Amargo café*, pp. 86–88.

[183] USDW, *1899 Census*, pp. 152–54 and p. 354, table 39.

TABLE 1.8
Distribution of Farms by Size, 1899

Size (cuerdas)	Number of Farms	Percent of All Farms	Area Cultivated (cuerdas)	Percent of Cultivated Area
0–4	22,327	57.2	50,374	10.5
5–9	7,417	19.0	48,875	10.2
10–19	4,503	11.5	58,760	12.3
20–49	2,929	7.5	83,783	17.5
50–99	994	2.5	64,942	13.6
100 or more	851	2.2	171,392	35.9
Total	39,021	99.9	478,126	100.0

SOURCE: USDW, *1899 Census*, pp. 354, 355, tables 39 and 40.

number) occupied 35.9 percent of the land under cultivation. In fact farms fifty cuerdas or larger—less than 5 percent of all farms—occupied about the same amount of cultivated land as did the other 95 percent of farms. And while it was true, as often noted, that at least 91 percent of Puerto Rico's cultivated land was occupied by its owner in 1899, as compared to only 43.5 in Cuba, this should not be taken as evidence, as it sometimes is, that land was relatively equally distributed, but only that landowners, large and small, did not rent their land out to other producers and become truly absentee owners, though many may also have maintained part-time residences in the city.[184] As table 1.8 shows, land was very unequally distributed: there were many small holdings and many small owners, while the largest farms controlled the bulk (and the best) of the productive land.

By way of summary, figure 1.2 presents a schematic diagram of the development of Puerto Rico's social formation from the sixteenth through the nineteenth centuries.

In the early part of that era, slave production existed alongside the independent production of peasants and agregados. In the late eighteenth and nineteenth centuries, hacienda production emerged and grew, as did pockets of capitalist organization. Hacienda production, especially after the 1830s, evolved in two directions. Some hacendados were able to organize on a capitalist basis, a process that gained momentum in the last decades of the nineteenth century as both internal developments and the weakness of Spanish control provided openings for growth. But the internal structure and the external forces were not sufficiently altered to

[184] USDW, *1899 Census*, p. 151.

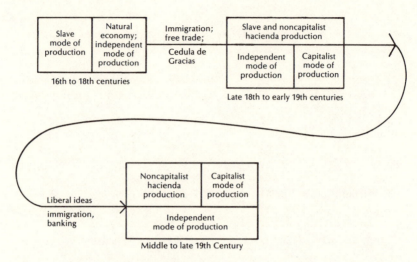

Figure 1.2 Development of the Social Formation from the 16th to the 19th Century

permit capitalist production to become the dominant mode of production, so, while capitalism became stronger and more apparent, it coexisted with noncapitalist hacienda production, which used agregados, jornaleros, and family labor. This type of production is not easily or usefully categorized as either feudal or capitalist. Instead, it represented a transitional form of production embodying both feudal (servile) and capitalist characteristics at the same time and in varying degrees, depending upon the location and size of the hacienda, the crop produced, the access to credit, the proximity to urban areas, and other factors.[185] Independent peasants and small-farmer production continued, but their existence was threatened by the growth of capitalist production on the haciendas. However, this threat was moderated by the growth of coffee production, which slowed down the process of proletarianization of small producers, even though coffee haciendas used wage labor in increasing quantities and found their labor problems ended by the 1880s and 1890s.[186]

A drive toward expanded capitalist relations and production methods thus existed in the coffee and sugar sectors (as well as in tobacco manufacturing) in the last decades of the nineteenth century. There were, however, countervailing forces—the decline of the sugar economy during the last quarter of the century, the ability of small coffee growers to survive

[185] A system similar to this in West Bengal has been referred to as "semi-feudalism" in Bhaduri, "Agricultural Backwardness." The patterns of tenant farming, sharecropping, debt, and irregular consumption seem nearly identical.

[186] Bergad, *Coffee and the Growth of Agrarian Capitalism*, p. 175; and "Coffee and Rural Proletarianization," pp. 96–99.

alongside large hacienda producers, and the remaining institutional barriers of Spanish mercantilist policy—which prevented the dominance of capitalist production. But it is essential to keep in mind that objective forces were at work that strengthened the trend toward capitalist methods of production and wage labor as the primary source of the labor supply.

POLITICAL DEVELOPMENTS

The nineteenth century also saw the growth of a political movement and the birth of political parties, manifestations of a divergence of economic interests between the Spanish and the creole Puerto Ricans and among other classes. In 1809, Puerto Rico elected Ramón Power y Giralt as its first representative to the Cortes, the Spanish parliament. Napoleon had invaded Spain, and the Spanish government had granted representation to the colonies in an effort to maintain their loyalty. Power, who owed his election largely to the creole elite, carried with him a list of twenty-two proposals which he had been directed to ask the Cortes to act upon. The contents of the proposals were evidence of the impact of rising liberal sentiment among the native hacendados and professionals, as well as the increasing tension between creole producers and Spanish immigrants that had been created by Spain's restrictive mercantile policies. Among them were requests for freer trade, lower taxes, more roads, the appointment of native Puerto Ricans to public posts, the provision of public education, and regulations designed to control free and agregado labor.[187] These proposals clearly were designed to benefit the local classes already possessing some measure of economic power, at the expense of economically weaker creoles as well as Spanish hacendados and merchants.[188] Some of the requests were satisfied with the opening of ports and then the proclamation of the Cédula de Gracias in 1815; others were acted upon later through the laws governing vagrancy, the movement of labor, and agregados. (Mass public education, however, was never instituted.) These steps marked the beginning of the weakening of Spanish colonial power vis-à-vis the hacendados and professionals on the island. At the time, Spain had little choice but to accede: Puerto Rico was one of her last remaining colonies; it had no effective separatist movement; and Power was the sole deputy from any overseas territory present at the opening of the Cortes.[189] Puerto Rico had no political parties or other means of organized political expression at the time of Power's election,

[187] Cruz Monclova, *Historia* 1:24–26.
[188] Figueroa, *Breve historia* 2:24–27.
[189] In recognition of this, Power was elected first vice-president of the Cortes; three days later Venezuela declared independence: Cruz Monclova, *Historia* 1:28, 33.

but the articulation of demands objectively in conflict with Spanish colonial interests was the first clear expression of nationalist or liberal autonomist sentiment by the politically and economically frustrated creole
owning class.[190]

This is not to say that there were no political responses or struggles
outside official channels. Slave revolts and conspiracies were quite common and greatly feared by slaveowners and the colonial administration
alike. Some of these were grandly planned and well armed.[191] Baralt has
identified some twenty-two planned slave rebellions between 1795 and
1848, fourteen of which actually took place. The greatest number of rebellions occurred around Ponce, and they generally involved recently arrived African slaves (*bozales*) rather than native born Puerto Rican slaves.
Cane fields often were burned in these uprisings, sometimes as a diver-
sionary tactic for an attack on armories, other times to attract and kill
those trying to quench the flames. Attacks on hacienda stewards (*may-
ordomos*) and slaveowners were common, especially after 1848.[192] Other
than rebellions, individual escape was the most common form of resistance. Several legislative acts in the first half of the century—e.g., Gov.
Miguel de la Torre's 1824 decree and Gen. Juan Prim y Prats's *Bando
contra la Raza Negra* (Decree against the Black Race) of 1848, which
specified the death penalty for slaves attacking whites—were directed at
controlling slave activities such as social gatherings and dances, where
uprisings could be planned.[193] As an incentive to help the colonial government prevent slave rebellions, it offered a reward of up to 500 pesos
and freedom for those slaves who denounced conspiracies being planned
by their comrades.[194]

[190] Bayrón Toro, *Elecciones y partidos políticos*, conveniently summarizes the election
results and the philosophical and political tendencies represented by the voting. In the early
1800s, liberals or reformists were generally creoles who wanted greater autonomy. Conser-
vatives were generally large Spanish merchants, colonial administrators, and some large
landowners: Cruz Monclova, *Historia* 1:31.

[191] Díaz Soler, *Historia de la esclavitud negra*, chap. 9.

[192] Baralt, *Esclavos rebeldes*, pp. 63, 122–24, 144, 149–50, 155–59. Baralt's work provides the fullest picture of the continuity of slave rebellions and the ingenuity of slaves in
maintaining contact with one another and the outside world despite efforts by the colonial
officials to block communications. See also *BHPR* 1:144, 3:347–49, and 8:106–7 for information on other slave rebellions.

[193] Baralt, *Esclavos rebeldes*, pp. 68–71, 129–31, 141. De la Torre's decree provided
extensive regulations on behavior and the carrying of arms and machetes, imposed a 10:00
P.M. curfew, and set penalties for hiding escaped slaves: *BHPR* 2:32–44. General Prim's
bando was issued in response to the rebellions and violence against whites that followed
emancipation in nearby Martinique and Guadeloupe. For the text of this bando, see *BHPR*
2:122ff.

[194] Slaves did not always receive the money, however. Santiago, a slave informer, gained
his freedom, but it was his owner who was paid the 300-peso reward: *BHPR* 2:128–29.

By 1810, a separatist movement had appeared, which made known its sympathy for Bolívar's independence movement and particularly the struggle in Venezuela. Colonial governors attempted to suppress it, but it continued to manifest itself sporadically. As a result of the suppression, and also because of the weakness of the economic base, independence forces during this early period remained small, clandestine, and battered.[195] It is interesting, though, that among the proposals that Power was authorized to present to the Cortes was one favoring Puerto Rican independence, approved by the municipal government of San Germán five months before Venezuela's revolution. Power, however, never did present this request.[196]

In the course of the nineteenth century, the hacendado, merchant, and professional creole elites, steadily developed an interest in, as well as an economic need for, greater self-rule. Their greater involvement in the political affairs of the colony was evident, for example, in the arguments and counterarguments around the question of slavery and abolition. In 1868, the anti-Spanish sentiments held by a group of hacendados and intellectuals culminated in Puerto Rico's only, and but briefly successful, revolution, the so-called Grito de Lares (Scream of Lares) uprising. It was organized by a French-trained doctor, Ramón Emeterio Betances, who had spent much of his life in exile because of his independence activities on the island, but it was carried out by creole hacendados, merchants, and workers intimately connected to the coffee economy. Betances, like most liberals of the intellectual elite, had been influenced by Bolívar and the independence movements in the rest of the Americas. First in New York, then in Santo Domingo, and finally in St. Thomas, Betances attempted to coordinate plans for a revolution. In November 1867, a leaflet, *Los Diez Mandamientos de los Hombres Libres* (The Ten Commandments of Free Men), was distributed with Betances's name on it. It listed ten demands: the abolition of slavery, the right to reject all taxes, freedom of religion, freedom of speech, freedom of the press, freedom of commerce, the right to assemble, the right to bear arms, the inviolability of citizens, and the right of Puerto Ricans to elect their own authorities.[197] Although these were stated as demands that would have to be met if Puerto Rico were to remain in association with Spain, it is clear

[195]Cruz Monclova, *Historia* 1:301–7; see also n. 35 above, and Silén, *Historia*, pp. 83, 94–95. Secret societies were organized in support of independence in Mayagüez, Ponce, Aguadilla, and Arecibo as well as in other areas: Figueroa, *Breve historia* 2:239ff., and Lidin, *Independence Movement*, vol. 1.

[196]Figueroa, *Breve historia* 2:25–26. The text of the San Germán resolution is in Cruz Monclova, *Historia* 1:517–21.

[197]*BHPR* 7:20–21; see also Wagenheim, *Puerto Ricans*, pp. 79–80, and Suarez Díaz, *El doctor Ramón Emeterio Betances*, p. 51.

that the actual aim was separation, for Betances must have known full well that they could not be met without breaking the colonial structure apart. These demands were "radical," however, only within the colonial framework; today, they seem quite reasonable, measured, and humane.

Betances worked hard throughout the Caribbean to collect arms, men, and money for an uprising. Secret committees on the island issued statements, organized men, and prepared for revolution. September 29, 1868, was selected as the date, but the Spanish authorities learned of the plans by infiltrating one of the secret groups, forcing the act of insurrection to be advanced to September 23 if a strike was to be made before the Spanish forces could be mobilized. Though Betances was stopped from leaving St. Thomas with the small invasion force and the arms he had collected, the revolt proceeded, anyway. In an attack begun near midnight, the mountain town of Lares was captured by a force of nearly a thousand rebels, a Republic of Puerto Rico was proclaimed, and the flag of the new republic was raised. Libretas and debt books of the largest, Spanish-owned tiendas were burned, a proclamation abolishing slavery was issued, and a new governing council for the city was named, in the first, and almost the only, acts of the revolution. An attack the next morning on the nearby town of Pepino (now San Sebastian) was a failure, and the Spanish moved in and quickly crushed the revolt, dispersing the rebels. After a few days of further skirmishing, the revolt was over. Betances was expelled from St. Thomas, and the pursuit of all who were associated with the rebellion, or even suspected of complicity, was undertaken.[198]

The fact that the Lares uprising failed so quickly and the obvious reasons for its failure (a lack of mass support, for example) are of much less importance than the fact that such a rebellion took place at all. It had been planned and led by members of the coffee hacendado and smaller merchant classes: Manuel Rojas, one of the leaders of the rebellion, was the largest coffee-grower in Lares, and Andrés Pol, another leader, was the owner of a number of small pulperías. Their decision to act was influenced not only by the liberal ideas of the nineteenth century but also, and probably more importantly, by their subordinate position within the economic structure of Lares and the threats to even that position from land concentration, the often huge debts they owed to the large merchant houses, and other problems resulting from the near-total dominance of commerce and finance by peninsulares, whose business acumen, contacts, and ruthlessness squeezed creole coffee-growers and small mer-

---

[198] Cruz Monclova, *Historia* 2; Lidin, *Independence Movement*, chap. 12; Silén, *Historia* pp. 95–104; and Figueroa, *Breve historia* 2:231–55. Amnesty was declared on January 20, 1869, for those participating in the Lares rebellion: *BHPR* 9:327–28. Jiménez de Wagenheim, *Puerto Rico's Revolt*, is an admirable and detailed study of the rebellion.

chants alike. The Lares revolt thus reflected the changing and maturing class positions and struggle, which pitted creole against peninsular. The Grito de Lares was a concrete manifestation of the attempt by members of the more powerful creole class to end the dominance of the hated Spanish merchants.[199]

This conflict erupted into violence again in the late 1880s and early 1890s, when attacks were made on peninsular-owned haciendas and tiendas, again in the Lares area. And after the American occupation of Puerto Rico in 1898, properties like that of the Mallorcan merchant and hacendado Juan Castañer were occupied and debt books were destroyed and burned, this time by jornaleros and agregados. But such attacks were directed only toward the outward signs of the causes of rural poverty—the immigrants who supported and benefited from Spanish colonialism at the expense of their workers and the creole growers and merchants. The underlying cause itself, the exploitive system of nascent agrarian capitalism, was left untouched.

Puerto Rico did not develop an independence struggle at the same time as the rest of Latin America because it lacked a strong or large enough economic class (or classes) whose interests were in fundamental conflict with the colonial structure or who were being ruined by economic change. On the contrary, the hacendados, native and immigrant alike, had depended upon colonial power to consolidate their position; the colonial government had responded to their needs by, for example, attempting to expand the supply of labor and by liberalizing trade and other regulations. Spain also provided the repressive force that landowners could not individually muster to control labor and mobilize productive forces. For a long period, then, the local economic elite needed the colonial power to be able to build its own power base.

Eventually, however, as the economic strength of the large landowners and small merchants increased, Spanish domination, and in particular peninsular control over the largest commercial establishments and credit, became an obstacle rather than an ally to members of this class, as well as to educated professionals, just as it had in the rest of the New World. Lares represented the point at which the development of Puerto Rico's productive forces came into fundamental conflict with Spain's sociopolitical domination. The same forces that had led to successful independence movements in the rest of Latin America, however, failed in Puerto Rico

[199] See Bergad, "Grito de Lares," for an excellent analysis of the productive and class forces leading up to the rebellion, and see also Díaz Hernández, *Castañer*, pp. 41–45. Immigrants did not become a part of the society that enriched them. Rather, they remained aloof, treating the island much as the early colonizers had; to them, it was little more than a place to get rich in order to return to Europe in style.

in the face of Spain's greater and more concentrated force. Historically, though, Lares proved to be a turning point in the development of nationalist, autonomist sentiment among the creole elites. The repression that Spain unleashed against the Lares rebels and the persistent persecution directed against separatist sympathizers was not lost on other members of these classes. Their later nationalist struggles did not take the road of violence, but were channeled into the legal parties and organizations that Spain soon would permit to form.

One effect of the Lares rebellion, and of the revolt in Cuba that began in the same year, was to motivate Spain to grant Puerto Rico the right to send more deputies to the reestablished Cortes (fifteen in 1874), and to permit the election of local municipal administrators.[200] The first legal political parties were organized in November 1870: the Liberal Reform party (Partido Liberal Reformista) and the Conservative party (Partido Conservador, later called the Partido Español sin Condiciones, the Unconditional Spanish party).[201] This period of Spanish liberalism ended abruptly, however, in January 1874, with the suppression of the 1869 constitution. In 1876, a new constitution extended provincial and representative status once again to Puerto Rico, but an 1877 electoral law restricted the franchise to Spanish male citizens 25 years and older who had a profession or who had paid at least 125 pesetas in taxes. (Prior to that, there had been nearly universal male suffrage for white, male citizens.)[202]

The majority within the Liberal Reform party was in favor of greater autonomy for Puerto Rico and articulated the interests of creole sugar hacendados and of some coffee producers, particularly those interested in expanding trade with nations other than Spain, as well as of educated professionals and artisans. There also was an "assimilationist" faction within the party, which urged that Puerto Rico be made a province of Spain. The Conservative party, on the other hand, desired continued close association with Spain short of complete integration. It represented the interests of peninsulares and the supporters of Spanish colonial policy—many large merchants, the clergy, the military, and the large coffee hacendados whose markets were predominately in Spain or Spanish posses-

[200] The parliamentary system had been ended in 1837. López, "Socio-Politico Developments in a Colonial Context," pp. 75ff., discusses these developments more fully. See also Silén, *Historia*, pp. 109ff., and Quintero Rivera, *Conflictos de clase*, pp. 17ff. At the same time that there was some liberalization of Spanish colonial policy toward Puerto Rico, repression of reform and its advocates also escalated. In 1869, the rural Civil Guard was formed and press censorship and other restrictions followed.

[201] Bayrón Toro, *Elecciones y partidos políticos*, pp. 52–53, 79.

[202] Ibid., pp. 65–66, 76–77, 80. In 1873, there were 46,042 registered voters; in 1881, there were but 3,306.

sions like Cuba. The political positions of the parties thus developed from the economic base, the power, and the status interests of their supporters and the relation of these interests to Spain. Neither party, however, had a mass base. Both represented the interests of economically and politically powerful minorities engaged in a struggle for hegemony among themselves and with the colonial administration.

Political differences arose within the Liberal Reform party, and in 1887, it became the Puerto Rican Autonomist party (Partido Autonomista Puertorriqueño).[203] The assimilationists had left, and so the new party was uniformly nationalistic. Yet its supporters desired to remain within the Spanish empire; they were autonomists, not *independentistas*. The split between "Puerto Ricans" and "Spaniards" was opened wider with this new party, though there were "Spanish Puerto Ricans" and "Puerto Rican Spaniards"—that is, the division was essentially a class, not a national, question. Combined with the activities of secret societies which practiced a boycott against Spanish merchants,[204] this split thrust separatism forward as a movement which was perceived by the Spanish colonial authorities as a serious threat to their rule. The response to the demands for greater autonomy has gone down in Puerto Rican history as "The Terrible Year of 1887," in which the Autonomist party, its leadership, and suspected supporters were severely and brutally repressed.[205]

A part of the Autonomist party, however, survived the purge and terror and, as the Liberal Fusionist party (Partido Liberal Fusionista Puertorriqueño), became the institutional base from which Luis Muñoz Rivera (publisher of the influential newspaper, *La democracia*), negotiated an autonomy agreement with the Spanish Liberal party under Práxedes Mateo Sagasta. In January 1897, Muñoz and Sagasta agreed that Puerto Rico would be granted greater autonomy should Sagasta come to power. Sagasta did become prime minister (for the fourth time) later that year, and he fulfilled his promise on November 25, 1897. It had become clear that increasing numbers of Puerto Ricans supported the autonomist demands and were willing to defend their interests with force if necessary.[206] Spain, weak and tired from fighting but wishing to hold on to what was left of

[203] *BHPR* 6:275–95.

[204] *BHPR* 5:17, 20; Cruz Monclova, *Historia* 3, part 1: 70–75, 199–202; and Silén, *Historia*, pp. 116–18. Silén points out that these secret societies enjoyed the support of peasants, agregados, and workers in the southwest.

[205] Pedreira, *El año terrible*; Lidin, *Independence Movement*, chap. 14.

[206] Silén, *Historia*, pp. 122–26, describes two widely supported protests in 1894 aimed at Spain's power to grant rights of distribution and production. One incident was concerned with match sales and the other with oil distribution, and in both cases, Spain was forced to back down in the face of popular pressure. See also Cruz Monclova, *Historia* 3, part 2:210–25.

its empire, gave in to the moderate demands of Muñoz and the Liberals in an effort to prevent more radical demands from being made.

The Autonomist Charter gave Puerto Rico full representation in the Cortes and extensive rights to make commercial treaties and to control trade and tariffs. The island was to continue to be headed by a Spanish-appointed governor, but a bicameral legislature—consisting of a Chamber of Deputies of thirty-two members and a fifteen-member Administrative Council—was to have power over internal affairs. On March 27, 1898, voters went to the polls to choose the deputies and the eight elected members of the council.[207] Munoz's Liberal party won twenty-five of the seats in the Chamber, and on July 17, 1898, the Puerto Rican legislature held its first session. Eight days later, however, U.S. military forces invaded Puerto Rico, and on July 28, less than two weeks after its opening, the legislature held its final meeting. Autonomy was more short-lived than anyone could have imagined.[208]

LABOR ORGANIZATIONS

Another part of the political picture was the embryonic labor movement, which eventually became the base for the Socialist party. In the nineteenth century, however, the political expression of labor's interests remained mostly latent. The existence of nascent labor organizations and related elements of working-class consciousness is consistent with the evolution of capitalist production in the last half of the century. Just as some hacendados and professionals had been influenced by the liberal ideas that emerged from the capitalist revolutions on the European continent, so too was the thinking of Puerto Rican workers influenced by anarchist and socialist ideas and the workers' struggles in Europe.[209] Puerto Rican workers, without land or capital, confronted the same conditions and problems of work, control, and alienation that all workers face. Ideas about capitalism, accumulation, exploitation, and alienation reflected the changes that workers in Puerto Rico were experiencing, and these ideas were read, discussed, and adapted to the local situation. Organizations of artisans—printers, carpenters, cigarmakers—appeared in the cities.[210] They

[207] Cruz Monclova, *Historia* 3, part 3:192–95.

[208] The Autonomist government retained official power until October 18, but that was of little practical or functional significance, given the military occupation: USDW, *1899 Census*, p. 21.

[209] Bakunin's *Federalism and Socialism* was circulated in Spanish translation as early as 1890 among artisans and was later published by a worker's organization: Quintero Rivera, *Workers' Struggles*, p. 216.

[210] Quintero Rivera, *Workers' Struggles*, p. 209, n. 2. Free associations of workers appeared at least as early as 1866, though Spain did not legalize them until 1873: Gómez Acevedo, *Organización y reglamentación*, p. 349, and García and Quintero Rivera, *Desafío*

published newspapers and essays,[211] and they organized strikes.[212] Organizations of rural workers came only very much later.

In 1897, the first national union was established. Its core group of leaders—men like Ramón Romero Rosa and José Ferrer y Ferrer—as well as the momentum toward collective action were on the scene before the arrival in Puerto Rico in 1896 of Santiago Iglesias, who is often but erroneously, seen as the founder of the Puerto Rican labor movement. Iglesias was but one of several leaders of a movement that preceded him and would have developed without him. Though he no doubt contributed to the rapid expansion of the movement, especially in its formative stages, he did not create it; its creation was an outgrowth of capitalist production, which generated the conditions of work that led to a strong, militant, and active labor movement to oppose them.

Conclusions

The nineteenth century was a period of fundamental and rapid change in Puerto Rico. After centuries of little or no growth, a process of economic and social development began and was intensified. Spain's restrictive mercantilist policies and neglect of Puerto Rico as a colony came to an end with the independence movements in the Americas that cost Spain the bulk, and the richest part, of its empire. With the granting of the right to private property in land, trade liberalization, and immigration, the door was opened to changes in production and trade. Yet the potential gains from these liberalizing measures were never fully attained. Colonial domination continued to thwart the full development of the forces that the liberalizing policies had set in motion. The absence of the necessary supportive institutions or infrastructure—banks, a generally accepted currency, roads, communications, and so on—made it difficult to achieve the reorganization of production that was required to meet the competition on the world market. The enduring problem of obtaining sufficient labor also slowed the process of capitalist transformation and bedeviled hacendados for most of the period.

---

y solidaridad, pp. 21, 24, 30. Most of the early organizations were mutual-aid societies; they began to replace the guilds (*gremios*), which had represented skilled and independent artisans but did not meet the needs of unskilled jornaleros or the rapidly increasing labor force in the urban areas.

[211] The first workers' newspaper, *El artesano* (The Artisan), appeared in 1874. It was followed by *El obrero* (The Worker, 1889), *El eco proletario* (The Proletarian Echo, 1892), and *Ensayo obrero* (Workers' Essays, 1897). The successive titles reflect the changing composition of the work force, from skilled artisans to unskilled workers.

[212] In 1897, Spain made organizing for higher wages or better working conditions illegal, indicating its concern over this form of protest.

But over the course of the century, the tendency toward change and progress was unmistakable. Puerto Rico increasingly was connected to, dependent upon, and subject to the pressures of the market and the exigencies of reaching for maximum profit and producing at minimum cost. Inserted into the world market by trade liberalization, but lacking a sound internal institutional base, production—first in sugar, then in coffee— began to suffer the cycles familiar to capitalist production. Throughout the last half of the century, the forces of market, trade, population growth, and competition, combined with the impact of bourgeois modernizing ideas from Europe and North America, exerted pressure on the structure of production and the class relations. In the transformation that followed, the colonial government was the unwitting servant of its ultimate destruction. Choosing or forced to grant concessions to the landed class, the colonial authorities passed laws and created regulations, like the libreta system, which enhanced the economic power of the landowners and fueled their desire for still greater economic, and then political, power. Spain's attempts to control these economic and political forces were ineffectual, though colonial policy prevented the revolution in production and class relations characteristic of other developing nations. The base for such a revolution did emerge in Puerto Rico, but the island paid—and would continue to pay—a price in the form of retarded economic, social, and political progress.

The Early Period of U.S. Control, 1898–1930

INTRODUCTION

In 1895, the second Cuban war for independence was launched under the leadership of two of Cuba's most revered heroes, Antonio Maceo and José Martí. The goal of the Cuban revolutionaries was not only to free Cuba from the colonial dominance of Spain but also to put a halt to the increasing influence of the United States in Cuba.[1] In the new expansionary perspective of the United States, however, Cuba was much too valuable a prize to be permitted an independent course of action. Cuba's drive for independence threatened U.S. economic and strategic interests in the Caribbean and Latin America, interests U.S. policy makers made no attempt to disguise or apologize for and which focused on the hemisphere's resources, markets, and cheap labor.

By the late nineteenth century, Spain was weak and nearly broken as an empire, and she did not fare well in the war against the committed and well-organized rebel forces in Cuba. U.S. businesses with interests in Cuba, especially sugar companies, were worried, and what worried them likewise worried U.S. policy makers.[2] The war and Spain's inability to contain it raised fears about U.S. investments on the island and whether an independent Cuba would respect them. And, too, there was anxiety about the possibility of a suspension of sugar imports, an important part of the total U.S. supply; as much as 80 to 85 percent of U.S. consumption was provided by imports from Hawaii, Cuba, Puerto Rico, the Philippines, Santo Domingo, and a few other places.[3] Thus, business

[1] See the excellent analysis by Foner, *Spanish-Cuban-American War*.

[2] Already by 1821, two-thirds of U.S. exports to Latin America went to Cuba. Charles Beard, the noted American economic historian, pointed out that at the time of the war 95 percent of Cuba's sugar exports were going to the U.S. and there was perhaps $50 million of U.S. investment in Cuba. President Cleveland, in an address to Congress in 1896, referred to the rapidly deteriorating "industrial value" of Cuba due to the Spanish-Cuban war: Berbusse, *U.S. in Puerto Rico*, p. 60. (Berbusse believes, however, that these interests were less important in getting the U.S. involved in the war than was the hysteria whipped up by the press: pp. 61ff.)

[3] Luque de Sánchez, *La ocupación norteamericana*, p. 34.

and public interest converged in concern over the likely repercussions of a Cuban victory. Day by day, a growing segment of the population—or at least an influential group—pushed the United States closer and closer to involvement in the war.

The events surrounding the eventual entry of the United States into the Spanish-Cuban War are still shrouded in uncertainty. The events as they unfolded, however, certainly coincided with U.S. interests as defined by big business, the leading newspapers, and the government. Some facts are uncontroverted. On February 15, 1898, a U.S. naval cruiser, the *Maine*, which had sailed into Havana Harbor at the direction of President Mc-Kinley on January 25, exploded and sunk to the bottom of the bay, taking the lives of 266 men. While many believed the explosion had been an accident, other suspected sabotage.[4] Warmongers in the United States, unwilling to await or trust an official investigation of the incident, demanded that the United States immediately declare war against Spain. The Hearst newspaper syndicate—proclaiming the slogan, "Remember the Maine, to hell with Spain!"—was a leader in the campaign to stir up prowar sentiment among the general populace, a strategy that at least prepared people for a war that soon would send the U.S. military to defend the interests of absentee landowners, banks, and importers, as well as, of course, the "national" interest.

For some people, the *Maine* "incident" was most opportune. Influential policy makers had long made it known that the United States wanted Cuba and meant to have it. Captain Alfred T. Mahan, who was president of the Naval War College, had asserted in his publications (the most famous being *The Influence of Sea Power upon History*) the importance of Cuba to U.S. defenses. He justified overseas expansion as "national destiny" rather than the more distasteful and objectionable need and desire to advance and protect the economic position and wealth of the already powerful. Mahan's thesis of the "need" to conquer and control the seas and their islands presaged Frederick Jackson Turner's "frontier" thesis, which would argue that new frontiers were essential to the political and economic progress of the United States and justify the taking of land from Native Americans and other settlers.[5]

So anxious was the United States to get control of Cuba that there was even an effort to force Spain to sell Cuba immediately as indemnity for damages to the *Maine*, an exchange Spain refused to make, especially before the results of the investigations into the cause of the sinking had

---

[4]The latter was the position, for example, of Theodore Roosevelt, then assistant secretary of the navy: see Foner, *Spanish-Cuban-American War* 1:chaps. 11, 12.

[5]Ibid., pp. 300–10; Luque de Sánchez, *La ocupación norteamericana*, pp. 24–25. For a readable discussion of Mahan, see Tuchman, *Proud Tower*, chap. 2.

even been made known. But the major effort of the McKinley administration, even while negotiations were proceeding, was directed toward war preparations.

.... [E]ven before the reports of the Court of Inquiry on the *Maine* disaster were submitted, the United States government had chosen war against Spain, had even worked out the strategy with which this was to be carried into effect and had decided upon the issue—humanitarianism—which was to justify military intervention.[6]

Ultimately, the reports of the U.S. and Spanish commissions of investigation reached differing conclusions, with the U.S. commission giving no explicit answer to the question of which side had sabotaged the vessel, though the implication was obvious. But sabotage it almost surely was. No amount of argument from the international community was able to stop the momentum that had been built up in the United States for a declaration of war on Spain. A resolution to that effect was passed in Congress by overwhelming votes and was signed by the president on April 25, 1898. The Spanish-Cuban-*American* War became a reality. The nascent U.S. empire, until then restricted in its expansion to its own continent, was making a bid for world power.

None of Spain's other colonial possessions was immune from intervention once the United States declared war. Government lawmakers and business leaders had never made it a secret that, besides Cuba, they were interested in wresting control of Puerto Rico and the Philippines from Spain. For a time, however, military operations concentrated on crushing Spanish opposition in Cuba. It did not take long. By August 12, 1898, the war in Cuba was virtually over: Spain accepted defeat and the United States ceased military operations. The Philippines also passed from Spain to the United States.

Before the long period of Spanish dominance ended, and despite the handwriting on the wall, Puerto Rico autonomists, led by Muñoz Rivera, had tried to obtain greater concessions from the Spanish crown and to some extent had succeeded (see chapter 1). But the U.S. had other plans, and autonomy was cut short almost before it had had a chance to begin. On July 25, an invasion of Puerto Rico was launched at Guánica on the south coast, with the purpose of expelling the Spanish and of gaining Puerto Rico for the U.S. empire.[7] Independence for the island was not a serious

---

[6] Foner, *Spanish-Cuban-American War* 1:243. The findings of the inquiry, and the conclusions to be be drawn from them, are summarized in ibid., pp. 243–47.

[7] An earlier attempt by the U.S. Navy to sail into San Juan Harbor had been repelled by Spanish forces from the El Morro and San Cristóbal fortresses. The navy then attacked the less well defended south coast.

objective of U.S. policy, notwithstanding the hopes of the Puerto Rican members of the Cuban Revolutionary party in New York.[8] By October 18, 1898, what little Spanish resistance there had been was over, and the U.S. flag flew over La Fortaleza, the governor's mansion in Old San Juan. The autonomous government, which had witnessed the U.S. invasion only eight days after its opening session, was ended officially on February 6, 1899, by order of Maj. Gen. Guy Henry, but the local government had ceased to have meaning long before. Puerto Rico belonged to the United States, and U.S. rule was to prevail for decades without the trouble of autonomy, local elections, and local interference.

POLITICAL INTEGRATION

Puerto Rico was "obtained" from Spain, a spoil of war as compensation for damages suffered (though the United States also paid Spain $20 million), under the Treaty of Paris ending the Spanish-Cuban-American War. The treaty was signed on December 10, 1898, and ratified by Congress on April 11, 1899. As might easily be imagined, Puerto Ricans had no voice or role in this transfer of colonial control. Spain and the United States decided the fate of Spain's former colonies (including the Philippines, Cuba, and Guam) without bothering to consult the "colonial subjects." The United States, with its new overseas colonies (including Hawaii, which had been annexed in 1898), now officially wore the badge of "empire builder." This expansion was no mere aberration.

. . . [T]he United States did not set out on an expansionist path in the late 1890's in a sudden, spur-of-the-moment fashion. The overseas empire that Americans controlled in 1900 was not a break in their history,

---

[8] Members of the Puerto Rican section of the Cuban Revolutionary party in New York, headed by José Julio Henna, had met with various U.S. officials, including President McKinley, after the declaration of war against Spain in Cuba to encourage the U.S. to act in Puerto Rico as well. They provided maps of military locations, the numbers of Spanish soldiers, and other vital information, for which Assistant Secretary Roosevelt thanked them. The Puerto Ricans of course expected (or hoped) that the U.S. would drive the Spanish out and leave the island independent, but the outcome must be recorded as one of history's sad ironies. Betances, the organizer of the failed Grito de Lares, who was by this time in exile in Paris, uttered a note of caution against placing too much trust in the U.S.; sensing the threat of U.S. expansionism, he wrote that "if Puerto Rico does not act rapidly, it will be an American colony forever": quoted in Berbusse, *U.S. in Puerto Rico*, p. 64. See also Lewis, *Puerto Rico*, p. 86; Andreu Iglesias, *Memorias de Bernardo Vega*, pp. 119–20; and Luque de Sánchez, *La ocupación norteamericana*, pp. 53–55.

but a natural culmination. . . . Americans neither acquired this empire during a temporary absence of mind nor had the empire forced upon them.[9]

The U.S. undoubtedly had what could be called "strategic" interests in Puerto Rico, interests which became even more important after the U.S. failed to buy St. Thomas from Denmark in 1867. Puerto Rico was important for the protection of the proposed canal across Central America; at a time when sea lanes and sea power still were decisive, the island was situated ideally for defense of the seas, as it had been for the Spanish. But strategic interests are not suspended in a vacuum. They are strategic only in relation to some referent—that is, to some objective. In the most abstract and official sense, the United States has always claimed this referent to be "political freedom." In its operational sense, however, it has been freedom *of enterprise and investment*—a very different sort of freedom, even if U.S. policy and the dominant school of economic thought have continually (and perhaps not accidentally) confounded the two concepts. At root, strategic interests were the protection of specific economic interests and a way of life: capitalism, consumerism, and commodity production.

From October 1898 to April 1900, Puerto Rico was governed by the U.S. military forces that had occupied the island after defeating the Spanish. Many Puerto Ricans welcomed the invading forces, since to them the United States promised a democratic alternative to the oppressiveness and backwardness of Spanish domination. Few expected Puerto Rico would become a colony of the United States; most felt there would be greater freedom, both politically and economically, in any association with the United States. This view was certainly held by many large landowners, but Puerto Rico's intellectual elite also looked upon the United States as a bastion of democracy and progress. Muñoz Rivera and other liberal leaders made known their admiration of the United States and the hopes they held for annexation in the pages of the newspaper *La democracia*.[10] Their vision was shared by sugar, tobacco, dock, and other workers who believed that U.S. labor laws and democratic practices would be extended to the island and would protect them from the often arbitrary actions of

[9] Walter LeFeber, *The New Empire: An Interpretation of American Expansionism, 1860–1898* (Ithaca, N.Y.: Cornell University Press, 1963), p. viii, quoted in Maldonado-Denis, *Puerto Rico*, p. 67.

[10] Negrón-Portillo, *El autonomismo*, pp. 36–43. As Negrón-Portillo very effectively shows, the perspective of the liberal autonomists toward the U.S. changed with continued U.S. control.

their employers and bring them greater rights.[11] This impression was reinforced by Gen. Nelson Miles, the leader of the U.S. invasion, who stressed in a speech to the people that the United States was intent not on oppressing them, but on bestowing "the advantages and blessings of enlightened civilization."[12] Later, some political leaders expressed more doubt about the benefits of increased U.S. influence,[13] but others saw nothing to fear from closer association with the United States and looked forward to territorial status and eventual statehood.

Three successive military governors (Maj. Gen. John R. Brooke, Major General Henry, and Brig. Gen. George W. Davis) administered the new colony from October 18, 1898, until May 1, 1900, and oversaw efforts to improve the abysmal living conditions which the U.S. occupying forces found. Access to education was broadened, with the proviso that English-language instruction be provided. In 1898, there had been 529 public schools, most of them in makeshift quarters; at the end of 1901, the number of schools had risen to 733, with 31,172 enrolled students, though this still represented only about 10 percent of the school-age population. By 1910, the number of lower schools, most of which went up to the fifth grade, had increased to 1,025, and enrollment to 121,453, and the level of illiteracy had declined to 66.5 percent from the 79.6 percent of 1899. There were nineteen high schools with 636 students, but only three of them offered four years of education. Improvements also were made in health care, communications, roads, and the civil service, though it must be said that these changes did not greatly alter living conditions for most Puerto Ricans.[14] But the military occu-

[11] For the views of workers, see Quintero Rivera, *Conflictos de clase*, pp. 124–28, and the "Tyranny of the House of Delegates," in Quintero Rivera, *Workers' Struggles*, pp. 51–66. Luque de Sánchez, *La ocupación norteamericana*, chap. 2, provides a wide range of perspectives on the meaning of U.S. control.

[12] The complete text of General Miles's rather overstated speech is in Wagenheim, *Puerto Ricans*, pp. 123–24.

[13] Consider, for example, an editorial in *La democracia* in late 1898, which began: "With annexation to the United States, what will we get? A change of pain and nothing more. We will continue being exploited colonials." The entire Spanish text can be found in Silén, *Historia*, pp. 137–38, and an English translation in Maldonado-Denis, *Puerto Rico*, pp. 61–62.

[14] Colton, *Report to the Governor*, pp. 33–34, 153, 156–57; Quintero Rivera, *Conflictos de clase*, p. 43, table 1; USDL, *Labor Conditions*, p. 12; and Negrón de Montilla, *Americanization*, pp. 43, 59. English was the sole language of instruction in 112 of the rural schools in 1910, a point noted with pride in Governor Colton's annual report. Negrón de Montilla's work is a useful study of the influence of the U.S. in educational policy making and especially of the unremitting efforts by U.S. commissioners of education to have English taught as the vehicle, indeed the essence, of Americanization. See also Berbusse, *U.S. in Puerto Rico*, pp. 210–24. On roads, see Hunt, *Second Annual Report*, pp. 38, 214.

pation also shattered any illusions Puerto Ricans might have had about the promise of liberalism and democracy in U.S. relations with the new possession. The first peacetime military governor, Major General Brooke, for example, ordered that the name of the island be changed to "Porto" Rico, an Americanized corruption of Spanish that remained the official spelling until 1932. On February 6, 1899, the last remaining institution of local government, the Insular Council, was dissolved by the United States as being "not compatible with American methods and progress."[15] Newspapers that opposed the military government were censured (*La democracia*) or closed (*La metralla*).[16]

Resentment and opposition to military rule began to grow. Many of Puerto Rico's elite began traveling to Washington—much as they and their predecessors had gone to Madrid—to plead their case and to present their demands for change before the War Department, which at the time administered colonial policy, and before Congress. Besides the degrading and undefined status of military occupation, which dismayed and confused Puerto Rico's leaders, the other major concern was with tariffs, which all the island's politicians and businessmen wanted lowered; in fact, the two issues were intimately related. It was precisely because U.S. policy makers had not resolved the issue of Puerto Rico's legal status vis-à-vis the United States that tariffs on the goods that flowed between them remained in place and in some cases were actually increased, since Puerto Rico was technically still a foreign country. Spain and Cuba also had raised their tariffs on Puerto Rican goods, for they, too, now treated the island's products like those of foreign nations. For example, tobacco shipped to Cuba before 1898 had paid a tariff of 15 to 20 cents per pound; after the end of the Spanish-Cuban-American War, the tariff was increased to a devastating $5.00 per pound to protect Cuban tobacco producers. Coffee paid a prohibitive tariff of $12.15 per kilogram in Cuba, a nearly fourfold increase over the prewar level.[17] Thus, the markets for key exports were being closed, and no new markets were opening. Imports into Puerto Rico also were adversely affected, particularly by the tariff law which went into effect on January 20, 1899.[18] Puerto Rico's leaders clamored for relief through the extension of free trade to open the massive North American market to the island's products.

[15] This was done by Major General Henry: Berbusse, *U.S. in Puerto Rico*, pp. 81–82, 91–92, 106. Offices were abolished and people discharged, supposedly to make the colonial administration more efficient. These dismantled local institutions had been representative in a limited sense only, however. Suffrage was not universal; women were excluded from voting entirely, and men had to meet economic and literacy requirements.

[16] On the suspension of newspapers, see Berbusse, *U.S. in Puerto Rico*, pp. 94–95.

[17] Luque de Sánchez, *La ocupación norteamericana*, pp. 45, 63, 76, 78.

[18] Berbusse, *U.S. in Puerto Rico*, pp. 132–33.

Muñoz Rivera, who had been involved in the bargaining that had resulted in the Autonomist Charter of 1897, argued in Washington the position of the autonomist faction within the elite, grouped in the Partido Federal Americano, which wanted Puerto Rico to be associated on more nearly equal terms with the United States as a territory or a state and, in either case, for Puerto Ricans to be United States citizens.[19] Many other different groups and individuals also appeared in the U.S. capitol to ask for special favors, including business representatives, bankers, and mayors.[20] Others, like Eugenio de Hostos, went to demand independence, a position that did not meet with much sympathy in Washington. The military government did grant some tariff concessions to meet some of the demands and mitigate the dissatisfaction, but it did not introduce free trade. In 1899, the tariff on rice had been reduced from $1.85 to 60 cents and on flour (by 50 percent), cheese (60 percent), beans (56 percent), and lard (25 percent), but the tariffs on other goods remained in place and the prices of ham, bacon, butter, and other imported products increased.[21] While the lower tariffs on the former goods generally helped low-income consumers, the increases in the price of the latter products, with no tariff relief, adversely affected higher-income consumers, who, ironically, were the ones making the case for free trade in Washington.

However, the autonomist, independence, and free-trade arguments were lost. Pressures on Congress from all sides led to maintenance of strict control over the new colony, which was held to be U.S. property, rightfully obtained—a sentiment soon to be inscribed in law.

THE FORAKER ACT

Congress decided that Puerto Rico was and would remain a colony, but that a civilian government would replace military rule. The new government structure was created by the Foraker Act (the first Organic Act, or constitution), which went into effect on May 1, 1900.[22] Although supposedly a temporary measure, it remained in force until 1917. It provided for rule primarily by U.S. civilians, appointed by the War Department and the president and approved by Congress. The governor was to be presidentially appointed (until 1946, all the appointees were North Americans) and, in turn, had the power to name certain other government officials.[23] The supreme decision-making body was the Executive Coun-

[19] Raffucci de García, El gobierno civil, pp. 112–13.
[20] Luque de Sánchez, La ocupación norteamericana, pp. 64ff.
[21] Ibid., pp. 65.
[22] The official title of the law was "An Act Temporarily to Provide Revenues and Civil Government for Porto Rico and for other Purposes." See García Martínez, Puerto Rico, pp. 129–51, for the text.
[23] Luque de Sánchez, La ocupación norteamericana, p. 126.

cil (*Consejo Ejecutivo*), which served as a cabinet to the governor as well as the chief law-making body, an obvious violation of the separation of executive and legislative powers. The Executive Council had eleven members, appointed by the president and approved by Congress. No more than five had to be native Puerto Ricans, so North Americans were able to exercise effective veto power within the council. More important, top officials were appointed by the president, who regularly named North Americans to such key policy-making positions as attorney general, treasurer, auditor, and commissioner of education. These were the positions in which the day-to-day policies were made that influenced the direction of socioeconomic development and ideological training.

The Foraker Act also created a House of Delegates (*Camara de Delegados*) which functioned like the lower house of a legislature. Its thirty-five members were to be elected for two-year terms.[24] The governor had the power to veto any of its decisions, and Congress had ultimate veto power over all legislation. The U.S. court system was introduced, and Puerto Ricans were "given" Puerto Rican citizenship, an internationally undefined status.[25] All U.S. laws were made applicable except those specifically exempted.

The act also created the position of "resident commissioner," who was

[24] The franchise for these elections was quite restricted—a regression from the nearly universal male suffrage that had been introduced in the Autonomist Charter of 1897. The vote was limited to males aged twenty-one and over who could read and write or who had paid taxes. (One argument for these provisions was that they would "excite a desire to acquire property and education in order that the right to suffrage may be enjoyed": Raffucci de García, *El gobierno civil*, p. 91.) The overall level of literacy in Spanish was 22.7 percent, though it was higher in urban than in rural areas, in the professions that in agriculture, and among men than among women. As a result of these restrictions, about three-quarters of the men (and of course all women) were disenfranchised. The number of registered voters in 1900 was 123,140. See Quintero Rivera, *Conflictos de clase*, pp. 34, 36–38; Berbusse, *U.S. in Puerto Rico*, pp. 41, 106; USDW, *1899 Census*, pp. 22, 63, 79; and Bayrón Toro, *Elecciones y partidos políticos*, p. 115. A Senate report in 1900 stated that literacy in Spanish was probably no greater than 12 percent and in English less than 0.1 percent: Gould, *La Ley Foraker*, p. 32.

[25] Puerto Rico's leaders had asked that U.S. citizenship be granted, and the original version of the law did so. The argument over citizenship revolved around the question of whether a tariff could constitutionally be levied on U.S. citizens residing in a U.S. territory. Since Congress was determined to levy tariffs on imports from Puerto Rico, it decided that the island would be an "unincorporated territory," that the U.S. Constitution would not apply to it, and that Puerto Ricans would not be U.S. citizens. The best discussion of these complexities is in Raffucci de García, *El gobierno civil*, esp. chap. 4. Until the issue of citizenship was resolved, Puerto Ricans were in a very real sense a people without a country. They were not eligible for a U.S. passport nor for any other, and thus they could not legally travel, even to the U.S. The issue was not finally resolved until 1904: Luque de Sánchez, *La ocupación norteamericana*, pp. 75, 135, 184–87.

elected to a two-year term and served in Washington. The functions of this official, however, were only vaguely defined. The commissioner could speak to issues of importance to the island before federal departments but not before Congress. The U.S. territory of Hawaii, on the other hand, had a delegate to Congress, with both a seat in and a voice before that body, though without a vote.[26] The slight to Puerto Rico and Puerto Ricans was not lost on the island's leaders, and the limited role of the resident commissioner created conflict and resentment in San Juan. In 1902, the commissioner was granted the right to enter the House of Representatives (but not to take part in its debates), and in 1904, the right to speak in the House, though still not the right to vote on the issues.[27] Even then, the restriction on the participation of Puerto Rico in the policy making of the colonial power represented a step backward from the representation and voting power obtained in the Spanish Cortes during the more liberal periods of Spanish rule.[28]

The island's status and political rights were finally and legally settled when the U.S. Supreme Court ruled that Puerto Rico was a "non-incorporated territory," a formula that Senator Foraker had proposed in the congressional debate. The Court agreed that the provisions and protections of the Constitution did not automatically apply to Puerto Rico.[29] By this decision, Puerto Rico "belonged to," but was not part of, the United States. The decision and the ambiguous status it gave to Puerto Rico were acidly commented on in a San Juan newspaper at the time:

We are and we are not an integral part of the United States. We are and we are not a foreign country. We are and we are not citizens of the United States. . . . The Constitution covers us and does not cover us . . . it applies to us and does not apply to us.[30]

[26] Within the bounds of the congressional debate and the constitutionality of the Foraker Act, the decision not to allow Puerto Rico a voice in Congress followed a certain logic. Puerto Ricans were not U.S. citizens, the island was not part of the U.S., and the constitution therefore did not automatically apply. It made little sense, as one senator remarked, to have a Puerto Rican delegate swear before being seated in Congress to uphold a Constitution which did not extend to the island: Raffucci de García, *El gobierno civil*, p. 88.

[27] Luque de Sánchez, *La ocupación norteamericana*, pp. 173–81. Further details on the Foraker Act may be found in ibid., pp. 126–29.

[28] "In thus creating a form of civil government for the people of Puerto Rico, Congress gave little regard to the principles of consent of the governed or the right of a people to participate in the determination of its own affairs": Hunter, *Puerto Rico*, p. 3.

[29] The decision was handed down (on a 5-to-4 vote) in *Downes v. Bidwell* (1901). For discussions of relevant court cases, see Luque de Sánchez, *La ocupación norteamericana*, pp. 172–73; Berbusse, *U.S. in Puerto Rico*, pp. 168–69; and Gould, *La Ley Foraker*, pp. 147ff.

[30] *San Juan News*, May 29, 1901, quoted in Carr, *Puerto Rico*, p. 38.

Congress was to decide which constitutional guarantees were to be applicable and which were not; it decided, for example, that Puerto Ricans did not have the right to trial by jury.

The Foraker Act was not simply a political document, however; it was also an economic instrument designed to control Puerto Rico's economic life.[31] Under the act, Puerto Rico was prohibited from negotiating commercial treaties with other nations. It was prohibited from determining its own tariffs; after a short initial period with tariffs equal to 15 percent of those prevailing in the United States on foreign products, it was to share "common tariffs" with the United States.[32] All goods that moved between the island and the mainland were to be carried by U.S. shipping lines. Puerto Rico was to be part of the U.S. monetary system, with the Puerto Rican peso retired at the rate of 60 cents to the peso. Corporations, but not individuals, were restricted to owning less than 500 acres of land; Clarence Senior has suggested that this was a reflection of the power of the populist movement in the United States at the time,[33] but if so, neither the populists nor anyone else was powerful enough to see to it that the restriction was enforced until some four decades later.[34]

Prior to passage of the Foraker Act, less than 16 percent of Puerto

[31] See the speech of Senator Foraker, quoted in Maldonado-Denis, *Puerto Rico*, pp. 89–90, in which he said in part: "We have reached the point in the development of our resources and the multiplication of our industries where we are not only supplying our home demands, but are producing a large surplus, constantly growing larger. Our greatest present and prospective commercial need is for markets abroad." See also Berbusse, *U.S. in Puerto Rico*, pp. 60–61, for additional statements to the same effect.

[32] During the initial period, some items, including capital and intermediate goods, directed toward large corporations, were exempted from tariffs. The tariff revenues were to be returned to the Puerto Rican government for its administrative expenses. These provisions were to remain in effect only until the insular government devised means to finance its operations locally and in no case were to extend beyond March 1, 1902 (they actually ended on July 25, 1901): Gould, *La Ley Foraker*, p. 39, nn. 20, 21, and Hunt, *Second Annual Report*, pp. 332–34. The tariff was important to the passage of the Organic Act, since interests in the U.S. opposed to free trade might have blocked it otherwise. As might be expected, merchants were in favor of free trade, but U.S. producers of sugar, tobacco, and fruit were less "liberal." U.S. beet-sugar producers opposed free trade not only because of an immediate fear of competition, but also because of the possible precedent for policy toward Cuba and the Philippines: Gould, *La Ley Foraker*, chap. 5; Luque de Sánchez, *La ocupación norteamericana*, chap. 4; and Raffucci de García, *El gobierno civil*, p. 67. Also see the critique of the tariff as a means of financing the Puerto Rican government that appeared in the *Nation* in 1899, quoted in Wagenheim, *Puerto Ricans*, pp. 136–139.

[33] Senior, *Santiago Iglesias*, p. 43.

[34] Governor Hunt expressed the opinion of the sugar overlords in his 1903 report: "Investments in sugar plantations should not be limited to 500 acres. The capitalist finds this statute an impediment, and it has been the opinion of the executive council for some time that Congress could wisely allow an ownership of not to exceed 5,000 acres": *Third Annual Report*, p. 40.

Rico's exports and 22 percent of imports had been carried on U.S. ships,
even though more than 80 percent of its trade was conducted with the
United States.[35] Following its passage, the prices of imported goods rose,
because the U.S. merchant fleet was more expensive than that of other
countries. Meanwhile, incomes were substantially lower in Puerto Rico
than in any state in the United States. Because Puerto Rico was denied
the right to make commercial pacts with other nations, it could not enter
into stabilizing arrangements for the island's products, a prohibition from
which coffee especially suffered. The island's farmers and manufacturers
were subjected to the same market forces as the larger U.S. agricultural
growers and firms and were confronted with the necessity of competing
with the products of some of the largest and most powerful firms on the
world market. By the provisions of the Foraker Act, then, Puerto Rican
producers were forced to face in the market the most rapidly developing
capitalist country in the world without the possibility of protecting domestic production and industries through the use of the tariff barriers and
commercial treaties that were available to independent countries (and that
had been available to Puerto Rico as well, however briefly, under the
Autonomous Charter). The local economy was left defenseless against
the inflow of U.S. products and capital—which, in fact, was precisely
what the Foraker Act intended.

The extension of the U.S. monetary system to the island also had an
adverse impact on the local economy. During the military occupation,
there had been a multiple currency system on the island; Puerto Rican,
U.S., and other monies were in circulation. In January 1899, exchange
rates for all currencies were made official to facilitate business transactions, but the multiple monetary system continued.[36] The rate of 60 cents
to the peso was chosen as a compromise between the intrinsic value of
the peso (the value of its silver content, about 40 to 42 cents at the time)
and its value as generally accepted in transactions (66⅔ cents). In the
hearings that preceded passage of the Foraker Act, debt-laden landowners
had asked for an exchange rate as low as 50 cents, so that they could
more easily liquidate their debts, while bankers had pleaded for a higher
conversion rate (as much as 75 cents) to avoid the negative effects of
devaluation.

The Foraker Act's conversion rate of 60 cents constituted a de facto
devaluation from the peso's value of 66⅔ cents at the time. It had the
effect of increasing prices, by some estimates as much as 40 percent, due

[35] Berbusse, *U.S. in Puerto Rico*, p. 150.
[36] For the presidential order on exchange rates, see *BHPR* 6:104–5. Other rates besides
the official ones were commonly used in transactions, however: Ramos Mattei, "Las inversiones norteamericanas," p. 58.

to both the conversion rate itself and the scarcity of money created as pesos were removed from circulation. Many merchants, whether out of ignorance or greed, quoted identical prices for goods in dollars after the changeover as they had in pesos before, which meant a substantial increase in prices. Wages, however, quickly adjusted to the lower exchange rate, and hence the purchasing power of income was reduced for most workers. The Foraker Act also ended the multiple currency system and made the U.S. dollar and U.S. monetary decisions dominant.[37]

Devaluation no doubt facilitated the large land purchases by U.S. sugar corporations which followed the invasion. The scarcity of local credit, long a problem, intensified upon the contraction of the money supply, and it became even more difficult and expensive for small growers to borrow. But U.S. banks soon entered to make loans to "qualified" applicants. The first U.S.-owned bank to operate in Puerto Rico was the American Colonial Bank, which in 1901 already was the second largest bank on the island and by 1910 had become the largest. "Qualified" borrowers turned out to be, not surprisingly, mostly American sugar companies with the collateral to back their loan requests, something that small Puerto Rican landholders could not offer except by mortgaging their land, which was then often lost to the banks or sold off to the sugar corporations when loans could not be repaid, contributing further to a decline in local control of land and production which took place at a rapid pace during the first decade of U.S. control.[38] Many land sales, increasingly to U.S. sugar corporations, were made to avoid increasing debt and thus were seemingly "voluntary," but it is important to understand that they took place in a context of U.S. decisions and laws affecting the

[37] Berbusse, *U.S. in Puerto Rico*, p. 136; Silén, *Historia*, pp. 146–47, 150–51; Luque de Sánchez, *La ocupación norteamericana*, pp. 66ff; and Herrero, *La mitología del azúcar*, pp. 10–16. Sánchez Tarniella, *La economía*, pp. 79–80, writes that on the world market the Puerto Rican peso was valued at 75 cents, which would have made the effective devaluation resulting from the Foraker Act 20 percent, rather than the 10 percent that would be calculated from a value of 66 ⅔ cents. No evidence, however, is given to support his statement.

[38] V. Clark et al., *Porto Rico and Its Problems*, pp. 374–77. A local law of February 12, 1899, forebade land foreclosures for debt repayment, precisely to prevent land from being lost due to the problems brought on by exchange conversion, the lack of credit facilities during the change of power, high interest rates, and abuses in land transfers. However, since land could not be foreclosed on, banks and other lenders refused to accept land as collateral; hence, many farmers ended up selling land to obtain funds that would normally have been provided through credit channels. Thus, a law designed to protect small farmers proved to be ill designed and actually had the opposite effect of forcing many to sell part or all of their land, further contributing to land concentration: Herrero, *La mitología del azúcar*, pp. 17–18, and Berbusse, *U.S. in Puerto Rico*, pp. 93, 131–32. This law was soon overturned.

money supply, taxes, and credit arrangements. There was nothing inherent in the situation that required a turn of events in which so many lost
their land to so few.[39]

The Foraker Act thus established Puerto Rico as a sphere of U.S. influence, open to exploitation by its more powerful neighbor, by denying
to Puerto Ricans control of the process of political and economic development. Subjected to the same economic and monetary forces, Puerto
Rico suffered the movements and fluctuations of the North American
economy, typically with greater severity. The mechanisms of colonial
control facilitated the efforts of the United States and its monopoly enterprises to assert their economic power. At the same time, the island served
as a strategic military location for the protection of those interests in the
Americas. Puerto Rico was to rapidly become a location for profitable
production by U.S. firms, with a captive labor force ready to be employed.

The Foraker Act also confirmed the colonial status of Puerto Rico and
denied to it the possibility of independent capitalist economic development. It blocked the growth of an indigenous entrepreneurial class, which
might have been able to pursue such a path. That, of course, was one of
the implicit objectives of the act. The Puerto Rican capitalist class, small
but beginning to develop before 1898 in the sugar and coffee regions and
in urban factories, was destroyed before it could fully emerge. The em-
bryo of national capitalist development died in the womb, but capitalism
and capitalist production relations were to blossom under foreign control.[40]

A report by the authoritative Brookings Institution in 1930 admitted
that, under the Foraker Act, "mainlanders controlled the government,"
but, it went on to say:

> The Foraker Act was designed to assure the people of Porto Rico
> full opportunity to express their will in all public matters through reg-
> ularly elected representatives, but to prevent their political inexperience
> from provoking crises or engaging them in unwise public projects.[41]

---

[39] Bergad, "Agrarian History," pp. 74–75. In 1902, an acre of good sugar land sold for
about $150, high even in comparison to land prices in the U.S. Coffee land sold for $10 to
$15 an acre, a measure of its lower productivity on the market and the decline already
apparent in the industry: Hunt, *Second Annual Report*, p. 30.

[40] By the end of 1909, 142 foreign corporations with a total capital value of $299,354,439
had entered the local economy. There were 119 registered domestic corporations (not all
locally owned), with a total capital value of $21,911,570, only 7.3 percent that of the
foreign firms: Colton, *Report to the Governor*, p. 5.

[41] V. Clark et al., *Porto Rico and Its Problems*, p. 94.

This blithe assessment neglected the facts that the ability of Puerto Ricans to express their will was severely constrained by voting restrictions on the franchise and by the subordination of the only elected body, the House of Delegates, to the triple veto of the Executive Council, the governor, and Congress. The belief that Puerto Ricans were not "ready" to govern themselves accurately mirrored the paternalistic opinion many North Americans held about Puerto Ricans. They were seen as backward and uncivilized, wholly unfit (at least for some time) for home rule. Colonial control was "for their own good."[42] Contrary views were put forth in reports by three officially commissioned investigators—Dr. Henry Carroll, Father Thomas J. Sherman, and U.S. Consul Philip C. Hanna, who, besides detailing many urgent needs for Puerto Rico, also argued that the island was ready for and should be granted self-rule—but these views were disregarded.

On the other hand, Congress did see fit to implement many of the recommendations made in these reports for improved health care, better education and communications, road building and repair, and liberalized banking laws, among other things. Even these acts had another aspect, however, one that was inextricably tied to the maintenance and usefulness of Puerto Rico's colonial status. The Foraker Act and its implementation can be understood as creating the infrastructure necessary for the success of U.S. business on the island. American business entrepreneurs and administrators could come to Puerto Rico to produce and sell goods without fearing disease and with the assurance of finding a reasonably healthy and minimally educated population to labor in the cane fields and the factories. Roads to move goods would exist, and communication would be easier. There can be no doubt that Puerto Ricans benefited to an extent from these expenditures on infrastructural development, but it ought to be recognized that their welfare was not the sole motivating force behind them.

The hope that Puerto Rican leaders had had for the extension to their land of the benefits of U.S. liberal democracy began to sour as the "temporary" Foraker Act began to appear more and more permanent. Regardless of whether they favored statehood, greater autonomy, or independence, nearly all were offended by the restrictions of the act and outspoken in their objections. Perhaps the only exception was the Partido Republicano, led by José Celso Barbosa, which was a staunch supporter of the status quo, from which many of its members personally benefited as of-

---

[42] See, for example, the statements of this position made by various U.S. officials in their capacity as military governors or as witnesses at the committee hearings on the Foraker Act, in Berbusse, *U.S. in Puerto Rico*, pp. 88-89, 98, 151-52, 154.

ficials of the colonial apparatus. Barbosa's party was adamantly opposed
to Muñoz's Federal party, and this split within the creole elite manifested
itself not only in ideological struggle but also in violence directed against
Federal party members and the offices of *La democracia* and other pro-
autonomy publications. Attacks by mobs under the control of the Republicans, and with the tacit consent of the colonial government, escalated
beginning in 1900 and lasted until at least 1903; people were hurt, some
were killed, and property was damaged.[43]

Muñoz Rivera, meanwhile, expressed the feelings of his fraction of the
creole elite in these words, spoken in 1904: "In 1901, only a few of us
distrusted the United States. Today all are beginning to realize that we
have been deceived. We no longer worship everything that comes from
the North."[44] The longer the Foraker Act remained in force, keeping
Puerto Ricans as second-class, or worse, subjects of the U.S. empire, the
more widely shared was that view and the more did resistance to and
discontent with U.S. control grow. Interestingly, this would lead the autonomists full circle, as they would come to declare themselves in opposition to the U.S. citizenship that they had so wanted in the early years
of U.S. control. Instead, they would insist on maintaining Puerto Rican
citizenship, and Spain and Spanish culture were soon to be raised to new
levels of significance as North American culture and accelerated capitalist
development began to threaten old customs and beliefs, including the
traditionally subordinate role of women.[45]

Ironically, perhaps, it was labor and labor organizations which gained
most from early U.S. colonial domination. Under Spanish law, workers
had been permitted to form mutual-aid societies and social clubs but had
been prohibited from joining together to attain higher wages, reduced
working hours, or better working conditions (see chapter 1). In plain
language, unions were illegal. Labor organizing took place, nonetheless,
but at a price: leaders were jailed and strikes broken by the authorities,
often with considerable violence. Santiago Iglesias, one of Puerto Rico's
better-known early labor leaders, was in prison at the time of the U.S.
invasion for precisely the "crime" of organizing workers. He had been
imprisoned by the autonomous government in 1897, and popular legend
has it that he escaped during the U.S. invasion when an exploding shell

---

[43] Negrón-Portillo, *El autonomismo*, pp. 52–59.
[44] Quoted in Golding, *Short History*, p. 116. The disenchantment of the "transitional"
generation of intellectuals and the elite of leaders is evident from the selection of their
writings in section 2 of Závala and Rodríguez, *Intellectual Roots*.
[45] This change in attitude is well documented in Negrón-Portillo, *El autonomismo*, pp.
81–95. See also the revealing letter written by Muñoz Rivera in 1914: *BHPR* 6:207–11.

made a hole in his cell through which he fled. The true story, rather less colorful, is that he was released by the new military government on October 5, 1898, as part of a general armistice.[46] Iglesias immediately began to agitate for workers' rights, under the protection of the new military government. He was jailed twice again under Spanish law during the military occupation on an old charge, but finally, in 1902, with the support of the American Federation of Labor (AFL) and its president, Samuel Gompers, and of U.S. liberal opinion and the governor, labor was guaranteed the right to organize into unions.[47] This was done in the belief that an organized, legal labor movement operating within well-defined legal channels was more predictable, more easily controlled, and a better guarantee of business stability than the tendency toward labor anarchy which had existed to that point.[48] Such an enlightened view was not shared by Puerto Rico's domestic elite, however; they saw in the working-class movement the seeds of class struggle, whereas they wished to continue to believe in *la familia puertorriqueña*, the idea that all Puerto Ricans were one family. The process of capitalist development, which during the coming decades of the twentieth century would create ever more members of the propertyless working class, made this little more than an early nineteenth-century dream.

Iglesias, who was a self-proclaimed socialist, an ardent advocate of statehood, and a paid organizer for the AFL in Puerto Rico, no doubt succeeded in winning protection and important advances for organized labor, but this occurred without presenting any fundamental challenge to the dominance of business and capital. U.S. investors, who would soon become the most important owners and employers, would be able to reap their profits in a more stable (though not trouble-free) atmosphere, while Iglesias became a "respected" politician as a result of his activities.

Puerto Rico's indeterminate status as a nonincorporated territory led members of the elite to redefine and rethink their strategy and positions vis-à-vis the United States. Political parties jockeyed for control of insular politics; they split and created alliances and coalitions, often of improbable kinds, while new parties developed to fill voids the older ones

---

[46] Galvin, *Organized Labor Movement*, p. 37.

[47] For an extremely sympathetic short history of Iglesias and his work, see Senior, *Santiago Iglesias*. Galvin, "Early Development," provides a broader and more sober view of Iglesias's work, and Galvin, *Organized Labor Movement*, pp. 46, 52, has the story of the later arrests.

[48] Negrón-Portillo, *El autonomismo*, pp. 79–81, and Galvin, *Organized Labor Movement*, pp. 53–54. The *San Juan News*, a newspaper with a metropolitan perspective, supported Iglesias as one who favored "order instead of disorder."

left or to serve new needs.[49] These parties and their leaders—the Union party under Muñoz Rivera and José de Diego (formed in 1904), the Republican party under Roberto Todd and Barbosa, and even Iglesias's Socialist party after a time—represented the Puerto Rican elites from which their leaders came, and they articulated the elites' special problems and concerns. Each party tended to respond, of course, to different groups: the Union party to local coffee producers, the Republican to foreign sugar entrepreneurs and professionals with connections to the United States.[50] The Union party tended to favor autonomy and independence, while the Republicans were solidly pro-American. The Socialist party began as a workers' party, but because of the desire of its leadership to maintain association with the United States in order to protect labor's rights, it chose in 1924 to join a coalition with dissident elements of the Republican party who represented the most reactionary landowners. Upon the formation of this coalition, what worker orientation remained in the Socialist party disappeared.

What all the parties lacked, even when "in power," was effective control over political and economic events on the island. The Foraker Act put the U.S. government squarely in control of politics and opened the door wide for U.S. capital's dominance of the economy. As Gordon Lewis noted, the North Americans could truthfully say: "You are in office, but we are in power."[51] The members of the local elite recognized their ultimate weakness; some reconciled themselves to it, others fought it. In either case, they continued to work within the rules set by the very system that was oppressing both them and all other Puerto Ricans. More trips were made to Washington, and ever more requests for a loosening of the colonial ties were filed. Some preferred statehood. Others pleaded for greater autonomy and, in some instances, eventual independence. Many still wanted the "equality" of U.S. citizenship.[52] What they obtained, however—along with all other Puerto Ricans, including those whose class interests were quite different—was the Jones Act, Puerto Rico's second Organic Act, which became law on March 2, 1917.

[49] There is no pretense made here at covering the complex development of political parties. The best source, though one which must be read with caution, is Pagán, *Partidos políticos puertorriqueños.*

[50] See Silén, *Historia*, pp. 141–83, and Mattos Cintrón, *La política y lo político*, chap. 2, for more details.

[51] Lewis, *Puerto Rican Revolution*, p. 108.

[52] In 1912, a committee made up of José de Diego, José Coll y Cuchi, Roberto Todd, Arturo Gómez Brioso, Santiago Iglesias, and Luis Muñoz Rivera had proposed to President Taft and Congress that Puerto Ricans be granted U.S. citizenship: Silén, p. 165. There were earlier and later such requests, both official and private.

THE JONES ACT

The Jones Act created a new, bicameral, and wholly elective legislature for Puerto Rico. Its upper house, the Senado, was to have nineteen members, five of them elected *por acumulación*, or at large. In effect, it took over the law-making powers of the Executive Council. The lower house was called the Cámara de Representantes; it was to have thirty-nine members, four elected por acumulación. Suffrage was extended to all males twenty one-years and over, with no property or literacy requirements. Women, however, remained disenfranchised, as they were in the United States.[53] The governor continued to be presidentially appointed, as were the attorney general, auditor, and commissioner of education, all of whom also served on the eleven-member Executive Council, which was now to act exclusively as a cabinet. The other eight members of the council were named by the governor, subject to approval by the Senado. Puerto Ricans finally were granted U.S. citizenship; those wishing to remain Puerto Rican citizens had to renounce U.S. citizenship within six months and would lose many of their civil rights, including the right to vote by doing so—a costly act of defiance, which 287 people nevertheless undertook.[54] The governor retained veto power over all acts passed by the insular legislature, though the veto could be overridden by a two-thirds vote of both houses. The U.S. president, however, retained a final, unconditional veto power over all legislation, even over decisions of the governor, and Congress had the right to veto any legislation, even after it had been signed by the governor. There were no changes from the Foraker Act relative to immigration, trade, money, tariffs, commercial treaties, shipping, communications, the judicial system, or defense.[55] Even the dead-letter 500-acre restriction on corporate land holdings remained. The local government continued to be financed principally from customs collected on goods entering Puerto Rico and through the return of federal revenues collected on Puerto Rican tobacco, rum, and other products sold in the United States.[56]

[53] A movement for female suffrage began to be organized in 1917. The labor movement had supported the vote for women from its beginnings: T. Clark, *Puerto Rico*, pp. 39–46.

[54] On the relation of the Jones Act to U.S. involvement in World War I, see ibid., pp. 35–39. During the war, 17,855 Puerto Ricans were inducted into (segregated) military units.

[55] See García Martínez, *Puerto Rico*, pp. 153–98, for the complete text of the act. One provision called for Puerto Ricans to express their wishes on the sale of alcoholic beverages; they did so on July 16, 1917, and prohibition began in March 1918, almost two years before prohibition in the U.S. The effect of the ban in Puerto Rico was negligible: T. Clark, *Puerto Rico*, pp. 31–35.

[56] V. Clark et al., *Porto Rico and Its Problems*, pp. 99, 162, and Hunt, *Second Annual Report*, p. 188.

The Jones Act reaffirmed Puerto Rico's colonial condition, though the local Republican party supported it wholeheartedly while the Unionists simply tolerated it. Commenting on the Organic Acts, Gordon Lewis has pointed out that "85 percent of the basic areas of government that constitute national sovereignty in any generally understood definition of that term remain[ed] under the jurisdiction of the U.S. Congress. . . . The government of Puerto Rico, in effect, governs practically nothing."[57] Most Puerto Rican leaders capitulated to this defeat, even if they tried to believe they had scored a victory. The elites chose not to fight back; in fact, they were too weak. They became accomplices to and servants of the colonization that debilitated them and the mass of workers and semi-independent farmers. The opinion that had appeared in the newspaper *La correspondencia* in September 1903 had not lost its meaning for the discouraged, dejected, and displaced colonial elite in 1917: *no sabemos lo que somos*—"we do not know what we are."[58]

ECONOMIC REPERCUSSIONS

The colony the United States "inherited" in 1898 had already experienced profound internal transformations in its production and class relations (see chapter 1). Though the economy had been bounded by the backwardness and inflexibility of Spanish colonial policy, indigenous capitalist development had begun in agriculture and some industries and had begun to be an important force for change and progress in the last third of the century. Credit became more regular with the founding of banks, which permitted further expansion of production. Technology improved as financing made its purchase easier, and production became more "rationalized" as a result—i.e., made more efficient in terms of the output/cost ratio. There was a growing working class, increasingly accustomed to the rigors and demands of wage labor. Capitalism was still of relatively small scale in the late nineteenth century and capitalist production methods and relations were not the dominant economic forces. It would be idle speculation to wonder whether, under the move toward autonomy that began in 1897, national capitalist development would have come to prevail if the United States had not invaded. A tendency in that direction was certainly there and developing; what the U.S. invasion and capital did was to accelerate that change and direct it toward U.S. interests.

The flow of capital that followed the U.S. flag began to turn Puerto

---

[57] Lewis, *Puerto Rican Revolution*, p. 14.
[58] Quoted in Luque de Sánchez, *La ocupación norteamericana*, p. 143.

Rico into a classic monocultural colony, directed by U.S. business interests and dominated by capitalist methods of production, with sugar again becoming the leading export crop. The U.S. tariff wall erected around the island contributed to this dominance. Within the legal channels provided by the Foraker Act and then the Jones Act, there was nothing that could have been done to prevent this, and legality was respected by the island's elected leaders. As a consequence, Puerto Rico's economic life became increasingly tied to and dependent on the decisions of U.S. capitalists and on the U.S. economy.

THE DECLINE OF COFFEE

The discussion in chapter 1 explained how coffee became the leading cash crop for export, surpassing sugar in the closing decades of the nineteenth century. This process was reversed after the American occupation. The causes of the decline in the importance of coffee were both natural and manmade. The most important natural cause was a severe hurricane, San Ciriaco, which struck the island on August 8, 1899. Millions of dollars of property were destroyed and more than 3,000 persons were killed. Perhaps as much as 80 percent of the coffee crop, worth between $5.5 and $6 million, was lost; even worse, many, perhaps 55 to 60 percent, of the coffee plants and associated shade trees were destroyed.[59] Coffee plants require from four to six years to reach maturity, and for many small farmers, who depended on their coffee crop for at least a portion of their livelihood, this physical destruction was devastating; many of them were pushed into the ranks of landless wage workers, and others joined the first wave of migrants, hungry and jobless, to depart for Hawaii, Cuba, Santo Domingo, and other locations, where they were often abused and exploited.[60]

But it was the manmade causes that ultimately were more destructive to the coffee economy. Puerto Rican coffee, unlike sugar, had chiefly found its export markets in Cuba, France, Spain, and Germany. During the 1890s, on average, less than 1 percent of coffee exports had gone to the United States.[61] Puerto Rican coffee was highly regarded in Europe for its rich, deep flavor, and it commanded a relatively high price in those countries as a result. After the transfer of its colony to the United States, however, Spain considered Puerto Rico a foreign country, and it therefore increased its import tax on Puerto Rico's coffee, which had enjoyed a

[59] Saldaña, *El café*, pp. 17–18.
[60] Berbusse, *U.S. in Puerto Rico*, pp. 103, 105. The U.S. contributed about $1 million in food and medical aid after the hurricane.
[61] CENEP, *Taller*, p. 55, table 3.

semiprotected market until then.[62] Cuba also quadrupled its tariff, and, since production of Cuban coffee was increasing and was less expensive, purchases of Puerto Rican coffee virtually ended.

The loss of the markets for coffee in Spain and Cuba, which Puerto Rican products had entered without paying the tariff charged to producers from other countries, was not compensated by the new tariff relationships with the United States. The United States had no tariff on coffee imports, since there were no domestic producers to protect against foreign competition. Puerto Rican coffee thus entered the U.S. market on the same terms as any country's coffee, but it was more expensive than South American coffee.[63] Besides, North Americans had become accustomed to the taste of the weaker South American coffees, especially Brazil's, so that at its higher price Puerto Rico's stronger, richer coffee—U.S. consumers considered it bitter—was not popular on the mainland. No consideration was given to instituting special tariff protection for Puerto Rican coffee, on the ground that Puerto Rico was not part of the United States. But, as will be seen below, that argument did not prevent tariff protection for sugar. The fact is that Puerto Rican coffee growers were sacrificed to other, more powerful, interests.[64]

The abrupt drop in the relative value of coffee exports can be seen in table 2.1. Already by 1901, it had almost slipped back to the level of 1876 (compare table 1.4). The year before the beginning of the Great Depression in 1929, it had fallen to 2.5 percent, and it stood at an almost insignificant 0.3 percent in 1935. The continued decline during the twenties and thirties is explained by two additional factors: first, World War I further disrupted the European markets; and second, on September 13, 1928, the island was struck by another hurricane, San Felipe, which wrought about $85 million of damage, including destruction of 80 percent of the coffee crop and perhaps 50 percent of the plants.[65] The U.S. pro-

---

[62] Luque de Sánchez, *La ocupación norteamericana*, p. 78. In the late 1890s, from 25 to 30 percent of Puerto Rico's coffee exports had been sold to Spain. The tax thus affected a sizeable portion of the island's market: CENEP, *Labor Migration*, p. 71, table 3.2.

[63] Brazilian coffee cost $8–$10 a sack, while Puerto Rican coffee sold for $14–$15: Luque de Sánchez, *La ocupación norteamericana*, pp. 167–68.

[64] Some U.S. businesses had financial interests in Brazilian imports, and they had no desire to see any tariffs imposed that would have increased the price of Brazilian coffee. Given such interests and the lack of concern for Puerto Rican producers, it was unlikely that a tariff would be imposed merely to protect Puerto Rican coffee, though there was no reason why one could not have been put in place. Years later, Rexford G. Tugwell, governor from 1941 to 1946, wrote of these events: "So we had, in effect, taken away her livelihood and then had required her to support, out of her impoverishment, the far more prosperous farmers and processors in our States." Tugwell, *Stricken Land*, p. 284.

[65] Saldaña, *El café*, p. 21.

TABLE 2.1
Percentage of Total Export Value
in Selected Products, Selected Years, 1881 to 1935

Product	1881	1897	1901	1914	1928	1935
Agricultural						
Coffee	54.5	59.7[a]	19.5	19.0	2.5	0.3
Sugar	28.9	21.6	54.9	47.0	52.7	60.0
Tobacco	—	—	4.4	7.7	16.6	9.0
Manufactured						
Cigars	—	—	1.6	13.0	3.5	1.7
Textiles and garments	—	—	0.1	—	9.3	18.5

SOURCES: CENEP, *Taller*, p. 121; Bergad, "Agrarian History," pp. 65, 69. See V. Clark et al., *Porto Rico and Its Problems*, pp. 606–7, for detailed figures for exports, 1901–29. Other export products of lesser importance (and showing no particular trend) were molasses, fruit, and hides.

[a] 1895.

vided about $10 million in relief, but it was not enough to save the coffee industry or to compensate for much of the loss. As a result of the destruction of the plants, it was actually necessary to import coffee from 1929 to 1934 to meet the local demand.[66]

The decline of the importance of coffee exports does not mean that coffee production came to an end, however. In fact, in some years when the *relative* value of coffee exports decreased, the *absolute* value and quantity of coffee exports increased. The decline in relative value must be attributed at least partly to an astounding increase in sugar production and exports, to be discussed. As can be seen in table 2.2, there was a precipitous drop in both the volume and the dollar value of exports in 1901, as a result of the loss of markets and the 1899 hurricane, but they resumed their rise during the first two decades of the twentieth century. However, the cumulative devastation caused by the loss of markets, higher tariffs, the 1928 hurricane, and the Great Depression can be read in the export volume figures for 1928 and 1929. The coffee industry never recovered. Interestingly, through all these fluctuations, the amount of land devoted to coffee production remained fairly constant (table 2.3). The fall in production after 1925 came about principally because of a drastic decline in output per cuerda.

Conditions of work and life for those in the coffee sector were poor. In 1917, the Bureau of Labor reported that there were 156,700 persons

[66] Perloff, *Puerto Rico's Economic Future*, p. 94; PRDAC, *Statistics, 1943–44*, p. 205, table 147.

TABLE 2.2
Volume and Value of Coffee Exports,
Selected Years, 1881 to 1935

	Volume (lbs.)	Value ($)
1881	47,182,029	—
1895	39,683,160	5,640,055
1901	12,157,240	1,678,765
1905	16,949,739	2,141,019
1910	45,209,792	5,669,602
1914	50,311,946	8,193,544
1920	32,776,754	9,034,028
1925	23,782,996	6,575,635
1928	7,837,800	2,596,872
1929	1,278,666	458,924
1935	799,950	207,739

SOURCES: CENEP, *Labor Migration*, p. 94,
table 4.1; PRDAC, *Statistics, 1934–35*, p. 152.

in the coffee industry, including workers and individual owners (compared to 191,750 in sugar). Wages were low; in fact, of workers in the
three leading agricultural sectors (sugar, coffee, and tobacco), coffee
workers were the lowest paid: during the busy season, wages ranged from
50 to 60 cents a day for men, 18 to 32 cents for women, and 15 to 28
cents for children.[67] Hours were long and work was seasonal, like most
agricultural work, so even these minimal sums often were not earned in
the "dead season," when there was no harvesting to be done. Coffee
producers, many of them small and trying to preserve their independence
and a traditional life style, struggled to survive in the face of adverse
market conditions and in the face of the calculated policy and benign
neglect of the United States. But the combined forces were too strong,
and by the 1920s and 1930s, the coffee sector was in serious decline.
Coffee growers began to abandon their land, often moving to the coastal
plains to work on the large, sugar plantations then being formed—a reversal of the migration trends of the late nineteenth century, and a welcome development as far as the new sugar barons were concerned.[68] The
relative decline of coffee exports in the early period of U.S. control became an absolute decline of production in the twenties and thirties, and
the shift toward rural capitalist production and wage labor gained further
momentum in consequence.

[67] USDL, *Labor Conditions*, pp. 13, 37.
[68] Bergad, "Agrarian History," pp. 75–76.

TABLE 2.3
Area of Land in Coffee Production,
Selected Years, 1862 to 1935

	Area (cuerdas)
1862	57,000
1897	122,358
1899	197,031
1909	186,875
1919	193,561
1929	191,712
1935	182,316

SOURCES: CENEP, *Labor Migration*, p. 98, table 4.4; Perloff, *Puerto Rico's Economic Future*, p. 83, table 21A. See also Gayer, Homan, and Jones, *Sugar Economy*, p. 21, table 2.

THE ASCENT OF SUGAR

In contrast to the case in coffee production, sugar production rocketed upward, as U.S. capitalists invested in and began to dominate the industry.[69] Sugar quickly regained the position of predominant export crop and largest sector in the economy. Its potential market expanded, production methods were improved, and land ownership was concentrated. In the struggle over the provisions of the Foraker Act, some of the mainland sugar entrepreneurs led the forces opposed to free trade with Puerto Rico and to common tariffs for Puerto Rico and the United States. Representatives of beet-sugar producers feared not only that Puerto Rico cane sugar would take away part of their current and future markets if it were allowed to enter unrestricted, but also that a free-trade precedent would be applied to other sugar-producing territories under the U.S. flag. They therefore advocated import tariffs on Puerto Rico's sugar.[70] There were other entrepreneurs in the mainland sugar business, however, who saw the potential gains from free trade if they could control and reap the

[69] In 1879, production of sugar had been 170,679 tons, the highest level until the American occupation. By 1898, it was down to 60,285 tons. See Gayer, Homan, and Jones, *Sugar Economy*, p. 79, table 30 (production figures from 1828 to 1935), and Perloff, *Puerto Rico's Economic Future*, p. 70, chart 2.

[70] Berbusse, *U.S. in Puerto Rico*, pp. 154, 157–58. Mainland tobacco producers also expressed concern over the impact of free trade with Puerto Rico, for substantially the same reasons.

benefits of the island's cane production, and they made the argument in favor of free trade in congressional hearings.[71] The free-traders won out, and as a result, Puerto Rican sugar gained a privileged market in the United States, while foreign sugar producers were subjected to a tariff. Puerto Rican sugar was thus shielded, like mainland-produced sugar, from the full force of foreign competition.[72]

The increase in sugar production under the U.S. occupation was nothing short of spectacular, as table 2.4 shows. Production in 1930 was more than ten times the level of 1900. The increase in production was not uninterrupted; the 1928 hurricane adversely affected the sugar crop in 1929, and there were downturns in other years as well. But by the late 1920s, *annual* production was greater than total production had been during the entire last *decade* of Spanish rule.

Table 2.1 showed that sugar accounted for over half of all export value in 1901 and for 60 percent in 1935. It can now be seen in table 2.4 that the bulk of sugar was produced for export, and this was almost exclusively for the U.S. market.[73] Thus, the island's exports were increasingly dominated by one crop, produced primarily *for* export and sold virtually entirely in one market. The danger of such "monodependence" is apparent. A failure in the sugar crop due to bad weather or disease, a decrease in the price of sugar, recession in the United States, or any of a host of other factors could reduce the quantity and/or value of sugar exported and thereby threaten the ability to import the increasing quantity of goods the island consumed but did not produce.

Most of what was exported was raw sugar, not the refined product that ultimately reached the consumer. Except for small quantities used for local consumption, refining was done in the United States by the U.S. sugar companies, which imported raw sugar from many different loca-

[71] See ibid., pp. 151–54, for some of these arguments. The U.S. consul in San Juan received thousands of letters of inquiry from U.S. businesses after the takeover of the island. They had heard that Puerto Ricans were "not a class of people acquainted with strikes . . ." Thus, Puerto Rican workers, less organized and class-conscious than U.S. workers, seemed to promise an attractive climate for firms wishing to escape labor demands and protests on the mainland: Lewis, *Puerto Rico*, p. 87.

[72] The levels of tariff advantage enjoyed by Puerto Rican sugar producers over foreign producers and over the partially protected Cuban raw and refined sugar from 1903 to 1949 can be found in Perloff, *Puerto Rico's Economic Future*, p. 73. On raw sugar, the tariff reached its maximum of 2.5 cents per pound in 1930; it was high when the world price of sugar was low, and low when the world price was high. In most years, Cuba's tariff was 80 percent of the full tariff, though in some years it was less than 50 percent. See Herrero, *La mitología del azúcar*, p. 25.

[73] By comparison, from the end of the U.S. Civil War until 1898, the U.S. had purchased an average of 64.4 percent of Puerto Rico's annual sugar output: CENEP, *Taller*, p. 53, table 2.

TABLE 2.4
Production and Export of Sugar,
Selected Years, 1895 to 1930

	Production (tons)	Exports	
		Volume (tons)[a]	Value ($)
1895	66,073	—	—
1900	81,526	—	—
1902	100,576	92,000	5,890,302
1904	151,088	130,000	8,690,814
1906	206,864	205,000	14,184,667
1908	277,093	235,000	18,690,504
1910	349,840	284,000	23,545,922
1915	345,490	294,000	27,278,754
1917	503,081	489,000	54,015,903
1919	406,002	352,000	48,132,419
1921	491,000	409,000	72,440,924
1923	379,000	355,000	46,207,276
1925	660,003	572,000	53,261,895
1927	629,133	575,000	54,756,984
1929	586,760	471,000	35,224,056
1930	866,109	—	53,670,038

SOURCES: Gayer, Homan, and Jones, *Sugar Economy*, p. 79, table 30; V. Clark et al., *Porto Rico and Its Problems*, p. 606; PRDAC, *Statistics, 1934–35*, p. 11.
[a] To nearest thousand.

tions so as to minimize the risk to their supply. This meant that Puerto Rican sugar exports depended not only on the U.S. market but also on refining capacity located in the United States, and that the value added in production was created within the U.S. economy and accrued to U.S. companies.[74]

The increase in sugar production was the result of both expansion of the industry and its rationalization or "modernization," and both these processes imply that production was increasingly being put on a capitalist footing. Huge grinding mills or *centrales*, which processed the cane from a large surrounding area, installed the most modern technology available, and cheap labor was readily found to work in them. Large sugar plantations became even larger, covering the coastal plains. Cane production

[74] V. Clark et al., *Porto Rico and Its Problems*, p. 457.

eventually moved into the interior valleys and low foothills as well, and irrigation brought formerly inappropriate and marginal land into use. Consequently, the area devoted to sugar-cane production increased dramatically: from 72,146 cuerdas in 1899 to 145,433 in 1909 and 237,758 in 1929. Some of this additional land came from pasture converted to cane production, but part of it came into use at the expense of domestic food crops.[75]

CONCENTRATION OF LAND AND CAPITAL

The ownership of land in general, and not just of that in sugar production, became more highly concentrated under U.S. control, a pattern that was firmly in place by the end of the first decade of political domination (table 2.5). In 1899, nearly 90 percent of all farms had less than 20 cuerdas, and they cultivated about one-third of the land in production. Farms of 100 cuerdas or more cultivated about the same proportion of land, though they constituted only 2.2 percent of the number of farms. By 1910, the proportion of farms with 100 or more cuerdas had risen to 6.4 percent, and they now owned more land (62.7 percent of the total) than the other 93.6 percent of farms combined. Little changed in the next decades: farms of over 100 acres continued to own more land than all other farms combined, though the specific proportions varied slightly. It is especially interesting to note the amount of land in farms with 500 acres or more: in 1930, though they were only 0.7 percent of all farms, they owned 33.7 percent of all land. Many of these farms, as corporations, were in violation of the 500-acre limitation that was part of both the Foraker and Jones acts. The area of land under cultivation nearly doubled between 1899 and 1930 as new cane lands were planted, though the total land area in farms had declined between 1920 and 1930 by 2.1 percent (from 2,022,404 to 1,979,474 cuerdas).[76]

An accelerating tendency toward absentee ownership and a separation of ownership and control also appeared during this period. A census in 1930 found that managers operated 6.4 percent of all farms, accounting for 34.1 percent of the land in use. In 1910, only 19.3 percent of the land had been manager-operated. Conversely, the area in farms operated by owners fell from 69.9 percent in 1910 to 59 percent in 1930. (The remainder were renters.)[77] Thus, not only did land ownership became more concentrated; control over production decisions shifted toward hired managers, a sign of the spread of capitalist methods of production.

[75] CENEP, *Labor Migration*, p. 98, table 4.4.
[76] Gayer, Homan, and Jones, *Sugar Economy*, p. 114, table 45.
[77] Ibid., pp. 22–23.

TABLE 2.5
Percentage Distribution of Farms and Farm Area by Farm Size,
1899, 1910, 1920, and 1930

Size (cuerdas)	1899		1910		1920		1930	
	No. Farms	Area[a]	No. Farms	Area	No. Farms	Area	No. Farms	Area
0–19	87.7	32.7	72.0	12.4	62.3	10.6	71.0	14.1
20–49	7.5	17.3	15.2	12.9	20.6	12.6	16.7	13.4
50–99	2.6	14.5	6.4	12.0	8.5	11.1	6.3	11.4
100–499	} 2.2	35.5	5.5	31.0	7.4	29.7	5.3	27.4
500 or more			0.9	31.7	1.2	36.0	0.7	33.7
Number of farms	39,021		58,371		41,078		52,965	
Cuerdas under cultivation	482,272		—		719,970		835,460	

SOURCES: Gayer, Homan, and Jones, *Sugar Economy*, p. 24, tables 7 and 8, and p. 114, table 45; CENEP, *Labor Migration*, p. 96, table 4.2; Perloff, *Puerto Rico's Economic Future*, p. 406.

[a] For 1899 only, distribution by area of land under cultivation.

The pattern of concentrated land ownership was most visible in the sugar industry, which became the favored location for U.S. investment. In 1935, there were 7,693 sugar fincas of all sizes; these contained 38.7 percent of all farm land and 31.4 percent of all cultivated land.[78] The 156 farms with more than 500 acres (2.1 percent of all sugar farms) owned 65.2 percent of all land in sugar farms (table 2.6), nearly twice the proportion of farm land in general owned by farms of that size (see table 2.5). In fact, these same 156 plantations, just 0.3 percent of all farms, owned 25.2 percent of all farm land. The best sugar lands (e.g., in the municipio of Santa Isabel in the South) tended to show the highest concentration of ownership.

The small and medium semi-independent farmers (*colonos*) who grew cane had it ground at one of the large centrales located on the large sugar plantations. This critical function gave the large plantations a degree of control over sugar production that extended beyond their own holdings.

[78] Ibid., p. 22. The figures for some other crops as a percentage of cultivated land were: coffee, 25.3; corn, 9.3; tobacco, 7.0; sweet potatoes and yams, 6.3; beans, 5.4; cotton, 1.4; rice, 0.7.

TABLE 2.6
Distribution of Sugar Farms by Size, 1935

Size (cuerdas)	No. Farms	% of Farms	Area Cuerdas[a]	Percentage	Average Size (cuerdas)
0–5	2,558	33.2	7,093	0.9	2.8
6–10	1,222	15.9	9,618	1.3	7.9
11–25	1,526	19.8	25,704	3.4	16.8
26–50	897	11.7	31,998	4.2	35.7
51–200	1,058	13.8	104,641	13.7	98.9
201–500	276	3.6	87,729	11.5	317.9
501–1,000	90	1.2	61,647	8.0	685.0
over 1,000	66	0.9	436,945	57.1	6,620.4
Total	7,693	100.1	765,375	100.1	99.5

SOURCE: Gayer, Homan, and Jones, *Sugar Economy*, p. 103, table 43.
[a] Of the total land area on sugar farms, only 299,384 cuerdas were planted in cane: Smith and Requa, *Puerto Rico Sugar Facts*, p. 122, table 11.

Without a central to buy cane and to grind it into raw sugar, the colono's crop was worthless; the relations that developed between colonos and mills worked to the benefit of the large and powerful central owners.

During the last third of the nineteenth century, the number of grinding mills, most of which had been relatively small, had declined—to 446 in 1888 and 345 in 1899[79]—as a result of the weakness of the sugar industry discussed in chapter 1. After the U.S. occupation, the number of mills further declined, to 146 in 1910, but now as the result of greater concentration and monopolization of the grinding process. Of the 146 mills, 41 were classified as centrales, and they produced 97 percent of the sugar output, exporting 96.4 percent. The 91 ox-driven ingenios, on the other hand, sold all of their output locally. By the 1930s, the centrals had the capacity to grind more than twelve times the cane of the small mills which had been in existence in 1888, which meant that they had a voracious need for cane if they were to operate at a profitable scale.

Of the forty-one centrals in the 1930s, eleven were owned by four large U.S. corporations: Central Aguirre (three mills), South Porto Rico (one), Fajardo (two), and United Porto Rico/Eastern Sugar (five).[80] These

[79] V. Clark et al., *Porto Rico and Its Problems*, p. 614, and USDW, 1899 *Census*, p. 155.
[80] Central Aguirre Associates was organized as a Massachusets trust in 1901 and was reorganized in 1918 and 1928 as a holding company for Central Aguirre Sugar Co. In 1920,

four corporations dominated the industry; they owned or leased 23.7 percent of all cane land in 1930 and 46.3 percent of all land organized in corporations. The extent of their landholdings is shown in table 2.7. The amounts owned represented approximately 35 to 58 times the legal limit of 500 acres, and the amounts controlled 75 to 100 times the limit.[81] By 1934, these four U.S. companies controlled a total of 211,761 acres.[82] More than 51 percent of total ground sugar output was produced by these four companies in 1927–28, from cane grown on their own land or on that of colonos who sold their cane to them. This was an increase from 35.2 percent of total output in 1922 and 26.4 percent in 1913.[83]

In 1928, total foreign investment in Puerto Rico (ownership of government debt, loans, land, direct investment, etc.) was somewhat greater than $176 million, most of it from the United States. More than 22 percent of this total, or $40 million, was directly involved in the sugar industry. At that time, the total wealth of Puerto Rico was estimated to be approximately $650 million; thus, more than one-quarter (27.1 percent) of Puerto Rico's total wealth was foreign owned. Furthermore, as the Brookings Institution report pointed out:

These figures gain added significance from the fact that the share belonging to foreigners represents active, productive capital; whereas the

---

it purchased Central Machete. It was allied with Luce and Co., a limited partnership, and Henry de Ford and Co., which made extensive investments in Puerto Rico immediately after the U.S. invasion. A financial institution set up by the de Ford group held deposits of the colonial administration. Central Isabel was also part of this complex, and it also owned the Ponce and Guayama Railroad Co.

South Porto Rico was organized in New Jersey in November 1900 and was linked to Russell and Co., another limited partnership "whose profits are distributed to common shareholders of South Porto Rico Sugar Co."; it operated Central Guánica, the largest mill on the island and in the Caribbean. Fajardo Sugar Co. was incorporated as a New Jersey company in 1905 and later (1919) in Puerto Rico; it controlled the Fajardo Sugar Growers Association and operated Central Canóvanas and the Fajardo mill. Eastern Sugar Associates grew out of a reorganization of United Porto Rico Sugar Co. in 1934; it controlled the Santa Juana, Defensa, Juncos, Cayey, and Pasto Viejo centrales. There had been about 32 centrales in 1898: Gayer, Homan, and Jones, *Sugar Economy*, pp. 62, 63 (n. 10), 104; Diffie and Diffie, *Porto Rico*, pp. 46–50; V. Clark et al., *Porto Rico and Its Problems*, pp. 614–15, 643–45; and Ramos Mattei, "Las inversiones norteamericanas," pp. 54–56, 61 (n. 43), 64–65.

[81] Some corporations attempted to circumvent the legislation by acting as holding companies for partnerships which owed land or by holding land in the name of individuals, but these efforts fooled no one. Other corporations simply ignored the legislation, which was never enforced.

[82] Quintero Rivera, *Conflictos de clase*, Cuadro 7, p. 66.

[83] K. A. Santiago, "La concentración," p. 155, table 13.

TABLE 2.7
Area of Sugar Farms Owned and Controlled by
U.S. Sugar Corporations, 1929
(in cuerdas)

Company	Owned	Controlled[a]
South Porto Rico	17,635	49,635
United Porto Rico	28,843	44,030
Central Aguirre	22,269	39,269
Fajardo	25,741	37,741
Total	94,488	170,675

SOURCE: Diffie and Diffie, *Porto Rico*, p. 52.
[a] Includes land owned, leased, or held under long-term contract.

share belonging to Porto Ricans includes personal property as well as productive capital.[84]

This is not to deny that there were not large Puerto Rican land holders—there were in fact quite a number[85]—but U.S. capitalists were the dominant holders of Puerto Rico's productive forms of wealth.

The sugar corporations were extremely profitable for their absentee owners. In 1920, a boom year for the industry, Central Aguirre paid a dividend equal to 115 percent of equity. From 1923 to 1930, the return on capital of the mills of the four largest U.S. corporations averaged 22.5 percent per year. From 1920 to 1935, Central Aguirre, South Porto Rico, and Fajardo distributed $60,562,000 in dividends to their shareholders while accumulating a surplus available for reinvestment of another $20,500,000. Thus, these three companies invested about one-quarter of their profits and distributed 75 percent to absentee, mostly U.S., shareholders over that period.[86] Since the cost of production of Puerto Rican sugar was higher than that of sugar from Cuba and the Philippines (though lower than that of Louisiana sugar), the tariff advantage that the sugar

[84] V. Clark et al., *Porto Rico and Its Problems*, p. 418. The details of these holdings are given in ibid., pp. 416–18.
[85] Quintero Rivera, *Conflictos de clase*, pp. 65–67.
[86] Bird, *Sugar Industry*, pp. 40, 96–97. According to Gayer, Homan, and Jones, *Sugar Economy*, p. 155, table 60, Aguirre, Fajardo, and South Porto Rico had averaged after-tax returns on investors' equity (which is not the same as capital invested) of 10.2 percent from 1923 to 1935. This compared to returns of 3 percent on equity for Puerto Rican–owned

companies enjoyed in the U.S. market was essential to those large profits.[87]

However, the wage workers and colonos in the sugar industry did not share in the prosperity. The average daily wage of plantation workers in Puerto Rico was 63 cents in 1917; in Hawaii, by comparison, the daily wage was 97 cents, and in Cuba, $1.26. On one plantation studied in 1928, almost 85 percent of the workers (excluding the cane cutters, who were better paid) earned less than $1.00 a day (the corresponding figure for all workers, including cutters, on a sample of plantations studied in 1929, was 57 percent), while in Honduras the daily wage averaged between $1.25 and $1.50. Mill workers, generally with some special skills, earned more: 80.6 percent earned between $0.75 and $1.49 a day in 1928.[88] (The return on capital of the three largest centrales that year was 30.6 percent.) In 1935, the average weekly wage on sugar plantations was $3.34. About 94 percent of this was spent on food, the largest item of expenditure being for imported polished rice. For a family of four, that works out to about 12 cents per person per day for food, at a time when a federal agency had found that, even buying in quantity at wholesale prices, a day's supply of adequately nutritious food could not be bought for less than 20 cents.[89]

---

firms (ibid., p. 154). See V. Clark et al., *Porto Rico and Its Problems*, p. 641, for details of assets, capital, and earnings for Central Aguirre, Fajardo, and South Porto Rico from 1922 to 1927. High returns continued to be earned in spite of adversities like the Great Depression, which in fact was a strong period for the U.S. companies in Puerto Rico, as Cuban sugar production fell rapidly and Puerto Rican sugar filled the gap.

[87] In 1930–32, average costs of production per pound at the mill were: Cuba, 1.33 cents; Philippines, 1.97; Puerto Rico, 2.54; Hawaii, 2.54; Louisiana, 3.77: Gayer, Homan, and Jones, *Sugar Economy*, p. 85. Also see V. Clark et al., *Porto Rico and Its Problems*, p. 631, for the 1913–23 period. Puerto Rico's yields per acre, on the other hand, were relatively high in comparison to other sugar-producing areas, though Hawaii had the highest yields: Perloff, *Puerto Rico's Economic Future*, p. 72; table 15; and Smith and Requa, *Puerto Rico Sugar Facts*, p. 123, table 12.

[88] For other years, see V. Clark et al., *Porto Rico and Its Problems*, p. 635. These wages are for the grinding season; for wages in the dead season, which were lower, see ibid., pp. 637–39.

As a later governor was to remark, the tariffs protected the profits and inefficiences of the large sugar producers without resulting in a better standard of living for workers in Puerto Rico in comparison with those in other sugar-producing areas: Tugwell, *Stricken Land*, pp. 33–34.

[89] Diffie and Diffie, *Porto Rico*, p. 86; V. Clark et al., *Porto Rico and Its Problems*, pp. 637–39; and Bird, *Sugar Industry*, pp. 40, 42–43, 46. In Asia at the same time, about 90 percent of income went to food, 80 percent in Europe, and 30 percent in the U.S.: Diffie and Diffie, *Porto Rico*, pp. 176–77.

Wages were nearly insensitive to changes in profits or prices. From 1913 to 1932 (leaving out the special cases of very high prices in 1920 and 1921), wage elasticity with respect to prices was .09—that is, a 1 percent rise in price increased wages by only .09 percent.[90] This lack of wage sensitivity was probably due to three factors: a surplus of labor in rural areas; a near absence of effective labor organizing; and the insignificance of the local market. These factors need to be examined in more detail.

In contrast to the situation for most of the nineteenth century, the first decades of the twentieth century saw an "oversupply" of agricultural labor. The abundance of job seekers made it easy for purchasers of labor power to push wages downward, which in turn forced other family members to enter the labor market, increasing the labor supply and further depressing the wage level. To the extent that a family still had access to land, the deficiency in wages could be made up by home production, but sugar workers tended to have less access to land than other agricultural workers.

The lack of effective labor organizations, and the power of the sugar companies to defeat their efforts even when they did exist, blocked most collective action by workers. There were strikes and protests, but it was easier for the companies to last out a strike than it was for the workers, who, being too poor even to pay dues to their union, lacked a strike fund. Unions of agricultural workers nevertheless did form in the early decades and they did go on strike, but not often successfully.[91]

Not only the sugar industry but virtually the entire Puerto Rican economy was oriented toward exports. The markets for sugar, coffee, tobacco, fruits, and manufactured products were abroad, predominately (with the exception of coffee) in the United States. Since profits were therefore realized outside of Puerto Rico, it was in the producers' interest to maintain wages as low as possible. From their perspective, wages were nothing more than a cost; they did not at the same time represent purchasing

[90] Stahl, "Economic Development," p. 15, and K. A. Santiago, "La concentración," p. 156, table 14.

[91] The U.S. Department of Labor, drawing on earlier reports by an Industrial Relations Commission, said that there had been seventy-eight strikes, involving 25,000 workers in 36 towns, from July 1, 1917, to May 31, 1918, and it quoted the commission as having written: "The strike of agricultural laborers and other workers, which began in January, 1915, was not only justified but was in the interests of the progress of the island. The long hours, low wages, and exploitation of the laborers could not have been relieved except by their organized action" (USDL, *Labor Conditions*, p. 19). It was statements such as this that continued to give workers faith in the U.S. government's ability to put a stop to the abuses of absentee owners, but it was to be some time before that faith was vindicated: Galvin, *Organized Labor Movement*.

power for the commodities produced, since nearly all of the output was exported.[92]

The large sugar companies were of course interested in presenting themselves in the best possible light, and there were many individuals working for the companies who provided justifications for the actions of their employers. Economists argued, for example, that the value of production from each unit of cane land greatly exceeded the value that could be obtained from alternative uses of the land—for example, if it were devoted to subsistence or locally marketed food crops. With the higher income earned from sugar, even more food could be imported than could be locally produced, with gains for everyone. However, as Raymond Crist has pointed out, this argument made little sense in Puerto Rico:

> Although it may well be true that the cash income from a single acre planted in cane is equal to the income that could be derived from as many as four to twelve acres planted in food crops, nevertheless the advantage is of little practical benefit to the mass of poorly nourished Puerto Ricans, who have little share in the sugar income.[93]

The defense on the ground of opportunity cost, then, was a specious argument to uphold the profits of the sugar companies and excuse the continued poverty and exploitation of sugar workers.

THE COLONOS

The other large category of producers besides wage workers were the colonos, or semi-independent farmers. In the early 1930s, colonos occupied 48.7 percent of the cultivated sugar land and produced 35.5 percent of the cane.[94] The farms owned by colonos had anywhere from just a few to more than a thousand cuerdas; most, however, were relatively small though large colono farms produced the bulk of all colono sugar and profits, and colonos often hired wage workers just as the larger corporations did.[95] What distinguished them from the sugar plantations was their reliance on the centrals for financing and for grinding their raw

[92] Bird, *Sugar Industry*, p. 12. "The laborer, who was the largest contributor to the value created, lived in extreme poverty, and during some months of the year, lived on the verge of starvation. Yet millions were being made around him": Ibid., pp. 9–10.

[93] Crist, "Sugar Cane and Coffee," p. 471.

[94] Gayer, Homan, and Jones, *Sugar Economy*, p. 78, table 29. The American companies cultivated 23.3 percent of the cane land and produced 31.2 percent of the cane in the 1934–35 growing season; Puerto Rican-owned centrals cultivated 28.0 percent of the cane land and produced 33.3 percent of the cane, an indication of the importance of large local centrals and their owners. This is a subject that merits further study.

[95] For the report of a study of farm size, production expenses, and revenues on thirty-one colono farms in 1929, see V. Clark et al., *Porto Rico and Its Problems*, pp. 622–26.

cane. This asymmetrical relationship, in which the centrales acted as monopsonists vis-à-vis the surrounding colonos, was specified in the contracts between the two parties. The details of these contracts were important to both colono and central. Cut cane rapidly loses its sucrose content, so colonos needed firm contracts at a nearby central so as to be able to sell their output when it was ready to be cut. They also needed loans for consumption and supplies to tide them over until the crop was harvested, and the large growers were the most important source of such funds, just as they had been during the nineteenth century. The central, on the other hand, needed the colonos so that the mills, with their huge capacity, could be used efficiently and because the purchase of colono cane permitted greater profits. In 1934–35, colonos supplied 29.6 percent of the total cane ground by the eleven U.S. centrals; the thirty locally owned mills were even more dependent on colono cane, which accounted for 40.2 percent of the total that they ground.

Colono contracts ran from one to several years in duration. Besides setting terms for crop loans, interest rates (usually from 9 to 12 percent), delivery dates for cane, and fertilizer and irrigation use, they sometimes also gave certain rights to the central owners, such as the right to inspect colono cane in the field to check its condition and readiness. But the most important part of the contracts concerned the method of payment for cane delivered. They specified how the returns from selling the processed sugar would be divided between the colono and the mill, with the dollar return of each party dependent upon the price of sugar in the New York market at the time the sale was made and the quantity of sugar obtained in the grinding stage. In the early contracts, a common method of expressing returns was in terms of the weight of the ground sugar. For example, if 100 pounds of cane was expected to yield 12 pounds of raw sugar in the grinding process, the contract might specify that the colono would receive the value of 7 pounds and the mill the value of 5 for each 100 pounds of cane delivered. In practice, this method worked to the disadvantage of the colono. If more than 12 pounds of raw sugar was obtained, the colono still received the value of only 7 pounds; whereas if less than 12 pounds resulted, the colono's share would fall, usually so that the mill would still receive the value of its 5 pounds.

By the 1930s, sophisticated techniques were being used by the mills to measure the sucrose content of cane and to base the colono's share on that measurement. This procedure was designed to encourage colonos to produce cane with a high sucrose content, but it turned out that it typically increased profits for the centrales. Most methods, like the so-called Guánica table, penalized low sucrose content heavily, yet set an upper limit on the amount that could be marginally gained by producing cane with a high sucrose content. This method also was open to considerable abuse, since the sucrose analyses were done by the centrals themselves. In 1937, a law was passed requiring that colonos receive a fixed 65 percent of yield, measured (by the centrals) in terms of sucrose content.[96]

There is no doubt that the centrals benefited most from the colono contracts. In 1931–32, the price paid for colono cane averaged $3.75 per ton, while the centrales' cost of production averaged $4.60 per ton.[97] It is true that a study by the U.S. Tariff Commission reported that colono costs at that time were lower than central costs.[98] However, the measured costs in the study probably understated the contribution of the colono's labor by not counting it at its potential market value. Furthermore, costs were lower for colonos in part because they paid their wage workers even less than did the corporate farms. Studies of independent farmers and peasants in other countries have found that they often "exploit" themselves and their workers far more than wage workers are exploited in large capitalist enterprises. This happens because the goal of small farmers is not simply profit but the maintenance of their quasi-independent status. They may even earn negative returns on their land, tools, and other "investments," a phenomenon which, if it persists, is difficult to understand within the conventional economic framework of "rational behavior." Such producers are not irrational, however; their goal is not maximum profit.

Although colonos bore 72 percent of the total cost of sugar production in the early 1930s, they received a return of only 65 percent of the value of the yield in the centrales with the lowest yields and only 54 percent in those with the highest yields.[99] Colonos were paid only for the direct sugar yield of the cane; they did not share in the substantial returns from the by-products of grinding and processing. For example, from every ton of cane ground in 1928, centrales were able to make five gallons of molasses, in addition to the raw sugar obtained. This resulted in additional revenues of $830,891 for the mills but nothing for the colonos. Bagasse, another by-product, was used for fuel in the mills; thus, colono cane helped the mills to reduce their fuel costs, but the colonos received nothing in return.[100]

---

[96] Ibid., pp. 613–26, and Gayer, Homan, and Jones, *Sugar Economy*, p. 77, table 28.

[97] Gayer, Homan, and Jones, *Sugar Economy*, pp. 87, 89. In 1930–31, the colonos' average costs of production were $4.79; the reduction had come primarily from lower labor costs.

[98] Ibid., p. 87.

[99] Bird, *Sugar Industry*, p. 11.

[100] Diffie and Diffie, *Porto Rico*, pp. 69–70.

TABLE 2.8
Area of Land in Tobacco and Sugar,
Selected Years, 1899 to 1935
(in cuerdas)

	Tobacco	Sugar
1899	5,963	72,146
1909	22,142	145,433
1919	39,068	227,815
1929	52,947	237,758
1935	45,720	254,154

SOURCES: Gayer, Homan, and Jones,
Sugar Economy, p. 21, table 2; CENEP,
Labor Migration, p. 98, table 4.4.

OTHER PRODUCTS

Like sugar, Puerto Rican tobacco enjoyed tariff protection in the U.S. market, as there were domestic producers to be protected from foreign competition. Consequently, the tobacco industry prospered for a time after the U.S. takeover. In fact, by 1918, tobacco was the second most important export product, replacing coffee. Table 2.8 shows the expansion of land devoted to tobacco in comparison with that devoted to sugar. The number of cuerdas devoted to tobacco increased nearly fourfold from 1899 to 1909 and more than doubled again by 1929. After that, however, the amount of tobacco land declined. By 1939, only 28,584 cuerdas were being cultivated, barely half of the 1929 level.

The value of leaf-tobacco exports also rose quite rapidly (table 2.9). It tripled from 1901 to 1910, even though the quantity exported actually decreased slightly, and it had increased another 847 percent by 1930, while the quantity exported was increasing about seven times. However, this boom did not last. Puerto Rican leaf tobacco was used chiefly to make cigars, in factories either on the mainland or in Puerto Rico (cigar factories on the island used Cuban and other tobaccos as well). But cigarettes were becoming more popular than cigars, and in the 1930s, the cigar industry began to decline rapidly. In 1910, 244.4 million cigars were produced, 62 percent of which were exported. In 1931, 220 million were produced, and 78 percent exported. By 1939, production had fallen to 66 million, just 30 percent of the 1931 level, and only 3 percent of it was exported.[101] Tobacco growing, like coffee production, had been the

[101] Perloff, *Puerto Rico's Economic Future*, p. 91, n. 5, and Colton, *Report of the Governor*, p. 10. In 1910, some 407 million cigarettes were produced in Puerto Rico, but they were primarily for the domestic market (394 million, or 96.8 percent). The type and quality of Puerto Rican cigarettes were not those desired in the U.S. market.

TABLE 2.9
Value of Leading Exports in Selected Years, 1901 to 1930

	Tobacco	Cigars[a]	Coffee	Sugar	Fruit	Cotton Goods[a]
1901	375,000[a]	306,000	1,678,765	4,715,611	109,801	8,000
1905	438,000[a]	2,152,000	2,141,019	11,925,804	255,900	36,000
1910	1,258,317	4,480,000	5,669,602	23,545,922	1,635,817	37,000
1915	3,204,423	6,016,000	7,082,791	27,278,754	3,441,157	—
1920	13,416,388	11,614,000	9,034,028	98,923,750	3,900,930	807,000
1925	9,870,076	7,105,000	6,575,635	53,261,895	4,923,029	6,207,000
1930	11,916,505	3,848,000[b]	151,550	53,670,038	7,890,404	15,337,000[b]

SOURCES: V. Clark et al., *Porto Rico and Its Problems*, pp. 606–7; PRDAC, *Statistics, 1934–35*, p. 11. See tables 2.2 and 2.4 for exports of coffee and sugar for other years.
[a] To nearest $1,000.
[b] 1929.

domain of small growers, who constituted perhaps as much as 80 percent of all growers and who sold their crop to middlemen who often cured the crop as well as marketing it. Cigar production had begun as an artisan enterprise before the U.S. occupation, but by the 1930s, about 75 percent of the industry had been mechanized, and cigar makers formed a substantial part of the early proletariat in the urban areas.[102]

The tobacco economy employed a large number of women workers. In the agricultural phase, more women were employed on tobacco farms than in the production of any other crop; in the industrial phase of cigar production, women workers were the largest and most rapidly growing segment of the wage-labor force in the early decades of the century.[103]

Even though tobacco farming and growing was small scale and predominately done by Puerto Rican owners, about 80 to 85 percent of the manufacturing end of the business was controlled by U.S. capital after 1898. The Porto Rican-American Tobacco Company of New Jersey (which began production in 1899 by buying four local firms) and the New York

[102] Diffie and Diffie, *Porto Rico*, pp. 96–97, and Quintero Rivera, "Socialist and Cigarmaker," pp. 31–33. Already by 1910, three-quarters of tobacco workers in the manufacturing phase were employed in factories of more than 100 workers; the only firms with more than 1,000 employees were in cigar and cigarette production and the preparation of leaf for export. Nearly 80 percent of all tobacco production was carried out in firms organized as corporations, indicating how rapidly the artisan nature of the industry was destroyed. (By comparison, 64 percent of output in the sugar industry and 10.4 percent in other industry was produced by corporations.) By 1920, nearly 80 percent of tobacco production took place in factories with more than 500 workers: Quintero Rivera, "Socialist and Cigarmaker," pp. 31–33.
[103] Azize, *Luchas de la mujer*, pp. 6–19.

Tampa Cigar Company (incorporated in Delaware in 1921) were the most important companies.[104] In 1928–29, Porto Rican-American Tobacco alone bought half the island's tobacco crop and operated ten manufacturing plants, two of which were located in the United States. It also served as a buyer in Puerto Rico for other cigar manufacturers located in the United States.[105]

Table 2.9 also shows that exports of both fruits and cotton goods increased after the U.S. occupation. The cultivation of fruits, especially of citrus fruits, which are ideally suited to the local climate, began to develop in 1905. About a third of the industry's exports were controlled by absentee owners, and most of those who established fruit farms were mainlanders.[106]

The manufactured cotton goods that were exported included women's dresses, skirts, blouses, underwear, and handkerchiefs, and other items in smaller quantities. Much of this production was carried out in the home, with contractors and subcontractors overseeing the work, and it typically was completed for export to a mainland firm. There were also some small factories in operation. The type of work done ranged from complete production, to assembly, to the addition of embroidery on already-produced items.[107] During World War I, embroidery became an important part of this industry, and indeed Puerto Rican embroidery became known for its quality. Production was performed mostly by women and children, either in a factory or at home, and payment was by the piece. Women making embroidery and lace in factories generally earned only about 20 to 60 cents a day, and since most women did not work full time, weekly wages in 1918, for example, were only about $2 to $3.[108] Wages for home production are not available, but it is likely that they were lower, for two reasons: first, to the extent that such work was contracted and subcontracted out, a portion of what would otherwise have been wages was skimmed off by labor contractors; and second, the amount of production done in the home was probably less than in factories, where at least a minimum of work discipline could be enforced.

It is interesting to note that educational policy at the time was designed to meet the needs of this U.S.-dominated industry. In elementary school, girls spent half their time at more or less traditional subjects, but the other

[104] Diffie and Diffie, *Porto Rico*, p. 95.

[105] V. Clark et al., *Porto Rico and Its Problems*, p. 433.

[106] Diffie and Diffie, *Porto Rico*, pp. 99–100, and V. Clark et al., *Porto Rico and Its Problems*, pp. 485–88.

[107] V. Clark et al., *Porto Rico and Its Problems*, pp. 467–74.

[108] USDL, *Labor Conditions*, p. 40. This report admits that most women worked because they had to do so to supplement low family income, but adds that it is a "gross injustice" that they are paid so little (p. 41). A full study of this industry is badly needed.

half they devoted to learning needlework skills.[109] The process of education was thus a part of the wider process in which the U.S., as the colonial state, provided the training, skills, and knowledge necessary for capital accumulation and profitable production to U.S. capitalists and to a few Puerto Rican entrepreneurs who associated themselves with this process.

EXTERNAL TRADE

Not only did U.S. capital rapidly enter the economy and transform production methods and relations, but the provisions of the Foraker and Jones acts also guaranteed that Puerto Rico would trade almost exclusively with the United States. First, because the United States and Puerto Rico shared common tariffs, U.S.-made products had a price advantage in Puerto Rico and Puerto Rican goods were cheaper for the U.S. market than for markets in other countries. Second, the requirement that shipping between the United States and the island be done on ships of U.S. registry made trade with other countries more difficult, since foreign ships could not stop in Puerto Rico and then continue on to the United States to deliver goods, or vice versa. The export-oriented pattern of U.S. investment on the island was, of course, intimately related to these provisions and intensified the trade dependence of Puerto Rico on the United States.

As can be seen in table 2.10, during the last decades of Spanish control, the proportion of total trade with the United States fell, as sugar exports declined and coffee, increasingly the key export, was sold in other markets. In 1897, the year prior to the occupation, only 19 percent of total trade (exports plus imports) was conducted with the United States. But in 1899, the year after the island became a U.S. colony, this share already had nearly doubled, to 37 percent, and by 1900, it had jumped to 68 percent.[110] In 1930, trade with the United States accounted for 94.3 percent of Puerto Rico's trade with the world. This is precisely the classical pattern of colonial trade dominance which Spain had tried to impose by directly prohibiting trade with other countries. The United States obtained the same result from the provisions of the Organic Acts, the predominance of U.S. capital, and U.S. political control. By 1910, the small island of Puerto Rico was the twelfth largest consumer of U.S. goods in the world. Puerto Rico's trade relations thus moved back more than a century in time and in fact worsened, since never before had the island

[109] Rivera Quintero, "Educational Policy," pp. 350–51.
[110] CENEP, *Taller*, p. 108, table 1.

TABLE 2.10
Exports to and Imports from the United States,
Selected Years, 1848 to 1930

	Exports			Imports		
Year	Total ($)	To U.S. ($)	% of Total to U.S.	Total ($)	From U.S. ($)	% of Total from U.S.
1848	—	—	44.1	—	—	19.5
1855	—	—	40.7	—	—	16.4
1860	—	—	51.8	—	—	25.4
1865	—	—	40.6	—	—	25.7
1870	—	—	56.8	—	—	33.8
1879	—	—	27.2	—	—	20.4
1885	—	—	37.8	—	—	24.2
1890	—	—	23.3	—	—	21.1
1896	—	—	13.9	—	—	21.7
1897	—	—	15.2	—	—	21.0
1901	8,583,967	5,581,288	65.0	8,908,136	6,955,408	78.1
1905	18,709,565	15,633,145	83.6	16,536,259	13,974,070	84.5
1910	37,960,220	32,095,645	84.6	30,634,855	27,097,654	88.5
1915	49,356,907	42,311,920	85.7	33,884,296	30,929,831	91.3
1920	150,811,449	133,207,508	88.3	96,388,534	90,724,259	94.1
1925	94,818,944	84,411,792	89.0	90,504,601	79,349,618	87.7
1930	99,566,205	95,097,640	95.5	83,922,829	73,078,799	87.1

SOURCES: CENEP, *Taller*, pp. 52, 108; PRDAC, *Statistics, 1934–35*, p. 7.

been dependent on one market for its exports. As the Brookings Institution report remarked:

This growth of foreign trade in proportion to population is the result of the transforming of a more largely self-sufficing island economy into one which is integrally related with the commerce of the rest of the world, particularly . . . of the United States.[111]

Not only did the share of trade with the United States increase after 1898, but the total volume of trade also increased dramatically. From 1836 to 1877, total trade averaged $22 million per year. In the decade from 1901 to 1910, the average nearly doubled, to $42 million. In the next decade, it almost tripled, rising to $119 million, and it reached $183 million in the decade of the twenties.[112] Puerto Rico's external trade in

[111] V. Clark et al., *Porto Rico and Its Problems*, p. 403.
[112] CENEP, *Taller*, p. 110, table 2, and Curet Cuevas, *El desarrollo económico*, p. 34, table 13.

TABLE 2.11
Composition of Imports, Selected Years, 1901 to 1935
(in percentage of total import value)

Category	1901	1914	1920	1928	1929	1935
Foodstuffs	49.9	40.7	39.5	32.1	35.3	36.6
Apparel	23.8	18.2	24.9	19.8	21.7	21.0
Household goods	7.9	9.7	8.7	8.2	9.4	11.3
Building materials	11.1	13.4	9.8	9.5	13.2	8.1
Motor and other vehicles	0.8	1.5	2.5	9.5	8.8	7.2
Manufacturing machinery	5.8	6.3	7.1	6.0	4.9	7.9
Agricultural machinery	—	2.1	3.7	8.4	4.4	3.6
Others	0.7	8.1	3.8	6.5	2.3	4.3
	100.0	100.0	100.0	100.0	100.0	100.0

SOURCE: V. Clark et al., *Porto Rico and Its Problems*, p. 407.

the thirty years preceding U.S. control had been virtually stagnant; in the thirty years after, the value of trade exploded, increasing more than eight times by 1930.

Gross domestic product (GDP) was certainly growing during this period (though there are no good estimates of its magnitude), but not all of the potential benefits of growth accrued to residents of the island. The large outflow of profits to absentee, primarily U.S., shareholders represented sums not available for local income, investment, or further production.[113] Output expanded rapidly as production methods were improved and the total amount of capital was increased, and capitalist development, though foreign controlled, began to spread, though it still was not a generalized phenomenon. Only certain sectors of the economy were changed significantly, most dramatically in those areas of production where U.S. capital was most evident—sugar, cigar production, and some needlework.

It is instructive to consider not only the total volume of imports but also the specific items being imported. As table 2.11 shows, nearly one-half of all imported goods by value were foodstuffs in 1901. This percentage declined over time, though in 1935 foodstuffs still accounted for

[113] "While it cannot be denied that the inflow of capital has increased the efficiency of production and promoted general economic development, it does not follow that the benefits of this have accrued to the working people of the Island": V. Clark et al., *Porto Rico and Its Problems*, p. 420. In other words, the economy's output grew, but it did not raise living standards for the majority because of the concentration of ownership of productive resources by absentee U.S. owners, which drained income from the island economy to the U.S. This phenomenon will be analyzed in greater detail in chap. 5.

TABLE 2.12
Area of Cultivated Land in Food and Other Crops,
Ten-Year Intervals from 1899 to 1929
(in cuerdas)

Crop	1899	1909	1919	1929
Beans	—	20,652	34,907	40,902
Corn	18,093	56,640	58,785	70,217
Sweet potatoes and yams	51,465	—	31,457	47,616
Other[a]	133,291	110,931	74,971	115,490

SOURCE: Gayer, Homan, and Jones, *Sugar Economy*, p. 21, table 2.
[a] Both food and nonfood, but excluding sugar, tobacco, and coffee.

more than one-third of imported goods by value. The decline, however, was the result of an increase in the value of imports overall. The *absolute* value of imported food increased: in 1901, it stood at $4.5 million, and in 1935, at more than $25 million.[114] There are two ways to intepret this. First, it could be an indication of a rising living standard, as people are buying greater quantitites of food. This was the view most compatable with the sugar companies' argument noted above, about the higher value of sugar production relative to other crops.[115] Second, increased food imports may simply have compensated for the decline in domestic food production due to land concentration and displacement. Though imports per capita did increase during the period, that is not sufficient evidence for the conclusion that the standard of living was higher. Rising food imports, whether measured in aggregate or per capita terms, are only half of the picture. The total food *supply* is the critical measure.

In 1899, at least 42 percent of cultivated land was used to grow crops for local consumption; in 1929, the figure was only 28 percent. While it is true that the *absolute* amount of land devoted to locally consumed crops increased (table 2.12), the increase was only about 28 percent; population grew during the same period by more than 60 percent. Thus, the amount of land per capita devoted to food crops declined.[116] This could have been offset, of course, by improvements in technology resulting in greater efficiency of production. This, however, did not happen;

[114] V. Clark et al., *Porto Rico and Its Problems*, p. 407.
[115] This is the interpretation given in Smith, *Standards* (a report made in 1937 for the Association of Sugar Producers). See also Cordero, *El progreso económico*, which reports only the positive aspects of U.S. domination (e.g., growth).
[116] Gayer, Homan, and Jones, *Sugar Economy*, pp. 18, 21, 32. The figures presented by Bergad, "Agrarian History" pp. 63, 76, show an increase of approximately 30 percent in land devoted to food crops over the same period.

improvements in technology were concentrated in the dynamic, capitalist, and chiefly foreign-owned export sectors. As a result, the share of the total food supply that was imported increased to 60 percent in 1929.[117] It seems safe to conclude that the absolute increase in food imports was not an indication of an improved standard of living. Instead, it was the result of the lopsided organization of the economy, which favored cash crops for export and reduced the economic possibilities for growing food locally as land values increased, squeezing out low-profit crops and low-income landholders, whose land was turned over to cane production.[118]

The decline in the cultivation of food crops was not due to any physical inability to expand production. During the later months of World War I, when food shipments were interrupted and undependable, there was a successful government-sponsored effort to increase food production. Land planted to food crops increased from 137,000 acres to 335,000, with no reduction in the land area devoted to export crops. After the war, however, the crops grown on this land could not meet the compelling test of profitability that was coming to dominate economic decision making, and the land reverted to its earlier uses. The test of profitability was not balanced by considerations of distributional equity. Sugar cane, more highly valued by the market, displaced food crops, which returned lower profits but distributed them to a larger number of Puerto Ricans.[119]

One of the most important items in the budgets of low-income Puerto Ricans was rice. Per capita imports of rice rose from 43.8 pounds in 1901 to 134.6 in 1929. Given the relatively poor nutritional quality of polished and hulled rice, the growth of such imports was not necessarily an advance in the standard of living. Fish, on the other hand, which the poor consumed from time to time, showed no regular growth pattern; but between 1895 and 1927–28, per capita consumption fell 10.3 percent. This suggests something like the Irish potato famine: poor Puerto Ricans increased their consumption of rice because they could not afford anything else, and that is why total imports rose. Meat consumption per capita did rise, from 5.7 pounds in 1901 to 20.7 in 1929, but because the bulk of the population rarely was able to afford meat, this is more a measure of

[117] Gayer, Homan, and Jones, *Sugar Economy*, p. 32. Substitution was rapid and costly. In 1900, rice imports from the U.S. amounted to $153,882; by 1902, they had reached $2,255,429: Hunt, *Third Annual Report*, p. 23.

[118] Between 1830 and 1909, total cultivated land increased 4.5 times, but land devoted to export crops increased more than 10 times, while land cultivated for food crops increased only 2.3 times. The more rapid expansion of land for export than for food crops during this period indicates that economic reorganization had been taking place even before U.S. control was established and that the U.S. accelerated, but did not initiate, the export orientation of the economy: Perloff, *Puerto Rico's Economic Future*, p. 83, table 2.1.

[119] V. Clark et al., *Porto Rico and Its Problems*, pp. 489–94.

the skewed income distribution and of the better consumption of the upper class and professionals in the cities than of improvements in general conditions.[120]

As table 2.11 shows, there were increases in the import shares (and hence of course in the absolute values) of motor and other vehicles and agricultural machinery, until the Great Depression. These two categories of imports were obviously related to the growth of agricultural production for export, and the increases indicate the extent of capitalization that was taking place, especially in and around the sugar industry. Large sugar corporations often owned their own railways to transport cane to the grinding mills. Of 1,485 kilometers of rails in the 1930s, 924 kilometers (62 percent) were owned or controlled by the sugar companies.[121] These capital imports, then, could hardly be considered "Puerto Rican"; control over them and the income deriving from them lay to a great extent with U.S. owners.

CHANGES IN THE SOCIAL FORMATION

It was lust for gold which spurred the early Spanish colonialization, and it was "white gold"—sugar—which made U.S. colonization so profitable and determined so much in the first decades of U.S. control. Puerto Rico began to take on many of the properties that characterized sugar monocultures in the West Indies and elsewhere, not because of the functioning of "comparative advantage," much less because of any inevitability, but as the result of U.S. policies and the actions of U.S. sugar producers and investors.[122]

The sugar-grinding mills were, of course, factories in the ordinary sense of the term: large and complex facilities using modern machinery. The work was done by hired laborers, some of them full-time, year-round workers, but most of them working only irregularly and often not at all in the dead season, which extended from June or July to December. The work was demanding and exhausting. Until 1935, there was no effective law limiting the hours of work, though an eight-hour day had been on the books since the beginning of U.S. control. In the 1932–33 season, the average work week in the mills was an astonishing 79.8 hours. Dur-

---

[120] Ibid., pp. 34, 608–9.

[121] Bird, *Sugar Industry*, p. 23.

[122] Eduardo Galeano has written of the commanding role of "King Sugar" in many tropical and semitropical lands: *Open Veins*, chap. 2. In *The Poverty of Philosophy* (1847), Marx wrote: "You believe, gentlemen, that the production of coffee and sugar is the natural destiny of the West Indies. Two centuries ago, nature, which does not trouble herself about commerce, had planted neither sugar cane nor coffee trees there." Quoted in ibid., p. 77.

TABLE 2.13
Changes in Size of Population between 1899 and 1910

Region	% Change	Deviation from Island Average
Puerto Rico, total	17.3	
Guánica (largest sugar municipality)	121.4	+104.1%
17 municipalities with largest concentrations of sugar production	45.4	+ 28.1
Municipalities with concentration of coffee production	−4.2	− 21.5

SOURCES: CENEP, *Taller*, p. 106; Quintero Rivera, *Conflictos de clase*, p. 53.

ing the grinding season, the centrals ran two twelve-hour shifts, seven days a week. For field workers, the average work week was 50.4 hours.[123]

Many of these wage workers, as was pointed out earlier, were former independent or semi-independent producers. In the first decade of the U.S. occupation, Puerto Rico's population increased by slightly more than 17 percent, but population growth in the leading sugar-producing regions was much greater than that, as table 2.13 shows. (Guánica was the largest sugar municipality on the island.) This suggests that there was a large migration of population to the sugar regions. Landless laborers were moving to the sugar lands, the more so as it became increasingly difficult to survive in the coffee and tobacco economies of the highlands. Sugar-cane production, the sector of most active U.S. interest and investment, both created these landless people and drew them to the plantations, where they became members of a growing rural proletariat.

The number of males who migrated to the sugar regions was typically larger, often by as much as 50 percent, than the number of females.[124] This strengthens the conclusion that it was a forced and socially disruptive migration. The necessary labor for production, which the Spanish colonial administration had attempted to obtain via the libreta system and the destruction of the agregado, was created by the United States via the concentration of land, the expansion of the sugar economy at the expense of other sectors, and the increasing monetization of the entire fabric of society.[125]

The shift from a predominately precapitalist social formation to one dominated by capitalism was swift. By 1930, the Brookings Institution

[123] Gayer, Homan, and Jones, *Sugar Economy*, p. 177.
[124] Quintero Rivera, *Conflictos de clase*, p. 55.
[125] Wessman, "Is There a Plantation Mode of Reproduction?," p. 37.

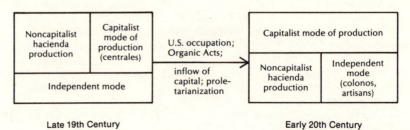

Late 19th Century   Early 20th Century

Figure 2.1 Development of the Social Formation from the Late 19th to the Early
20th Century

report observed that nearly 80 percent of those in rural areas lived as
". . . a community of agricultural laborers. . . . They own neither the
land that they till nor the crops that they raise. . . . It is a country where
the masses depend . . . upon the goodwill of the landowner . . ."[126]
The development of the social formation during this early period is shown
in figure 2.1.

In the first decades of U.S. control, foreign-owned and foreign-con-
trolled capital became dominant in the Puerto Rican economy. It has
already been noted that four U.S. corporations controlled about half of
all sugar production and that U.S. tobacco companies controlled some 85
percent of the cigar-manufacturing industry. But in addition, by the 1920s,
about 50 percent of public utilities (telephones, electric power, etc.) were
foreign owned; railroads were 60 percent foreign owned; shipping, nearly
100 percent. Four banks that were 95 percent foreign owned—American
Colonial Bank, National City Bank of New York (which bought American Colonial in 1930), Bank of Nova Scotia, and Royal Bank of Canada—in 1929 held 50.2 percent of the assets of the eighteen banks then
in existence ($44,333,167 of a total of $88,185,102), not to mention the
indebtedness of Puerto Rican owners of land and factories. Even in the
locally owned banks, foreign participation exceeded 26 percent.[127] Furthermore, the degree of interlock between the financial institutions and
the productive sector was quite extensive.[128]

This did not mean there were no local capitalists at all. In the sugar
industry, there were large owners whose power approached that of the
smaller U.S. corporations, and collectively the centrals owned by Puerto
Ricans processed about half the sugar output. But in general, the fortunes, for Puerto Ricans who aspired to them, were to be made as ser-

[126] V. Clark et al., *Porto Rico and Its Problems*, p. 13.
[127] Diffie and Diffie, *Porto Rico*, pp. 116, 133–35, and V. Clark et al., *Porto Rico and
Its Problems*, pp. 375–77.
[128] K. A. Santiago, "La concentración," pp. 146–47.

vants to U.S. capital: as lawyers, engineers, merchants, or bankers, members of what Quintero Rivera has disparagingly called the "antinational bourgeoisie."[129] The contradiction of the Spanish colonial period, in which creole hacendados and emerging capitalists had economic but not political power, was resolved in a way that excluded them from both. After the U.S. occupation, both the polity and the economy were dominated by and for the interests of U.S. big businesses, especially the sugar and tobacco trusts. The transfer of power from Spain to the United States provided the necessary but until then missing framework and support institutions for the rapid advance of capitalist organization and the capitalist mode of production. Capitalism developed and became the most important form of economic organization, but the initiative resided with U.S. capital. It is difficult to disagree with the Diffies' conclusion that "the real American Rule is the economic penetration which has taken place."[130]

LIVING CONDITIONS

In its 1930 report, the Brookings Institution team asserted, on the basis of its study of the Puerto Rican economy, that "the condition of the masses of the Island people remains deplorable."[131] Rural family income from all sources averaged at most $250 to $275 a year. Urban workers tended to earn somewhat more than rural laborers; perhaps half of the skilled workers earned from $1 to $2 a day in the 1920s, though about half of them were employed only twenty or fewer days a month. Of course, in urban areas, where 27.7 percent of the population lived in 1930, the cost of living was higher and there was little possibility to grow one's own food. In both rural and urban areas, women workers, whose labor was becoming more integrated with the market, earned less then men at whatever they did. In the industries examined by the Brookings Institution team, there were more women workers than men overall; in the tobacco trades, almost 80 percent of workers were women, and in garment production, 85 percent.[132]

Meanwhile, the cost of foodstuffs and other staples in Puerto Rico was

---

[129] Quintero Rivera, *Conflictos de clase*, p. 62. Quintero's analysis of these class relationships is most insightful.

[130] Diffie and Diffie, *Porto Rico*, p. 44.

[131] V. Clark et al., *Porto Rico and Its Problems*, p. xix.

[132] Ibid., pp. xix, 45–49. Women were working for the same reasons as men: the demands of economic survival and changing economic conditions forced them from the home, though without freeing them from "their" home responsibilities: Azize, *Luchas de la mujer*, p. 50 and passim.

inflated by the requirements imposed on the island in the Organic Acts, especially the provision that imports be carried exclusively by U.S. shipping lines, which were relatively expensive.[133] Thus, on seventeen articles which comprised 65 percent of the food items normally consumed by the poor, prices were 8 to 14 percent higher in Puerto Rico than in New York City, even though wages in Puerto Rico were on the average less than $1 a day, while they were about $4 to $10 in New York.[134]

Housing conditions were wretched. The average dwelling accommodated nearly eight persons. More than half the houses had only one or two rooms—and the two-room houses typically were one room with a divider that did not reach to the ceiling. The houses were crudely built and generally lacked furniture. Hammocks served as bedding or people slept on the floor, and cooking facilities were located outside, as were toilet and bathing facilities in most cases. The wooden structures deteriorated rapidly from the effects of rain and sun. Slums had already begun to appear in the cities, but there was also better housing there for professionals, merchants, bankers, and others connected to U.S. and Puerto Rican capital.[135]

Health care, on the other hand, showed some significant improvements under U.S. control, in part as the result of such measures as smallpox vaccinations and mosquito control. In other respects, much remained to be done. Tuberculosis, for example, was still a major killer, and in 1910 the governor's report could still note that all of the island's drinking water was contaminated.[136] The overall mortality rate declined immediately after the U.S. gained control, but it did not decline further after the first three

[133] See the detailed table in Diffie and Diffie, *Porto Rico*, pp. 124–25. Especially revealing are the comparisons with the Philippines, which, though a U.S. colony, was not subject to the same shipping restrictions. For example, to ship 100 pounds of sugar from Puerto Rico to New York cost 15 cents, or 10.7 cents per 1,000 miles; it cost 27 cents from the Philippines, a distance of about 10,000 miles, or 2.7 cents per 1,000 miles. For canned fruit, shipping costs from Puerto Rico to New York were 30 cents per 100 pounds, or 21.4 cents per 1,000 miles; from the Philippines, the corresponding costs were 45 cents and 4.5 cents.

[134] Ibid., pp. 155, 213. Smith, *Standards*, argues that Puerto Rico should not be compared to the U.S. in terms of consumption goods, because tropical and semitropical climates make lower demands for clothing, shelter, and heating. While this is true to some extent, Smith carries it so far as to make it seem as if such things are virtually unnecessary. In the comparisons that Smith makes with Latin America—e.g., in literacy rates and productivity—Puerto Rico fares quite well.

[135] V. Clark et al., *Porto Rico and Its Problems*, pp. 14–21, 40–43.

[136] Colton, *Report of the Governor*, p. 213. The Brookings Institution team wrote: "The impoverished state of the masses is in no small measure responsible for the prevalence of disease, and in turn disease and ill health react directly upon economic conditions": V. Clark et al., *Porto Rico and Its Problems*, p. 55.

or four years, and the rate continued to average about double the rate in the U.S.[137]

One of the more prevalent diseases was uncinariasis, or hookworm. Given the lack of sanitary facilities for human waste disposal and the poverty that prevented large numbers of people from owning shoes, hookworms abounded and entered cracks in the feet, causing a general weakening of the body. In severe cases, anemia ensued. Before U.S. control, perhaps 90 percent of the rural population had been infected with hookworms. While the incidence of deaths directly attributable to uncinariasis declined from 7,369 in 1899 to 1,339 in 1909 and to 483 in 1928, a study in 1925 found the incidence of the disease itself had not fallen dramatically.[138] Attempts were made to impress upon people the importance of constructing and using sanitary facilities, with some success. But shoes would have been effective as well. However, in 1930 only one person in four had ever worn shoes; a pair of shoes cost twice their cost plus transportation charges.

Under Spanish domination, there had been little interest in education. The situation improved with U.S. control, but the impact was uneven. Though in the mid-1920s, 97 percent of urban children between five and fourteen years of age were registered in school, only about 40 percent of rural children were in school. In the rural areas, most children attended school only half day, and only about 16 percent attended beyond the third grade. A major cause of failure to attend was lack of clothing. The 1920 census reported that 61 percent of all persons over ten years of age were illiterate.[139]

From the U.S. viewpoint, important reasons for expanding education in Puerto Rico were to teach and to inculcate "American values." The swings in policy as to how often English would be taught, in what grades and what subjects, and to what extent it would be a separate subject or the language of instruction occupied a large part of the time of the commissioners of education. The forced teaching of subject matter in English to Spanish speakers had devastating effects on the education process and is believed to have lowered the overall quality of education.[140] Of course,

---

[137] V. Clark et al., *Porto Rico and Its Problems*, pp. xxiv, 68.

[138] Ibid., pp. 65–66, and Colton, *Report of the Governor*, pp. 38–39, 213. Observers often noted that Puerto Rican workers seemed tired, "lazy," and lacking in initiative. These observations were rooted in real material conditions: the intestinal hookworm, by eating its host's food, robbed him or her of strength. The Brookings Institution report suggested it "often reduces their earning capacity by as much as 50 or 75 percent."

[139] Ibid., pp. 77–78. Many landowners opposed increased education out of the fear that no one would then wish to do unskilled, low-paid agricultural work.

[140] Negrón de Montilla, *Americanization*.

it was not neglected that wider availability of education would be supportive of business interests:

. . . technical and industrial education here will give us a corps of young Puerto Ricans, trained in both the English and Spanish language and in our industrial and commercial methods who will be valuable pioneers in extending our trade in South America. . . . they ought to accomplish much in extending our commerce and in creating markets for our manufacturers.[141]

By 1933, the rate of illiteracy had been reduced to 41.3 percent, but it remained much higher in rural than in urban areas.[142]

UNEMPLOYMENT

Since the beginning of U.S. colonization, Puerto Rico has had a growing unemployment problem. To an extent, the nature of the sugar and other agricultural industries was responsible, since they provided permanent employment to relatively few, while requiring large numbers during the harvesting periods who were unemployed for the rest of the year, even though they wanted to work. This seems to contravert the conventional economic theory of the equilibrium wage, which holds that, in the absence of artificial barriers, wages will adjust until there is no involuntary unemployment—that is, until there is no one who wishes to work at the prevailing wage but cannot find work.

Although there are no reliable unemployment data for the period, table 2.14 provides some useful information. Even taking into consideration that not all of those ten years of age and older and not in school are actually in the labor force, the proportions with "no economic activity" are quite high. The decline in the percentages of "no economic activity" for females shows that increasing numbers of women were being incorporated into the labor force, at the same time that there was increasing inactivity (i.e., unemployment) among men. This is to be expected with increasing modernization, and it does not necessarily indicate that women were displacing men. Rather, women had to work to supplement the low, irregular, or nonexistent incomes of the male members of their families, who typically were involved in different economic sectors.

---

[141] This statement was made by Victor S. Clark, who had been director of the Bureau of Education under the military government in Puerto Rico: quoted in Berbusse, *U.S. in Puerto Rico*, p. 214. Later, Clark was director of the Brookings Institution team whose investigation in the late 1920s is such an important source of information.
[142] Smith, *Standards*, p. 17, table 5.

TABLE 2.14
Economically Inactive Population, Selected Years from 1899 to 1935

	Total Population	Population 10 yrs. +	With No Economic Activity[a]	
			No.	Percent[b]
1899				
Male	472,261	322,567	45,173	14.0
Female	480,982	336,727	283,677	84.2
1910				
Male	557,301	386,516	20,765	5.4
Female	560,711	395,084	279,276	70.7
1920				
Male	647,825	447,777	52,343	11.7
Female	651,984	456,646	329,395	72.1
1930				
Male	771,761	544,184	97,461	17.9
Female	772,152	549,239	362,057	65.9
1935				
Male	861,635	615,983	149,006	24.2
Female	861,899	621,966	408,518	65.7

SOURCE: CENEP, *Labor Migration*, p. 107, table 4.5.
[a] Having no paid employment and not attending school.
[b] On base of population 10 years +.

EMIGRATION

The hypothesis that unemployment became an increasing problem in the early decades of U.S. control is corroborated by what is known about migration flows. In 1900–1901, some 5,300 persons left Puerto Rico to work the sugar plantations of Hawaii. Many people were preyed upon by the labor contractors who recruited workers for the plantations there and in Cuba, the Dominican Republic, and other locations. Many of these contractors deceived the migrating workers, and the contracting relationship sometimes came close to bondage.[143] Between 1914 and 1930, there

[143] Maldonado-Denis, *Emigration Dialectic*, pp. 60–61; CENEP, *La migración puertorriqueña* and *Puerto Rican Migration*. On their way to Hawaii and after traveling by boat to New Orleans, migrants were brought by train, in boxcars, across the southwestern U.S.; they were locked up on sidings at night away from towns to prevent escapes. In 1901, there were at least eleven large-scale migrations to Hawaii, and many Puerto Ricans managed to escape, some in California: CENEP, *Labor Migration*, pp. 108, 110. Rosario Natal's *Exodo* is a superb narrative history, drawing on many of the documents in the works cited above.

was a net population outflow from the island of 51,986 persons (3.4 percentage of the 1930 population).[144] Between 12,000 and 13,000 were brought to the United States by the government during World War I to relieve labor shortages. Many died on the trip or in work camps in the states, and this led to some mild reforms in contracting conditions without substantially altering the attempts to relocate Puerto Ricans.[145] However, most Puerto Ricans who went to the United States did not do so under contract or through official relocation. They left individually and with families and friends, most of them for New York, in the hope of finding regular work. The importance of this migration accelerated after World War II (see chapter 5 for further detail).

It is fitting and revealing to end this evaluation of social conditions with the opinion of Secretary of the Interior Harold Ickes, who oversaw policy for Puerto Rico and the territories. He wrote, in 1935:

> Puerto Rico . . . has been the victim of the *laissez faire* economy which has developed the rapid growth of great absentee owned sugar corporations, which have absorbed much land formerly belonging to small independent growers and who in consequence have been reduced to virtual economic serfdom. While the inclusion of Puerto Rico within our tariff walls has been highly beneficial to the stockholders of those corporations, the benefits have not been passed down to the mass of Puerto Ricans. These on the contrary have seen the lands on which they formerly raised subsistence crops, given over to sugar production while they have been gradually driven to import all their food staples, paying for them the high prices brought about by the tariff. There is today more widespread misery and destitution and far more unemployment in Puerto Rico than at any previous time in its history.[146]

It is little wonder that a system which its highest administrator could so strongly criticize would come under increasing attack from within Puerto Rico, ultimately reaching a point at which U.S. colonial dominance was threatened.

SUMMARY

The first three decades of U.S. colonial control brought about decisive changes in the Puerto Rican economy and its class and social structure. U.S. capital flowed into the sugar industry and led to a substantial in-

[144] Rosario Natal, *Exodo*, p. 78, and Perloff, *Puerto Rico's Economic Future*, p. 201, table 72.
[145] CENEP, *Labor Migration*, pp. 110–11.
[146] Quoted in Mathews, *Puerto Rican Politics*, p. 215.

crease in land concentration during the first decade. Large and economically viable centrales were constructed which consumed large quantities of cane from corporate plantations and colonos alike. Sugar and tobacco prospered, being inside the U.S. tariff wall, but Puerto Rican coffee had no such advantage and, pushed along by natural disasters as well, it declined in importance.

More than a quarter of Puerto Rico's total wealth, and substantially more of its productive wealth, was owned by foreigners, primarily U.S. businessmen. The Organic Acts guaranteed that political decisions would be governed by the interests of the United States, while U.S. capital investments reoriented the economy. There were some large local capitalists—in sugar, for example—but U.S. dominance in political, economic, educational, and judicial affairs was unquestionable.

The influx of U.S. capital was rapid and dramatic in its effects. The tendency toward capitalist organization and relationships of production was accelerated, and the proletarianization and semiproletarianization of an expanding proportion of the population was one result. On sugar plantations, in the cigar factories, in needlework operations, the Puerto Rican economy was integrated into the U.S. economy, money and monetary relations increasingly influenced decisions and behavior, private and public institutions were "rationalized" and put on a profit-loss footing, and in general the market system and its peculiar logic and time horizon came to regulate the pace and measure the pulse of economic life.

Though total national income increased over the period, due to the rapid growth of sugar production and exports, and per capita income also grew, there is little evidence to suggest that the average income figures meant improvements in the standard of living of the mass of working and nonworking people. There were gains in health care, but the health problems associated everywhere with poverty and human degradation continued.

The rise to dominance of capitalist production in Puerto Rico created a society immensely distant from its Spanish past, and even from its Caribbean and Latin American neighbors. Legally, perhaps, Puerto Rico was not part of the United States, but only legally. Economically, politically, and culturally, the forces of U.S. capitalism weighed ever more heavily on the Puerto Rican social formation.

The displacement of traditional values has commonly accompanied the rise of capitalism. In other respects, however, the process was different in Puerto Rico from what it had been in other societies. First, a historical change which elsewhere occurred over a period of centuries was compressed into decades, making it that much more wrenching. Second, the new form of production was transplanted from and controlled by interests residing in an already advanced and developed capitalist country, the United States, rather than developing indigenously within the previous social formation. Third, it was monopoly capitalism, with large-scale, concentrated production using relatively sophisticated and expensive technology, not the more competitive capitalism that had spurred development in Western Europe. Finally, Puerto Rico entered upon its development process late in historical time, confronted in an unprotected marketplace by the leading capitalist power.[147] The implications of these differences will be explored in the next chapter.

[147] Gerschenkron, *Economic Backwardness*, has commented on the significance of this "delayed entrance" in a more general context.

3

The Thirties: Crisis and Transformation

INTRODUCTION

After three decades of bringing sweeping changes to Puerto Rico's economic, political, class, and social structure, the underpinnings of U.S. control were threatened for the first time by the events of the 1930s. The decade that began with the Great Depression challenged the viability and resiliency of all Western capitalist nations—their ability to respond to the threat of collapse and social instability which accompanied the crisis begun in the United States. It would take expanded war preparations and another world war, however, and not the timid and tentative Keynesian-type reforms and programs that were instituted, to rekindle prosperity and create the next boom period.

Puerto Rico experienced the dislocations of the depression years in all their manifestations. There was a breakdown in the functioning of the predominately monocultural, agricultural model of growth, which led to open and at times violent class struggle and demands for change. Such events laid the base and created the conditions that would accelerate the transformation of the economy from a rural, agricultural-based capitalism to an urban, manufacturing-oriented capitalism, an evolution completed to a great extent by the 1950s. In the early depression years, sugar workers, the largest sector of the rural working class, rebelled against the working conditions imposed on them by the large sugar companies and centrales, in the process abandoning their own union leaders, who had chosen collaboration with the sugar companies over representation of their members. The Nationalist party became a visible and militant force and a danger to U.S. interests in Puerto Rico with its demand for unconditional and immediate independence. The standard of living for the great majority of the population, and particularly agricultural workers, worsened during the early years of the decade as unemployment increased, wages and incomes declined, and prices of necessities increased relative to wages. The "deplorable" conditions reported by the Brookings Institution team at the end of the 1920s became the increasingly impossible and stagnating situation of the 1930s.

Very broadly, the legitimacy of U.S. control in Puerto Rico was now

being questioned by a wide spectrum of society as a consequence of the
economic collapse. The thin gloss of legitimacy which U.S. colonial rule
had managed to maintain until that time, and which had been generally
accepted, was threatened with being wiped away, thus exposing to scrutiny the full extent of U.S. domination of the island's economy, politics,
and people. In the profound economic and social crisis of the world capitalist system, the extent of colonial domination of Puerto Rico and its
position in the international economy increasingly became the focus of
discussion, concern, and defiance. Steps were taken to restore voluntary
acceptance of the legitimacy of U.S. colonialism, but more repressive
and less democratic means were also used to demand and ensure compliance.

The thirties were a turning point for Puerto Rico, and not only because
of the open and often brutal form that resistance to continued U.S. domination took. Struggles by workers, nationalists, and students emerged
when they did because the colonial model of development itself was in
severe crisis. Partly, of course, this was due to the impact of the worldwide depression, but the signs of crisis in the development model had
been evident well before that: high and increasing unemployment, low
incomes and rising prices, the contrast between the high profits of the
absentee owners and the poverty of their workers, structural dependence
on one agricultural export commodity, and a high level of trade dependence. The coming of the Great Depression simply made manifest the
severity of the conditions that debilitated the island economy; it did not
create or invent them. The problem that confronted the colonial administrators in Washington and San Juan was how to transform the colonial
development model and improve its functioning in such a way as to preserve the colonial relation.

IMPACT OF THE GREAT DEPRESSION

For most businesses in the U.S. and elsewhere, the decade of the twenties was a period of bright prosperity, darkened only by the 1921 downturn. Workers did not always fare as well, but the impression of well-
being lingered throughout the decade until, on October 29, 1929, the
bottom fell out of the stock market. The prosperity of the late 1920s had
come to an end, and it was soon realized how illusory it had been all
along. By 1933, U.S. gross national product (GNP) had dropped to $56
billion from its high of $104.4 billion in 1929 (in nominal dollars). Con-
sumer prices fell by about 25 percent, and workers' real wages, or their
purchasing power, declined about 15 percent. Unemployment reached a
staggering 24.9 percent of the work force in 1933, and the real rate of

unemployment was certainly even higher.[1] And although the depression was triggered by events in the United States, its effects reverberated throughout the world capitalist system.

In Puerto Rico, the decline in output was not as severe as in the United States, at least partly because income and production were so low to begin with. Puerto Rico's GNP fell from $176 million in 1929 to $134 million in 1933, a decrease of 23.9 percent, compared to the 46.4 percent decrease in the United States.[2]

The impact of the crisis was far from uniform in the different sectors of the economy (table 3.1). Agriculture's share of the national income fell substantially in both absolute and relative terms, while the government sector more than doubled its share and, by the close of the decade, was the most important sector in the economy in terms of generating income. There can be little doubt that this increasingly prominent role of the government set the stage for the transformations of the 1940s, when the state's involvement became central to the dynamic of the island's economy. Indeed, with the decline of productive values in both agriculture and manufacturing, if there had not been a substantial increase in the state's participation in the economy, national income in 1939 would have been below its 1929 level, illustrating the importance of the new role for government.

Similarly, not all groups in society suffered equally. From 1929 to 1933, wages and salaries declined from $131 million to $95 million, dividend payments on stocks and bonds remained unchanged at $3 million, and net interest and rent actually increased, from $6 to $7 million. Enterprise profits as a whole declined 19.4 percent, though some large corporations, especially in sugar production, actually increased their profits during the crisis.[3]

The dislocations caused by the Great Depression came on the heels of the 1928 hurricane, long before the island had recovered from that tragedy. Then, in 1932, another hurricane, San Ciprián, struck, killing 225 people and causing damage estimated at $30 million. Much as in the U.S. Midwest's "dust bowl" of the 1930s, natural calamity could not have struck at a less opportune time. Production of sugar and sugar exports, however, suffered less than other sectors during the early 1930s for two reasons: first, the hurricanes did not cause long-term damage to the cane, as they did to coffee, tobacco, and fruit plantings; and second, because of the decline in world sugar prices that had begun even before the

[1] Fite and Reese, *Economic History of the U.S.*, chap. 27; Robertson and Walton, *American Economy*, pp. 405–6, chap. 24; and Dowd, *Twisted Dream*, chap. 4.
[2] Quintero Rivera, "La base social," p. 52, table 3.
[3] Ibid.

TABLE 3.1

Shares of National Income by Economic Sector,
1929, 1934, and 1939

Economic Sector	1929		1934		1939	
	Dollars (millions)	Percent	Dollars (millions)	Percent	Dollars (millions)	Percent
Agriculture	87	49.4	71	43.3	59	30.1
Manufacturing	16	9.1	12	7.3	14	7.1
Services	10	5.7	15	9.2	21	10.7
Government	25	14.2	34	20.7	63	32.1
All others	38	21.6	32	19.5	39	20.0
Total	176	100.0	164	100.0	196	100.0

SOURCE: Dudley Smith, *Puerto Rico's Income* (Washington, D.C.: Association of Sugar Producers of Puerto Rico, 1943), p. 18, as quoted in Quintero Rivera, "La base social," p. 46, table 1.

depression, Cuban sugar production, lacking the tariff protection that Puerto Rican sugar enjoyed, fell off dramatically, and Puerto Rico was able to expand its market by gaining what Cuba lost.[4] Thus, there was a seemingly anomalous situation of boom conditions for some sugar companies in Puerto Rico in the depths of the depression. For example, Fajardo Sugar, one of the U.S.-owned corporations, tripled its profits between 1931 and 1932, while increasing its production of raw sugar by 26,000 tons. Fajardo, in fact, was one of only seven corporations in the entire United States to make more than a minimal profit in 1932, and that despite the low sugar prices.[5]

WORKING AND LIVING CONDITIONS

Per capita income worsened during the early 1930s and only began to approach the 1930 level again, in nominal value, toward the end of the decade (table 3.2). By 1933, per capita income was nearly 30 percent below what it had been in 1930. For sugar workers in the fields, wages fell from 90 cents a day to 50 to 60 cents in 1931–32, about equal to what they had been at the turn of the century.[6] When changes in purchasing power are considered, the decline was even greater. Whereas in the U.S. prices generally fell, prices in Puerto Rico for many necessities actually increased in some years. According to the Chamber of Commerce, prices of basic necessities, and the cost of living in general, rose approximately one-third between 1932 and 1933, while per capita money income was falling more than 12 percent. Rice, a staple of the Puerto Rican diet, sold for $2.40 per 100 pounds in December 1932; a year later, the price was $4.10. Imported beans increased from $3.00 per 100 pounds to $5.25; bacalao, from $19 to $28; lard, from $14.50 to $18. The price of a quart of milk rose from 5 to 14 cents, of a pound of bread from 4 to 10 cents.[7] Income levels began to rise by the middle of the decade, but this was due to the extension of federal emergency relief and the New Deal programs to the island (to be discussed below), not to any substantive recuperation of the viability of the colonial development model.

A consideration of the changes in income by sectors makes their extent and effects clearer. A study of 11,325 field workers in the cultivation of

[4] Sugar prices (including the U.S. tariff) had reached a peak of 21.58 cents per pound in May 1920. Two years later, the price had dropped to 2.59 cents: Serralles, *Farm Prices*.
[5] Mathews, *Puerto Rican Politics*, p. 131, and Mattos Cintrón, *La política y lo político*, pp. 197–98, n. 136. See also Bird, *Sugar Industry*, pp. 39–41.
[6] Gayer, Homan, and Jones, *Sugar Economy*, p. 221.
[7] Mathews, *Puerto Rican Politics*, p. 137. To give an idea of the importance of rice consumption and the impact of higher prices, it need be pointed out only that in Puerto Rico over the period 1931–35, per capita consumption averaged 137.7 pounds, compared to U.S. consumption of 5.5 pounds: Smith, *Puerto Rico's Trade*, p. 24.

TABLE 3.2
Per Capita Net Income, 1930 to 1940

	Per Capita Net Income (dollars)	% Annual Change	% Deviation from 1930 Income
1930	122	—	—
1931	108	−11.5	−11.5
1932	98	− 9.3	−19.5
1933	86	−12.2	−29.5
1934	108	+25.6	−11.5
1935	104	− 3.7	−14.8
1936	115	+10.6	− 5.7
1937	120	+ 4.3	− 1.6
1938	121	+ 0.8	− 0.8
1939	113	− 6.6	− 7.4
1940	122	+ 8.0	0.0

SOURCE: Perloff, *Puerto Rico's Economic Future*, p. 160, table 49.

sugar cane found that their average wage was 11.1 cents per hour in 1932 and that by 1933 this had decreased to 9.6 cents. Weekly earnings fell from $3.80 to $3.55, even though the average number of hours worked was increasing. Agricultural workers in tobacco, one of the lowest-paid sectors, received an average hourly wage of 4.3 cents in 1933 and worked an average of 29.5 hours per week, resulting in average earnings of $1.27 per week. Differences in income by sex, as always, were sharp. For men in tobacco production, the average weekly wage was $1.46, while for women it was $0.97. Needleworkers in factories averaged 8.9 cents an hour and $3.32 a week.[8]

To roughly measure the cost of living, the designers of the study from which the above figures were taken asked a physician at the University of Puerto Rico to determine the caloric requirements for various jobs. Hand needleworkers, he reported, required 1,800 calories a day, while farm laborers, whose work was more arduous, required 3,200 to 4,100 calories. (It could well be objected that the requirement for needleworkers was too low, since most were women and their labor in the home was not considered.) By comparing the caloric content of foods eaten by Puerto Ricans with these requirements, it was estimated that, for food alone, the cost of an adequate diet was $3.19 per person per week in 1933, and the food budget for a family of four was $11.17 per week. When this is put against the facts that in most industries the average weekly wage was $3

[8] Rodríguez, *Wages*, pp. 5–7.

TABLE 3.3
Average Weekly Wages for
Various Occupations in Three Industries, 1933–1936
(in dollars)

Industry and Occupation	1933–34	1934–35	1935–36
Sugar			
Field workers	4.44	—	3.75
Overseers	19.62	—	—
Foremen	6.97	—	—
Wagon loaders	6.13	—	—
Cane cutters	4.25	—	—
Weeders	3.66	—	—
Mill (factory) workers	—	7.53	6.78
Chemists	44.08	—	—
Sugar mixers	6.12	—	—
Unskilled laborers	5.02	—	—
Tobacco			
Field work (cultivation)	—	—	2.18
Factory work (stripping)	—	—	4.76
Coffee			
Field work (cultivation)	—	—	2.33

SOURCE: Gayer, Homan, and Jones, *Sugar Economy*, pp. 194, 205 (table 94), 206–7 (table 95), 210 (table 98).

NOTE: These figures are yearly wages calculated as weekly averages; they thus take into account differences in periods of unemployment. In the sugar industry, mill workers were more likely to have year-round employment than field workers.

or less, and that no account was taken of the costs of housing, clothing, health care, or other expenses, the difficulties experienced by the great majority of persons become vividly clear.[9]

Some useful comparative data on wage levels are presented in table 3.3. Workers in the sugar industry were better paid than those involved in either tobacco or coffee production, though this advantage was par-

[9] Ibid., pp. 9–11, 14. Own production of food could, of course, substitute for purchased food, reducing the cash outlay for rural workers with access to land. In the mid-1920s, families living on cane farms had an average of .076 cultivated cuerdas and those on coffee and tobacco farms, .342 cuerdas. There is no reason to think that these figures increased in the 1930s, and it is reasonable to conclude that own production, while of some importance, did not greatly improve the standard of living for agricultural workers: Quintero Rivera, *Conflictos de clase*, p. 141, graph A.

tially offset by their more restricted access to land for their own production. In each industry, factory workers had higher weekly wages than field workers, though this is a somewhat deceptive statistic, since hours per week worked in factories, especially in the centrals, often significantly exceeded hours worked in the fields. During the grinding season, the mills operated two twelve-hour shifts, seven days a week.[10]

Significant differences in hourly wages also existed. In 1932–33, sugar field workers averaged 9.8 cents an hour and mill workers, 11.3 cents; in 1935–36, the respective hourly wages were 12.1 cents and 16 cents. In tobacco production, the differences were even greater: in 1935–36, hourly wages for cultivation averaged 5.7 cents and for leaf stripping, 12.5 cents. In coffee, hourly wages in the field averaged 6.3 cents.[11]

Weekly wages decreased after the eight-hour day went into effect in November 1935, requiring payment of double time for more than eight hours work per day. By 1935–36, the average number of hours worked per week in sugar mills had dropped to 53.4, just two-thirds of the 1932–33 average. Higher hourly earnings failed to compensate for this shorter work week, although there were also fewer accidents in 1935–36 than in previous years.[12]

WOMEN WORKERS

Women consistently earned lower incomes than male workers. For example, men earned an average of $4.76 a week in 1935–36 as leaf strippers in the tobacco factories, while women received $2.59, barely half as much. Outside the agricultural sector, salaries were somewhat more nearly equal. In a survey of office workers in 1936–37, men were found to be earning an average of $20.04 per week and women, $12.79, or a little less than two-thirds as much.[13] Despite their lower average incomes, women's participation in the labor force increased during the 1930s. Between 1930 and 1940, the number of employed women grew 17.9 percent (from 122,488 to 144,360). About a third of working women were employed in home needlework production. Home needleworkers (who included many children as well as women) were the lowest paid of all workers; more than 60 percent of them earned 2 cents per hour or less, and only 6 percent earned 4 cents or more in 1934. In 1936, these wages had increased very little: 46.5 percent of the workers still earned less than

---

[10] Gayer, Homan, and Jones, *Sugar Economy*, p. 177.
[11] Ibid., p. 210, table 98. The much higher wages of some skilled workers in the sugar mills also helped pull the average wage upward in that industry. The most common wage— that is, the modal one—was below the arithmetic wage.
[12] Ibid., pp. 176–80.
[13] Ibid., p. 197; PRDL, *Annual Report, 1936–37*, pp. 48–50.

2 cents an hour and 30.5 percent from 2 to 4 cents. Such low wages were due not only to the piecework nature of home production and the fact that women felt forced to accept work at any wage to supplement family income, but also to the nature of the organization of the production process, in which subcontractors and even sub-subcontractors recruited workers and monitored their production. The contractors received their commissions from the funds provided to them to pay labor costs, and these commissions averaged 22 percent of the total funds.[14]

In the factories and workshops where sewing and embroidery were done in a more centralized manner, wages for women were lower than for men but higher than for needlework done in the home. The ratio between men's and women's wages ranged between 1.4 to 1 and 2.3:1. Since men were more likely to be supervisors and foremen, however, these differences reflect not merely differences in wages for similar work but also the hierarchical structure of the workplace.[15] In general, factory work was better paid and more regular for women than agricultural work, which often provided only three or four months' work during the year.[16]

THE NEW DEAL IN PUERTO RICO

While the New Deal programs of the Roosevelt era did not fundamentally alter the base of the capitalist economic system in the United States, they did forge, and legitimize, a larger role for government activism within the economy. This expanded role was oriented primarily toward creating sufficient aggregate demand, or total spending, to keep private production profitable and to assure sufficient capital accumulation to employ the labor force. The New Deal was not a socialist program, as many of its critics charged it was; the government did not enter into production in competition with or as a substitute for private-sector production. Instead, the federal government attempted to ensure that the economy would be stable enough to allow profits to be made that would be adequate for the attainment of full employment.

The theoretical foundation for greater intervention by government was provided by John Maynard Keynes and the Keynesian economists, and even earlier by Michal Kalecki and Knut Wicksell. In this theoretical

[14] Silvestrini, "La mujer puertorriqueña," pp. 69 (table 1), 70 (table 2), 80, 82–83.

[15] Ibid., p. 81, table 3. In the production of children's clothing, women earned $3.18 weekly and men $9.66 in 1933–34; handkerchiefs, $3.02 and $4.42; men's clothing, $4.70 and $6.68; women's undergarments, $3.02 and $6.89. In 1936, incomes of all workers in the production of men's clothing averaged $6.57 per week, while in the U.S., they averaged $31.05: PRDAC, *Statistics, 1935–36*, p. 182.

[16] Silvestrini, "La mujer puertorriqueña," p. 77.

144 CHAPTER THREE

perspective, the cause of the Great Depression was not the lack of any physical or technical ability to produce, but the absence of any incentive to produce on the part of profit-oriented private firms. At the bottom of the depression in 1932, less than one-half of the productive capacity of industry was in use; firms were not producing because it was not profitable for them to do so, given the level of effective demand in the economy.[17] The Keynesian solution was to increase total spending in the economy, so as to motivate firms to increase production and thereby increase profits by meeting the newly created demand. Unemployment will then fall as more workers are hired to produce the increased output. This sequence of events can be initiated by government through an appropriate combination of fiscal and monetary policies.

Whatever the merits of Keynesian demand stimulation for already developed capitalist economies with an extensive stock of productive capacity, Puerto Rico's situation was substantially different. Its problem was not one of economic rehabilitation, as in the United States, but of economic construction; not the stimulation of demand but the more fundamental task of developing a productive and dynamic economic base in the first place. Because of the common tariffs and the high degree of economic integration with the United States, Puerto Rico was a very "open" economy; the impact of increased spending there would have much of its income-multiplier effect not in the island's own economy but in the United States, where the spending would flow for the purchase of imported goods.[18] New Deal expenditures in Puerto Rico by the federal or colonial government could help to relieve the grinding poverty by distributing funds and providing relief, temporary jobs, and the wherewithal for current consumption. Such spending, however, would not be more than a temporary palliative; it promised no long-term solution to the need for a viable productive structure capable of meeting the needs of the local population. In short, there was in Puerto Rico an incomplete productive structure in place unable to respond to Keynesian demand stimulation.

[17] Dowd, *Twisted Dream*, p. 104. Productive capacity in use had declined from about 85 or 95 percent in the 1920s to 66 percent in 1930 and 42 percent in 1932, and it then rose to 52 percent in 1933.

[18] "It was estimated that sixty cents out of every dollar spent in Puerto Rico returned to the United States on the first turnover": Mathews, *Puerto Rican Politics*, p. 227. If this ratio remained constant in all further turnovers, and assuming all income was spent (a not unreasonable assumption for that period), the maximum value of the multiplier of increased spending would have been 1.7—that is, for every dollar of new spending, total production and total income would have increased by $1.70. However, assuming a marginal propensity to consume of only 0.5 in the U.S., to account for leakages, the original $1 of spending in Puerto Rico would create $2 of income in the U.S., through import purchases and the multiplier effect.

When the Great Depression struck, Puerto Rico was relatively fortunate to have Theodore Roosevelt, Jr., the son of the former president, as colonial governor. In his own distinct, certainly paternalistic, way, he had been attempting to administer the colony as an imposed outsider, to maintain democratic pretensions, and all the while to accomplish some good within an essentially adverse political environment.[19] Roosevelt had been appointed by President Hoover in April 1929, and he had brought with him Hoover's essentially classical economic policies. To cope with the depression, at hand, he sought to balance the island's budget by reducing government expenditures, at a time when Puerto Rico needed more spending in the right places, not less. To his credit, Roosevelt did try to come to grips with some of the most serious problems he encountered. He was proud of his efforts to learn and speak Spanish—something most U.S. governors had never bothered themselves with—and he openly, and self-deprecatingly, admitted to making often humorous and embarrassing errors, which probably further endeared him to many Puerto Ricans.[20]

Also in classical economic fashion, and in the face of declining government expenditures, Roosevelt appealed to U.S. charities and private individuals to provide aid to the island, and he succeeded in raising about $200,000 in 1930–31, though this was trivial compared to the magnitude of the problems. A school-lunch program was begun, and a 500-bed hospital for tuberculosis patients was built (but more than 3,000 persons were dying from the illness every year).[21] Roosevelt also took some positive steps in education, especially to reduce the use of English as the primary language of instruction. He saw to the creation of a Department of Labor and set up an office in New York to attempt to attract additional U.S. capital investment, to promote Puerto Rican products, and to stimulate tourism. The fact that this office opened in 1930 may have shown bad timing and a lack of foresight on the governor's part, but certainly not bad faith.[22] Roosevelt was perhaps the first colonial governor to un-

[19] Gordon Lewis, *Puerto Rico*, p. 113, has characterized the dilemma of U.S. governors in Puerto Rico in this fashion: "Spain had been an autocracy behaving autocratically; the United States was a democracy behaving autocratically."

[20] See Roosevelt, "Colonial Policies," p. 173, where he notes that he once said to an astonished school group that he himself had given birth to four children and that on another occasion he introduced a startled general to an equally startled audience as a "tapeworm" (*solitaria*) rather than a "bachelor" (*soltero*).

[21] Mathews, *Puerto Rican Politics*, pp. 17–18. Roosevelt himself wrote of a previous hospital which had a capacity of only 247 patients, while at least 40,000 people were suffering from tuberculosis: "Colonial Policies," p. 169.

[22] Chap. 6 of T. Clark, *Puerto Rico*, deals with Roosevelt's tenure as governor. The New York office was called the Bureau of Commerce and Industry; its success was, as could be expected, very slight: Ross, *Uphill Path*, pp. 19–21.

derstand that Puerto Rico's problems were economic at their root and to
act within the colonial restraints and his own ideological perspective to
begin to resolve some of them. However, his efforts were too weak and
too late to initiate any measurable, enduring transformations within the
economy or society, and in January 1932 he left Puerto Rico to become
governor of the Philippines, a bigger diplomatic plum. Puerto Rico's
problems remained behind, unsolved and mostly untouched.

THE FIRST EFFORTS

Severe economic crises like the Great Depression tend to erode faith
in the ruling orthodoxy. President Hoover, guided by classical economic
theory, believed in the automatically self-adjusting nature of capitalist
market economies. An important part of this view was the idea that "that
government is best which governs least," particularly in economic affairs. These theories, however, became more and more questionable and
difficult to adhere to as the depression worsened. Against his ideological
bent, Hoover in January 1932 approved the creation of the Reconstruction
Finance Corporation, which was to extend credit to selected, qualifying
businesses and later to states for public works projects. Puerto Rico qual-
itifed for such aid, and by May 1933, some $1 million had been spent
on irrigation and water systems and had created 3.5 million hours of work
for about 1,200 men in forestry and other activities. The major innovations in the interventionist role of the capitalist state and in federal aid,
however, had to wait for Franklin D. Roosevelt and his "brain trust" of
academic advisers.

President Roosevelt took office in March 1933, and two months later,
in May, the Federal Emergency Relief Administration (FERA) was created to make grants to state and local agencies for relief and public works
projects. The federal government would provide one dollar for every three
dollars advanced by local governments. The Puerto Rican Emergency
Relief Administration (PRERA) was created to administer the program
on the island, and in August 1933, James Bourne, a friend of Roosevelt's, was appointed to head it. Until Bourne's appointment, Puerto Rico
had not even applied for funds to the FERA. Even after the birth of the
PRERA, Puerto Rico's governor—Robert H. Gore, who on his appointment is supposed to have claimed to have had no idea where Puerto Rico
was—and the island legislature failed for many months to appropriate any
local funds to be able to qualify for the federal matching money.[23] During

---

[23] The newly appointed Governor Gore did not attend the briefing session on the FERA
in Washington, even though he was in the U.S.; instead, he sent an unprepared surrogate.
This is perhaps, an indication of his attitude toward his appointment and toward the people
and problems of Puerto Rico. For the story of Governor Gore's turbulent five months in

1933, the PRERA did manage to receive $770,000, but with barely one-third of the population employed, this amount was wholly inadequate to the magnitude of the problem, as is indicated by the number of people applying for assistance. In September 1933, the PRERA handled 5,000 direct relief cases; in the following months, it struggled with 50,000 cases a month, of which 93 percent were families, with an average of five persons each. Through the PRERA's efforts in its short life, roads were built, malaria control was advanced, more needlework centers were set up, 120,000 pounds of pork were distributed, and a core of young professionals were trained in survey, census, and other techniques which were to be vitally important skills for future development. This training ground for Puerto Rico's own "brain trust" was perhaps the PRERA's most enduring contribution to the island.[24]

But nothing the PRERA could do with its meager resources was enough to blunt the harshness of the depression conditions. As noted above, prices of basic necessities rose by one-third from December 1932 to December 1933. Much of this increase was the result of a processing tax placed on agricultural products as part of the Agricultural Adjustment Act (AAA), passed by Congress in May 1933. The explicit purpose of this legislation was to raise farm prices by encouraging farmers to plant and produce less; the processing tax was to be used to pay farmers for restricting output, while consumers were forced to pay higher prices for agricultural products so as to create the funds to be able to increase farm prices to the levels prevailing in 1900–1914.[25] The device was, however, a crushing burden to ask Puerto Rican (as well as U.S.) consumers to bear.[26]

In January 1934, as the cane-cutting season just was beginning, a wave of strikes swept the island's sugar farms as workers demanded higher wages. There were other issues involved, which will be examined later, but the decline in purchasing power was a major one. These strikes, and the reaction of the colonial government to them, were critical incidents in the development of colonial relations and in providing an impetus for changes in the development model in the 1940s.

For most of the early period of U.S. rule, responsibility for the admin-

---

office, see Mathews, *Puerto Rican Politics*, chap. 3. At a time of deteriorating living conditions, when Puerto Rico required creative leadership and responsiveness, the Gore episode showed how easily the functioning of the colonial government could be brought to a standstill.

[24] Ibid., pp. 117–22, 127, 130–31.

[25] Robertson and Walton, *American Economy*, pp. 429–30, and Fite and Reese, *Economic History of the U.S.*, p. 520.

[26] Mathews, *Puerto Rican Politics*, p. 137. The AAA was declared unconstitutional and the processing tax "invalid" by the U.S. Supreme Court in January 1936.

istration of Puerto Rico had been located in the Bureau of Insular Affairs of the War Department.[27] On July 28, 1934, after more than a year of wavering by Roosevelt, jurisdiction was transferred to the Interior Department (then headed by Secretary Harold Ickes), within which the Division of Territories and Island Possessions was created. Ernest Gruening became its first director in October.[28] At the time, this seemed to many to be a fundamental reorientation of colonial policy, since it removed administration of Puerto Rico from the military and put it into the hands of a civilian agency with a well-known liberal at its head. What actually followed was one of the most repressive periods of U.S. rule; Gruening quickly shed his liberal image when colonial authority was challenged by the Puerto Rican Nationalist party. But in the initial stages, the appointment of Gruening, and his association with Puerto Ricans sympathetic to the New Deal, especially Luis Muñoz Marín, seemed promising for stimulating the economy and relieving the hardships that had been made even worse by the depression.

The political situation in Puerto Rico was less than propitious for the extension of New Deal programs. While in the United States it could be said that the Roosevelt administration had a mandate as a result of the 1932 election, the same was not true in Puerto Rico. There, the 1932 election gave the coalition of the Socialist and Republican Union parties a majority in the insular legislature over the new Liberal (formerly the Union) party.[29] The coalition brought together seemingly strange bedfellows. The Republican Union party represented the interests of business and especially the sugar companies, including the absentee U.S. corporations. The Socialist party ostensibly represented the interests of workers and was intimately connected, via overlapping leadership with the Federación Libre de Trabajadores (Free Federation of Workers, or FLT), a labor union allied with the AFL. What the two parties (or at least their leaders) had in common was a desire for continued close relations with

[27] The Bureau of Insular Affairs was created on July 15, 1909: Colton, *Report of the Governor*, p. 3.

[28] Ibid., pp. 172, 186. Gruening had been editor of the liberal magazine, the *Nation*. Note the name of the division: It clearly made a distinction between "territories," like Alaska, and "possessions," like Puerto Rico, which were not territories but colonies with indefinite future status.

[29] The Socialist party received a total of 97,438 votes; the Republican Union party, 110,794; the Liberal party 170,168; and the Nationalists, 5,257 votes. The coalition held fourteen of the nineteen seats in the upper house and thirty-one of the thirty-nine in the lower house. Santiago Iglesias, the Socialist leader, became resident commissioner in Washington. Luis Muñoz Marín was elected senator for the first time, as a Liberal. This also was the first election in which women who met a literacy requirement could vote, as a result of Law 74 of 1929. It was not until the 1936 elections that there was universal suffrage: Bayrón Toro, *Elecciones y partidos políticos*, pp. 177–78, 185; Silén, *Historia*, p. 199.

the United States and, eventually, statehood. This, plus the lure of power, brought them together in opposition to the Liberals, who spoke of independence as a possible solution to the island's status question. However, as will become clearer in a later section, the leadership of the Socialist party gradually moved toward the right and by the 1930s was socialist in name only.

The coalition, backed by the large sugar interests, was hostile to the Roosevelt administration and the New Deal programs; the Liberal party, on the other hand, was favorable to the new Washington administration. Governor Gore professed support in public but never demonstrated an active commitment in practice. With the coalition in power in the legislature and Gore in La Fortaleza, the New Deal found an unfriendly environment on the island. Introduction of its programs was an uphill battle from the beginning, attended by political infighting and intrigue and hurdles at every step.[30] This conjuncture of hostile forces was to remain in place until the 1940 elections ushered in a whole new era.

THE CHARDÓN PLAN

The outline of a more effective New Deal plan emerged in late 1933 and early 1934. Its main supporters—Rexford Guy Tugwell, Luis Muñoz Marín, and Carlos Chardón—are important personalities, who had a significant impact on Puerto Rico's later development.[31] They were representatives of a more liberal and enlightened capitalism, in which the stranglehold of the absentee sugar monopolies would be broken, permitting the growth of local capitalism and the retention of more of the benefits of expanded production within the island economy. The plan for economic recovery they envisaged was one that would create small-scale capitalists who would be able to compete on the world market and who would exercise local control over capital, production, and economic decision making. It was believed that only through such a development strategy could a national base for development be built that could break out of the cycle of colonial underdevelopment and perhaps out of colonialism itself.[32]

[30] Mathews, *Puerto Rican Politics*, esp. chaps. 6–8. Mathews, in the preface to his *Puerto Rican Politics* (p. xi), wrote that by the end of 1938, the New Deal had "definitely lost its renovating drive on the island . . . at this time it was not renovating, but in some ways was reactionary in its character."

[31] Tugwell became, in 1941, the last non–Puerto Rican to be appointed governor of Puerto Rico. Muñoz Marín, son of Muñoz Rivera, forged a new political party and became the first elected governor; Chardón, a respected educator and scientist and chancellor of the University of Puerto Rico, was the main author of the island's reconstruction plan.

[32] This was at least Muñoz's position at first. He was a staunch supporter of independence in the early thirties and had written the independence statement for the Liberal party in the

The sequence of events leading up to the birth of the New Deal plan for Puerto Rico is revealing. In January 1934, writing in *La democracia,* Muñoz Marín outlined his views on the necessity of reorienting the economy. Soon afterward, Eleanor Roosevelt and a group of U.S. officials made an inspection tour of the island; and at a briefing specifically for Mrs. Roosevelt on March 10, Carlos Chardón revealed, to the surprise and shock of many of those present, his own plan for the fundamental reorganization of the sugar industry as the key to reconstruction, a plan which Tugwell, Muñoz, and other New Dealers found to their liking. In April, Tugwell, who was then assistant secretary of agriculture, brought this plan to the attention of his superiors with some additions of his own. All the proposals shared some basic features: the diversification of agriculture; the creation of a group of small, independent farmers; the breakup of the large sugar corporations through enforcement of the 500-acre restriction of the Organic Acts; promotion of new industries appropriate to the island, such as fishing and forestry; and achievement of a more reasonable balance between the island's purchasing and producing powers.[33]

On the basis of reports by Tugwell, Mrs. Roosevelt, and the AAA administrator for Puerto Rico, James A. Dickey, all of whom stressed the special situation in Puerto Rico and the critical need for much more than relief aid, President Roosevelt authorized the formation of a Puerto Rican Policy Commission (PRPC) to study the island's particular needs and to formulate an integrated plan for economic rehabilitation, revitalization, and reconstruction. Chardón and two other Puerto Ricans were appointed to the commission. Muñoz Marín, while not a member (though he had asked to be appointed), was permitted to participate in the hearings and meetings, which were held in May and June 1934 in Washington, to avoid interference from local special interests, especially the sugar corporations. The specific purpose of the PRPC, as stated in the presidential directive, was to determine how to make use of the revenues from the AAA's processing tax. But the commission's report, drawn up in

---

1932 elections. But he was also a practical and political man who was interested in seeing Puerto Rico develop economically. It may have been that independence, up until the advent of the New Deal, seemed the only way to solve the island's economic problems. For Muñoz, the New Deal must have been viewed as a means by which to attain the level of economic development necessary for a self-sustaining and viable independent economy. He was one of the island's foremost New Deal supporters, was privy to most key decisions, and had the ear of leaders at the highest levels in Washington.

[33] Mathews, *Puerto Rican Politics,* pp. 151–52, 156–58, 162–63. Tugwell also favored a birth-control program, something Puerto Ricans delicately avoided suggesting. The question of "overpopulation" will be taken up in chap. 5. It dominated the thinking of many North Americans, who often saw excessive reproduction as the major problem confronting the island.

June 1934 and known popularly (and sometimes unpopularly) as the Chardón Plan, went far beyond that limited scope and became the basis for future reconstruction plans and the center of debate and controversy for much of the remainder of the decade.

Starting from the premise that economic reconstruction was possible without any fundamental political or institutional change in the existing colonial framework, the Chardón Plan proposed a reorientation of the economy via the development of appropriate industries, relocation of small farmers to better and more productive land, the purchase of at least one sugar central to be run by the government, and increased emigration. The objectives of the plan were to reduce unemployment; to end the monopoly of land, especially by absentee corporations; to reduce the flow of profits, interest, and dividends going to the United States; and to diversify the productive structure of the economy.[34]

The heart of the Chardón Plan was its recommendations for the sugar industry, but before turning to that in detail, it will be useful to consider briefly some of its other points. Greater industrial development was to be encouraged and was to be concentrated in labor-intensive production or in production using agricultural raw materials that either were already produced on the island or could readily be promoted. Sugar refining was to expand, displacing the export of raw sugar, and the commission also suggested the canning of fruit and vegetable products; the bottling of fresh orange juice for export; the use of bagasse to make boards, paper, and similar products; the expansion of shoe, furniture, and ceramic production; the manufacture of a variety of containers to be used in local industry; and the promotion of tourism from the mainland. Also recommended was the production of an alcohol-gas blend that would use sugar waste and would be less expensive than gasoline alone—a remarkably farsighted proposal (and one which was ignored). In the broadest sense, what the Chardón Plan urged was the building of industry around labor, which was plentiful, and an emphasis on developing products related to sugar and other agricultural crops, which could broaden and deepen the local industrial base. Protective tariffs were recommended for these infant industries, though they were to be phased out after an initial period or, if the tariffs were retained, the firms so protected were to be regulated as public utilities.[35] Besides initial tariff protection, tax credits were to be offered to attract industry, the amount of the credits to depend upon the company's labor bill—that is, upon its specific and direct contribution to the generation of employment—and on the nature of the industry.[36]

[34] Ibid., pp. 173–74, and PRPC, *Report.*
[35] PRPC, *Report*, pp. 63–69, 74.
[36] Ibid., p. 2.

152   CHAPTER THREE

The Chardón Plan also made recommendations for the revitalization of
coffee production as a means of rural relief and assistance, and it called
for greater attention to citrus and tobacco cultivation. In both the coffee
and the tobacco regions, which had been to an important extent the domain of the small farmer, it was suggested that subsistence farms be
created by extending government assistance to former producers who had
been forced to migrate in search of work after these commodities had lost
their importance as income-producing crops.[37]

But it was in its vision for the future of the sugar industry that the
Chardón Plan was both at its boldest and its most threatening to powerful
economic interests. Under the plan, the government was to buy the most
productive, primarily corporate, sugar lands and redistribute them to small
colonos who were working marginal, low-productivity land. The land
vacated by the colonos was to be permanently withdrawn from cane production; subsistence farms were to be created on them and offered to the
landless sugar workers displaced by the redistribution of the corporate
land. Thus, colonos would benefit by being relocated to more productive
land on which they could grow sugar cane, while landless agricultural
workers would gain by being able to provide for their own consumption
and would also contribute to the supply of locally grown food.

As if these proposals for purchasing or expropriating the huge corporate sugar plantations were not controversial enough, the Chardón Plan
also proposed that the government buy one or more centrals, the control
of which had been so important to the monopsony power of the sugar
corporations. These were to be operated as semipublic corporations, selling their output at cost plus a normal profit, and hence they could serve
as yardsticks, or benchmarks, for judging the appropriateness of the prices
and profits of the privately operated mills. The centrals not only were to
be self-financing; they would also have the added benefit of enabling the
government and the colonos to capture a part of the surplus and economic
rent being transferred to the United States by the absentee sugar companies. This surplus then would be available to the local economy for productive investments. Most of the funds to be used to purchase the centrals, and the corporations' sugar land, was projected to come from the
processing tax collected on sugar grinding.[38]

The attractions of the Chardón Plan for Puerto Rico's development and
control were broad and compelling, both economically and politically.
Land was to be distributed to the landless, and subsistence farms were to

[37] Ibid., pp. 38–53.
[38] Ibid., pp. 3, 12–14.

be created.[39] Colonos would be able to sell their cane to a semipublic corporation and would thus be assured of receiving a fair price. The existence of the "yardstick" centrals were expected to increase competition among the remaining private centrals, though an element of local monopsony, due to transportation problems, would remain. There would very likely be an increase in the return accruing to colonos selling to private centrals as well, since they would have to offer higher prices to attract colono cane. Conversely, it was expected that the privately owned centrals would earn smaller profits, with obvious benefits to consumers and to resource allocation in general. The surplus of revenues above costs remaining to Puerto Ricans would be increased, at least initially, and thus the volume of funds available for locally controlled investment and development would be substantially enlarged.

The Chardón report estimated that land redistribution would result in a net reduction in unemployment of 17,000 persons and that, at a maximum, industrialization might provide an additional 50,000 jobs. The plans for coffee, fruit, and tobacco rehabilitation would absorb perhaps another 10,000 to 20,000 of the unemployed, but these were generous and long-term estimates, and since 150,000 heads of families were then out of work, a great deal of unemployment would remain.[40] As a solution, the commission proposed encouraging emigration by developing "mass colonialization projects in under-populated regions of tropical countries similar to Puerto Rico. . . . These emigrants should go to settle farm lands, not to be exploited as wage laborers."[41] Although such "colonialization" projects were never carried out, the belief that it was impossible to employ the total labor force within the structure of the island economy certainly underlay the thinking and the policy proposals of the commission.

Land redistribution required that large landholdings be broken up. The report suggested two ways of achieving this: (1) The 500-acre clause of the Jones Act could be enforced, though the commission recognized that

---

[39]The report did not neglect the details of how these were to be formed. Each subsistence farm (of about ten cuerdas) was to be supplied with a house, a shed, and livestock. Payment was to be made by the new owners over a period of twenty-three years, with no payment of principal during the first three years and exemption from property tax during the first five years. Farms were to be located in communities of 250 houses and were to be under the direction of an agrarian specialist to ensure their viability. Four cuerdas of the land were to be used for pasture and food production for the livestock, two cuerdas for subsistence-crop production, and the remaining four cuerdas for cash-crop production. The value of each farm, including house and livestock, was estimated to be $1,000: ibid., pp. 17–18, 21.

[40]Ibid., p. 4.

[41]Ibid., pp. 6–7.

doing so might be quite disruptive to the economy. (2) The Jones Act could be modified so as to: (a) prohibit any future acquisition of land by corporations already owning 500 acres or more; (b) create a fund that would allow the government to purchase land exceeding the 500-acre restriction when offered for sale by its current owners; and (c) authorize the insular government to exercise its right of eminent domain at three-year intervals in order to acquire 10 percent of the area of all farms over 500 acres, until such time as redistribution was completed.[42] These proposals aroused terror in the offices of the sugar corporations.[43]

THE PRRA

The proposals contained in the Chardón Plan were not immediately made public, nor was the plan approved by the secretary of agriculture, whose approval was required since the plan proposed the use of revenues from the agricultural processing tax. However, President Roosevelt, who was given an outline of the plan, accepted it in principle, and he proceeded to approve the creation, on June 16, 1934, of an Inter-Departmental Committee for the Economic Rehabilitation of Puerto Rico, which implied to many that the Chardón Plan was to be implemented. The Inter-Departmental Committee, one of whose members was Tugwell, also was charged with the responsibility of coordinating all federal programs on the island.[44]

The subsequent fate of the Chardón Plan is a tale of intrigue and deception, in which the sugar interests did everything possible to prevent its implementation—from defaming the character of the plan's supporters to "influencing" the members of a supposedly independent and objective team of investigators who had come to Puerto Rico to study the feasibility of putting the plan into operation.[45] Among other roadblocks, legal questions and complications were raised concerning the possibility of creating the semipublic corporation that would operate the centrals and about the proper use of the sugar-processing tax.[46] At the end of 1934, no substan-

[42] Ibid., p. 32.

[43] The sugar corporations had had a hint of what was to be in the report, since Chardón had already revealed his hand in the briefing for Eleanor Roosevelt (and Tugwell) in March 1934. They were quick to mobilize their resources to block any effort to implement the Chardón Plan.

[44] Mathews, *Puerto Rican Politics*, pp. 173–74. President Roosevelt declared his support for the Chardón Plan on a visit to Puerto Rico in July 1934 and again in a radio broadcast on December 22, 1934, from Washington, with a translation read in Spanish by Muñoz Marín. From all evidence, the president seemed committed to the plan.

[45] Ibid., chaps. 5 and 6, presents several stories of the maneuvers of the powerful. Their attempts to either control or prevent the implementation of the Chardón Plan included machinations by Santiago Iglesias.

[46] Ibid., pp. 197–99 and chap. 6.

tial progress toward economic rehabilitation or toward implementation of the Chardón Plan had been made; even President Roosevelt's influence seemed not to have any effect. In part, the struggle was over whether the reorganization should be locally or federally directed, but it was the question of who was going to benefit from and who was to pay for the reorganization which dominated and shaped the debate. At stake, in other words, were fundamental conflicts of class interests. The struggle—among local forces in Puerto Rico, among federal agencies in Washington, between the PRERA and Washington—was often unscrupulous and heedless of facts.

Finally, to get the new development strategy moving, President Roosevelt created, by executive order on May 28, 1935, a Puerto Rican Reconstruction Administration (PRRA) and appointed Ernest Gruening to head it. At last, or so it seemed, there was in place an agency committed to long-term economic and social reconstruction on the island.[47]

But the PRRA's success was limited. Gruening asked for $75 million to finance the agency, but he received only $35 million and a promise from President Roosevelt for more later. Furthermore, the PRERA was made a temporary subdivision of the PRRA, so that a portion of the $35 million had to be directed to relief, the PRERA's primary responsibility, rather than to reconstruction, the PRRA's principal function[48] This dilution of funds certainly hampered the new agency's effectiveness during its first year of operation, as did the political attacks leveled against it by the Republican-Socialist coalition.[49]

The PRRA did realize some achievements. Perhaps its most important project was an island-wide electrification program; not only did this improve living conditions, but it was also an essential first step in any attempt to increase the degree of industrialization. Producer associations for coffee and fruit were organized to assist in the rehabilitation of these crops and to raise the incomes of small farmers, and a model coffee farm was organized in 1937 on Hacienda Castañer. Health care was improved; rural clinics were established and preventive disease programs were initiated. Some families actually were relocated on small (five-to-ten-acre) farms, and a few rural communities with new cement houses in place of the old wooden ones, were begun. A program of reforestation was inaugurated and another to combat soil erosion. Rural educational facilities

---

[47] Ibid., pp. 223–25.

[48] Ibid., pp. 228, 234–35. The PRERA's life was extended until June 1936, after which it ceased to exist.

[49] Because of their opposition, coalition supporters did not receive many jobs in the PRRA, while Liberal party supporters, who were in favor of the Chardón Plan, made up most of the agency's payroll. This was a constant source of tension.

156

were improved and extended to more areas. The PRRA designed and
built a cement plant, which later was sold to the government, and it
undertook feasibility studies for such industries as bottle and cardboard
manufacture, which would use local products or by-products, though these
studies were not acted upon until government-sponsored industrialization
began in the mid-1940s.[50] The PRRA made an important contribution to
the reduction of unemployment; in 1936, it employed about 60,000 persons, equivalent to roughly one-half the number of people employed in
the sugar industry.[51] However, many of its programs were experimental
and never went beyond that stage. When the PRRA's money ran out in
the late 1930s, these programs simply disappeared, leaving no permanent
legacy.[52]

The fulcrum of reconstruction as conceived by Chardón and others
was, of course, the sugar industry, and in this critical area, the record of
the PRRA was poor. The plan to have the government purchase a mill
encountered funding problems, legal roadblocks, and objections in the
U.S. Senate, which echoed the sentiments of the sugar corporations that
such an entity would constitute "unfair competition" for the private centrals.[53] One legal complexity, for example, arose out of the proposal to
move colonos from marginal land to more productive plantation lands.
Most colono land was heavily mortgaged, having been used as collateral
for obtaining loans, or else title to the land was not clear at all. How
were transfers involving such encumbered landholdings to be carried out?
Without a change in the legal status of these small farms, or some mechanism for paying off the debts, the proposed land redistribution could not
be accomplished on any significant scale. For similar reasons, the proposal for the semipublic central was altered and diluted so many times
that by the time a working project emerged, the colonos who were expected to gain most from it had withdrawn their support.[54]

[50] Hanson, *Transformation*, pp. 145–46.
[51] Quintero Rivera, "La base social," p. 50.
[52] Mathews, *Puerto Rican Politics*, pp. 243, 282–83, 323–24. In mid-1937, funds were
cut back, and in 1939, the PRRA received only $7 million. Some aspects of the PRRA's
activities (e.g., health care, sanitation, and education) were then turned over to the local
government, but the lack of funds at that level led to reductions in service, anyway. In
November 1938, the PRRA handled 222,606 direct relief cases, which provided aid to
1,121,935 persons, or more than 60 percent of the population. Appropriations for the PRRA
were ended by Congress in 1941, by which time some $72 million had been spent: Perloff,
Puerto Rico's Economic Future, p. 31.
[53] One senator expressing this view was Millard Tydings, who later played a prominent
role in legislation affecting Puerto Rico: Mathews, *Puerto Rican Politics*, p. 283.
[54] The project began in 1937 in the form of a cooperative at Central Lafayette in southeast
Puerto Rico, with some 10,000 owned cuerdas and an additional 8,000 leased. Land not

Another test of the reconstruction plan was its ability to deal with the 500-acre law. This law had always been somewhat of an anomaly, stating a policy but failing to provide any enforcement powers or other measures to obtain compliance. Moreover, it seemed to be an infringement on the rights of ownership of private property, the fundamental basis of a capitalist economy, and was also a restriction unknown in the United States or in its other territories. Foreign and domestic corporations had circumvented it in a number of ways, for example by holding land under the names of private individuals or in partnerships, though just as often they violated it quite openly (see table 2.7). But no legal steps had ever been taken against any corporation for violating the law; indeed, despite periodic rhetorical outbursts, it was not until the Chardón Plan that there was any serious threat to enforce it.

Even prior to the creation of the PRRA, and frustrated by the delays involved in getting the Chardón Plan into operation, Gruening thought he had found a means of initiating enforcement of the 500-acre limitation. In March 1934, United Porto Rico Sugar was sold to the National City Bank of New York, which had branches in Puerto Rico. United Porto Rico had sustained three continuous years of losses beginning in 1930, and prices of its stock had plummeted as a consequence. It was reorganized by new owners as Eastern Sugar Associates, but the new corporation ran into difficulties in trying to register its extensive landholdings. Gruening decided that this would be the appropriate time to attempt to apply the 500-acre limitation, to convince the U.S. corporations especially, and also the Puerto Rican people, that the legislation was not a dead letter. His strategy was to initiate quo warranto proceedings against

used for pasture was divided among former laborers and colonos into 314 farms of various sizes, most of them between five and ten cuerdas. The grinding mill was operated cooperatively. The Asociación Azucarera Cooperativa Lafayette had been organized the year before to operate the project; it was to pay the PRRA the purchase price of $1.3 million over a twenty-year period. One difficulty the project ran into was that the farmers could not borrow, since they did not own the land and could offer no collateral. A second cooperative, Los Caños, was later organized in Arecibo with 24 persons: Mathews, *Puerto Rican Politics*, p. 284; Gayer, Homan, and Jones, *Sugar Economy*, chap. 17; Sánchez Dergan, "La industria azucarera," pp. 34–35. Lewis, *Puerto Rico*, p. 128, attributes the failure of the Lafayette project to a lack of funding, but it was much more complex than that. The Chardón Plan was virtually impossible to carry out, with money or without, because of the existing power relations and organization of the socioeconomic system. Economic reconstruction was defeated not by a lack of money, though there never was enough, but first and foremost by resistance from the powerful classes, who were able to defeat any plans for substantive change. The Chardón Plan was not a socialist plan, as was often charged, but its redistributive character was radical enough to arouse the concerted opposition of vested interests.

Eastern Sugar Associates in the Puerto Rican Supreme Court.[55] Gruening
asked the governor, Blanton Winship, to take the necessary legal steps,
but Winship did nothing. The attorney general in Puerto Rico, also a
North American, questioned the law on the ground of its supposed vague-
ness and suggested instead that the limit be extended from 500 to 6,000
acres, based on the efficiency considerations set forth in the Brookings
Institution report of 1930. Not only did the attorney general go beyond
his duties in even making such a suggestion, but he approached being
unethical when he attempted to obtain supporting evidence for his position from the sugar companies themselves. Ultimately, a special assistant
was appointed to the attorney general's office in March 1935 to make the
government's case, but nothing came of the effort, anyway.[56]

After the PRRA was created, it did not move toward enforcement of
the 500-acre law. In fact, it did not even have the power to do so. It was
not until January 28, 1936, that the first definitive action was undertaken,
when the Puerto Rican government filed a complaint against the Rubert
Hermanos Company in the Puerto Rican Supreme Court. This local corporation owned more than 12,000 cuerdas, and the complaint sought a
judgment and dissolution. Nearly two and one-half years later, on July
30, 1938, the court upheld the validity of the law and affirmed the right
of Puerto Rico to act to enforce compliance. On appeal, the U.S. District
Court of Appeals in Boston overturned this decision on September 27,
1939, but on March 5, 1940, the U.S. Supreme Court ruled in favor of
the origianal decision handed down by the Puerto Rican Supreme Court.[57]
This decision was to be key, not to economic reconstruction in the thirties, however, but to the plans of the new political party and government
which came to power in Puerto Rico in 1940.

EXTERNAL TRADE

The absolute level of exports and imports decreased in the early
depression years and did not return to its 1930 value until 1936, only to
record declines again in 1938 and 1939 (table 3.4). Imports fell more

[55] A quo warranto is "a demand made by the state upon an individual or corporation to
show by what right such individual or corporation exercises some franchise or privilege
appertaining to the state which, according to the constitution and laws of the land, cannot
be legally exercised in the absence of a grant of authority from the state": Anderson,
Ballentine's Law Dictionary, pp. 1049–50. In other words, quo warranto proceedings would
demand that the corporations show why they were not in violation of the Jones Act and
why they should not be subject to prosecution. See also Black et al., Black's Law Dictionary, p. 1131.

[56] Mathews, Puerto Rican Politics, pp. 161–62, 214–17.

[57] Hanson, Transformation, pp. 141–42.

TABLE 3.4
External Trade, 1930 to 1939

	Exports ($000,000)	Imports ($000,000)	% of Exports to U.S.	% of Imports from U.S.
1930	99.6	83.6	95.5	87.1
1931	98.4	76.4	96.4	89.0
1932	86.5	61.3	96.8	86.1
1933	75.4	54.7	97.3	89.4
1934	86.5	63.9	96.9	90.0
1935	79.7	70.0	97.4	90.9
1936	99.3	84.1	97.9	92.4
1937	115.0	98.9	98.2	91.3
1938	82.1	93.3	97.2	91.1
1939	86.5	82.7	98.0	91.5

SOURCE: Perloff, *Puerto Rico's Economic Future*, pp. 123, 407–8.

rapidly than exports, because of the drop in the island's income already noted. The 1928 and 1932 hurricanes adversely affected export values, and of course the United States, Puerto Rico's chief customer, was also experiencing reduced purchasing power, but the terms of trade, as measured by the ratio of average import prices to average export prices, were much worse for Puerto Rico in the thirties than they had been in the twenties and earlier (table 3.5). Export values fell in some years because of lower prices for Puerto Rico's exports rather than because of a drop in export volume. The unfavorable turn in the terms of trade meant, for example, that Puerto Rico needed to export 36.2 percent more in volume in 1937 to purchase the same quantity of imports as it did in 1910–14.[58] Nevertheless, Puerto Rico maintained a positive balance of trade for most of the 1930s. In fact, since 1913, it had had a positive balance of trade ever year but two (1924 and 1929), and in the century before 1940 it had had a negative balance only six times.[59] Beginning in 1940, however, imports would regularly exceed exports.

When table 3.4 is compared to table 2.10, what is especially striking is the increase in Puerto Rico's dependence on the U.S. economy. By 1939, all but 2 percent of Puerto Rican exports were sold to the United States and 91.5 percent of its imports were purchased from the United

[58] Quintero Rivera, "La base social," pp. 43–45. Because of the importance of imports in Puerto Rico, particularly of food and other consumer goods, they are sensitive to changes in income (i.e., elastic): Perloff, *Puerto Rico's Economic Future*, p. 124, and p. 125, chart 7.

[59] Perloff, *Puerto Rico's Economic Future*, p. 123, table 36, and p. 124.

TABLE 3.5
Index of Terms of Trade,
Selected Years, 1912–13 to 1939–40
(1935–39 = 100)

	Index[a]
1912–13	78.7
1914–15	62.1
1916–17	72.2
1919–20	51.9
1924–25	90.0
1929–30	108.7
1932–33	87.9
1934–35	104.8
1937–38	93.4
1939–40	90.4

SOURCE: Perloff, *Puerto Rico's Economic Future*, p. 135, table 38.
[a] Ratio of average import prices to
average export prices.

States. At the same time, the island had also become important to the
U.S. export trade: Whereas in 1923 it had been the ninth largest market
in the world for U.S. food exports, by 1935 it was the third largest; in
1900, it had been the twenty-sixth largest buyer of total U.S. exports,
and in 1936 it was the seventh largest. Because of this high level of
dependence ("practically all" of Puerto Rico's clothes and at least half
of its food supplies came from the United States), and because of the
common tariff structure, Puerto Rico was also a more stable market for
U.S. exports than many other countries. Between 1929 and 1933, U.S.
exports to the island declined 14 percent in volume and 42.5 percent in
value, while sales to other countries fell by 47 percent in quantity and
68.5 percent in value.[60] For much of its Spanish past, the island had been
little more than a strategic military location; it continued to play that role
for the United States in protecting the Panama Canal and the sea lanes,
but it was also becoming important as a market for U.S. exports and
hence as a source for realizing corporate profits. This economic role was
to become even more important in the future.

THE NATIONALIST PARTY AND THE LABOR MOVEMENT

The Great Depression created the climate for growing dissatisfaction
with U.S. colonial control and absentee ownership, but it is equally true

[60] Smith, *Puerto Rico's Trade*, pp. 8, 25, and p. 23, table 7.

that the nationalist movement in Puerto Rico was an important force for change in the colonial relationship. This has not always been well understood, and the Nationalist party either has been roundly condemned as backward-looking or romanticized to excess.[61] The Nationalists openly and forcefully challenged the legal and moral basis of U.S. colonial rule, and they did so in ways that provoked a serious reaction from the United States. Perhaps it was coincidental that the demise of the New Deal reconstruction program in Puerto Rico occurred at this time, but it seems more likely that it was connected with attempts to suppress the Nationalists.[62]

The Nationalist party (Partido Nacionalista, or PN) had been formed in September 1922 by a group of dissidents who left the Union party out of opposition to its acceptance of a new annexionist formula and the elimination of independence from the political program.[63] The Nationalist party's primary goals were independence and the creation of a sovereign Republic of Puerto Rico. It was not until the 1930s, however, that the party became a leading player in the island's history. Until then, it was nearly inactive, except in some towns and municipios. But on May 12, 1930, the party members elected Pedro Albizu Campos as their president, and with that act, the PN began to make a name for itself, not just in Puerto Rico but on the world stage.

Albizu Campos had joined the PN in 1924, after leaving the Union party when it had allied itself with the conservative, pro-statehood Republican party. In 1926, he was commissioned by the party to make an extended visit (it lasted some two and one-half years) to the Dominican Republic (Santo Domingo), Haiti, Cuba, Mexico, Panama, Venezuela, and Peru, where he came in touch with political leaders and the works and ideas of other nationalist and anti-imperialist thinkers.[64] By the time

[61] The former position can be found in Lewis, *Puerto Rico*, p. 136. Traditional histories of Puerto Rico condemn the Nationalists not only as backward but also as a fringe group of ill-motivated and discontented terrorists. (That was also the position of the U.S. government at the time.) Other historians have created, or perpetuated, myths about the Nationalists that make them seem larger than life; this view is seen, for example, in Maldonado-Denis's introduction to P. Albizu Campos, *La conciencia nacional*, and in Peoples Press, *Puerto Rico*. A more balanced treatment can be found in Silén, *Albizu Campos*. Mattos Cintrón, *La política y lo político*, pp. 73–93, develops an interesting case for the impact of the Nationalists on the New Deal.

[62] Mattos Cintrón, *La política y lo político*, pp. 76, 84, actually refers to the early thirties as the "first stage" of the New Deal, which ultimately ended in failure because of the actions of the Nationalists.

[63] Silén, *Historia*, p. 174. Interestingly, what the Union party had approved was a formula to create a permanent U.S. protectorate in Puerto Rico, to be known as the Estado Libre Asociado—which became the official name for the commonwealth status adopted in 1952. In 1932, the Union party was reorganized as the Liberal party.

[64] L. de Albizu Campos, *Albizu Campos*, pp. 27–33; P. Albizu Campos, *La conciencia nacional*, pp. 17–20; and Silén, *Albizu Campos*, pp. 20–35.

of his return from this official pilgrimage early in January 1930, Albizu had become a militant and outspoken supporter of the anticolonial struggle. This was not an entirely new political position for him: Albizu, or Don Pedro, as he came to be commonly known, had shown his distaste and contempt for U.S. rule before, as for example on one occasion in 1925 when he removed a number of small American flags from an assembly stand where he was speaking. As early as 1924, his public statements were taking on a more militant tone,[65] but his greater outspokenness and more open renunciation of U.S. colonialism were heightened and solidified by the contacts he made with other Latin American movements. There has been much speculation about possible other reasons why Albizu, a Harvard Law School graduate who had been in the Reserve Officers Training Corps and had served briefly in the U.S. Army, became radicalized—the racism he encountered at Harvard, his admiration for the Irish struggle, the influence of his Peruvian wife[66]—but it is sufficient to know that he and the party he headed became dedicated enemies of U.S. colonialism in Puerto Rico, advocating armed struggle as the necessary means of liberating the island.

The Nationalist program followed in the tradition of Latin American nationalism and populism. It was determinedly anticolonial and anti-imperialist, but it was neither anticapitalist nor prosocialist. It rejected foreign domination of Puerto Rico's resources, politics, and labor in favor of ownership and power vested in Puerto Ricans. But the party made no demands for a reorganization of the economic structure beyond the transfer of ownership of the means of production to Puerto Rican capitalists.[67] Albizu argued that the Treaty of Paris, which had transferred sovereignty from Spain to the United States, was null and void; it had been imposed on Puerto Ricans without their consent or participation. Hence, Albizu reasoned, all instruments of U.S. power and domination—all institutions, laws, and offices in Puerto Rico—existed illegally. He proposed the convening of a constituent assembly, which would decide, unilaterally, Puerto Rico's future status.

The Nationalist demand for an independent Puerto Rico with Puerto Rican instead of foreign capitalists represented the interests of those Puerto Ricans—displaced or threatened small landowners, professionals, intellectuals, and others—whose economic base and social position were being

[65] Silén, *Albizu Campos*, pp. 21–22, 25.

[66] Ibid., pp. 26–29.

[67] P. Albizu Campos, *La conciencia nacional*, pp. 21–22, n. 1. The nationalist program did call for distribution of land to the landless, but this was far from being a radical demand for the time and was indeed something that, as was seen above, the Chardón Plan and the Department of the Interior also proposed. See also Maldonado-Denis, *Puerto Rico*, pp. 118–19.

eroded by U.S. political and economic domination. The PN did not put forward a program for agricultural recovery or on behalf of industrial workers but focused instead on the ideological and almost mystical, albeit appealing, conceptions of *la familia puertorriqueña* and *la patria* (the fatherland). Albizu was not concerned with classes or class conflicts; rather, he emphasized the community of Puerto Ricans as Puerto Ricans, believing that their common experience alone was sufficient to bind them together.

The depression of the 1930s gave the Nationalist Party its forum. Given the deteriorating living conditions, the patriotic plea of the PN found a wider audience than it would have had in the more stable, though still difficult, 1920s. Its message of nationalistic pride and economic and political independence seemed an attractive alternative to the traditional parties' subservience. Independence, the Nationalists promised, would bring economic autonomy, political self-determination, and personal dignity. In the terrible thirties, these promises reached a desperate and responsive constituency, which extended far beyond the electoral arena.

THE SUGAR STRIKES

As discussed above, conditions for workers had worsened in the early part of the decade, and sugar workers, who formed the largest part of the agricultural work force, suffered along with the rest. The sugar companies claimed that, because of the depression, they could not afford to pay even as much as before. Strike activity increased (see table 3.6), especially when the FLT seemed to be less and less on the side of the workers and increasingly in favor of industrial peace and cooperation, a movement that was accelerated when the Socialist party, with which the FLT was closely allied, joined the governing coalition after the 1932 election. From July to December 1933, there were eighty-five strikes or actions by workers in tobacco, sugar, needlework, baking, and transport, and on the docks, and by *publico* drivers. (The publico is a private automobile operated along a regular route by an independent driver-owner.) These strikes were directed not only against employers but also against the government for failing to do anything to alleviate unemployment and suffering. Workers at Central Monserrate, for example, went on strike to protest their wage of 50 cents a day for twelve hours or more of work with no time allowed for lunch. A common complaint of workers on the large farms was that the company store often sold inferior products at inflated prices and that the workers were often paid in kind or in script, rather than in cash, thus obliging them to make their purchases at the company store.[68]

[68] Silvestrini de Pacheco, *Los trabajadores*, pp. 55, 62, 66–67. Merchants sometimes joined the workers in demanding an end to this system, since cash payment of wages would increase their own sales: Bird, *Sugar Industry*, pp. 54–56, and Taller, *Huelga*, chap. 2.

TABLE 3.6
Strike Activity from 1931–32 to 1936–37

	No. Strikes	No. Workers Involved
1931–32	10	3,355
1932–33	14	13,594
1933–34	18	33,333
1934–36	—	50–60,000
1936–37	40[a]	13,119

SOURCES: Gayer, Homan, and Jones, *Sugar Economy*, p.
223, table 101; PRDL, *Annual Report, 1936–37*, pp. 62–63.
[a] Includes "conspiracies."

However the sugar industry was extremely difficult to organize. There
was a large and growing surplus of landless workers who had few if any
opportunities for other kinds of work, so that employers could replace
strikers out of the pool of the unemployed. During the dead season on
the haciendas, many workers migrated elsewhere or were simply unemployed. Government efforts to enforce protective labor legislation were
weak and ineffectual when they conflicted with the wishes of the sugar
companies, even when a Socialist party member, Prudencio Rivera Martínez, was heading the Department of Labor. In fact, government policy
was strongly influenced by the sugar corporations to begin with.

The FLT did try to organize the sugar workers, but its efforts were
less than overwhelming and any *convenio* or agreement rarely lasted into
the next season, so each year the difficult process of organizing had to
begin anew.[69] Even when convenios were ratified, the companies did not
always comply with them, the government did not always act to enforce
compliance, and even the FLT sometimes failed to support its members
in their efforts to get the companies to abide by the agreements. This
failure of the FLT leadership to stand behind its membership provoked
discontent with the union and with the Socialist party and was one cause
of the major sugar strike of 1934.[70]

On December 6, 1933, the workers of Central Coloso struck for higher
wages. The strike spread quickly to other corporate mills, including Central Guánica, the largest on the island, at the critical time when they were
being prepared for the upcoming cane harvest. The island's chief of po-

[69] In 1934, the FLT represented a total of 50,337 workers in many different industries,
including sugar. But there were some 125,000 sugar workers alone, which gives some
indication of the limited extent of organization in the sugar industry by the FLT: Taller,
Huelga, pp. 13–14.
[70] Galvin, "Early Development," pp. 25–26.

lice, E. Francis Riggs, made special police protection available to the
centrals to maintain "industrial peace" and also intervened personally,
talking to workers in an effort to bring the strike to an end.[71] Labor
Commissioner Rivera Martínez initiated negotiations with the company—
but, significantly, not with the workers—to try to settle the strike, while
the FLT attempted to negotiate a contract with the sugar corporations that
would cover workers in the entire industry for the first time. The FLT
was successful in obtaining such a convenio, and it was signed on January 5, 1934, by the Unión de Trabajadores Agrícolas de Puerto Rico
(Union of Agricultural Workers), a part of the FLT, and the Asociación
de Productores de Azúcar de Puerto Rico (Sugar Growers Association).
The contract provided for a workday of eight hours for field workers and
twelve hours for mill workers; wages for cane cutters were to begin at 90
cents a day, while the most skilled mill workers were to receive $2.75.
Other elements of the convenio are listed in table 3.7.

The workers' reaction to this agreement, which had been made without
their participation or consultation, was swift and negative. They felt it to
be even worse than the status quo, because it called for minimum wages
lower than what many of them were already receiving and lower than
what they believed they needed. The union's explanation that the convenio prohibited the companies from reducing wages that were already
above the minimum did not console the workers, whose experience had
led them to distrust promises by the FLT to compel the companies to
abide by their word. Furthermore, the FLT had said it would demand an
eight-hour day for all workers, but the convenio retained the twelve-hour
shifts in the mills.[72]

The sugar workers were thus outraged both with the corporations and
the FLT, and on January 6, 1934, the day after the convenio had been
signed, they struck again. Beginning at Central Aguirre in Guayama, the
strike quickly spread to other centrals elsewhere on the island; twenty-
nine of the forty-one centrals were struck at one time or another. Other
unions lent their support and encouragement and as a result, the 1934
harvest was prevented from beginning on time.[73]

The sugar workers in Guayama organized their own union, the Asociación de Trabajadores de Puerto Rico (Workers' Association) to replace
the FLT.[74] The demands they presented to the operators of Central Aguirre

[71] Taller, *Huelga*, pp. 41, 58–59.
[72] Silvestrini de Pacheco, *Los trabajadores*, pp. 66–72. See the document in Quintero
Rivera, *Workers' Struggles*, pp. 132–40, esp. p. 135, and see also Mathews, *Puerto Rican
Politics*, pp. 139–40.
[73] Taller, *Huelga*, pp. 12, 19.
[74] Ibid., pp. 124–25.

TABLE 3.7
Provisions of Sugar Convenio of 1934

1. Work Day:

In the field, eight hours per day, and not more than forty-eight hours per week. In the mills, twelve hours per day; pay for hours over that amount is to be at time and a half. A Comité Conjunto de Patronos y Obreros (Joint Committee of Owners and Workers) is to be created to study the most practical means of moving toward an eight-hour day.

2. Hours of Work:

Work hours in the field are to be from 7 A.M. to 11 A.M. and from 12 P.M. to 4 P.M.

3. Minimum Daily Wages[a]:

Weeders	$0.80
Cane cutters	0.90
Cart drivers	1.00
Unskilled mill workers	0.90
Machinists	1.40
Mechanics and electricians	2.45
Carpenters and masons	2.75

4. Payment for work by the piece or job is abolished.

5. Form of Payment:

Wages are to be paid every Saturday after 1 P.M. and are to be in legal U.S. tender. Payment in stores or other establishments of the employer is prohibited, as are reductions in pay as a result of debt.

SOURCE: El Mundo, January 6, 1934, p. 7, as quoted in Taller, Huelga, pp. 186–90.

NOTE: There were five other provisions in the convenio, not shown here; the most important of these was one which guaranteed workers the right to organize.

[a] Selected categories only, for centrals located on the coast. Minimum wages for interior centrals were less by 5 to 10 cents a day at the lowest wages rates up to 25 cents at the highest. The minimums were not to affect any current wage that exceeded them. Mill wages greater than the minimum in the first week of the last harvest were to be increased by 10 percent. All wages were to be increased by 10 percent with each 25-cent increase in the price of sugar above $3.25. The minimums (but only the minimums) applied to both men and women.

were: payment in cash; no work day longer than eight hours; an end to piece and task work; and an increase of 40 percent in wages above prevailing wages, payment of time and a half for overtime, and equal pay for women throughout the wage scale.[75] This last demand, for equal pay

[75] Ibid., appendix B, pp. 190–91. A list of wages, ranging from $1.25 to $3.50, was also included.

for women at all levels, is especially interesting and revealing. First, it indicates the importance women were beginning to assume in the work force. Second, it suggests the greater participation of women in the union movement. And third, it indicates that this new independent union was relatively advanced, since its members were evidently able to put divisions of sex behind them to promote their common interests.

The workers at Guayama wired the Nationalist leader, Albizu Campos, on January 11, asking him to speak to them and to lead them. Albizu came, spoke to some 6,000 workers at a rally in Guayama, and then went on to Fajardo, Luquillo, Ponce, Toa Baja, and other places.[76] He promoted their cause in speeches and articles, and he encouraged them to be firm in their demands against both the owners and the FLT, but his efforts were unavailing. The strike ended when the workers, too poor to stay out any longer and confused by an FLT strategy of dividing them, returned to their jobs.[77] Little was done to apply even the convenio that had been signed, and in any case it did not last beyond that season.

It is not unfair to say that the sugar workers, increasingly aware of the class nature of their struggle, understood the underlying forces of the 1934 strike better than any of the established political and union leaders. However, the colonial administration and the powerful economic interests on the island recognized how much of a threat the strike had been to U.S. economic and political domination, and they feared what would happen if such a threat emerged again under different leadership. To avert that possibility, they developed a two-pronged strategy. First, there was an effort to improve conditions, initially through implementation of the Chardón Plan and then, when that collapsed, through creation of the PRRA. The plans for these measures began to be made early in 1934, not long after the sugar strikes. In 1935, the eight-hour day was enacted into law and a workers' compensation bill was passed to provide payments for job-related injuries or deaths.[78] Second, steps were undertaken to repress the Nationalists, who were believed to have stirred up the strikers and used their struggle to support the demand for independence. The failure of the Chardón Plan and the PRRA to get economic reconstruction under way has already been discussed. The violence directed against the Nationalists proved to be an obstacle to reconstruction as well.

---

[76] Taller, *Huelga*, pp. 14, 123, 134, 139, 183.

[77] The strike ended at different centrales at different times, some as early as mid-January, though it was not unusual for new protests to break out afterward for short periods. For the most part, however, the sugar strike of 1934 was over by early February.

[78] A bill to provide unemployment insurance was also approved by the lower house but did not receive final approval: PRDL, *Annual Report, 1936–37*, pp. 22, 25–26.

THE NATIONALIST CHALLENGE

For most of 1933, the colonial administration was under constant attack from all sides. The year has been dubbed "Gore's Hell," not out of sympathy for the governor but because of the problems and controversy he caused.[79] Gore was replaced in 1934 by General Winship, who was chosen specifically because of his military experience; he was expected to rule with a firm hand over conditions that were more disorderly than they had been since the beginning of U.S. control.[80] He met the expectations. It was he who appointed E. Francis Riggs, also a former military officer, as island police chief, and he also increased the numbers and arms of the insular police force. Winship was evidently preparing for a battle.

The first encounter occurred on October 24, 1935, near the University of Puerto Rico campus in Río Piedras. Students had planned a meeting to protest allegations made in a speech by Albizu Campos about their patriotism and masculinity. The police placed guards at the entrances to the campus to prevent any disturbances by Nationalist party members who might try to disrupt the meeting. A car in which a number of young Nationalists were riding, allegedly with bombs, was intercepted near the campus; on the way to the police station, with the police riding on the running boards, a gunfight ensued in which four youths (and one bystander) died. Albizu and the PN vowed revenge at their graves, and on February 23, 1936, Colonel Riggs was assassinated.[81] Two young Nationalists, Hiram Rosado and Elías Beauchamp, were accused of his murder and were taken to the San Juan jail. There, supposedly in an escape attempt, they too were killed.[82]

The repercussions from this series of events extended far beyond the question of the violation of rights, as serious as that was; the entire re-

---

[79] Mathews, *Puerto Rican Politics*, chap. 3, covers this most disgraceful period, in which Gore raised the incompetence and holier-than-thou attitude that had characterized most U.S. governors to a new level.

[80] Even the usually tolerant and understanding James Beverly, who was serving as acting governor early in 1934, felt that political conditions called for a strong hand. It was he who suggested the appointment of General Winship: ibid., p. 112.

[81] Ibid., pp. 39, 249–50, and Silén, *Albizu Campos*, pp. 52–54. In 1932, Albizu had promised in a speech that if any Nationalist died at the hands of the police, the chief of police would pay with his life. It is of some interest to note that Riggs had been in St. Petersburg during the Bolshevik Revolution, and his car was used by Kerensky, the deposed prime minister, in his escape: Ross, *Uphill Path*, p. 47.

[82] The explanation was not widely accepted. In fact, the police involved were brought to trial, but four were acquitted and there was a mistrial in the case of the other. Governor Winship asked for a promotion for one of the officers, and when it was denied, he had him transferred to an easy position at La Fortaleza: Mathews, *Puerto Rican Politics*, p. 255.

construction project was placed in jeopardy, particularly when Muñoz Marín, who was close to the liberal U.S. administrators in Washington, was unwilling to condemn the killing of Riggs, as Gruening asked him to do, without a comparable statement from the U.S. government condemning the police for killing the two Nationalists in their custody. From that time on, Gruening cooled both toward Muñoz and toward the quest for economic recovery in Puerto Rico. Chardón, who had been regional director of the PRRA, was removed from that position, and other members of the Liberal party were also dismissed from their jobs in the agency, effectively depriving it of its most committed and talented workers and for all intents and purposes ending the PRRA's activities—which was probably what Gruening intended, as punishment for Muñoz's "disloyalty."

Further actions were taken against the Nationalists. Federal charges of "sedition and conspiring to overthrow the federal government" were brought against Albizu Campos and seven others in the wake of the Riggs assassination.[83] The first trial, held with a jury of seven Puerto Ricans and five North Americans, resulted in a hung jury. In a second trial, the jury consisted of ten North Americans and two Puerto Ricans, and it found the defendants guilty—by a vote of ten to two. Albizu Campos and the others were ultimately sent to the federal prison in Atlanta.[84]

Another consequence of the Riggs assassination was the introduction of a bill in Congress in 1936 to grant immediate independence to Puerto Rico if Puerto Rican voters expressed that as their preference in a referendum to be held in November 1937. Introduced by Senator Millard Tydings, who had nominated Riggs for island police chief and was a close friend, the bill had been discussed by President Roosevelt, Secretary Ickes, and Gruening, and very likely had been drafted by them. The bill provided for a transition to independence on terms favorable to the United States and excessively harsh for the island. For example, Puerto Rico would have become subject to full U.S. tariffs after a phase-in period of only four years.[85] To accept independence on such terms meant almost

---

[83] Besides Albizu, the other Nationalists brought to trial were Juan Antonio Corretjer, Erasmo Velázquez, Juan Gallardo Santiago, Julio H. Velázquez, Pablo Rosado Ortiz, Clemente Soto Vélez, and Luis Florencio Velázquez. The charge of sedition was brought because there was no evidence to show the accused were accomplices to murder and because as a federal charge it gave jurisdiction over the case to the U.S. judicial system rather than the Puerto Rican. Even the prosecutor thought the charges were improper and were designed simply to get a conviction against the Nationalists. The American Civil Liberties Union (ACLU) agreed with this opinion, contending that the trial was a political, not a criminal, prosecution: Ibid., pp. 251–52, 267–68, and Maldonado-Denis, *Puerto Rico*, pp. 124–25.

[84] P. Albizu Campos, *Obras escogidas*, pp. 9–10.

[85] Mathews, *Puerto Rican Politics*, pp. 253–61.

certain economic disaster;[86] to reject it, however, meant a tacit if not explicit acceptance of continued U.S. colonial domination. There were nevertheless many popular expressions of support for the bill, and several of the political parties (including the conservative Republicans, who actually hoped for the defeat of the independence proposal) conditionally expressed their support for a referendum while recognizing the onerousness of the bill's provisions.[87] However, Congress took no action on Tydings' proposal, and it died after the session adjourned. Gruening's desire to punish Puerto Rico subsequently took the form of the cutbacks in New Deal programs, which have already been discussed.[88] In effect, Puerto Rico's economy was cast adrift to founder on its own.

Out of this neglect by the colonial administration in Washington, reinforced by the turn of attention to preparations for war at the end of the decade, there emerged an opportunity for Puerto Ricans to begin to exercise a greater measure of local initiative and control over their own affairs. The intense struggles of the thirties weakened colonial rule and resolve sufficiently to raise the possibility that Puerto Ricans could capture greater local autonomy while remaining within the bounds of the colonial framework.[89] The Nationalists, whose leadership was in prison and whose ranks had been decimated by official violence, were not going to play a role in the efforts toward that end.[90] Yet there were others who were prepared to come forward to assume leadership of the fragmented society.

[86] Chardón declared, for example, that it would have resulted in a doubling or tripling in cases of starvation as markets that had developed because of the colonial relation were closed: Ibid., p. 258.

[87] The Liberal party came close to sending a message of support for the measure, but Muñoz Marín, who proposed a substitute and more favorable bill, was able to prevent this action. For Muñoz, acceptance of the Tydings bill during a period when so many Puerto Ricans depended on federal relief, which the bill would have ended, would have been political suicide. In fact, the Tydings bill did not really envision full independence; e.g., the U.S. was to retain certain rights over foreign affairs and the U.S. federal court was to retain its jurisdiction. What was proposed was to make Puerto Rico a protectorate, which would have been nothing more than a disguised form of colonialism. This alone should have been sufficient reason for independentistas to reject the bill; Mathews, *Puerto Rican Politics*, p. 256; García Passalacqua, "Muñoz Marín," p. 14; Silén, *Historia*, pp. 208–9; Lewis, *Puerto Rico*, p. 137.

[88] Tugwell commented that Gruening's "progressivism which, until this experience, had been largely literary, and so untested, melted quickly in the heat of tropical politics": *Stricken Land*, p. 5.

[89] This is, for example, the position of Navas Dávila, *La dialéctica*, p. 68, and Mattos Cintrón, *La política y lo político*, pp. 92, 99.

[90] Silén, *Albizu Campos*, p. 49, says that the Nationalists lost their chance of leadership even before the sugar strike: "La huelga del 34 es a todas luces el punto culminante del nacionalismo" (The 1934 strike is undoubtedly the culminating point of the nationalist movement).

TABLE 3.8
Quota for and Production of Puerto Rican Sugar, 1934 to 1939

	Quota (000 tons)	Production (000 tons)	Excess of Production over Quota (%)
1934	807	1,104	+37
1935	788	773	− 2
1936	909	926	+ 2
1937	847	996	+18
1938	816	1,077	+32
1939	807	852	+ 6

SOURCES: Sánchez Dergan, *La industria azucarera*, p. 43, table 1; Smith and Requa, *Puerto Rico Sugar Facts*, p. 115, table 1.

CHANGES IN PRODUCTION AND CLASS STRUCTURE

THE SUGAR INDUSTRY

On May 9, 1934, Congress passed the Jones-Castigan Law, which set quotas on the imports of sugar in order to reverse the price decline for U.S. sugar producers resulting from the glut of sugar on the world market. Puerto Rico's quota for 1934 was based on the proportion of total U.S. sugar purchases it had supplied during the period from 1925–1933. During that period, hurricane damage had reduced Puerto Rico's output, and the island had supplied only 12.4 percent of the U.S. market.[91] Based on projections of future demand, its 1934 quota was set at 802,842 tons of raw sugar, later revised slightly upward after some bargaining. The quota was established, however, well after the harvest had begun, and so actual production of sugar that year exceeded the quota by 37 percent. Quotas and production levels for the rest of the decade are shown in table 3.8.

An important part of the Chardón Plan, formulated with the quotas in mind, had been to convert to subsistence farming the marginal sugar lands cultivated by colonos. If the plan had been implemented, it would have eased the transition to the shrunken market the quotas imposed and would have shifted the impact of the decline mostly onto the sugar corporations. Instead, without the plan, the brunt of the change was borne by the colonos. The centrales would of course process cane from their own land

[91] By comparison, in 1935 Cuba provided 30.7 percent of U.S. sugar purchases: Gayer, Homan, and Jones, *Sugar Economy*, p. 71. Lewis, *Puerto Rico*, p. 130, suggests that the quotas were an effort to favor Cuba so as to increase U.S. exports to that country.

TABLE 3.9
Number and Size of Sugar Farms, 1929, 1935, 1938, and 1939

	No. Farms	Land Devoted to Sugar Cane (acres)	Average Size of Sugar Farm (acres)
1929	7,103	251,018	35.3
1935	7,693	299,384	38.9
1938	9,201	300,567	32.7
1939	11,381	303,055	26.6

SOURCE: Smith and Requa, *Puerto Rico Sugar Facts*, p. 122, table 10.

first, and only then would they grind colono cane, and only to the extent that corporate production fell short of the quota plus any local demand they supplied. The absence of the semipublic mill which the Chardón Plan had proposed meant that the colonos were at the mercy of the large private centrals.[92]

The imposition of quotas closed off any growth prospects for exports to the U.S. markets and made expanded investment in the sugar industry substantially less attractive, and the sugar strikes reinforced this outlook. The flow of investment capital to the island virtually halted in the thirties (though not only in the sugar industry). Ironically, however, the number of farms producing sugar cane increased throughout the thirties, and their average size declined (table 3.9), suggesting that even more marginal and less productive sugar land was being brought into production by colonos trying to eke out a livelihood in nearly the only industry that was viable, though even there earning a living was more and more difficult.

Despite the quotas, sugar was still the most important export crop at the end of the decade; it had, in fact, become relatively even more important. By 1940, sugar exports accounted for 62 percent of total export value, compared to 55.3 percent in 1931.[93] This was not due to any vitality in the sugar industry, but was the result of even more severe crises in other sectors of the economy. At the end of the thirties, exports were lower than they had been at the beginning of the decade (see table 3.4), so the larger share for the sugar industry at the end of the decade was of a smaller total amount of trade.

[92] In 1939, each central ground the cane of an average of 317 colonos; in 1898, each had ground cane for an average of only 7 colonos. This greater structural dependence is what gave the centrals their monopsony power: Smith and Requa, *Puerto Rico Sugar Facts*, p. 8.

[93] Perloff, *Puerto Rico's Economic Future*, p. 137, table 39.

TABLE 3.10
Percentage of Export Value by Commodity, 1931 and 1940

Commodity	1931	1940
Sugar and molasses	56.6	62.9
Tobacco	17.5	6.6
Needlework	14.2	1.6
Fruits	4.4	17.0
Coffee	0.6	0.5
Rum	a	6.0
Others	6.7	5.5
Total value	$98,401,000	$92,347,000

SOURCE: Perloff, *Puerto Rico's Economic Future*, pp. 136–37, table 39.

a An exact figure for the value of rum exports in 1931 is not available, and the amount is not included in the total, but rum exports did not become important until 1936.

THE TOBACCO INDUSTRY

With the shift in consumers' preferences from cigars to cigarettes, Puerto Rico's industry was adversely affected, since its tobacco for the U.S. market was used primarily for cigar production, and most of the leaf tobacco was shipped to the United States to be processed. From 1920 to 1933, U.S. per capita consumption of cigars declined by nearly one-half, and by 1940 cigar consumption was 38.5 percent below the 1920 level.[94] Puerto Rico's production of tobacco and cigars and exports of tobacco for filler and manufactured tobaccos fell to pre-1920 levels.[95] By 1940, exports of tobacco products were 6.6 percent of total export value, down from 19.3 percent of the total in 1921 and 17.5 percent in 1931 (table 3.10).

Puerto Ricans, too, were affected by changing consumption patterns. Whereas the island had been able to provide virtually all of the demand for cigarettes out of local sources early in the century, by 1922 only 73.2 percent of local demand was locally produced, and that figure declined further to 31.1 percent in 1930 and to 7.9 percent in 1937.[96] Meanwhile,

[94] Ibid., p. 92, and p. 93, table 22. In 1920, per capita consumption of cigars in the U.S. was 1.66 pounds; in 1930, it was 1.18 pounds; and in 1940, 1.02 pounds. Meanwhile, per capita consumption of cigarettes tripled, from 1.29 pounds in 1920, to 2.73 in 1930, and to 3.88 in 1940.

[95] Ibid., p. 89, chart 3, and Quintero Rivera, "La base social," p. 48, graph 3.

[96] Quintero Rivera, "La base social," p. 47, table 2. Quintero's figures come from a 1939 U.S. Department of Agriculture report.

TABLE 3.11
Coffee Production and Export, 1928, 1929,
and 1935 to 1939
(in thousands of pounds)

	Production	Exports
1928	32,393	7,838
1929	18,446	1,279
1935	8,000	800
1936	20,000	—
1937	20,536	—
1938	16,639	—
1939	18,949	—

SOURCES: Descartes, *Basic Statistics*, p. 26,
tables 3-7; PRDAC, *Statistics, 1934–35*, pp.
151, 152.

employment in tobacco manufacturing fell precipitously, from 7,543 in
1909–10, to 5,583 in 1919–20, and to but 539 in 1939–40.[97] Most affected by the decline in employment were women workers.

THE COFFEE INDUSTRY

Coffee exports, as can be seen in table 3.10, had "dwindled almost to
the vanishing point" by 1940.[98] Yet, as Perloff has pointed out, coffee
production remained an important cash crop for many small farmers of
the interior. Total coffee production actually remained relatively constant
over the decade (table 3.11), but most of this was destined for the local
market. The large decrease in output between 1929 and 1935 was the
result of the hurricanes in 1928 and 1932; in fact, between 1929 and
1934, Puerto Rico became a net importer of coffee. However, in a country where coffee drinking is nearly a national passion, production was
maintained for local consumption, and the area devoted to coffee remained greater than for all crops except sugar.[99] Nevertheless, at the end
of the decade, the production of coffee was less than half of the level of
44,194,219 pounds at which it stood in 1921, when exports still played
an important role.[100]

---

[97] Quintero Rivera, "La base social," p. 57, table 5.
[98] Perloff, *Puerto Rico's Economic Future*, p. 94.
[99] Ibid., pp. 93–94.
[100] PRDAC, *Statistics, 1934–35*, p. 151.

THE NEEDLEWORK TRADE

The needlework industry had begun to develop during and after World War I (see Chapter 2), and by 1930, needlework exports were third in importance by value (table 3.10). In terms of contribution to net income in manufacturing, textile products, primarily needlework, became second only to sugar refining: 22.1 percent of manufacturing net income in 1940 was generated in this sector, which was the manufacturing sector demonstrating the most "significant expansion" over the decade.[101] Much of the needlework involved adding simple designs, borders, and the like to products such as handkerchiefs manufactured in the United States and reexported for sale. Simple assembly and sewing were also commonly done.

Wages, hours, and working conditions in the needlework factories and workshops were very poor, and wages for the more than 40,000 workers who were employed at home were even worse. At the end of August 1933, women workers in Mayagüez, the center of the needlework industry, went on strike for better wages. In a clash with police and strikebreakers, two persons were killed, a woman and a three-year-old girl; seventy others were injured, including strikers and police. Such actions strengthened support among women workers for increased organization, and by 1934 at least 75 percent of the workers in the factories and shops were unionized, as were some 3,000 home workers, in nine unions organized by the FLT.[102]

The especially poor working conditions and low salaries in the needlework industry resulted in its becoming one of three industries in Puerto Rico subjected to a code of conduct under the NIRA, which was made applicable to the island in July 1934.[103] This code set a 44-hour work

[101] Ibid., p. 99. It is useful to know what was meant by "manufacturing" in the thirties. Perloff (*Puerto Rico's Economic Future*, pp. 99, 101) notes that "aside from the processing of a few agricultural products and the manufacture of a relatively small number of chemical, metal, wood, leather, stone, clay, and glass products, Puerto Rican manufacturing has been largely of a handicraft nature," and that "industrialization of the advanced type is extremely limited."

[102] Silvestrini, "La mujer puertorriqueña," pp. 80, 84–85.

[103] The NIRA was passed in June 1933. Its purpose was to raise wages and prices (i.e., "reflate" the economy) and to spread work by reducing the work week. A "code of fair practice" was to be prepared for each industry, governing wages, prices, and labor-management relations. Section 7A of the act was one of the most controversial, since it gave labor the right to bargain collectively, which was less than appealing to employers in either the U.S. or Puerto Rico. In effect, the NIRA "legalized price and production agreements that had been illegal under the antitrust laws," which were suspended. The NIRA was declared unconstitutional in May 1935, but the sections dealing with collective bargaining

week, and a minimum salary of $2.00 a week for home needleworkers and from $3 to $5 a week for workers in factories and workshops, depending upon whether labor was done by hand or by machine. This was, in fact, a restatement of existing policy. On June 9, 1919, minimum wages had been set by the Puerto Rican legislature at $4 a week for women under the age of 18 and $6 a week for women 18 and older. This policy was reaffirmed by the commissioner of labor in his 1937 report, though these wages did not apply to home needleworkers.[104]

CHANGES IN EMPLOYMENT

The number of workers involved in agriculture, forestry, and fishing (the latter two categories accounted for less than 0.5 percent of the sector) declined by 12.8 percent over the decade of the 1930s, while manufacturing employment grew by 2.6 percent (table 3.12). The most rapid growth in employment in absolute terms occurred in trade, services, and government—an increase of 30 percent, while total employment was growing but 2 percent. As an illustration of the importance of government employment, at the end of 1938, more than 50 percent of those who had graduated with degrees in business administration between 1931 and 1938 were employed by the public sector. On the other hand, 43.8 percent of the 1929 graduates from the University of Puerto Rico, and 55.6 percent of the 1930–31 graduates, were unemployed in 1932.[105] It cannot be said, however, that any changes in the class structure took place during the thirties beyond the trends already evident in the first decades of U.S. control.

POLITICAL DEVELOPMENTS

The most significant political development, besides the surge and then repression of the nationalists, was the emergence of the Popular Democratic party (Partido Popular Democrático, or PPD) at the end of the decade. It was to be this party, under the leadership of Luis Muñoz Marín, that would lay the base for the new model of capitalist development in the 1940s that promised to extract Puerto Rico from the economic morass of the 1930s while holding out renewed hope for autonomous develop-

---

and the rights of labor were passed as part of the Labor Relations Act (Wagner Act): Fite and Reese, *Economic History of the U.S.*, pp. 517–19, 524–25, and Robertson and Walton, *American Economy*, pp. 415–16, 494–95.

[104] Silvestrini, "La mujer puertorriqueña," p. 84, and PRDL, *Annual Report, 1936–37*, pp. 12–16.

[105] Quintero Rivera, "La base social," p. 61. There are no other reliable unemployment figures for the period.

TABLE 3.12
Employment by Sector, 1930 and 1940

	1930		1940	
Sector	Number Employed	% of Total	Number Employed	% of Total
Agriculture, forestry, and fishing	263,577	52.4	229,901	44.9
Sugar cane	—		123,886	24.2
Tobacco	—		18,171	3.5
Coffee	—		25,594	5.0
Other	—		62,250	12.2
Mining	364	0.1	1,181	0.2
Construction	12,766	2.5	16,037	3.1
Manufacturing	98,150	19.5	100,693	19.7
Sugar refining	11,446	2.3	19,731	3.9
Tobacco processing	15,508	3.1	6,121	1.2
Home needlework	42,122	8.4	44,731	8.7
Other textile	13,197	2.6	16,780	3.3
Other	15,877	3.2	13,330	2.6
Transportation and communication	17,137	3.4	20,238	4.0
Trade (wholesale and retail)	39,534	7.9	53,570	10.5
Finance, insurance and real estate	812	0.2	1,799	0.4
Services	55,736	11.1	65,989	12.9
Government	11,423	2.3	19,116	3.7
Other	3,260	0.7	3,690	0.7
Total	502,759	100.1	512,214	100.1

SOURCE: Perloff, *Puerto Rico's Economic Future*, p. 401.

ment. The breakdown of the 1930s gave rise to a situation in which the discontent with the prevailing order on the part of the majority of Puerto Ricans needed only to be unified to become a potent force. All the traditional parties, including the Socialist, seemed to be out of touch with the mass base of landless agricultural workers, the new core of factory workers, the threatened small landowners in tobacco, coffee, and sugar production, and the unemployed. The programs of the Liberal, Republican, and Socialist parties were more appropriate to an earlier period, before capitalist development had begun to alter the economy, the society, and its class structure. The Nationalists had never attracted mass support, probably because of their tactics, but their ideals of national pride and independence were no doubt attractive to many, and all parties except the Socialists had at some time included independence as a possible solution to the status question, though obviously with different degrees of emphasis and for different reasons.

The PPD was born of a rift within the Liberal party that became irreparable when the Tydings independence bill was introduced in 1936. First there was disagreement over what the Liberal party's response to the bill should be, and then there was disagreement over whether the party should participate in the 1936 local elections, which were likely to be viewed as a quasi referendum on independence. On both these questions, the head of the Liberal party, Antonio Barceló, and his chief rival within the party, Luis Muñoz Marín, were on opposite sides. Barceló, probably by virtue of his age as much as anything else, had a slight majority of party support, and on the question of whether to participate in the 1936 elections, Barceló's position won out over Muñoz's by a single vote, out of the 204 cast.[106]

Muñoz first formed a faction (Acción Social Independentista) within the Liberal party in September 1936, but the next year he was expelled from the party for his independent organizing actions. He then formed a rival party, the Partido Liberal Neto, Auténtico, y Completo (The Pure, Authentic, and Complete Liberal party), which in 1938 became the PPD, with Muñoz at its helm.[107]

The program of the PPD addressed the immediate needs of many who had suffered from developing capitalism and from the monocultural production of sugar, which had come to dominate the economy with such profound effects.[108] The traditional parties had long been preoccupied with the question of status—was the island to be a state, or independent, or to have some middle status?—without accomplishing much that concretely improved the lives of the majority of Puerto Ricans.[109] Muñoz

[106] Details of this power struggle can be found in Mathews, *Puerto Rican Politics*, chap. 8; Silén, *Historia*, pp. 210–23; and Muñoz Marín, *Memorias*, pp. 153–71.

[107] Silén, *Historia*, pp. 212, 220, 223; Bhana, *Status Question*, pp. 26–27, 33. The old Liberal party began to disintegrate after the split, a process that accelerated after Barceló's death in October 1938. Under its new leadership, independence as an alternative was dropped from its program, costing the party even more support: Mathews, *Puerto Rican Politics*, pp. 299, 307.

[108] See Quintero Rivera, "La base social," pp. 83–89, for a fuller discussion of the basis of the party's support.

[109] An exception to this was the Socialist party in its early years; it gained mass support among workers for its program of economic justice. However, over time, it was increas-

THE THIRTIES 179

had been a staunch and outspoken supporter of independence, but in his campaign in the 1940 elections, he declared that social and economic justice and economic rehabilitation would be the PPD's first priorities. As he put it, at that point, faced with crushing economic problems, status should not be an issue dividing Puerto Ricans.

If Puerto Rico ever was to be independent *and* prosperous, Muñoz argued, its economic structure must first be brought to the point where independence would be economically viable. Many observers interpreted this position as an abandonment of the goal of independence. Some, particularly the more radical writers, believe Muñoz was an opportunist bent on gaining power; the ideas he professed to believe in were thus subject to revision when more popular ones came along. Others believe he had always placed Puerto Rico's pressing economic problems ahead of the status question; it was just that, until the New Deal, he had never thought economic justice was possible without independence.[110] In any case, Muñoz and the PPD decided not to make status a principal concern and chose to focus instead on the problem of attempting to achieve economic justice within the existing political and economic structure of colonial domination.

For the agrarian and growing urban working class, for the small, semi-independent farmers, for the new professionals, and for all those who had suffered from four decades of unbridled capitalist expansion, the party's populist message and Muñoz's effort to gain the trust of the people offered the only hope in what had been a very bleak decade. At the same time, because the PPD put the status issue in the background, the party's emergence and growth did not threaten U.S. colonial hegemony. This could not have been but a welcome turn of events for the United States, since the PPD promised to channel the energies and angers stirred up by the Nationalists, the depression, and the absentee corporations in a direction that not only did not question the colonial relationship but that would work within it and strengthen it by pursuing economic recovery. It is unlikely that Muñoz or the PPD intended this result, but nevertheless the decision to accept the prevailing colonial relation would further cement that status if the PPD's program succeeded.

The PPD's slogan, "Pan, Tierra, y Libertad" (Bread, Land, and Liberty), and its promise of economic reconstruction struck a responsive chord among the disadvantaged. Muñoz focused their latent frustration on a very visible enemy: the foreign-owned sugar plantations. It was due to

---

ingly identified as an "American" party, and its decline was especially marked after the 1934 sugar strikes.

[110] Johnson, *Puerto Rico*, chap. 4, and Mathews, *Puerto Rican Politics*, pp. 292, 295.

them that the people lacked "bread, land, and liberty," and it was the corporations which corrupted the political process when it forced voters to sell their votes to keep their jobs and feed their families.[111] The PPD promised to rid the country of the worst evils of capitalist exploitation for which the absentee corporations were held responsible, to return the land to the people, and to restore the meaning of the vote.[112]

The PPD's populist program and rhetoric were anti-imperialist and anti-expansionist; they were not, however, anti-American or anti-capitalist. From the PPD perspective, Puerto Rico's problem was foreign political and economic domination, not the nature of the system itself, a position not very different from that of the Nationalists.[113] The PPD believed it possible to redirect capitalist growth in a progressive direction, more beneficial for Puerto Ricans, with the aid and protection of the United States acting in the best tradition of its democratic ideals.[114] That the United States had just gone through a period of violent official repression against the Nationalist party and that it had always had a tendency to consider its colonial subjects a bit less than "deserving" seem not to have dampened the faithful's beliefs. Perhaps at that time there seemed to be no other alternative to hoping for the benevolence of the United States; or perhaps, given the background of the PPD leaders as professionals who *had* benefited individually—in universities or while living and working in the

[111] Electoral corruption had been widespread. In the 1936 elections, closed-poll voting was instituted, in which all voters would go to their assigned polling place at a designated time, after which the doors would be closed and voters would then vote, one by one, as their names were called, until all had voted. This measure helped to stop multiple voting, but it did not prevent other abuses, especially the practice of buying votes for a couple of dollars or a pair of shoes. Muñoz campaigned against vote buying as the "theft of workers' democratic rights": Johnson, *Puerto Rico*, pp. 27–28, and Ross, *Uphill Path*, pp. 49–51.

[112] Muñoz promised "definitive enforcement of the 500-acre law, to distribute thousands of acres among workers and farmers, with the necessary facilities for their life on the land and for its cultivation": *El batey* (the PPD's campaign newspaper), March 1939, as quoted in Edel, "Land Reform" (October 1962): 30. The party's program was presented in a simple pamphlet, *Catecismo del pueblo* (People's Catechism); see Muñoz Marín, *Memorias*, pp. 265–67. For discussions of the PPD's ideology and examples of Muñoz's views on the absentee corporations and of the power of the PPD's message, see Navas Dávila, *La dialéctica*, pp. 75–87, and Muñoz Marín, *Memorias*, pp. 255–64.

[113] Lewis, *Puerto Rico*, p. 148, suggests that the PPD was the "first genuinely nationalist party" in Puerto Rico. More precisely, it was the first nationalist party acceptable to the U.S., since the PPD was not directly challenging the colonial status and remained within tolerable bounds on economic questions.

[114] The PPD's program was basically enlightened Keynesianism applied to an agricultural, underdeveloped, colonial setting. Though certain specific capitalist interests (the absentee sugar corporations) were to be sacrificed, the purpose of doing so was to liberalize and strengthen the capitalist structure over the long run by letting some of the benefits trickle down.

United States—it was impossible for them to think otherwise. The 1940 election brought the PPD, narrowly, to power. The changes the PPD was to bring would fundamentally alter, once again, the structure of the island's economy and society. By the 1950s, Puerto Rico would have left its agrarian past behind and become an urban, industrial nation.

SUMMARY

The decade of the thirties was another turning point in Puerto Rico's history. The stranglehold of U.S. business over the economy was sufficiently weakened by the depression and the war buildup to permit a new political formation and class alliances with a new plan for economic development to triumph in the 1940 elections. The Roosevelt New Deal had done little to create any long-term transformation of the Puerto Rican economy. Though federal relief expenditures and loans amounted to at least $230 million over the period from 1933 to 1941, Perloff commented that

> the federal contributions *as a whole* did little more than mitigate suffering and fill empty stomachs. They were essentially relief handouts. They did little permanently to strengthen the foundations of the economy or to solve the underlying economic problems.[115]

Even such relief as was offered was inadequate. In 1940, expenditures by the families of sugar workers were still no more than one-third of the minimum standard.[116]

Something had to change. The contrasts between the island and the United States and between what was and what could and should be were too great to prevent an alteration in the old order. For a time, it had seemed Puerto Rico would split apart with dissension, but the election of Muñoz and the PPD promised a new order in which Puerto Ricans would decide their own future and the poorest classes could hope to improve the conditions of their lives. The 1940s, then, promised a future not yet glimpsed under U.S. colonial control.

[115] Perloff, *Puerto Rico's Economic Future*, p. 32.
[116] Stahl, "Economic Development," p. 16. These figures were determined by a Works Progress Administration study.

4

The Origins of Industrialization:
From State Capitalism to
Operation Bootstrap

INTRODUCTION

The thirties had begun on a note of despair, but they ended in new hope for the great majority of Puerto Ricans with the Popular Democratic party's rise to power. Farmers and agricultural and factory workers who had been observers and victims of political maneuvering and economic exploitation were understandably wary of Muñoz's and the PPD's promises. Yet the moral tone of the 1940 political campaign, the resolve to discipline the absentee sugar corporations, and the respect shown the disinherited in building for the future were encouraging signs. Muñoz was able to channel the discontent of the majority, whereas Albizu Campos had aggravated class and colonial tensions. To the United States, Muñoz presented an opportunity for halting the social disintegration of the 1930s before it had gone too far. From a bare legislative majority in 1940, the PPD went on to score an overwhelming electoral victory in the 1944 elections.[1] If the thirties would be remembered as a decade of violence, decline, despair, and suffering, the forties would be a period of transition to a new level of capitalist development and industrialization amid great hope for the future.

Like earlier transformations in Puerto Rico, the shift from an agricul-

[1] In the 1940 election, the PPD received 37.9 percent of the total vote, compared to 39.2 percent for the Republican-Socialist coalition. However, the PPD won ten of the nineteen Senate seats, giving them a majority, and Muñoz became the Senate president. In the House, the PPD and the coalition each held eighteen of the thirty-nine seats. Muñoz was able to reach an agreement with two of the members holding the three deciding seats, so that they cast their votes with the PPD and gave the party a working majority. This arrangement was costly in terms of obligations incurred, and it was discontinued in 1944, when the PPD won a majority on its own with 64.8 percent of the 591,796 votes. The PPD won all but three seats in both houses and lost those only because it did not run enough at-large candidates: Tugwell, *Stricken Land*, pp. 625–26, 669; Curet Cuevas, *El desarrollo económico*, p. 197, n. 1, and p. 199, n. 3; and Bayrón Toro, *Elecciones y partidos políticos*, pp. 194–97, 202–5.

tural economy to an industrial one and from a rural society to an urban one was rapid. The gains were significant in many respects: higher levels of production and per capita income; a tendency toward product diversification and a definite reduction in the power of the absentee sugar corporations; land reform; and improved housing, health care, and education. These benefits were not won without costs, however. Some of these were tangible: greater unemployment and even isolation from the labor market for a significant proportion of the population; an increase in the number of migrants to the United States; greater trade dependence on the U.S. market; and increasing private and public debt. Other costs, though less amenable to quantitative measure, were no less real: the psychological shock of rural-urban migration; the implantation of the advanced consumerist ethic of the United States within an underdeveloped country; and cultural subjection to the U.S. media, tastes, work habits, and laws.

There is a sad irony in all this. Muñoz and the PPD were able to conceive, initiate, and support changes in the economic structure in the 1940s during a period of expanded autonomy which came about as a result of the depression, the crisis of hegemony in the 1930s, and then World War II. For the first time under U.S. rule, Puerto Ricans had an opportunity to increase their degree of autonomous control at the highest economic and political levels, and the PPD had a chance to move the economy toward the goal of independence. The opportunity was missed, however. Industrialization and the accompanying decline of agriculture after the late 1940s did nothing to expand and make permanent the relative autonomy of the early 1940s. Instead, the PPD program had just the opposite result: it laid the foundation for increased dominance by U.S. capital from the 1950s to the present. The PPD's goal of eventual political independence, after the attainment of social justice and a solution to the island's economic problems, faded further into the future and eventually disappeared altogether. It may be that Muñoz and the PPD never really were committed to independence, as many have suggested, but it is more likely that, as the PPD's redirection of the economy under Muñoz's leadership tied its destiny ever closer to that of the United States, what they had became what they wanted as what they had wanted slipped further and further from their grasp.

This chapter analyzes the changes in the economic and social structure from the period of state-dominated development in the early 1940s to the more traditional state-sponsored development of the famous Operation Bootstrap industrialization strategy begun in the late 1940s. That this was a period of profound transformation is clear; that it was a revolution, as some have suggested, is less certain.[2]

---

[2] Goodsell, *Administration of a Revolution*.

ELEMENTS OF STATE CAPITALISM

When Muñoz and the PPD assumed legislative control with their shaky majority in 1941, the economy was predominately agricultural and was still recovering from the dislocations of the Great Depression. Per capita income in 1940 was $122, exactly what it had been in 1930. By the time the PPD came to power and Puerto Rico finally had a local administration sympathetic to New Deal politics, hostility in Washington to the New Deal, Roosevelt's policies, and even Roosevelt himself was on the rise. This opposition to the new interventionist role of capitalist governments was mirrored to some extent in Puerto Rico. When the United States entered World War II, probably very few people realized that the island was on the brink of not just profound, but also progressive, change. Events and necessity, however, conspired to produce that result.

On September 19, 1941, Rexford Guy Tugwell became governor of Puerto Rico.[3] Tugwell had been a member of Roosevelt's early New Deal team, but he was later "exiled" to New York City, where he chaired the Planning Commission under Mayor Fiorello La Guardia. Tugwell was, for his time, an economic radical, but only in the sense that Thorstein Veblen in the United States or John Maynard Keynes in England were radicals. Tugwell did not believe that the right of private property carried with it the right to be socially irresponsible. For him and other institutionalists, laissez faire did not imply license. Society and its citizens had rights as well as responsibilities and so did business enterprises, and Tugwell, like Roosevelt and liberal political and economic thinkers in general, believed that government must not only protect the rights of private property, but must also balance such ownership against the needs and welfare of society in general.[4] Such thinking, of course, never fails to draw fire from the most reactionary of business interests, and the attacks that earlier had sent Tugwell packing to New York began almost immediately upon his arrival in Puerto Rico, and he was forced to endure them throughout his term as governor. He was branded at various times a so-

[3] On August 1, 1941, Tugwell had become chancellor of the University of Puerto Rico. He resigned this position after becoming governor. He had planned to hold both positions, but the opposition party in Puerto Rico objected; it preferred Tugwell as governor, where it was thought he could do less harm—an inaccurate expectation: Tugwell, *Stricken Land*, pp. 135, 143–48, and Ross, *Uphill Path*, pp. 53–54.

[4] Goodsell comments that, like many others, Tugwell believed that the emergence of large, oligopolistic corporations spelled the end of laissez-faire capitalism and the economy therefore required new solutions: "together government and industry must set prices and allocate capital investment in a rational, unified way. . . . all doctrinaire solutions must be rejected, including Marxian socialism": Quoted in Goodsell, *Administration of a Revolution*, pp. 17, 141.

cialist, a communist, and a fascist. He was none of these, of course, but rather was a pragmatic, liberal reformer. He was convinced that unregulated capitalism invited economic instability and social unrest and that such an order imposed unacceptable costs on the nation. Tugwell had no desire to do away with capitalism; he wished only to try to make it work better—which for him meant more humanely and more justly—even if unenlightened capitalists and their spokespersons did not see things in quite that light. Tugwell, like Keynes, wanted, and believed it essential, to save capitalism from itself without denying the fundamental basis and worth of the system. This line of thinking and action was completely compatible with Muñoz's and the PPD's perspective, and in this coming together of economic purpose and ideology, the PPD's plans for dealing with absentee owners and enhancing social justice had at least an even chance of success.[5]

The involvement of the United States in World War II was, after a fashion, a favorable circumstance for Tugwell, Muñoz, and the PPD, who were given a freer hand to reform by the president and the Department of the Interior, despite the constant efforts by special interests in Washington and San Juan to block them. Puerto Rico was believed important, perhaps essential, to the defenses of the United States in the Caribbean and of the Panama Canal, and there was a feeling, if not a firmly held belief, that greater economic progress was necessary to prevent unrest in the colony.[6] Fortuitously, the war did bring about significantly higher insular revenues, which went a long way toward financing the PPD's economic and social programs. Without the historically unique circumstances of a sympathetic governor and a colonial crisis begging for resolution, it is doubtful whether the road to economic reorganization could have been traveled as quickly as it was.

This reorganization took place in two distinguishable, but overlapping, phases. From 1941 to 1949, the government followed a program of land reform, control over and development of infrastructure and institutions, administrative reorganization, and limited industrialization through factories owned and operated by the government. In the period from 1945 to 1953, land reform and agriculture in general received less attention,

---

[5]Mattos Cintrón refers to this as the advent of the "creolized" New Deal: *La política y lo político*, pp. 81, 84, 96, 113. However, the state's involvement in production was significantly broader in Puerto Rico than was the case with the New Deal in the U.S., which is why this period is referred to here as "state capitalism" and not simply as Puerto Rico's New Deal.

[6]For a revealing exchange on Puerto Rico's strategic role among those with jurisdiction over the island, see the selection from the U.S. Senate hearings of 1943 in Wagenheim, *Puerto Ricans*, pp. 237–43. Tugwell often urged the need for the U.S. to gain the "tranquility, even the loyalty of its people": *Stricken Land*, p. 69.

the government-owned enterprises were sold to private firms, and a major effort was initiated to increase industrial production by attracting private, especially U.S., capital.

During both phases, however, the planning and promotion activities undertaken by the Puerto Rican government were the driving forces for change. The role of government as initiator was a constant, and this continuity of purpose is more important than the specific forms the government's role took. The colonial state performed the functions of a collective capitalist: it took risks and accumulated capital; it invested, made plans, and carried them out. Private capital and capitalists had not been performing these functions, and foreign capital, and much local capital as well, was locked into sugar-cane production, trade, and banking. The bulk of bank deposits were not even invested in Puerto Rico or used productively, but instead were used to purchase U.S. government bonds or simply sat idle (some $63 million). From 1942 to 1946, Puerto Ricans invested about $380 million in such bonds or in savings accounts in banks on the mainland. This unproductive use of savings hindered local investment and the development of a productive structure in Puerto Rico.[7] There was little effort by investors to branch into new lines of production, especially for the domestic market, with its low incomes and purchasing power.

These problems were exacerbated by World War II. The dislocations and uncertainty that accompanied it further discouraged local and foreign capitalists from undertaking investment. The war shut Puerto Rico off from its primary export market and source of imported goods, and meanwhile, there were no war industries to absorb surplus labor; consequently, unemployment increased. In such circumstances, the PPD's leaders felt they had to do something to overcome the effects of the isolation and disruption caused by the war; and if industrialization was to be furthered, the initiative and funding had to come from the government. Thus, the shift to private capital from public ownership in the second phase was not the essence of the state's role, nor does it even fully encompass the actual situation, since public corporations in transportation, electric power, banking, and other branches remained (just as private capital was encouraged in the earlier phase as well). The essence of the Puerto Rican government's role, rather, was that of collective capitalist, promoter, and

[7]PRPB, *Economic Development*, p. 20, and Tugwell, *Public Papers*, p. 171. Tugwell also commented on these idle funds, noted the necessity for government to mobilize the surplus when private capital was not doing so, and called attention to the adverse effect of mainland competition on industrialization: *Stricken Land*, pp. 254–55. This competition is said to have resulted in the closing of 350 local firms between 1940 and 1948: Silén, *Historia*, p. 301.

entrepreneur. As Teodoro Moscoso, the first director of the industrialization program, put it, the government's role in the development process was "purely pragmatic."[8]

Even before Tugwell's appointment as governor, the PPD-dominated legislature showed its will to reform by creating the Junta de Salario Mínimo (Minimum Wage Board), the Autoridad de las Fuentes Fluviales (Water Resources Authority, which generated and produced electric power), and the Autoridad de Tierras (Land Authority), among other important legislation passed in the regular session in early 1941.[9] After becoming governor, Tugwell called the legislature into a special session in late October and saw through the passage of forty-three bills, including one establishing the Comisión de Alimentos y Abastecimiento (Food and Supplies Commission) to control prices and ensure the availability of necessary goods as the war approached and shortages began to appear. Another bill gave the government control over all drinking-water systems, which at the time were operated by the municipalities and were often the source of illness and disease as the result of improper treatment.[10]

The key legislation for economic development, however, was passed during the regular 1942 session. It established a Compañía de Fomento (Development Company), which began operation in October 1942, and a Banco de Fomento (Development Bank), which began operation in December 1943.[11] From Tugwell's perspective, the creation of the Planning, Urbanizing, and Zoning Board (generally called simply the Junta de Planificación, or Planning Board), which was formed at his urging, was also an important step, though an incomplete one, in coordinating growth in

[8]T. Moscoso, "Orígen y desarrollo," p. 164. This talk was presented in 1966.

[9]The Land Authority was a cornerstone of the PPD's program for enforcing the 500-acre limitation. Governor Swope, who preceded Tugwell, signed it into law only on the last possible day. Under pressure from the sugar corporations, he had wanted to give it a pocket veto, but he was advised to sign by Washington and reluctantly did so. Electrical power was later nationalized under the War Powers Act to save on oil. Opposition to this was especially intense: Tugwell, *Stricken Land*, pp. 94, 345–46.

[10]Ibid., pp. 170–71; Silén, *Historia*, pp. 237, 239. The water system did not become islandwide until 1945, when the Autoridad de Acueductos y Alcantarillados (Aqueduct and Sewer Authority) was created.

[11]Ross, *Uphill Path*, p. 161, and Mundie, "Government Development Bank," pp. 35, 37–38. In 1913, 1916, 1921, and 1929, the Puerto Rican legislature had attempted to enact an Insular Bank Act, or similar legislation, to create an institution that would receive and use government deposits, offer lower-interest loans, and stimulate competition among private banks. The bills either failed to pass or were vetoed by the governor. The Brookings Institution report of 1930 had recommended against such an insular government bank with this reasoning: "In view of the fact that Porto Rico's economic life is intimately and inevitably closely con[n]ected with that of continental United States, its banking organization should be operated as an integral part of the credit system of the United States": V. Clark et al., *Porto Rico and Its Problems*, pp. 397–99.

the economy and collecting and analyzing data. Also important to Tugwell were the new Budget Bureau, the Central Statistical Office, and the
improvements that were made in the civil service system. There was
something of a division of labor in all of this, whereby Tugwell, by virtue
of his interest and training, concentrated on reorganizing governmental
administration while Muñoz and the PPD, by necessity, worked to put in
place the measures required for economic reconstruction.[12] The forging
of this entire network of infrastructural, planning, and coordinating institutions, built from scratch in the space of two years, was a remarkable
achievement. Without this far-reaching institutional change, the economy
very likely would not have been so profoundly transformed and certainly
not so rapidly.[13]

THE GOVERNMENT DEVELOPMENT BANK

The function of the Development Bank of Puerto Rico was to fill the
void left by the lending practices of private banks, which restricted their
loans largely to established enterprises in already profitable branches of
industry. The Development Bank was to lend money to enterprises that
it believed could contribute to the development and industrialization goals
of the economy and that met normal banking standards for loans but
found credit channels closed or unacceptably costly.[14] It operated at first
as a general-service commercial bank able to accept both private and
public deposits, but in a reorganization in 1948, the bank's name was
changed to the Government Development Bank (GDB), and it was prohibited from accepting private deposits or savings accounts. The bank
thus became the "government's bank," in that it held deposits of the
insular municipal, and federal governments, made payments for the insular government, and handled borrowing obligations for the public corporations, but it continued to make loans to qualifying businesses on the
same criteria as before.[15] The GDB made it possible to use government

[12] Tugwell, *Stricken Land,* pp. 172, 228, 258–59, and Goodsell, *Administration of a
Revolution,* pp. 142–45, 148–49. Tugwell had been skeptical about beginning a new economic program during the war, given the lack of resources, but Muñoz convinced him to
go along with the PPD's program. See Santana Rabell, *Planificación,* for a detailed history
of the development of planning under Muñoz Marín.

[13] González, *La economía política,* p. 74.

[14] The bank's initial appropriation of $500,000 was supplemented by an additional $5
million in 1944 and $15 million in 1945 through acts of the insular legislature.

[15] Mundie, "Government Development Bank," pp. 39–40, 45, 57–58, 62, and Montalvo, *External Investment,* p. 9. The GDB also acts as a discounting agent for locally
chartered banks that need loan funds, just as the Federal Reserve System in the U.S. serves
this function for its member banks. Since 1950, local banks have been permitted, if they so
choose, to become members of the Federal Reserve System. Under local law, the secretary

deposits to further social and economic goals, with funds that otherwise would have been deposited in private banks.

During the first decade of the GDB's operations, about two-thirds of its loans were made to local firms.[16] However, the great majority of these loans (almost 90 percent as of the middle of 1946) were for construction and trade, so the direct contribution of the GDB's operations to industrial development was slight. The degree of concentration in these sectors later declined somewhat, though most of the GDB's funds continued to go in the same direction.[17] In 1955, firms with loans from the GDB employed 18 percent (11,200) of all factory workers; these loans were concentrated in capital-intensive projects, so their impact on output was likely greater than on employment.[18]

THE PUERTO RICO DEVELOPMENT COMPANY

The leading institution for the promotion of industrialization was to be the Puerto Rico Development Company.[19] Teodoro Moscoso, who had been a pharmacist in Ponce and then an administrator for the Housing Authority, was named by the governor to head the company as its general manager.[20] The Development Company was set up as an independent public corporation, with an initial legislative appropriation of $500,000 and the right to borrow more to finance its operations, though it was expected to become self-financing eventually. Its functions under the original legislation were: (1) to carry out research leading to increased use of the island's natural resources in industrial production; (2) to conduct research and testing with respect to the marketing, distribution, and export of island goods; (3) to operate a design laboratory to provide information and assistance in the production of commodities using local raw materials or those adaptable to local production; (4) to establish and

---

of the treasury determines the required reserve ratio for locally chartered banks. Since 1958, Puerto Rico has been part of the New York Federal Reserve District for purposes of clearing checks. The GDB is headed by a seven-member board of directors appointed by the governor for four-year staggered terms.

[16] Mundie, "Government Development Bank," pp. 65–66, 70. A local firm is defined as one with a majority of its equity capital from Puerto Rican sources. Mundie details the types of loans the GDB makes, its loan operations, and its qualifying requirements.

[17] Ibid., p. 83.

[18] Ibid., pp. 101, 103.

[19] Ibid., p. 31.

[20] While working for the housing authority, Moscoso had introduced a method of improving slum living conditions: "utility units" were installed to serve every four houses. These included four showers, toilets, washbasins, and a sanitary drinking-water tap: Chase, "*Operation Bootstrap*," p. 38. Later, while John F. Kennedy was president, Moscoso was made director of the Alliance for Progress.

operate firms that would manufacture and distribute goods produced from local materials; and (5) to promote industrial participation by local entrepreneurs and local funds, with the goal of avoiding the problems created by large-scale, absentee capitalism.[21]

The most controversial area of the Development Company's proposed operations was point (4), the creation and operation of publicly owned enterprises or authorities *(autoridades)*. Corporate spokespersons—lawyers, conservative legislators, members of the Chamber of Commerce and the Rotary Club, and some economists—saw socialism written all over this provision. They believed that it threatened their immediate interests, and they feared the precedent it represented. But it was clear from the beginning, and it was stated explicitly as policy later, that any subsidiaries of the Development Company would not be in already existing industries, nor would they operate in competition with private capital. Rather, they were to service existing enterprises in those areas of production that private capital had not entered but that were important to the economy's overall development, particularly in the creation of linkages within a more integrated economy. The Development Company's first subsidiary was the Puerto Rico Cement Company, which had been organized by the PRRA and had assets valued at nearly $2 million when it passed into the Development Company's hands.

In spite of the objections raised, the Development Company moved ahead with studies of possible industrial projects, some of which had been begun even before the company had been authorized by the legislature. Earlier and still valuable PRRA studies were reviewed to determine their applicability and to avoid unnecessary duplication of effort. Some projects never went beyond the planning stages (e.g., production of yeast and vegetable oil), but four new enterprises did go into production—for glass products, shoes, paperboard, and clay building materials (as well as a hotel, the Caribe Hilton, and a textile mill that were financed but not operated by the government).[22] These can all be regarded as import-substitution industries, attempting to meet a local demand normally served by imports from the United States. In most development programs in the third world, import substitution has been a first step in the process of industrialization, in the belief that such production reduces the demand

---

[21] Curet Cuevas, *El desarrollo económico*, p. 208, and Ross, *Uphill Path*, pp. 62–63. The design laboratory came up with new ceramics, native rugs, and furniture locally designed and made from local materials, as well as other items, within its first year of operations: Tugwell, *Stricken Land*, p. 262. The Development Company focused its efforts on industry. Responsibility for agricultural development rested with the Land Authority and, later, with the Agricultural Development Company, which was formed in 1945 but which never played a prominent role in the development program.

[22] Ross, *Uphill Path*, pp. 64–73, provides a brief history of each of these subsidiaries.

for foreign exchange for imports and hence releases export earnings for other purposes, as well as being relatively safe because the products have a pre-existing market. In addition, all but shoe production had substantial backward and forward linkages with other sectors of production.[23]

The Puerto Rico Glass Corporation. Glass production was the first enterprise to be launched by the Development Company. The company was incorporated in February 1943, and plant construction began in May, but as a result of problems in deliveries of equipment caused both by the war and by glass producers in the United States who did not relish new competition, production did not actually begin until January 1945. A glass company seemed like an appropriate project. It used local raw materials, and as originally planned it was to produce bottles for the local rum industry. With the war, inbound shipping space was at a premium, and imported bottles had a relatively low priority. At the same time, the market for Puerto Rican rum in the United States was expanding, due to the difficulties of importing liquor from Europe and the reductions in U.S. whiskey production. A bottle factory to supply the rum industry thus promised to have broad benefits: the rum producers would increase sales and profits; the government would receive greater tax revenues from the increased sales; and the population in general would have the short-run advantage of more jobs and the long-run advantages that would come from greater funding for economic development and social programs.

Unfortunately, despite planning and logic, the project fared poorly from the beginning. As noted, the start of production was delayed, and a month after it did begin, the workers went out on strike and remained out for four months, until June 1945. By then, the war was virtually over. Imported bottles soon became available again, and Puerto Rican rum lost part of its market to the increased production of other liquors. The factory was also plagued by quality-control problems. The private rum producers, hostile to a government-owned bottle company on principle, and given the uncertainty caused by the start-up and labor problems, were glad to begin buying imported bottles again. The glass company's market was disappearing. In 1947, it began to produce containers other than rum bottles, but it was only years later, and after the company was privately owned, that these became an important part of its output.

In sum, resistance to government enterprise on the part of private producers in the United States and Puerto Rico, delays in starting production due to the war and a strike, and planning weaknesses all combined to

---

[23] Their use of local materials ranged from 70 to more than 99 percent by weight: Perloff, *Puerto Rico's Economic Future*, p. 105, table 30.

seriously damage the ability of the glass factory to function effectively and to contribute to the island government's social and economic goals.

The Puerto Rico Pulp and Paper Corporation. Planning for the paperboard factory was begun at the same time as planning for the glass factory. The hope was that it would sell its entire output to the privately owned Puerto Rico Container Corporation, which made the boxes used both by the new bottle company, and by the private rum industry. The paperboard plant was designed to recycle waste paper and to use bagasse, a by-product of sugar grinding, as additional raw material. Construction on the plant began in May 1944, and it was supposed to be in operation a year later. Production, however, was delayed until May 1946, again because of shipping and other problems encountered in receiving equipment from the United States. Besides what should have been the predictable problems that the middle-and upper-income mainlanders who were brought to run the factory had in adjusting to life on a still-poor island, it was discovered too late that the plant had been equipped with obsolete, second-hand machinery, which made it unable to compete with imported paperboard despite the high shipping costs, which, almost like a tariff, afforded a margin of protection to local production. As one observer has commented: "It appears that Puerto Rico had once more been the victim of dumping by mainland suppliers of substandard goods, this time with a new twist—not the product, but the productive facilities, were dumped."[24]

On top of this problem, a boycott of the paperboard company from two sides took a heavy toll. Local businesses refused to save their waste paper to sell to the government corporation, preferring to throw it away and forgo the extra revenues rather than to provide aid in any form to a government enterprise. On the other end, and more seriously, the Puerto Rico Container Corporation, which was owned by a member of the opposition party, refused to buy the firm's output, choosing instead to import its supplies, despite the added cost. The paperboard company was forced to sell its product below cost in the United States in order to recoup at least some of its production expenses.

The technical difficulties which the glass and paperboard factories met perhaps could eventually have been overcome, but the active hostility of private business interests to their existence was another matter. As long as rum producers and the box company could obtain their supplies from the mainland, they could and did, for primarily political and ideological reasons, boycott the output of the Development Company subsidiaries. Though it may have seemed perfectly logical to produce goods for the

---

[24] Ross, *Uphill Path*, p. 69.

local market which had previously been imported, as long as the government subsidiaries depended on the good will of virtually monopsony buyers to purchase their output, they were vulnerable to this form of sabotage. Even when the government companies could offer lower-priced goods, the political benefit to be gained by the private firms from the failure of the government enterprises was worth more to them than any short-term, marginal profits that they might have earned. That the insular government did not try to prevent this open and coordinated sabotage (e.g., by setting up public companies to produce boxes and to bottle rum) attests to the fact that there really was no intention to infringe upon the rights of private property or to work outside the confines of capitalism's boundaries. Thus, private firms retained the upper hand and the power to block the government's plans to import-substitute and to create greater integration within the economy. The acceptable planning boundaries were defined not by the PPD and the colonial government, but by the private interests of capitalist enterprises.

The Puerto Rico Shoe and Leather Company.   Construction began on the shoe plant in 1945, and it was in full production by February 1947. Shoe manufacture was a labor-intensive operation, in comparison with the making of glass or paperboard, and it resulted in a product, mass-produced shoes (with the trademark "Belma"), that Puerto Rico needed for health and other reasons. The original plan was to produce only a single style of shoes for local use, but the company quickly, and wisely, scrapped this decision—at the cost, however, of making the training time for the labor force correspondingly longer. Some shoes were exported so that the plant could take advantage of economies of scale, and by the beginning of 1948 it was operating at a profit and had good prospects for the future. In this instance, with a product sold directly to consumers, private capital had no means of blocking the plant's operations, and thus import substitution could readily take place, particularly since prices were kept low.

The Puerto Rico Clay Products Corporation.   The last public corporation to go on line was designed to produce construction brick, roofing and drain tile, and sewer pipes. Production began in August 1947, though construction of the facility had begun in July 1945. Once again delays were due to difficulties encountered in equipment shipments from the mainland. The output was easily sold to the growing construction industry, but the plant suffered from poor quality control (more than half the output was defective), and it consistently lost money. However, this was only a temporary condition, the result of inexperience. Once the quality problem was resolved, as it was during the 1950s, the postwar building boom and the government development program meant that marketing and demand would not be of major concern.

By mid-1947, then, the Development Company had four enterprises in production and was operating the previously existing and profitable cement company, and plans for other enterprises were under consideration. Yet there were continuing problems, some technical, others political and ideological. The concerted opposition of private capital to government-owned enterprises, combined with Moscoso's and the PPD's pragmatism rather than any strong ideological commitment to government ownership, was to lead to a reorientation of the development program that became fully apparent only after 1947, though the changeover began, as will be seen, much earlier.

LAND REFORM

The PPD came to power on the promise to enforce the 500-acre provision of the Jones Act and to return the land to those who worked it. Land reform would serve two purposes: first, it would weaken the power of the absentee sugar companies over the economy and government and increase the local surplus available for investment; and second, it would in itself make a contribution to social justice and economic transformation. The agency through which the 500-acre limitation was finally to be enforced was the Land Authority, created by the Land Law (Ley de Tierras), which was signed by Governor Guy J. Swope on April 12, 1941.[25] The preamble of the law stated: "It is the policy of the government of Puerto Rico that each person who works the land is to be the owner of the land that supports him."[26] Carlos Chardón, coauthor of the reconstruction plan of 1934, was appointed as the authority's first director. Significantly, the 500-acre restriction was applied by the legislature only to corporations, as the Jones Act had done; individuals were not prohibited from holding more than 500 acres. The Land Law, then, was not a law against large holdings per se so much as legislation aimed at the holdings of large corporations, especially absentee U.S. corporations.

---

[25] Edel, "Land Reform" (October 1962): 35–37. The way had been cleared for enforcement of the 500-acre law after a ruling by the U.S. Supreme Court in the case of *Puerto Rico v. Rubert Hermanos* (see chapter 3). The court argued that the absence of an enforcement mechanism in the Jones Act did not imply an intent by Congress not to enforce the limitation, and hence local legislation appropriate to the enforcement of the law was constitutional: Tugwell, *Stricken Land*, pp. 75–92, 101–5.

[26] "Es política del gobierno de Puerto Rico que cada persona que trabaje la tierra sea dueña de la tierra que la sostiene": Quoted in Sánchez Tarniella, *La economía*, p. 113.

THE LAND-PURCHASE PROGRAM

In the discussions before the Land Law was passed, as well as during the PPD's campaign, it had seemed that in any implementation of the 500-acre limit, the land purchased from corporations would be divided into small plots for individual colono production, as had been suggested in the Chardón Plan.[27] However, a central feature of the final form of the Land Law was a provision for "proportional-profit farms" (*fincas de beneficio proporcional*), which had previously been only a minor, nearly offhand, element, whereas the individual small-scale subsistence farm was given little importance in the final legislation. This turnabout can probably be traced back to the controversy on the nature of land reform that took place before the Land Law was passed. At the hearings of the Tugwell committee in March 1941 (when its chairman was still in the Department of Agriculture), on how the 500-acre limitation might be enforced, there had been heated disagreement over the impact of dividing the sugar corporations' lands into small plots for colono production. The sugar companies had argued that doing so would result in intolerable inefficiencies in an industry already at a competitive disadvantage on the world market. Tugwell shared this concern. The reason the companies made such an argument, of course, was to attempt to avoid indefinitely enforcement of the law by suggesting there would be a costly impact on productivity, output, and income. Supporters of the PPD program, on the other hand, believed that the social advantage to be gained from land distribution outweighed the purely economic factors and any inefficiencies that might result. The proportional-profit farm concept was a compromise between these views. It proposed to maintain efficient-sized farms but to have them run, though not owned, by their managers and workers, who would share in any profits. Where efficiency was of less concern, however, as on marginal lands, small plots would be distributed, since that would have no adverse effect on productivity.[28]

However useful the profit-sharing concept may have been as a means of maintaining large-scale production and at the same time giving workers some stake in the enterprise, neither this formula nor the Land Law itself did anything to reduce the dependence of the island economy on sugar production. Land ownership was to be transferred to the state, but

[27] There were expropriations with compensation from unwilling landholders, and the courts upheld this practice in a case involving Eastern Sugar Associates in Vieques: Edel, "Land Reform" (October 1962): 52.

[28] Distribution of small plots was never an important part of the land reform program in practice. It would seem that by the time of the final draft of the Land Law, and after the election, this formula for land redistribution per se had been shelved in favor of the proportional-profit farm.

the proportional-profit farms continued to be export-oriented and primarily one-crop producers of sugar, a commodity with a very narrow market and an even more uncertain future. This is vivid testimony to the limited purpose of the Land Law and land reform. The international division of labor and production which had turned so many Caribbean countries into sugar monocultures, and kept them so, was accepted as if it were somehow natural and immutable. To a large extent, in fact, land reform had not been envisaged as a way to revitalize agriculture, improve working and social conditions, and give power to those who worked the land; it was more a mechanism for Muñoz and the PPD to consolidate their power via popular reforms which, however, lacked significant content and would have little long-term impact on the economic and class structure.[29]

Interestingly and revealingly, the Land Authority did find some sellers who were willing to part with their land, though other corporations were almost impossible to deal with. Many relatively small landholders, who also had the opportunity of selling voluntarily under the law, welcomed the chance to do so. After it was clear the Land Law was going to be enforced, most delays by corporations in land transfers were due to disagreements over the price to be paid rather then over the 500-acre limit per se.[30] For those who believed the future of the sugar industry to be clouded (and not just in Puerto Rico), being able to sell their land, often at inflated prices, was an attractive and profitable alternative to a dim future.[31]

The first corporate farm to be purchased was that of Central Cambalache on the northwest coast, which had made known its desire to sell as early as 1939. In 1942, it signed the first consent decree in which a corporation agreed to accept the 500-acre limit. Six proportional-profit

[29] Tugwell, *Stricken Land*, p. 102, alludes to this; see also Edel, "Land Reform" (October 1962): 39. The exclusion of individuals from the 500-acre limit, when, as Tugwell argued, they were more exploitative and antilabor than the corporations, also suggests that the Land Law was less than a fundamental reform.

[30] Some corporations, like Central Cambalache, could see the handwriting on the wall and readily agreed to sell, but others, especially those which were mainland-owned, were quite creative in their attempts to avoid enforcement of the new law. For example, Central Aguirre, a mainland company, managed to avoid the intent of the law by playing its legal cards one at a time, forcing the government into expensive legal proceedings, and Eastern Sugar Associates followed the same delaying tactics: Edel, "Land Reform" (October 1962): 51.

[31] Prices paid by the government averaged $100 per cuerda, well above the market value for at least some farms. One of the participants in Tugwell's 1941 hearings on the 500-acre law noted afterward that the corporations were ready to be bought out at a "reasonable price" in the face of all the uncertainty: Tugwell, *Stricken Land*, pp. 90–92, and Edel, "Land Reform" (October 1962): 49.

farms were organized on the 9,519 cuerdas purchased in August 1943. In 1946, the average share of profit for the 8,838 workers on these six farms was $13.44.

Four more proportional-profit farms were organized on 5,700 cuerdas purchased from the Del Toa Sugar Company in late 1944. In 1945, the 3,976 workers on this farm shared 65 percent of the $71,109 profit, for an average of $11.63 per worker, though the actual amount varied with the number of days worked and the wage level. Less than $12 as an average share may not seem like much, but it must be remembered that wages in the sugar industry in 1941–45 averaged only 20 cents per hour.[32] For some workers the shared profits added nearly 20 percent to their wages.[33] Proportional-profit farms, engaging in single-crop agriculture, did not provide year-round work any more than the privately owned single-crop farms did, so workers' wages remained low. In fact, with the pressure of high unemployment during the war, there was a dramatic increase in labor use on the proportional-profit farms and a concomitant decrease in the number of days of work, and hence in the income, per worker. This was done in an effort to provide for as many workers and their families as possible by spreading the work, but the result was that the proportional-profit farms leveled individual income downward by making work irregular, even during the harvest, for all workers rather than just for some. Thus, the shared profits, small as they were, took on added significance.[34]

By the end of 1947, approximately 36 percent of corporate holdings of over 500 acres had been purchased, a total of 67,763 acres. The mill of Central Cambalache also was purchased and run as a proportional-profit enterprise, as was permitted by an amendment to the Land Law.[35] Another mill, Plazuela, was bought and operated by the government. In 1947, the total profits on all proportional-profit farms amounted to $560,350, with the 16,763 workers involved receiving an average profit share of $21.21.[36] Given that there were something like 130,000 sugarcane workers, including those employed, underemployed, and unemployed, and about 250,000 workers in all of agriculture, it is clear that the proportion of workers affected by this innovation in the land reform

[32] Perloff, *Puerto Rico's Economic Future*, p. 154, table 46.
[33] Edel, "Land Reform" (October 1962): 50.
[34] Edel, "Land Reform" (January 1963): 37–40.
[35] Ibid. (October 1962): 51–52.
[36] Koenig, *Comprehensive Agricultural Program*, p. 255, table 47. The worker share of profits was $355,347, or 63.4 percent. The rest of the profits were distributed as management incentives.

was quite small.[37] On June 30, 1950, the Land Authority owned 79,243 acres, of which 63,919 (81 percent) were under cultivation on forty-eight proportional-profit farms. In the fiscal year then ending, thirty-two of the farms earned total profits of $966,206, while the other sixteen farms had losses amounting to $351,296.[38] While more than a third of corporate land had been transferred to government control, nearly two-thirds had not, and noncorporate land remained untouched except to the extent that individuals voluntarily chose to sell.

Sugar continued to dominate production, and it continued to be responsible for about half of all agricultural output, employment, and income. The 1949-50 crop year saw one of the largest sugar harvests on record. In that year, 47.7 percent of all cultivated land was in sugar cane, compared to 22.9 percent for coffee, 3.5 percent for tobacco, 2.0 percent for plantains, and 0.7 percent for rice.[39]

The Land Authority had been underfunded from the beginning, and this certainly held back a more extensive effort to buy land. The expected deficiency of funds due to the island's low incomes and narrow tax base had been one reason that Tugwell and Gruening had thought federal enforcement of the 500-acre law would be necessary, a view that Muñoz also shared before the Land Authority actually was in place. No one expected the island government to to be able to generate sufficient revenue to finance large-scale land reform and still carry out its other essential functions. But when it became clear that federal money would not be made available because of congressional opposition to reform, the program was forced to depend on other sources. Fortuitously, greater wartime rum tax revenues collected in the United States were available, and they provided the largest share of the Land Authority's funds. The Land Law did permit the authority to issue bonds to finance its program, and some $5 million was borrowed. Borrowing above that amount, however, required that land be pledged as collateral. Since other Puerto Rican bonds already were encountering problems on the New York bond markets, and since two large corporations (Central Aguirre and Eastern Sugar) were still fighting enforcement, the search for further funding for the Land Authority was abandoned after 1945.[40]

At about the same time, attention to land reform and the breaking up

[37] Roughly 12 to 13 percent of all sugar workers and 6 to 7 percent of all agricultural workers: Perloff, *Puerto Rico's Economic Future*, p. 146, table 43, and Jaffe, *People, Jobs, and Economic Development*, p. 98, table 6.1.

[38] PRPB, *Economic Development*, pp. 78–79.

[39] Ibid., p. 19, and Koening, *Comprehensive Agricultural Program*, p. 35, table 11.

[40] Edel, "Land Reform" (October 1962): 38, 56–57.

of corporate land virtually ended, or, as Edel put it, the authority "discontinued its crusade."

After 1945 only one sugar company which had not already signed a consent decree was acquired. Its mill and land were purchased in 1946 after the company had attempted to sell them to mainlanders. By 1949 the last company which had signed a decree had sold its land to the Authority, which had no additional purchases planned. The president of the once-hostile Sugar Producers Association that year complimented the government on gaining necessary experience and discovering that his was "an honest and clean business like any other."[41]

The end of land purchases was the result of a number of factors. First, government funds for all uses became scarce, as the war ended and excise-tax collections fell, and there was no realistic expectation that they would return to wartime levels any time soon. Second, the land reforms already undertaken had given the PPD a symbolic victory, while reducing the influence of absentee capital in the sugar industry. The majority of Puerto Rican voters believed the PPD had carried out its promise of land reform, as indicated by the party's lopsided victory in 1944.[42] Nevertheless, enforcement of the 500-acre limitation was nowhere near complete.[43]

Third, the drive for industrialization in the postwar years was to draw both attention and funds away from agriculture. With the beginning of the industrialization program, based on private capital, agriculture not only took a back seat; it was even regarded as an obstacle to progress. In the cost-benefit calculus that came increasingly to dominate government decisions, land expropriations were perceived as doing little to bolster the confidence of business. Once economic growth and efficiency became the focus of policy, nonmonetary social goals and gains were given less weight than the tangible measures of output and monetary cost. Puerto Rico came to accept the trickle-down theory of the gains from economic growth, rather than following through on the "equity first, growth later" model of development which had characterized the first stage of state capitalism under PPD direction. Gradual though this reorientation was, it was en-

[41] Ibid., pp. 52–53.

[42] As in the Mexican Revolution, the reform in Puerto Rico had succeeded in consolidating the power of a new elite without the need to carry the reforms through to completion: Lewis, *Puerto Rico*, p. 181.

[43] Thirty-three corporations had been in violation of the limitation in 1940. Of these, seven sold out to the Land Authority and five others sold their land or part of it under federal government supervision to small owners. The remainder of the corporations were left untouched by the law: Edel, "Land Reform" (January 1963): 48.

forced on policy makers, many of whom were predisposed in that direction, anyway, by their greater reliance on the market and on private decision making and by the PPD's move away from the comprehensive economic and social planning that had been initiated during the war years.

AGREGADO RESETTLEMENT

Another innovation of the Land Law was the distribution of *parcelas*, or small pieces of land, to entitled recipients. The law provided a mechanism for the distribution to agregados of these plots, which would provide supplementary food production and permanent home sites. The agregado system had continued into the mid-twentieth century, providing landowners with a permanent source of cheap labor. Its victims, the agregados, poor, landless, and with no rights to the hovels in which they lived, often suffered exploitation, abuse, and capriciousness at the hands of their landlords.[44] Under the Land Law, each agregado was entitled to receive up to three cuerdas of land, at no charge but without the right of ownership, to prevent mortgaging the land or selling it during bad times. The Land Authority was given the right to purchase farms smaller than 500 acres for the purpose of creating communities of former agregados.[45]

It will be recalled that the 1849 libreta law also had attempted, unsuccessfully, to resettle agregados (see chapter 1). Then, the ostensible reason had been the desire to provide social services that could not be provided to families scattered over a wide area of the interior region; but there was also the element of domination and the drive to more closely control the labor of relatively independent agregados. The result of, if not the reasoning for, resettlement of agregados in the 1940s and afterward was to do what the century-earlier regulation had failed to accomplish: to make agregados into rural wage workers and to integrate them more fully into the labor force. The granting of small plots of land to agregados had the effect of destroying the remaining semiservile relations with their landlords while at the same time helping to ameliorate the worst conditions of their existence. The Land Law was thus an important step in dismantling the remnants of noncapitalist production relations.[46]

Agregado resettlement was accomplished more easily than was the organization of proportional-profit farms. The first resettlement project of

---

[44]Mintz observes that "in the period 1900–1944 the agregados on sugar plantations were subject to political repression and control. . . ": *Worker in the Cane*, p. 281.

[45]The idea of distributing subsistence plots was not new. The PRRA had distributed some 17,000 cuerdas in the 1930s, and the Farm Security Administration purchased and distributed 21,743 cuerdas in 590 farms between 1938 and 1945: Perloff, *Puerto Rico's Economic Future*, p. 39, n. 23.

[46]Edel, "Land Reform" (January 1963): 29–34.

Harvesting sugar cane near Guánica, 1941

Cutting cane, 1941

Remains of sugar mill "Rufina," near Guayanilla, 1982

Sugar cane worker, near Guánica, 1941

Street scene, San Juan, 1941

Entrance to town of Juncos, 1946 (Photo by Edwin Rosskam)

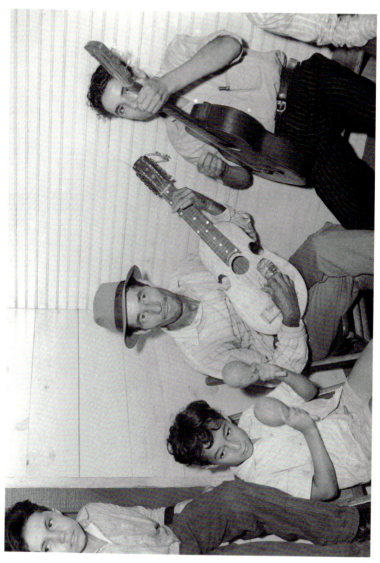

Musicians at Christmas party, near Yauco, 1940

Traditional thatched roof home (bohio), near Barceloneta, 1940

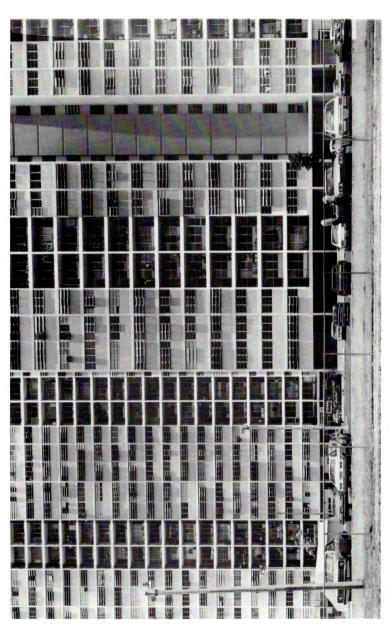

Modern condominium, San Juan, 1982

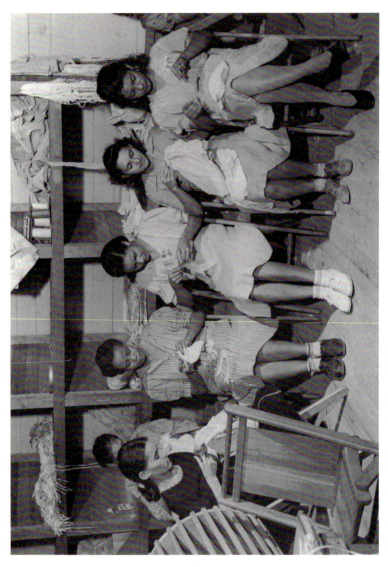

Small needlework shop, San Juan, 1941

Modern shirt factory, Las Piedras, 1982

295 families began on a noncorporate farm of 482 cuerdas in Sábana Seca, from which the U.S. Navy had displaced both owners and agregados in 1941. Edel notes that agregado communities were being established "at the rate of one village every ten days" by 1944 and that "by the end of the war, over 14,000 parcels had been distributed." By 1959, there were 304 of these communities with 52,287 families, involving about 10 percent of the total population. The original conception behind the provision of small plots had emphasized supplemental food production, but over time this aspect was given less and less attention than the development of cooperative communities that would engage in collective work and undertake community-betterment projects. As supplementary food producers, the parcels did not help much. In the late forties, the average value of their food production was about $50, or a little more than 13 percent of average family income.[47]

In 1948, the agregado resettlement program was placed under the direction of the Social Programs Administration, a new division of the Land Authority with its own finances and director and with a stronger orientation toward the creation of rural communities to provide the social services and amenities of life that might counter the tendency toward urban migration which had begun to accelerate during the 1940s. The most important and popular component of this effort involved aid to enable communities to build concrete housing at a cost to their owners of between $300 and $350, to be paid in installments. Perhaps ironically, however, by acclimating rural residents to urban life, albeit on a small scale, this move actually had the effect of stimulating migration rather than slowing it. Still, the program provided a certain amount of decent housing, replacing the inadequate shelters common before the forties, and thus made a positive contribution to the well-being of many families.

THE CRISIS OF THE FORTIES

Even in the best of times, life was difficult for the majority of Puerto Ricans. As the forties began, the island had barely recovered from the preceding decade's social disruptions and the near collapse of its economy. The U.S. entry into the war presented a new threat to living standards, and in the early war years the danger of starvation seemed very real. Puerto Rico was more than 1,000 miles from its mainland source of food, energy, and other basic supplies. The island depended upon shipping for its imported food, especially for such staples of low-income diets as rice and beans, and it also depended on ocean transport to deliver the

---

[47] Ibid. (October 1962): 48, and (January 1963): 32.

exports which paid for these imports. In the first year of the war, as shipping became problematical, all but the worst came to pass. In these circumstances, it might be asked why the island did not begin to grow more of its own food, to replace what could no longer be imported.[48] Tugwell has explained why this seemingly sensible solution encountered intense opposition in Puerto Rico:

> . . . the Farmers' Association (front for the sugar producers and roughly corresponding to that better-known American phenomenon, the California Farmers' Association) would never accept the suggestion of conversion from cane to food. It was their feeling that it was dangerous for it to get abroad that food could be raised in Puerto Rico. Cane was more profitable for them and their most earnest attention had always been given to lobbying for higher quotas on the ground that no other crop could be grown.[49]

For the sugar corporations, protecting profits and quotas were more important than the threat of hunger—which, of course, would not have directly affected their owners in any case.

During 1942, when Caribbean defenses were weak, German submarines regularly attacked ships en route to and from Puerto Rico. The island was isolated, and the cost of necessities increased as shortages loomed. And yet any attempt by the local or colonial government to set up supply and price guidelines or to procure and distribute food from other than the usual mainland sources met with almost total opposition in both San Juan and Washington from importers, other business interests, and their legal and political representatives.[50] The federal Office of Price

---

[48] It will be remembered that during World War I, the area planted in food crops had been increased nearly two and a half times to meet wartime shortages, though the area slipped back after the war ended: V. Clark et al., *Porto Rico and Its Problems*, pp. 489–90.

[49] Tugwell, *Stricken Land*, p. 215. The sugar companies were afraid of permanently losing their quota to competing areas if they reduced their output of cane. Ultimately, it was decided to guarantee their quota and to pay them the level of profits they would have received from sugar if they would agree to produce the food so desperately needed. Tugwell was able to get a $15 million appropriation from Congress for this subsidy, but it was never released for use because of personal opposition to him in Washington, and so the sugar companies did not convert to food production. In fact, the area devoted to sugar cane in 1942–43 increased 31 percent over the 1941 area. Between 1942 and 1947, the quotas on sugar were suspended, but because of shipping problems, it was not possible to export in excess of the former quota, and in many years less than half of what was produced was exported: Ibid., pp. 214–15; Tugwell, *Public Papers*, pp. 105–6, 166; Curet Cuevas, *El desarrollo económico*, p. 150, table 61; and PRPB, *Economic Development*, p. 51.

[50] Tugwell's relating of these incidents, including opposition from Puerto Rico's resident commissioner in Washington, is chilling. His book demonstrates the ease with which the powerful shaped events to suit their narrowly defined interests: Tugwell, *Stricken Land*, pp. 167, 169–70, 233–34, 324.

Administration began operations in May 1942, but it was never very effective in Puerto Rico in controlling prices or the abuses of the abundant profiteers.[51] For one period of almost three months, there was no rice, and there was another period of forty-one days during which only one ship arrived—and then only half of its cargo was for civilian use, the remainder being for the military.

Prices during this early crisis were increasing at an average rate of 5 to 6 percent a month for such goods as were available. Moreover, the inflation and shortages were beginning during the "dead time," when many sugar-cane and other agricultural workers were unemployed.

Prices of imported foods rose even faster than other prices; between 1941 and 1946, they increased by an average of 90 percent, while the prices of locally produced food were increasing by "only" 48 percent. Between 1941 and 1948, the price of imported rice increased 210 percent; prices of locally produced beef, milk, and coffee meanwhile increased a more modest 25 to 50 percent. From March 1941 to August 1948, the food-price index rose from 100 to 213.2.[52] The cost of dependence on the United States could not have been clearer.

Fortunately, by December 1942, as the war began to turn against the Germans and the Japanese, supplies of rice, beans, and other goods improved, though deliveries were still at about half their prewar levels. At least the immediate threat of starvation had passed—though, it must be said, without any help from private business interests.[53] Fortunately, too, the land-reform program had helped to increase the land area devoted to food production from 230,000 acres in 1940 to over 300,000 acres at the end of the war. Increases in output, however, were concentrated in starchy and not particularly nutritious vegetables like sweet potatoes, cassava, plantains, and yautia, the production of which doubled between 1940 and 1944. After the war, the area devoted to food crops declined once again to its prewar level, and the amount of imported food as a share of total

---

[51] As noted above, a local Food and Supplies Commission was created in 1941. It was supposed to buy necessities and sell them to merchants who would then resell them at fixed retail prices. This agency functioned until August 1942, when it was replaced by the Administración General de Suministros (General Administration for Supplies, or AGS), which operated at the same time as, though in a wider capacity than, the federal Office of Price Administration. The AGS had wide powers; for example, it prohibited the export of coffee in 1943 because of a local shortage, and it ordered the rationing of rice, backed by a stiff fine for violations: Santiago, "El control de precios," pp. 17–18, 20–21, 25, 28, and Tugwell, *Public Papers*, pp. 156–57.

[52] Perloff, *Puerto Rico's Economic Future*, p. 177, and PRPB, *Economic Development*, pp. 34, 48.

[53] The Puerto Rican Chamber of Commerce went so far as to accuse the insular government of "communism" for having undertaken emergency measures to prevent hunger: Tugwell, *Stricken Land*, pp. 386, 390, 408.

food consumption (by value) rose to 54 percent in 1950 (from 46 percent in 1940). By the end of the decade, the production of starchy vegetables had fallen 20 percent below its 1944 high.[54]

That few died of starvation did not mean there were no adverse effects of the food shortages or other deprivations. The poor, of course, were always short of nutritious food and a balanced diet, even when they received sufficient calories in more normal times.[55] In 1942–43, some 100,000 children under the age of seven, more than 20 percent of that age group, were found to be without enough to eat. Their average physical retardation was estimated to be 20 to 25 percent of normal growth. That much could be seen and measured. The damage done to these children's mental and social development, however, though less obvious, was no less real. Despite these tragic losses, few of the so-called "better" element seemed to care.[56]

However, total national income and real per capita income did increase in most years during the decade of the forties (table 4.1). Wages also rose, from an average of $1.10 to $2.75 a day in the sugar fields and from $0.75 to $1.25 in other agricultural work. Hourly rates in the sugar industry increased from 15.1 cents in 1940 to 39.5 cents in 1950; in tobacco, from 6.2 to 11.5 cents; and in all manufacturing, from 12.2 to 31.6 cents per hour.[57] Real per capita net income increased 48.4 percent between 1940 and 1950, though most of this increase took place in the first half of the decade. Some comparisons may make the figures in table 4.1 more meaningful. In 1940, when real per capita income was $122 in Puerto Rico, it was $203 in Mississippi (the poorest state in the U.S.),

[54] PRPB, *Economic Development*, pp. 28, 50, 52–53.

[55] In 1945–46, after the major crisis had passed, the volume of food available for consumption was 1,211 pounds per person; the minimum necessary for a nondeficient diet was estimated to be 1,400 pounds. However, the situation was actually worse than this shortfall indicates, since the diet was extremely unbalanced, with high concentrations of starchy foods and inadequate amounts of yellow, green, and leafy vegetables and dairy and meat products: Perloff, *Puerto Rico's Economic Future*, pp. 172, 313–17. One study noted that the diet was "markedly deficient in high-grade proteins, calcium, and in vitamins A, C, and riboflavins": Hanson and Pérez, *Incomes and Expenditures*, p. 16. See also Koenig, *Comprehensive Agricultural Program*, pp. 187–90.

[56] Tugwell, *Stricken Land*, pp. 429–31, and *Public Papers*, p. 168. According to Tugwell, his wife was instrumental in organizing a food-distribution program for children, using volunteer labor and federal surpluses of dried eggs, milk, and whatever else was available. It was difficult for business to attack the distribution stations, run primarily by women for children, that appeared in neighborhoods across the island. At the end of October 1942, there were 288 such stations, at which 59,017 children received food. Free school lunches reached 157,465 children aged six to thirteen. This program was funded by the U.S. Department of Agriculture: Koenig, *Comprehensive Agricultural Program*, p. 22.

[57] PRPB, *Economic Development*, pp. 50, 157, appendix table 7.

TABLE 4.1
Total and Per Capita Net Income,
1940 to 1950

	Total Net Income (current dollars, millions)	Per Capita Net Income (current dollars)	Price-Index Deflator	Real Per Capita Net Income
1940	227.8	$122	100	$122
1941	278.2	146	104.1	140
1942	359.0	184	112.5	163
1943	434.5	218	130.6	167
1944	477.4	236	145.9	162
1945	553.5	270	152.2	177
1946	565.0	271	156.9	173
1947	545.6	254	161.6	157
1948	556.5	256	167.0	154
1949	597.1	272	160.6	169
1950	613.6	279	154.5	181

SOURCES: Derived from data in Perloff, *Puerto Rico's Economic Future*, p. 160, table 49, and p. 383; Curet Cuevas, *El desarrollo económico*, p. 359, table 117, and p. 373. There are very minor differences between Perloff and Curet Cuevas, due to their use of different sources.

$270 in Alabama, and $317 in Georgia. For the U.S. as a whole, it was $575, nearly five times the level in Puerto Rico. By 1949, there had been a slight relative improvement: per capita personal income in Puerto Rico had risen from 21.2 percent of the U.S. level to 24 percent. On the other hand, by international standards, Puerto Rico did not seem so bad off, its $295 in 1949 putting it at 26th in level of per capita income, just behind Cuba with $296.[58]

Still, per capita real income actually fell 13 percent in the immediate postwar period and in 1950 was only 2.3 percent above its 1945 level. The reasons for the decrease after the war are not difficult to find. Two important ones were the drop in federal expenditures on the island and a sharp decline in rum sales in the United States, which resulted in a drastic reduction of the tax revenue returned to the island treasury (table 4.2).[59]

[58] Per capita real income for other countries in the region were $20 in Haiti (1941), $104 in Jamaica (1942), and $102 in Barbados (1942): Ibid., p. 164, and Perloff, *Puerto Rico's Economic Future*, pp. 3–4, n. 3, and p. 193, table 69.

[59] Excise taxes collected on Puerto Rican products sold in the U.S. (primarily rum), minus the costs of collection, are returned to the island treasury. U.S. custom revenues collected in Puerto Rico also go into the insular treasury.

TABLE 4.2
Federal Expenditures in Puerto Rico and U.S.
Tax Revenue Returned, 1940 to 1950
(in thousands of dollars)

Fiscal Year	Federal Expenditures[a]	Tax Revenue Returned[b]
1940	20,600	2,800
1941	33,300	4,500
1942	54,800	13,900
1943	101,500	14,000
1944	117,700	65,852
1945	133,600	38,579
1946	108,000	35,300
1947	50,000	19,800
1948	36,600	3,000
1949	41,600	7,400
1950	—	9,600

SOURCES: PRPB, *Economic Development*, p. 18 (tables 6 and 6a), p. 19
(table 7), and p. 79; Perloff, *Puerto Rico's Economic Future*, pp. 116–17,
table 35.
[a] Excluding transfers of funds to federal facilities in Puerto Rico and to
municipalities.
[b] Primarily from taxes collected on rum.

Between 1942 and 1944, federal expenditures in Puerto Rico amounted
to slightly less than one-quarter of total net insular income. By 1946–47,
this figure had fallen to 8.1 percent, and in 1948–49 it was down to 6.5
percent.[60]

OPERATION BOOTSTRAP

As a result of the problems encountered with the politically vulnerable
government corporations; of the weakness of agriculture in general and
of the uncertainty of the sugar industry in particular; and of the ever more
serious problem of unemployment; and in the absence of a firm commitment to government planning, the energies of development policy became
dedicated more and more to attracting U.S. private capital. However, it
is incorrect to claim that this was "the most fundamental policy change
in the history of the development program."[61] Rather, it represented a
shift of emphasis, beginning in 1945, toward what was thought to be the

---

[60] PRPB, *Economic Development*, p. 18.
[61] Ross, *Uphill Path*, p. 77. See also Sánchez Tarniella, *La economía*, p. 127.

most efficient way to increase economic growth and employment rapidly at the least cost to the government. As mentioned earlier, Moscoso, the director of the Development Company, declared that there was no ideological commitment to any particular method of reaching the PPD's goals of economic development and industrialization and, though of less direct importance now, social justice.

Within Puerto Rico's capitalist and colonial structure, the dominance of private U.S. capital was virtually guaranteed and could have been predicted at the time Muñoz and the PPD initiated state-owned production. It is possible that import-substitution firms in competition with mainland firms might never have been considered if there had been no war to make them necessary and feasible because of the interruption of normal supplies. But it is also true that neither Muñoz nor the PPD had ever expressed hostility to capitalism as a system or to private capital per se. What they had objected to was the blatant and unconscionable exploitation by the absentee sugar corporations. There is little to indicate there was a wider sensitivity to the potential abuses arising from concentrated corporate power. In 1945, the prewar power structure, despite all the positive social changes initiated by the PPD, remained more or less intact and still in the hands of U.S. capitalists.[62]

From the beginning, the program of the PPD had included industrialization as a goal. Part of its effort, as already seen, took the form of state-owned firms, but at the point in 1945 when the Puerto Rico Development Company was renamed the Puerto Rico Industrial Development Company (PRIDCO), increased interest was being shown in making Puerto Rico a more attractive location for mainland investors. It was soon discovered that "attractive" was not nearly enough: to get U.S. capitalists to invest, Puerto Rico had to be made *irresistible*. The enhancement of the investment and profit opportunities is the story of the development program from the late 1940s to the present.

In January 1945, the board of directors of the Development Company passed a resolution authorizing it to construct buildings for use by private firms. Wartime regulations and lack of funding prevented any substantial progress in that direction, but in May of that year, the island legislature earmarked $500,000 (less than 3 percent) of the Development Company's funds for buildings to be sold or leased to private firms at below-market rates as a means of attracting outside capital. In September 1945, the board of PRIDCO approved a more far-reaching plan, a building-subsidy

---

[62] Muñoz made a distinction between economic colonialism, practiced by the absentee sugar corporations, and political colonialism, which was not the policy of the U.S., in his view. In fact, he believed that the U.S. had gotten colonies not out of conscious policy but merely by chance: García Passalacqua, "Muñoz Marín."

program known as "Aid to Industrial Development" (AID). A PRIDCO office which had recently opened in New York became the primary agency for publicizing AID, although the original purpose for the office had been to promote the products of the government enterprises in the mainland market.

The first advertisement for the AID program appeared in *Fortune* magazine in February 1946. In the three months following, 726 inquiries were received by PRIDCO, none of which, however, resulted in an industrial relocation. Companies were curious, but not sufficiently impressed by the offer of a rental subsidy to risk a move to the island. The prospective savings from the subsidy were too insignificant in relation to the uncertainties of production in that location. In the first twenty months of the AID program, only three companies actually took advantage of the building subsidies, and all three—Red Cape Leather, Río Grande Artificial Flowers, and Ponce Candy—had been operating in Puerto Rico prior to the initiation of the program. During this period, the only effect of the program was to reduce the rental costs of three previously existing firms— and at a time when building space was in short supply and could easily have been rented at full value.[63]

By the beginning of 1949, however, the number of AID-subsidized projects had increased. Total approved financial assistance amounted to $13.5 million in sixteen different projects with expected employment of over 4,000 workers. It is not clear, however, that this represented a net gain in employment and production.[64] And even sixteen promoted projects did not constitute a prodigious success. Reduced rent apparently was still not a sufficient incentive to persuade many U.S. corporations to move their operations to Puerto Rico.[65]

As they became cognizant of the shortcomings of the AID program, government policy makers began to more consciously cater to the interests of mainland firms. In the process, perhaps unknowingly but certainly naively, the development process began to slip even further from whatever local control there had been. Soon, the wishes of U.S. private investors became of paramount concern. Once this policy direction became

[63] Ross, *Uphill Path*, pp. 84–95. The AID program also required that eligible firms not compete with already established local firms and that they have a wage bill at least equal to the rental subsidy provided by the government.

[64] At least, the figures in Perloff, *Puerto Rico's Economic Future*, p. 107, table 32, are not conclusive.

[65] The multinational movement, in which many large firms began to move their production facilities into other countries, began on a large scale only after World War II, without any special financial incentives to stimulate the process. It was a natural result of the pursuit of profit by oligopolistic, capitalist enterprises operating in an internationally competitive market.

codified programmatically, it became necessary to convince the mass of Puerto Ricans that their best interests also would be served by making the island a profit haven for U.S. investment. The argument used, of a harmony of interests among the different classes in society, is at least as old as Adam Smith's *Wealth of Nations*. Consensus around this view was obtained in Puerto Rico for a time, because living standards and social conditions did improve in an absolute sense, but, as will be seen, this occurred not because of the simple working of the marketplace, competition, or the trickle-down effect of a growing economy, but because of the particular interventionist role of the government in Puerto Rico and the nature of the colonial relation, which have permitted an improvement in living standards without a concomitant advance in institutional adaptation that could make such improvement permanent.

Concretely, what the Puerto Rican government and PRIDCO did was to take advantage of an opportunity that already existed in the legislation governing Puerto Rico's relations with the United States. Under article 9 of the Jones Act (and article 14 of the Foraker Act before it), individuals and corporations earning income in Puerto Rico were exempted from federal income taxes. Under section 931 of the Internal Revenue Code, subsidiaries of U.S. corporations were able to qualify as "possessions corporations" and were permitted to exclude their Puerto Rican income from their U.S. corporate tax bill (unless their profits were repatriated or otherwise returned to the United States). A possessions corporation was one which (a) obtained 80 percent or more of its gross income from sources within a U.S. territory, and (b) derived 50 percent or more of its gross income from the "active conduct of a trade business within a possession of the United States." These so-called 931 corporations, however, were, like all other corporations, subject to insular taxes, including the local corporate income tax (which had been in effect since 1913, the same year as in the United States), whose rates were very close to those prevailing in the United States. A U.S. corporation thus gained very little tax advantage from the 931 legislation by locating production on the island.[66]

To rectify this, in May 1947, the Puerto Rican legislature passed the Industrial Incentives Act, which not only exempted qualifying firms from property, excise, and municipal taxes and license fees, as earlier laws had done, but also provided complete exemption from insular income

---

[66] USDC, *Economic Study* 1: 73–74. Ross, *Uphill Path*, pp. 95–96, points out that the exemption from the the federal income tax had nothing to do with such lofty principles as "no taxation without representation" (other U.S. territories without representation pay the federal income tax), but was enacted because it was believed that Puerto Rico could not afford to pay any tax. The discussions preceding passage of the Foraker Act would appear to confirm this.

taxes until 1959 and partial exemption until 1962. The law extended this
exemption to all firms in an industry, not just the first, as had been the
case in earlier legislation.[67] Interestingly, because it demonstrates just
how early attention to U.S. capital promotion actually began, a virtually
identical tax-exemption bill had been passed by the legislature in 1944—
even before state-operated enterprises had begun production—but it was
vetoed by Governor Tugwell.[68]

Under the new law, firms manufacturing a good not produced in Puerto
Rico before January 2, 1947, or one already produced but on an approved
list drawn up by the government, could qualify for tax-exempt status.[69]
Besides the tax holiday, the government continued to provide subsidized
buildings and added work-training programs, "soft" (i.e., low-interest)
loans, and other aid. In May 1948, a new piece of legislation, the Industrial Tax Exemption Act, was passed, amending the 1947 law so as to
deny exemption to "runaways"— firms whose relocation in Puerto Rico
would cause the loss of U.S. workers' jobs. This restriction was added
in response to the concerns of U.S. labor organizations that the Industrial
Incentives Act might draw jobs away from the mainland.[70] With these
new laws and other incentives, the Puerto Rican government had initiated
"Operación Manos a la Obra," or "Operation Bootstrap," as it was
known in English, a program of "industrialization by invitation" that
attracted some 9,000 foreign observers between 1950 and 1959.[71] The
slogan for Operation Bootstrap, "the battle for production," made clear
that the intent of the new policy was no longer social justice, even narrowly defined. Growth of output, achieved on the basis of orthodox economic principles of behavior, was the new goal.[72]

---

[67] Stead, *Fomento*, p. 55. A 1936 law had exempted (from property and other taxes, not
from the income tax) only the first firm in an approved and designated industry, not all
firms in a new industry, as the new law did. In 1938, there were 98 such partially tax-
exempt firms: Ross, *Uphill Path*, pp. 44–45, 98–100.

[68] Tugwell makes no mention in his memoirs of his reasons for vetoing this legislation,
nor have others provided substantiated explanations.

[69] The industries on this approved list of industries already producing in Puerto Rico were
those that the government wished to promote because they used local imports or were highly
labor-intensive; there were forty of them, ranging from artificial flowers, candied citron,
and fishing tackle to women's outerwear. The complete list can be found in Perloff, *Puerto
Rico's Economic Future*, p. 108, n. 6.

[70] Baver, "Public Policies," p. 12. The direct impetus for this revision was the relocation
of Textron, the first major firm to move to Puerto Rico. It closed down six of its mills in
the U.S., laying off about 3,500 workers: NACLA, "Puerto Rico," p. 16.

[71] Mundie, "Government Development Bank," p. 138.

[72] The orthodox economic justification for providing tax holidays was that, since labor
was relatively unskilled for industrial employment, lower (though not necessarily zero) taxes
would help to compensate for lower profits during the training period. This assumes that

In 1950, the legislature created the Administración de Fomento Económico (Economic Development Administration), which became popularly known simply as Fomento. PRIDCO was brought under the administration of this new executive agency, becoming its subsidiary rather than continuing to function as an independent agency. The port authority, tourism, and other agencies also were brought under the direction of Fomento, and Moscoso was placed at the head of the entire operation.[73] Ross writes that this reorganization was necessary because the activities of PRIDCO were no longer to be self-financing; the development strategy had shifted from an emphasis on production in government-owned plants to "selling Puerto Rico as an industrial location."[74] Fomento was charged with the responsibility for implementing this new strategy. It proved to be quite successful, but, as shall be seen, with ambiguous and contradictory consequences for the economy and society.

On one level, the new tax laws, incentives, and promotion efforts showed immediate results. The financial press in the United States referred to the exemptions as a "bounty for industry" and to Puerto Rico as a "taxpayers' paradise."[75] During 1947, 9 U.S. firms (including Textron and Newberry Textile Mills) took advantage of the subsidies; in 1948, 16 more firms set up operations; and in succeeding years, the numbers were: 1949, 32; 1950, 37; 1951, 37; 1952, 74; and 1953, 83.[76] The share of total net income generated by manufacturing rose from 11.6 percent in 1940 to 14.5 percent in 1950 and to 17.6 percent in 1955—though these figures are not particularly revealing, since the two most important manufacturing industries were sugar grinding and needlework, which in 1949 were still responsible for 59 percent of manufacturing income. Income from construction of new factory sites, roads, and other infrastructure facilities

---

firms are conscious of marginal profit possibilities, but, Ross argues (*Uphill Path*, pp. 96–97) that this likely was not the case, which would help to explain why U.S. firms required large incentives for relocation and why full tax exemption, not just a marginal improvement in profitability, proved necessary.

[73] Stead, *Fomento*, pp. 16, 25–26, 28 (which includes an organization chart and structure for Fomento).

[74] Ross, *Uphill Path*, p. 126. However, PRIDCO, even as a subsidiary of Fomento, was still authorized to have full or partial ownership of enterprises, an indication that the door was not totally closed to state-run enterprises: Mundie, "Government Development Bank," pp. 33–34, 46.

[75] Perloff, *Puerto Rico's Economic Future*, p. 108, n. 7.

[76] Ross, *Uphill Path*, p. 129. These are the gross numbers of new firms, taking no account of plant closings. In June 1953, 229 Fomento-sponsored plants were in operation (25 of which were locally owned). Since Fomento had sponsored 261 enterprises by the end of 1953, this suggests that at least 32 firms (12.3 percent) had closed: Mundie, "Government Development Bank," p. 82, table 5. See also the convenient table in A. I. Rodríguez, "Inversión," p. 22.

TABLE 4.3
Average Monthly Employment in Manufacturing,
1939, 1940, 1947, 1949, and 1952 to 1957

	Total (000s)	Fomento-Promoted		Other	
		Number (000s)	Percent	Number (000s)	Percent
1939	32.0	n.a.	n.a.	32.0	100.0
1940	56.0	n.a.	n.a.	56.0	100.0
1947	50.0	1.0	2.0	49.0	98.0
1949	55.1	5.0	9.1	50.1	90.9
1952	56.7	16.2	28.6	40.5	71.4
1953	62.4	18.8	30.1	43.6	69.9
1954	65.7	22.0	33.5	43.7	66.5
1955	68.0	25.1	36.9	42.9	63.1
1956	72.2	31.7	43.9	40.5	56.1
1957	70.7	38.3	54.2	32.4	45.8

SOURCES: Jaffe, *People, Jobs, and Economic Development*, p. 45, table 3.2; Curet Cuevas, *El desarrollo económico*, p. 117, table 43.

NOTE: Figures do not include employment in home needlework. Some of the figures are estimates.

also increased in the course of servicing the new industries.[77] Employment in manufacturing increased, and employment in Fomento-promoted factories grew even more rapidly, but this came at the expense of growth in employment in other manufacturing sectors (table 4.3). This suggests that there was a substitution effect, in which manufacturing employment in non-Fomento firms was replaced by employment in government-aided enterprises.

Between 1947 and 1957, total employment in manufacturing rose by 20,700; employment in Fomento-promoted firms increased by 37,300 but decreased by 16,600 in all other manufacturing. Thus, nearly half (45 percent) of the employment growth that Formento could take credit for merely replaced jobs lost in nonexempt manufacturing firms, which were adversely affected by the tax policy. Since most Fomento-promoted firms were mainland-owned and most "other manufacturing" was locally owned, the overall growth in employment meant a shift away from local toward U.S. control. From 1948 to 1950 alone, net direct foreign investment in Puerto Rico grew by $14 million.[78]

[77] PRPB, *Economic Development*, pp. 19–20, and Curet Cuevas, *El desarrollo económico*, p. 111, table 39.
[78] PRPB, *Economic Development*, p. 32, table 18.

THE DECLINE OF STATE CAPITALISM

Opposition to PRIDCO's ownership and operation of industrial enterprises was strengthened by the technical and economic problems they encountered in getting started and in their early, somewhat poor, profit performance. The relentless verbal attacks by the press and business leaders began to take their toll, too, and with the new emphasis on tangible measures of success which had motivated Operation Bootstrap, the PPD, Moscoso, and PRIDCO began to back away from government ownership of the most controversial enterprises run by the government, restricting government ownership largely to the municipal bus service, electric power, water supplies, and sewage—all industries that were common areas for government operations in nearly all capitalist economies, including the United States.

From the perspective of a cost-benefit calculation alone, the import-substitution enterprises that the government had established did not measure up very well.[79] First, all the enterprises were running at a loss, except for the cement and shoe companies. While it is true that the profits of the cement plant about offset the losses from all the other enterprises, any losses made the government program vulnerable to charges of inefficiency, which were taken with increasing seriousness by the PPD. Second, the direct impact on employment of these enterprises was relatively small, and the employment multiplier was believed to be less in government-owned plants than in other areas of industrial promotion.[80] At first glance, the statistics seem to confirm this judgment. As of mid-1948, the five PRIDCO subsidiaries employed 992 workers on a total investment of nearly $11 million, or more than $11,000 per worker. In terms of direct expenditures, it appeared to be cheaper and more cost-effective to promote private capital as a way of increasing employment. For example, Perloff cites unpublished data showing that, with $13.5 million of financial assistance, the firms subsidized by the AID program were expected to employ 4,181 workers; the cost to the government per job created was

---

[79] "The weak and uncertain steps taken by non-competitive industries toward industrialization at this time were, excepting cement, fairly unsatisfactory, if judged, as they unfortunately and unwisely were, by laissez faire capitalist standards of profit margins and efficiency": Mathews, "Political Background," p. 15.

[80] The employment multiplier is the number of jobs created per dollar of spending, or, alternatively, the average investment cost of employing one worker. For example, if a $100,000 investment results in 100 jobs, the employment multiplier is 0.001—that is, it takes $1,000 to provide one job.

thus slightly more than $3,200, less than a third of the cost per job in the government-operated enterprises.[81]

Yet these figures and the conclusions drawn from them are to a certain extent deceptive. They relate only to AID expenditures, but by early 1949, there were also the expenses of industrial promotion on the mainland, running at about $2 million a year.[82] They also ignore the indirect cost of the government program, most particularly the tax and other revenues lost because of the exemptions, though this is perhaps but a small error.[83] More serious is the failure to take into account the loss of employment in other industrial sectors or, even more important, in agriculture. The superiority in cost-effectiveness of the promotion of private capital over the government enterprises is thus overstated in the figures presented above, though by how much is not clear.[84] However, the raw numbers—which showed 700 workers in ten Fomento factories at the beginning of 1947 and 9,000 in 128 enterprises at the end of 1951, producing such diverse commodities as drafting equipment, radios, synthetic hormones, and zippers—were much more persuasive to PPD policy makers than more complicated and sophisticated concerns such as how to precisely measure the true costs of promotion and the generation of employment.[85]

There was yet a third consideration that was making the government enterprises more burdensome from the PPD's perspective. The PPD had come to power on the votes of the dispossessed classes—urban and rural workers, peasants, intellectuals—but then found itself in the uncomfort-

[81] Perloff, *Puerto Rico's Economic Future*, p. 106, table 31, and p. 107, table 32. Ross's estimate is that the employment multiplier of the promotion of private capital was ten times that of government enterprises: *Uphill Path*, p. 84.

[82] Sánchez Tarniella, *La economía*, p. 131. Some proportion of the costs of infrastructure development (roads, sewers, electric power, communications, etc.) should be added, since such expenditures were required before many firms would consider relocation.

[83] Whatever this amount is (and it has not been estimated), it would be the difference between what tax revenues would have been in the absence of the exemption program and what they were with it. The amount of tax loss is obviously less than the taxes that would otherwise have been collected on the profits of promoted firms, since many firms would not have located in Puerto Rico without tax exemption. The extension of tax exemption to all firms in an industry once one firm received an exemption, as provided in the 1947 tax law, meant, however, that some firms already located in Puerto Rico no longer needed to pay taxes. While it is unlikely that this tax loss was zero, its actual size in this early period is difficult to ascertain: Taylor, *Industrial Tax Exemption*, p. 88.

[84] Moreover, as already noted, cost-benefit measures do not take in to account the possibility of gains in equity or autonomy, both of which were important components of Puerto Rico's earlier state-capitalist project.

[85] Chase, "*Operation Bootstrap*," p. 68. It had been estimated that the number of persons entering the labor force each year at that time was 10,000, so that even the 9,000 gross total of employment from private promotion represented a considerable shortfall from overall employment needs: Ross, *Uphill Path*, pp. 83–84.

able position of being an employer in the public corporations.[86] The PPD was thus forced to bargain with a subset of its own constituency and was faced with the necessity of enforcing industrial discipline upon the workers of the new state enterprises if these enterprises were to be competitive in the market place. The same problem did not exist in the government's water, sewage, and electric-power companies, for in those areas there were no, or only ambiguous, measures of efficiency, no competition, and hence less pressure to increase the "output" of workers. The glass, paperboard, ceramic, shoe, and cement companies, however, produced commodities for which efficiency measures could be devised and for which market competition existed. Indeed, the import-substitution strategy within which they had been conceived *demanded* that they be competitive with mainland firms.

The outcome of these combined pressures, which reflected the growing conformity of PPD policy to world market forces at the expense of planning, autonomy, and its other earlier social goals, was the decision in 1948 to sell the five subsidiaries controlled by PRIDCO and to attempt to recoup the government's original investment. From then on, the focus of government policy was to be on private U.S. capital investment.[87]

Although it had originally been planned to sell the five PRIDCO enterprises as a package to one buyer, the shoe company was separated from the others and sold to the Joyce Company, a mainland shoe manufacturer, in December 1949. Joyce would pay for only about 15 percent of the equipment, claiming that the rest was inappropriate for their operations, but it did use the building of the formerly government-owned company for its production facilities. The factory, however, suffered from a series of problems, including training difficulties for labor and management, that ended with the shutdown of the operation and then the closing of the plant in mid-1952. Fomento did not regain its investment from this venture.

The four remaining subsidiaries were sold to the Ferré family of Ponce for $10.5 million in September 1950.[88] The Ferrés already were million-

[86] Chase, "*Operation Bootstrap*," pp. 43–44, suggests this conflict as a possible reason for the sale of what he inappropriately refers to as the "nationalized" factories.

[87] It was only in 1947 that all five enterprises were finally in operation, so the decision to sell them less than a year later hardly allowed sufficient time for PRIDCO, management, and the workers to demonstrate decisively either failure or success. This tends to reinforce the suspicion that the decision to sell the subsidiaries was as much due to political considerations as to economic ones. The decision certainly indicated greater attention to narrowly defined business interests, at the expense of social goals, than had been the case in the earlier period.

[88] For a more detailed discussion of the process of finding buyers and negotiating the price and conditions of sale for all the companies, see Ross, *Uphill Path*, pp. 107–17.

aires, as their ability to make a $2-million down payment attests, and
they were the owners, among other enterprises, of Ponce Cement. The
purchase of these four enterprises gave the Ferrés a monopoly of cement
production on the island. (A legal challenge to the purchase, on the ground
that it violated the antitrust laws, was avoided through the subterfuge of
buying the firms through another Ferré company rather than through the
cement company.) In this sale, PRIDCO did recoup the original investment value of the subsidiaries, but at the same time, it strengthened the
economic and political power base of the Ferré family—who, to their
credit, succeeded in making all the enterprises show a profit.[89]

Some explanations of the turnabout in government policy stress the
roles played by Moscoso, who was without doubt the most keenly and
ideologically committed to promoting private enterprise, and by the absence of Tugwell as governor after 1946, since Tugwell was said to have
been "intractable" about the dangers of persuading private, especially
U.S., firms to move to the island.[90] This theory suggests that everything
depended on these two personalities, and it treats Muñoz and other PPD
leaders merely as passive conduits for the policies of more powerful individuals.[91] But what is even more serious, it underestimates the importance of the nature of the Puerto Rican economy and its power relations,
the changes occurring as a consequence of capitalist development in Puerto
Rico and elsewhere, and the island's colonial relation with the United
States.

The policy reorientation during this period can better be understood in
terms of the concept of "relative state autonomy" and its dynamic.[92]
When the PPD came to power in 1940, it did so in the midst of, and to
a great extent because of, an organic crisis which permitted it, with Tugwell's help, to function with greater autonomy, more boldly, and with

[89] In the case of the paperboard company, the Ferrés were able to do something Muñoz
had decided the government would not do: build a box factory, in direct competition with
the Puerto Rico Container Corporation, to buy the company's output. In this way, a vertically integrated firm was created for which supplies and a market were assured. Luis Ferré
admitted, though, that the plants probably would have become profit earners under Fomento
direction, though not as profitable as under private ownership: Chase, "*Operation Bootstrap*," pp. 115–16.

[90] Ross, *Uphill Path*, p. 112. See also p. 79, where Ross asserts that Tugwell "did not
accept the idea of peddling Puerto Rico, like a new brand of household detergent, to greedy
businessmen." This position was shared by Muñoz and the PPD.

[91] Ross portrays the manipulations of Moscoso as if the latter was engaged in a one-man
plot to promote private capital. See, for example, ibid., pp. 85–86, 100–102.

[92] Theories of the state and of government policy and action have been the focus of much
of the best recent Marxist scholarship. See Poulantzas, *Political Power* and *State, Power,
Socialism*; Jessop, "Recent Theories"; and Block, "Beyond Relative Autonomy," for an
overview and extension of these theories.

more initiative than during any period since the granting of the Autonomist Charter by Spain in 1897. This autonomy, however, was still limited
by its being exercised within the rules of a colonial and capitalist social
formation. The local government's power to effect changes was constrained by the limits on the kind of reform permitted in capitalist economies. Land reform, despite all the objections, had been radical only
from the perspective of the sugar companies. From the perspective of the
capitalist development process, some such action was required to break
the power of the land monopoly—which was blocking progress, especially toward industrialization—by releasing the productive surplus and
workers from the agricultural sector. The PPD's land reform did not deny
the prerogatives of private property in general; on the contrary, it stead-
fastly respected them. Expropriated land, where voluntary compliance
with the Land Law proved impossible (as in the Eastern Sugar case), was
always paid for. What the PPD policy did was not to narrow but rather
to broaden the avenues for private capitalist operations and capital accumulation.

The founding of government corporations in industries traditionally the
domain of private capital had been a bold move.[93] While neither PPD
nor Development Company policy anticipated massive public ownership,
the outrage expressed and the repercussions following upon the relatively
minor step of setting up a few import-substitution industries during the
crisis engendered by the war demonstrated the limits to the autonomy
which the Puerto Rican state could wield. Private companies in the United
States and Puerto Rico were able to sabotage the government enterprises
by refusing to buy their output, withholding their inputs, and mounting
ideological attacks. As World War II came to a close and the rum-tax
revenues declined, the limits of autonomy narrowed even further. Short
of a decisive break with capitalist development as the motor of growth,
and hence with the colonial relation, it became increasingly incumbent
upon the PPD to design policies that were acceptable to business, in order
to avoid future political and economic crisis. The Puerto Rican government was in the position of being a collective capitalist in a social formation without a large class of private capitalists willing or able to make
investments, and so it turned to U.S. capitalists to promote growth and
industrialization, for it was they who had a large surplus of finance capital, control over technology, and advanced managerial skills.

[93] Lewis, *Puerto Rico*, p. 172, suggests that the state enterprises had been designed only
as "showcases" to demonstrate the viability of manufacturing production to reluctant private investors. If that were the purpose, the policy can hardly be judged successful. But to
accept this as the basic explanation for state ownership in the early forties, it is necessary
to ignore other dimensions of the planning thrust of the PPD's program.

This, of course, was not the only course of action that was feasible within the bounds of the colonial relation. For example, an effort could have been made to increase the surplus available for internal investment by imposing and collecting taxes on income and property and through other measures (e.g., forced savings), with the resulting revenues to be used by Fomento and the GDB to promote local ownership and control; or the government could have continued to pursue the policy of creating public corporations, even in areas traditionally reserved to private capital, though certainly this would have been a greater challenge to the usual rules of behavior for capitalist governments than the first option. These choices—and others can be imagined[94]—would have had different long-run effects on Puerto Rico's growth and development, but it is impossible to know whether the result would have been slower or faster growth, higher or lower incomes, more or less employment, or more or less migration. In any case, they were not made. Instead, Muñoz and the PPD followed a development policy that had the effect of strengthening the colonial relationship, increasing dependence on the United States, and further integrating the Puerto Rican economy with that of the mainland.

At one time, among other possibilities, a Marxist explanation of the choice actually made would have been that the state in all capitalist social formations is but the instrument of rule by the capitalist class. This "instrumentalist" theory of the state, however, has been superseded by more sophisticated analyses, in which the state is seen as neither a simple instrument of capitalist class rule nor as a disinterested, pluralistic arbiter acting above classes. The capitalist state is both of these, yet at the same time it is neither. The state is contradictory in its actions, reflecting society's divisions but nevertheless relatively autonomous in its functioning, within the limits set by the rules of capitalism during noncrisis periods. Thus, capitalist states do tend to function to satisfy the reproduction of capitalist society and its relations of production—not because capitalists directly control the state but because the actions of capitalist governments are constrained by the limits imposed by the necessity to assure the functioning of the capitalist social formation and, particularly, the healthy functioning of the economy. There is no conspiracy of capitalists to rule. There is, however, a necessity for government to hold the system together, and that requires, to a great extent, that profits continue to be earned in satisfactory amounts and that capital accumulation proceed unabated.

Muñoz and the PPD had come to power in the midst of a crisis in the

[94]More radical and thoroughgoing programs might have included a movement for independence. Much of the leadership of the PPD (including Muñoz) was pro-independence, and many were socialists.

economy, in politics, and in ideology. The economy had not yet fully recovered from the depression; the traditional political parties were out of touch with the needs and demands of the new working class and the changing conditions created by capitalist development; and the prevailing ideology had not dealt with the conflicts engendered by the altered economic conditions, the depression, the actions of the Nationalists and the accompanying repression, the dislocations caused by the process of proletarianization, or the continued local political impotence. Muñoz's program in 1940 had responded to the needs of the majority of working Puerto Ricans, whose lives were little better in 1940 than they had been at the time of the U.S. invasion.

Yet, even while Muñoz and the PPD reaped the benefits of the shift in the balance of power in their favor, their goals and program respected the boundaries of capitalist reform and accepted the colonial restrictions on local power that were institutionalized by the Jones Act. It was these boundaries, in spite of any intentions the PPD had, which ultimately defined the direction of the development process. Puerto Rican autonomy could not go beyond these "invisible" limitations. To avoid political and economic crises that might have driven the PPD from power, it was necessary to respect the constraints of what was regarded as acceptable capitalist and colonial behavior. When the PPD strayed outside them, the market and private capitalists reined it in.[95] What Muñoz and the PPD were able to accomplish was important, but it was no more than what Gramsci has called a "passive revolution": a structural revolution from above, which left colonial dominance and capitalism intact and, in fact, actually strengthened them by introducing reforms that helped to resolve the crisis of the thirties.[96]

The reforms of the PPD and its efforts to improve social services, health care, education, housing, and the infrastructure certainly made the daily life of most Puerto Ricans better; they did so, however, without conferring on them a greater measure of political power or control over their working lives. The PPD launched its reforms and improvements from above, without changing the power structure that had been evolving since Puerto Rico had become a U.S. colony. The majority of the people

[95] This point is made in general by Block, "Beyond Relative Autonomy." He argues that decision makers of the state are interested in augmenting their power, prestige, and wealth and have a self-interest in being reelected. For the PPD, this meant undertaking needed reforms to improve the living standard, health, and hope of those who had elected them—that is, the traditionally weakest classes—but in a way that did not violate or challenge the colonial capitalist constraints. When the PPD policy did reach those limits, the reaction of business interests was a powerful force to be reckoned with.

[96] Boggs, *Gramsci's Marxism*, and Costello, "Capitalism," pp.7–8.

remained propertyless, and the privileged position of the powerful and wealthy minority was never in danger from the PPD. The attack on the absentee sugar corporations never went beyond what was necessary to reorganize the industry and was little more than symbolic reform necessary for the consolidation of the PPD's power. Better education, health care, transportation, and communications improved the people's standard of living, but they also provided the minimum requirements of a relatively healthy, literate labor force and the necessary infrastructure for capitalist industrial production, growth, and accumulation. What were without doubt popular reforms also cut another way: they were the means of creating a working class and the other prerequisites of an industrial society.[97]

The colonial relation was another factor that prevented Puerto Rico from pursuing a more autonomous course of development when the war ended. Lacking the power to impose tariffs to protect local industry from mainland competition, and given the dependence on U.S. firms for the technology with which to compete effectively in the mainland market, local industrialization was stifled by the impact of market forces, except in those areas in which the nature of the product provided inherent protection for local producers—e.g., construction and tourism.[98] Once the war was over and the flow of goods was normalized, any attempt to industrialize was destined to involve and depend on greater levels of U.S. investment. Of course, the terms of such involvement could have been different from what they turned out to be. Or, if Puerto Rico had chosen to industrialize in those areas where it had a comparative advantage (e.g., tropical fruits, vegetables, canning of these products), more local control might have been possible. But once the decision was made to industrialize along the path that had been followed by the United States and in those areas where U.S. firms had a clear advantage and head start, the needs of U.S. capital became the focus of policy so as to entice investors to the island. From that point forward, and without any conspiracy by U.S. capital or by the metropolitan state to control the Puerto Rican gov-

[97]Modern industries require, in particular, that a minimal "general training" (literacy, basic mathematical skills, acceptance of authority) be provided by the state so that workers can receive and understand the "specific training" of some particular industrial task. Individual firms would not pay the cost of general human capital formation that was transferable to any job, since they could not privatize the benefits, as could be done with more specific training.

[98]Of course, other countries face the problem of obtaining advanced U.S. technology, but the common tariff between the mainland and Puerto Rico means that purchase of technology will be more difficult for Puerto Rican firms, since the sale of technology to them will create direct competition unmediated by the tariff walls and other restrictions that can be placed on firms (including subsidiaries) in foreign countries.

ernment, the rules of capitalist development shaped what local policy had to be.

Even in comparison to other Latin American countries, the maneuverability of the colonial state was quite limited. Whereas horizontal import substitution, which replaces imported consumer goods with local production, was the initial phase of manufacturing in virtually all of them, Puerto Rico attempted this only in the production of shoes. The other government plants—in cement, glassware, paperboard, and construction materials—were examples of vertical import substitution, the production of intermediate goods to allow local producers to expand the industrial linkages within the local economy, the value-added accruing to it, and hence the income retained in it. Vertical import substitution is often regarded as the more "difficult" kind, and the experience of Puerto Rico confirms this judgment. It intrudes upon the production and distribution networks of existing firms, and of course they resist that, making the creation of an integrated industrial structure that much more difficult.

THE LABOR MOVEMENT

It was pointed out in chapter 3 that the FLT, the leading labor organization, had taken the path of cooperation with employers rather than representation of its members. The sugar workers' strikes in 1933–34 were an implicit rebuke to the FLT's leadership for signing a contract without the input of the workers, and these strikes were to be the last chapter in the FLT's role as the island's dominant labor organization. The FLT became less and less responsive to worker interests, at least partly because of its close connection with the Socialist party and the priority which the Socialists gave to remaining in the government. With the overlapping leadership between the FLT and the Socialist party, the tasks of defending workers and participating in the insular legislature became fused and, to a great extent, confused, to the detriment of the workers' interests. The vacuum thus created was not immediately filled, despite attempts by workers to form new, independent unions.

Strike activity, however, continued through the late thirties; in 1939, there were forty-five strikes involving 30,982 workers, and the result of one of these, by publico drivers, was an impetus toward the building of a new labor organization, the Confederación General de Trabajadores (CGT). The founding congress of the CGT, held in San Juan in March 1940, included representatives of 42 unions with a membership of some 72,000 workers. By the time of the next congress, in May 1942, there were 159 unions participating, and they represented 150,000 workers.[99]

[99] Silén, *Movimiento obrero,* pp. 105–7, 109–10, and Galvin, *Organized Labor Movement,* pp. 94–95.

The FLT did not disappear; in fact, for a time it continued to be the primary, though now even weaker, representative of the sugar workers. By 1943, however, CGT representation of sugar workers exceeded that of the FLT, and by 1945 the CGT had replaced the FLT as the dominant workers' representative.[100]

Thus, the rapidity of the PPD's growth had a parallel in the growth and influence of the CGT. It is crucial that the CGT was formed just prior to the 1940 elections, and it adopted a perspective on the role of a workers' movement that made the FLT all but obsolete. The FLT and the Socialist party had maintained a simple anti-hacendado policy more appropriate to the nineteenth century and, perhaps, to the very early years of U.S. control. But conditions had changed, and neither the FLT nor the Socialists were able to adjust. The CGT had a different conception of the problem of organizing labor—viz., that there was a new working class; that it was increasingly dispossessed of its access to land; and that those needing to be organized were now located not only in sugar and in cigar making, but in rum production, transportation, and services, and increasingly among the unemployed. While the FLT strategy of using its connection with the AFL and the U.S. labor movement may have made sense until the 1920s, it became an ossified, conservative, and pro-employer posture in the 1930s and 1940s, one that pushed the FLT and Socialist leadership into pro-U.S. and antiworker positions, especially when the Socialists participated in the governing coalition from 1932 to 1940.

The creation of the CGT was calculated to avoid the traps the FLT had fallen into. First, it was organized as an industrial union, representing all workers in a firm or industry regardless of occupation or skill. The FLT, on the other hand, was a craft union, so that a given firm and industry faced a multiplicity of unions representing different categories of workers. The CGT's strategy was to form one large union to increase the collective strength of the workers in the bargaining process.[101] Second, the CGT was conscious that, although a labor movement was also a political movement and would by necessity be involved in politics, it was crucial to avoid the co-optation of the labor movement by any particular political party. The policies of the Socialists had progressively consumed the FLT, and eventually the FLT was little more than the labor arm of the Socialist party. The CGT wished to organize as the representative of all workers, irrespective of political affiliation, with the single purpose of defending and extending the rights of all workers.

Third, the CGT acted on the premise that the struggle for the rights of

[100]Quintero Rivera, "La base social," p. 85.
[101]Ibid., pp. 82–83, and Quintero Rivera, *Workers' Struggles*, p. 142.

labor was a class struggle and, in Puerto Rico, an anticolonial struggle as well. The collaboration of the FLT's leaders with the AFL, their dependence for success on the application of U.S. laws, and their faith in the benevolence of the United States led to a pro-Americanism that became a virtual obsession, to the disadvantage of the labor movement and workers' rights in general.

The CGT, however, proved not to be immune to the forces that had thwarted the effectiveness of the FLT. Both Tugwell and Muñoz Marín encouraged the growth of the CGT: Tugwell, because he felt that the FLT was "totally corrupt"; Muñoz, because in the 1940 elections he and the PPD had benefited from CGT support.[102] Muñoz also was interested in controlling the new labor movement in order to get its support for the PPD's industrial program. He thus tried to attract CGT leaders into the government and to place PPD leaders in positions of influence within the labor organization.[103] To a great extent this strategy was successful, but because of the ensuing disagreement over relations between the PPD and the CGT, the union split in March 1945 into two factions, the "Government" faction (CGT Gubernamental) and the "Authentic" faction (CGT Auténtica). Other independent unions then sprung up as a result of this fissure; the goal of an independent, nonaffiliated union representing all workers faded away.[104] Subsequently, Muñoz actively blocked any legislation that attempted to increase the power of the union movement, on the ground that with him and the PPD in power protecting labor's interests, such legislation was unnecessary.[105] Having both the chief labor leader and the leading architect of Operation Bootstrap in La Fortaleza must have been reassuring to private investors. As Puerto Rico's Planning Board later noted, there were relatively few strikes in the late forties, and the largest of them occurred not in the new manufacturing sector but in the declining sugar industry.[106]

On the positive side for workers' rights and interests, in 1945 the Puerto Rican legislature passed the Insular Labor Relations Act. Though based on the National Labor Relations Act of 1935 (Wagner Act) in the United States, it was even broader, in that it guaranteed the right of collective bargaining to agricultural workers and employees of public corporations as well as to all other workers.[107]

[102] Galvin, *Organized Labor Movement*, p. 94.
[103] Silén, *Movimiento obrero*, pp. 112–13, and Quintero Rivera, *Workers' Struggles*, p. 156.
[104] Silén, *Movimiento obrero*, pp. 116–17.
[105] Galvin, *Organized Labor Movement*, p. 101.
[106] PRPB, *Economic Development*, pp. 46–47.
[107] Silén, *Movimiento obrero*, pp. 92–93.

THE NEEDLEWORK INDUSTRY

One of the most important industries in the new push toward manufacturing was textiles, including needlework, most of which was still done
in the home.[108] The home needlework industry, in which gloves, wom-
en's and children's clothing, embroidery, and other items were sewn in
the home, had its beginnings during World War I, when the usual European supplies and labor sources for U.S. companies had been cut off (see
chapter 2).[109] It was an industry predicated on poverty; as Ross remarks,
it was

> without roots, and without any foundation except misery. It could exist
> only on desperation wages. No one could make a living at it; but a
> woman whose husband is unemployed and whose children are starving
> will go to great lengths for the price of a few pounds of rice.[110]

In April 1940, there were 44,731 persons, mostly women, working in
the home needlework industry.[111] They accounted for more than 44 percent of all manufacturing employment (100,693); the industry was the
single largest one in the manufacturing sector. Eight years later, the number of home needleworkers had increased by nearly 16 percent, to 51,871,
of whom 98 percent were women. Two-thirds of the increase in manufacturing employment between 1940 and 1950 came in home needlework.[112] The importance of this industry is reflected in the value of its
output and in its share of total export value (table 4.4). Until the twenties,
needlework production was quite minor and exports were almost insignificant. From the 1920s to 1940, exports rose sharply in absolute and
relative value, accounting for about 15 percent of total exports on the

---

[108] In 1940, about 68 percent of persons counted as workers in manufacturing were actually home needleworkers or were employed in "tiny shops" rather than in what might
normally be considered factories: Jaffe, *People, Jobs, and Economic Development*, p. 106.
In April 1946, there were 308 manufacturing establishments, other than home needlework
sites, producing apparel, textiles, and the like, employing 10,967 workers, an average of
about 36 per factory. These firms accounted for 14.8 percent of all manufacturing firms and
22 percent of manufacturing employment: Perloff, *Puerto Rico's Economic Future*, p. 104,
table 29.

[109] V. Clark et al., *Porto Rico and Its Problems*, pp. 467–74, describes the industry in
the 1920s.

[110] Ross, *Uphill Path*, p. 17.

[111] Perloff, *Puerto Rico's Economic Future*, p. 55, table 9. The data on women workers,
especially those in the home needlework industry, are quite poor and it is likely that there
was substantial undercounting: Jaffe, *People, Jobs, and Economic Development*, p. 83,
table 5.4. Presser, "Labor Force Status of Puerto Rican Women," p. 4, indicates that for
1950 the undercount may have been on the order of nearly 50 percent of the reported
number of home needleworkers (54,000).

[112] PRPB, *Economic Development*, p. 55.

TABLE 4.4
Value of Needlework Exports and Percentage of Total Export Value,
Selected Years, 1901 to 1948

Fiscal Year	Value (thousands of dollars)	Percentage Total Export Value
1901	8	0.09
1911	12	0.03
1921	2,333	2.08
1930	13,335	13.38
1935	14,461	18.15
1940	15,696	17.00
1941	5,875	6.73
1945	21,004	18.08
1946	25,551	15.82
1947	39,268	21.99
1948	32,492	16.92

SOURCE: Perloff, *Puerto Rico's Economic Future*, p. 100, table 26, and p. 136, table 39.

NOTE: Not all of the value of exports represents value created in Puerto Rico. A substantial proportion is the value of the raw materials imported from the U.S.

average. Throughout this period, needlework was the second or third most important export, behind sugar and, in some years, tobacco.

Despite the importance of the needlework industry to the export trade, it brought little benefit to the local economy or to the women workers who were employed in it. This is illustrated by the fact that, although in 1940 home needleworkers accounted for 8.7 percent of all employment (and that is probably understated), the entire textile industry contributed only 2.6 percent of total net income.[113] Prior to the effective application of the minimum wage law in Puerto Rico, wage rates for home workers averaged from 1.5 to 4 cents an hour. The viability of the industry and its ability to continue to pay low wages was threatened, however, by a growing movement toward the application of uniform wage standards to the economy. In 1937, the U.S. Supreme Court upheld a 1919 law of the Puerto Rican legislature that set a minimum wage of $4 per week for women under eighteen years of age and $6 for women over eighteen. The legislation had been widely violated before, and later in 1937, the home needlework industry was exempted from it altogether. In 1938, a target rate of 25 cents an hour was set as a goal for all industries, and in

[113] Perloff, *Puerto Rico's Economic Future*, p. 97, table 23.

1940 this was made the minimum wage, rising to 75 cents in 1950. However, a loophole was added to the law that allowed exemptions for "hardship" industries. A 1940 amendment to the Fair Labor Standards Act of
1938 allowed industries to set lower minimum wages, though the target
wage for each industry remained the same.[114] As a result of such exemptions, in 1949 the minimum wage for home needleworkers was still only
15 cents an hour, which represented almost no gain in real income because of the rising price level. In 1955, it was 17.5 cents, and it increased
to 26 cents in 1957. By comparison, the minimum wage in the United
States at that time was $1.00 per hour. Throughout the early 1950s, me-
dian weekly earnings in home needlework were only slightly more than
$3.00, about one-fourth to one-third the median wage in all industry for
women workers and but one-tenth the weekly earnings of government
workers in Puerto Rico.[115]

The initial reaction in the needlework industry to the attempt to introduce minimum wages was to cut back production and to lobby, successfully, for exemption. In 1940–41, before an exemption was granted to
this industry, the value of exports of needlework was only $5.9 million,
a decline of nearly 63 percent from the previous year (see table 4.4).
After the exemption was granted, exports rose. Yet the industry, especially its home-production segment, was slated to recede into Puerto Rico's past. The government had a commitment to reasonable wages because of the high cost of living and union demands, and that spelled
decline for an industry that was so dependent upon cheap labor. The
home needlework industry took its business to countries that were even
poorer and more desperate than Puerto Rico. The number of home needleworkers began to fall: from the peak of 54,000 in 1950 to 43,000 in
1951 and then to 36,000 in 1952 and 34,000 in 1953, a decrease of 37
percent.[116] By 1957, there were but 15,000 such workers, and whereas
31 percent of all women workers had been employed as home needleworkers in 1940, by 1979 less than 1 percent of the female labor force
was so occupied.[117]

URBANIZATION AND MIGRATION

Along with the rapid economic growth of the 1940s, during which
GNP increased by 76 percent in real terms, Puerto Rico experienced a

[114] Ibid., pp. 152–58, and Ross, *Uphill Path*, pp. 41–44.

[115] Jaffe, *People, Jobs, and Economic Development*, p. 127, and p. 130, table 7.1, and
PRPB, *Economic Development*, p. 55.

[116] Jaffe, *People, Jobs, and Economic Development*, p. 83, table 5.4.

[117] Presser, "Labor Force Status of Puerto Rican Women," p. 7. In 1969, the median
income for year-round work for home needleworkers was $2,024, about $40 per week:
ibid., p. 8.

TABLE 4.5
Total, Rural, and Urban Population,
1940 and 1950

	1940	1950	Rate of Growth (percent)
Total population	1,869,255	2,210,703	18.3
Rural population	1,302,898	1,315,890	1.0
Rural as percent of total	69.7	59.5	—
Urban population	566,357	894,813	58.0
Urban as percent of total	30.3	40.5	—

SOURCE: CENEP, *Labor Migration*, p. 180, table 1, and p. 181, table 2.

demographic shift from rural areas to the cities—the usual pattern in the process of industrialization. But in Puerto Rico the rural-to-urban migration also took a more unusual form: migration from the island to the United States. This is an important difference, because coupled with the levels of unemployment that began to appear in the 1940s, it suggests that there was a weakness in the development program. Just when the most rapid growth of GNP was occurring, unemployment levels were rising and a growing number of people were migrating to the mainland in search of work.

The internal rural-to-urban shift is evident from table 4.5. Although the rural population did not decline in absolute numbers over the decade, its growth rate was far below that of the total population. Meanwhile, the urban population increased nearly 60 percent, expanding from 30 percent to more than 40 percent of the total.

The data on out-migration are shown in table 4.6. Migration had not been unknown before this period (see chapter 2), but the magnitude of the postwar migration was something quite new. In the decade from 1940 to 1950, net emigration from Puerto Rico was nearly 180,000 persons— more than in the previous four decades—most of it to the United States, and the number continued to increase thereafter.[118] Without this movement of people, total population would have increased 28 percent rather than 18.3 percent, and unemployment certainly would have been higher. As many have commented, without the ability to "export" its unemployed at the same time that capital was being imported, Puerto Rico's economic progress would have appeared much less impressive than the

[118] "In the year 1953 alone . . . almost as many persons left Puerto Rico for the mainland as in the entire 47 years between the time the United States took possession of the island and the end of World War II": Jaffe, *People, Jobs, and Economic Development*, p. 66.

TABLE 4.6
Migration to and from Puerto Rico,
1940 to 1949

Year (ending June 30)	Arrivals	Departures	Net Out-Migration
1940	23,924	24,932	1,008
1941	30,416	30,916	500
1942	28,552	29,480	928
1943	16,766	19,367	2,601
1944	19,498	27,586	8,088
1945	22,737	33,740	11,003
1946	45,997	70,618	24,621
1947	101,115	136,259	35,144
1948	104,492	132,523	28,031
1949	124,252	157,338	33,086

SOURCE: Puerto Rican Planning Board, *A Comparative Study of the Labor Market Characteristics of Return Migrants and Non-Migrants in Puerto Rico* (San Juan, 1973), as given in CENEP, *Labor Migration*, pp. 186–87, table 9.

usual statistics suggest. Such a situation might have forced a change in development policy because of the social and political crisis which very likely would have erupted. Thus the "safety value" of migration, which was available because as U.S. citizens Puerto Ricans could move freely anywhere within the continental U.S. and its territories, removed the necessity, for a time, to have to confront the failure of the growth model to provide adequate employment and income.

INCOME DISTRIBUTION

Table 4.7 shows the estimated distribution of income by quintiles for four years between 1942 and 1955. In 1946–47, the poorest 80 percent of families received only 44 percent of total income. However, though there are problems with the comparability and inclusiveness of the data, it would appear that there had been a redistribution in the direction of greater equality in the preceding years, during the PPD's early reforms, for in 1940, the poorest 86 percent of families had received only 29 percent of total income. On the other hand, there was very little further redistribution between 1947 and 1950, the period in which Operation Bootstrap was initiated and expansion of output began to take priority

TABLE 4.7
Distribution of Family Income in 1940,
1946–1947, 1950, and 1955
(percent of total income)

Quintile of Families	1940[a]	1946–47	1950	1955
Poorest 20%	⎧	3.5	4.5	5.0
Second 20%	⎨ 29	7.5	8.0	8.0
Middle 20%	⎩	13.0	12.5	13.0
Fourth 20%	71	20.0	20.0	22.0
Richest 20%		56.0	55.0	52.0
(Richest 5%)		(29.0)	(26.0)	(24.0)

SOURCE: Curet Cuevas, *El desarrollo económico*, pp. 23–24, and p. 364, table 120. See also Perloff, *Puerto Rico's Economic Future*, p. 166, table 54.
[a] Shares are for poorest 86 percent of families and richest 14 percent.

over social justice.[119] This suggests that there was a connection between development policy and the degree of equality of income distribution, though this is a very short time period in which to observe change. It is worth adding that the degree of inequality shown in table 4.7 is greater than that which prevailed in the United States at the time, though not greatly different from many underdeveloped countries and better than quite a few.[120]

One important argument justifying income inequality in capitalist economies has been that it provides an incentive to work by holding out the hope of higher income and thus increased consumption.[121] To the extent that people are so motivated, income inequality plays a functional role— a carrot to go along with the stick of unemployment. Table 4.8 shows the distribution of income for wage earner families alone (i.e., excluding

[119] In 1950, 47 percent of families had annual incomes of less than $1,000 and received 12.2 percent of total income; the richest 5.5 percent had incomes exceeding $5,000 (average income, $8,000) and received 27.2 percent of total income. Of those with incomes below $500 per year, 45 percent were in agriculture and 22 percent were families headed by women: Barton, *Family Incomes*, p. 13, table 3, and p. 32.

[120] In the U.S. in 1946–47, the poorest 20 percent of families received 5 percent of total income, and the richest 20 percent received 46 percent: Edward C. Budd, "Postwar Changes in the Size Distribution of Income in the U.S.," *American Economic Review* 60 (May 1970):249, table 1. For other countries, see World Bank, *World Development Report, 1979*, pp. 172–73, table 24.

[121] For an application of this argument to the U.S., see Thurow, *Zero-Sum Society*, pp. 156–58. Whether the prospect of increased consumption actually does have that effect is another question entirely, which is taken up in Scitovsky, *Joyless Economy*.

TABLE 4.8
Distribution of Income for Wage-Earner Families in
1941, 1952, and 1953
(percent of total wage-earner income)

Quintile of Families	1941	1952	1953
Poorest 20%	5.0	6.0	9.0
Second 20%	9.0	13.0	13.0
Middle 20%	12.5	17.0	17.0
Fourth 20%	20.0	22.0	25.0
Richest 20%	53.5	42.0	36.0

SOURCE: Andic, "Wage Earner Families," p. 19, table 3.

NOTE: Only the families of wage earners who worked at least 13 weeks in the year indicated are included in these figures.

recipients of salaries, profits, rents, and dividends, as well as the unemployed and some self-employed) for 1941, 1952, and 1953. This distribution was becoming somewhat more equal, as workers moved from relatively low-paying jobs in agriculture to higher-paying ones in manufacturing, construction, and government.[122] In 1941, the best-paid 20 percent of wage earner families received 10.7 times the income share of the poorest-paid 20 percent; in 1952, the ratio was 7:1; and in 1953, it declined to 4:1.

A much higher degree of inequality is manifested in the distribution of total income shown in table 4.7, which includes income from wages, salaries, profits, rents, and dividends, and also includes those without incomes. In 1946–47, the ratio between the highest and lowest quintiles was 16:1; in 1950, it was 12.2:1; and in 1955, it was 10.4:1. That does indicate an improvement in income distribution, it is true, but it also suggests that the degree of inequality in the distribution of total income was not entirely functional—that is, there could have been greater equality of total income without affecting the incentive to work, which is determined, to a large extent, by the degree of inequality of earned income.[123] There thus could have been greater taxation of unearned incomes,

[122] Andic, "Wage Earner Families," p. 24. See also Mann, "Economic Development," for criticisms of the literature on distribution and his interpretation.

[123] Migration probably had the effect of making total income more nearly equal than it would have been otherwise, since there would have been more unemployed or low-income persons otherwise.

and the revenue could have been used to continue working toward the PPD's earlier goals of social justice, greater local control over production, and reduced trade and financial dependence on the U.S. market.

There is little doubt that the PPD's social programs helped to improve conditions beyond what the income-distribution figures alone suggest. Better housing, improved drinking-water supplies, more extensive electrification and sewage systems, better education that reached larger numbers of children, and improved roads and transportation represented real gains. But these gains must be weighed against the fact that the development program did not create an economic structure able to sustain them or to provide sufficient employment. A welfare-type structure from above had been created; the means to support it locally had not.

POLITICAL DEVELOPMENTS

There were two significant political changes during this period: the passage of the Elective Governor Act and the creation of the Commonwealth of Puerto Rico.

Since the passage of the first Organic Act in 1900, Puerto Rico's governors had been presidential appointees. Often they were military men; too often, whether military or civilian, they lacked any knowledge about the island or, even worse, any willingness to learn. Most insulated themselves from a culture, language, and people they did not know or understand,[124] and few had more than the slightest positive impact, their tenure in office being little more than a holding action that perpetuated the inertia of the local government, dominated as it had been by the sugar interests until the 1940s. The chief exceptions were Roosevelt, who at least had made gestures of good will, and Tugwell, who more than any other governor was able to oversee changes in the economy and, to an extent, in the power structure, thanks to the conjuncture of events that made such change not only necessary but finally possible. Yet Tugwell was no less a North American for his sympathies; he was often paternalistic and condescending toward Puerto Rico and Puerto Ricans. He recognized, however, that the mere existence of a colonial, continental governor, when not ineffective and an irritant on the island, was becoming, or threatened to become, an embarrassment to the United States at the international level.

During the early months of the war, Tugwell had expressed the thought that having an elected governor might be a way to gain Puerto Rican

[124] Tugwell's pungent yet sympathetic observations on the archetypical mainland governor surely reflect some of his own experiences: *Stricken Land*, p. 80.

loyalty to the U.S. war effort.[125] He was a member of the Caribbean
Advisory Committee, which was meeting during the war to deal with the
problems of defense and food supplies of the multinational colonies in
the region. Unavoidably, the committee also discussed colonial policy
and its future, and one of its actions was to send a letter to President
Roosevelt supporting Tugwell's suggestion, made earlier directly to Roosevelt, that he ought to endorse an elective governorship for Puerto Rico
"to be set for 1944 when a general election is due. . . ." It also suggested that a constitutional convention be held within a year after the end
of the war to "settle the status of Puerto Rico in a permanent way."[126]
Roosevelt was agreeable to this initiative, as he had indicated in conversations with Tugwell and in a message to Congress, and he established a
special President's Committee in 1943 to consider revision of the Jones
Act, including the issue of an elected governor.[127] This committee did
recommend an elected governor, as well a plebiscite on status, a prohibition on unilateral changes in relations between Puerto Rico and the
United States and several other changes. But of the key suggestions, only
the elective governor proposal survived the Senate hearings, which, typically, were carried out in an atmosphere of hostility toward the island
compounded by ignorance.[128] The final version of the Senate bill actually
would have reduced Puerto Rico's autonomy even further, but it died in
the House of Representatives in early 1944 without coming to a vote.[129]

[125] "I should think that after the war the old colonialism would be dead. . . . I can't
help wondering what would happen here if an enemy landed in force. Exactly how would
Puerto Ricans divide if offered a new opportunity? I believe they feel more, but still not
nearly enough, part of us. I have been wondering whether it might not be strategic for the
President to support a new status for Puerto Rico now. I am writing him to suggest we
disassociate ourselves, by such a gesture, from the colonial empires . . .": Tugwell, *Stricken
Land*, p. 269 (from his journal entry for March 10, 1942). By "gesture," Tugwell did not
mean independence, but more autonomy under U.S. tutelage (pp. 324–25), and it is clear
from this quotation whose interests were paramount in Tugwell's mind.

[126] Ibid., p. 328 (from his journal entry for June 2, 1942). The letter from the Caribbean
Advisory Committee also recommended that, along with the elected governor, there ought
to be a "Presidential Delegate" to oversee the colony—i.e., a kind of "supergovernor,"
which certainly would have diluted the importance of the "gesture" of an elected governor
if it had been instituted. This provision was deleted from later proposals, though Tugwell
supported it as necessary to protect "the national interest" and to ensure U.S. sovereignty.
President Roosevelt agreed with him: Ibid., pp. 543–47.

[127] Ibid., p. 486. Tugwell's views on this committee, the goal of independence, and what
the aspirations of Puerto Ricans ought to have been can be found on pp. 486–97 and 508–
15. His perspective on the committee's deliberations and its final recommendations are on
pp. 538–61.

[128] Ibid., pp. 598–603.

[129] Efforts by the Puerto Rican legislature to unilaterally pass enabling legislation for an
elective governor and a status plebiscite when Congress had not done so were vetoed by

Tugwell assessed this debacle accurately with the comment: "The difficulty with the present policy is that it is not a policy at all. No one can say, no one can even guess, what the intentions of the United States are toward Puerto Rico."[130]

Tugwell had made it known that he planned to leave the governor's post in the fall of 1946 and return to teaching at the University of Chicago. President Truman took advantage of the opportunity this presented him and named Jesús T. Piñero as the first Puerto Rican governor on July 25, 1946. Piñero was the island's resident commissioner in Washington at the time and a leading member of the PPD. Following up on this initiative, Congress finally succeeded in passing a bill that provided for an elective governor. Truman signed it into law in August 1947; it set 1948 for the first election. It gave the elected governor the right to appoint the cabinet, but the president retained the right to appoint the auditor and members of the Puerto Rican Supreme Court. Furthermore, Congress and the president retained their veto power over all legislation, Congress maintained its right to unilaterally oversee and legislate for the island, and most of the other provisions of the Jones Act were retained.[131]

In the elections held under the new act in November 1948, the PPD won 61.2 percent of the total votes cast. Muñoz Marín became the island's first elected governor, and the PPD's candidates also won a majority in the legislature.[132]

The next political problem to be faced was resolution of the status issue to relieve the United States of its stigma as a colonial power and, in particular, to end the need to make regular reports to the United Nations on Puerto Rico, as required by the UN Charter of all nations for their colonial possessions. Concern with status had long dominated Puerto Rican politics and intellectual discussion. Muñoz had espoused independence since youth and had drawn up the Liberal party's platform on independence for the 1932 campaign. In the 1940 campaign, however, the party decided not to make status an issue; though Muñoz might still have favored independence philosophically, as a politician he came to feel that he could not risk a loss of support from those who had voted for him by attempting to implement what he now believed was his personal inclination and a preoccupation of intellectuals rather than a concern of the

---

Tugwell on the ground that, under the Jones Act, only Congress had the right to make such changes. Tugwell's veto was overriden by the Puerto Rican legislature, but President Truman upheld it, thus overruling the local government: Silén, *Historia*, p. 275.

[130]Tugwell, *Public Papers*, p. 153.

[131]Public Law 362; see García Martínez, *Puerto Rico*, pp. 199–203.

[132]Bayrón Toro, *Elecciones y partidos políticos*, pp. 210–14 (76.5 percent of those registered voted).

majority of poor Puerto Ricans, who did not have any strong preferences about the island's status.[133] Increasingly, Muñoz's desire to stay in power outweighed any ideological predisposition he might personally have had toward independence. He became a supporter, implicitly, of the status quo relationships with the United States—that is, colonialism—and he owed his political power to being able to make that status work and provide greater benefits to Puerto Rico, even if the gains were unequally distributed. His public stance, which may have had some validity, was that economic conditions were not sufficiently advanced to be beneficial to the island.

Hence, after being elected governor, Muñoz began to work for the institutionalization of the colonial status. In meeting with the press three days after being sworn in, Muñoz spoke of a new type of relation with the United States, neither as a forty-ninth state nor as an independent country, but a relationship that would provide the benefits of statehood without the obligation of paying federal taxes. In essence, what Muñoz was proposing was the existing status but with a greater degree of equality and autonomy vis-à-vis the states on the mainland and the federal government. It would be a colonialism acceptable to and validated by Puerto Ricans via a plebiscite—a colonialism "freely" chosen at the ballot box.

With Muñoz's impressive ability to command support and allegiance from his followers, this status option began to take shape as a genuine possibility. Tugwell, early in his tenure, had thought a "commonwealth, Dominion—call it anything indicating a half-way relationship" might be the best solution for the island's status problem, since it could be designed to reconcile the need for the dignity of self-rule with the aid from the United States that he believed essential to the island's progress.[134] In June 1946, Muñoz Marín wrote two articles for the newspaper *El mundo*, in which he claimed that statehood was impossible and independence "without special economic conditions" utopian, and in which he called for a new form of local government—he suggested it be called the Pueblo Asociado de Puerto Rico (Associated Community of Puerto Rico)—to

---

[133]Muñoz Marín, "Desarrollo de pensamiento político," p. 9, and *Memorias*, p. 186.

[134]Tugwell, *Stricken Land*, pp. 491–92, 495. Tugwell felt the greatest problem with such an arrangement was that it would "not satisfy the obsolete aspirations of the independentistas." Even though he believed that "independence would be ruinous" (p. 495), he also wrote that "the speeches made by the most extravagant independentistas sounded a good deal like those I had been taught to regard as a precious part of our own patriotic literature" (p. 25). Thus Tugwell, like Muñoz, saw independence as an ideal, but one that could not be realized without adverse economic consequences. He also believed that the island would be worse off as a state. The present status, with a different name and some minor changes, appeared to him to be the only possibility (pp. 495–96).

permit continued economic progress in association with the United States until a realistic choice between statehood and independence could be made.[135]

This suggests that Muñoz believed that both the expanded local autonomy that commonwealth status would bring and the continuation of colonialism were but temporary expedients during a necessary period of transition until, sometime in the future after "sufficient" economic development, a final reasonable decision could be reached. In 1946, he convinced his fellow leaders of the PPD to abandon independence as a goal, however, and they in turn gave Muñoz the responsibility for deciding "when to kill the hope for independence" among PPD followers.[136] On July 4, 1948, Muñoz declared that "the only serious defect" that remained in relations between Puerto Rico and the United States was the law that prevented the island from refining its own sugar.[137] This was a far cry from the young Muñoz, the vociferous advocate of independence in his essays, editorials, and poems who had decried colonial dominance of his country.

On July 4, 1950, President Truman signed Public Law 600, which permitted Puerto Rico to write its own constitution, replacing the Jones Act. The permission was made subject to certain conditions: that the form of government be a representative democracy, that the constitution stipulate neither statehood nor independence, and, perhaps most important, that it be approved by Congress before going into effect.[138] It was thus

[135] Silén, *Historia*, pp. 276–77, 293–95, and Johnson, *Puerto Rico*, p. 35. Muñoz believed that it would be at least fourteen years before economic problems would be sufficiently resolved to allow further consideration of the question of status. He had come to the conclusion that most people did not want independence, and any political party wishing to be elected had to avoid making independence a central issue. He clarified that position in a speech in 1953 in Barranquitas, "What I Learned from the People": García Passalacqua, "Muñoz Marín," p. 14.

[136] García Passalacqua, "Muñoz Marín," p. 14. Those members of the PPD who continued to support independence rebelled against this decision, and a fierce internal battle raged. When Muñoz won out, many independence supporters left or were expelled from the PPD: Silén, *Historia*, pp. 276–82, and Muñoz Marín, "Desarrollo de pensamiento político," p. 13.

[137] Silén, *Historia*, p. 294.

[138] García Martínez, *Puerto Rico*, pp. 205–6. The only vote in Congress against P. L. 600 was cast by Vito Marcantonio of New York, who supported independence and believed the law was a cover for colonialism. In Puerto Rico, the Independence party, the Nationalist party, the CGT (Auténtica), and the Unión General de Trabajadores (General Workers' Union, formed in 1947 in an unsuccessful attempt to heal the split within the CGT) opposed the law. At the end of October 1950, the Nationalist party took up arms against the authorities within Puerto Rico, attacking in various locations, including an attempt on Muñoz's life. In Jayuya, the National Guard used planes to bomb the Nationalists in order to block their advance. In the U.S., two Nationalists made an attack on President Truman on No-

236   CHAPTER FOUR

clear that the United States meant to retain sovereignty over the island;
despite the fact that Puerto Ricans were to be permitted to make their
own constitution if they chose to do so, the island was to remain a U.S.
colony.

A referendum was held on July 4, 1951—the date, of course, had
symbolic significance—in which Puerto Rico's voters were asked whether
they wanted to accept the offer to make their own constitution on the
terms set forth by the United States. Many *independentistas* urged boycott of the elections; other political figures, including those who favored
statehood, called for a negative vote. However, 76.5 percent of the 506,185
voters who participated in the referendum voted to accept the offer, although abstention was higher than normal (only about 65 percent of those
registered voted, some 22 percent fewer than had participated in the 1948
elections).[139] The convention opened in September 1951 with 92 delegates, three-fourths of them PPD members.[140]

The convention decided that the name of the intermediary status would
be the Estado Libre Asociado, which was to be rendered in English,
under Resolution 22 of the convention, as the Commonwealth of Puerto
Rico.[141] The convention approved the constitution it had developed on
February 6, 1952.[142] In comments before the assembled delegates, Muñoz Marín declared that with the document they had made, "the United
States of America ends every trace and vestige of the colonial system in
Puerto Rico."[143] In March, the constitution was presented to the Puerto
Rican people, who approved it overwhelmingly: More than 81 percent
voted to accept the constitution, though again participation was relatively
low (59 percent of those registered).[144]

---

vember 1. These efforts to foment a general uprising did not gain the backing of very many
people, but they did succeed in bringing to world attention the situation in Puerto Rico:
Silén, *Historia*, pp. 305–13.

[139] Bayrón Toro, *Elecciones y partidos políticos*, p. 215.

[140] Silén, *Historia*, pp. 322–23. The Independence party was not represented, by its own
choice, which meant that it was unable to influence the constitution's content.

[141] In 1921, Antonio Barceló, the leader of the Union (later Liberal) party, had supported
the establishment of an Estado Libre Asociado, which would have provided for a governor
to be chosen by the Puerto Rican legislature and overseen by a federal observer, similar to
what Tugwell proposed in the 1940s. The remaining provisions of the Jones Act were to
continue as before. This proposal was introduced into Congress as the Campbell project,
but it was not enacted. Only the name was the same, however, since this early plan provided even less autonomy than the Elective Governor Act of 1947: *BHPR* 9: 361–62.

[142] The differences of view expressed in different sections of the constitution and the
concessions made by the PPD to the other parties during the drafting process can be found
in Silén, *Historia*, pp. 324–27.

[143] Ibid., p. 327.

[144] Ibid., pp. 327–28, and Bayrón Toro, *Elecciones y partidos políticos*, p. 215.

When the constitution came before Congress for its approval, one section of the Bill of Rights was eliminated,[145] and a provision was added that any future changes in the constitution be in accord with the U.S. Constitution. While it was not required specifically that such changes be approved by Congress, the nature of the constitution as a "compact" implied the necessity of such approval. (Attempts in later years by Puerto Rico to make changes have regularly been rebuffed by Congress.) The revised constitution was sent back to the constituent convention for reapproval, and on July 10, 1952, the assembly accepted the changes. As the senate report on P. L. 600 had made clear even before the constitution had been written, it "would not change Puerto Rico's fundamental political, social and economic relationship to the United States," and as finally written it did not.[146] The constitution was concerned with issues of local government alone, and it defined those narrowly, leaving the essential colonial relations between Puerto Rico and the United States intact. Most of the provisions of the Jones Act remained in force, though now they were codified in the Federal Relations Law, which regulated the relations between Puerto Rico and the United States, thus replacing the Jones Act.[147]

On July 25, 1952, the fifty-fourth anniversary of the U.S. invasion, the Commonwealth of Puerto Rico was inaugurated. Puerto Rico had a new name for its status, but little else had changed. The island remained a colony, though now the United States could and did claim that the association of Puerto Rico with the United States was voluntary and had been approved by Puerto Rican voters, who had also written their own constitution. Thus, in 1953, the United States argued before the UN that it was no longer obliged to submit reports, since, by virtue of its voluntary association, Puerto Rico was no longer a colonial possession, and the UN accepted this explanation.

Originally, the commonwealth concept seemed to have been put forward as a transition stage during which Puerto Rico would develop economically to the point where it could choose independence or statehood from a position of strength and equality. Soon, however, commonwealth status was projected as a permanent "third way" for the island. This

[145] The constitution's Bill of Rights was very advanced. The section eliminated had included the rights to a free education, a job, an adequate standard of living, and aid to mothers and children, among others: García Martínez, *Puerto Rico*, pp. 229–30.

[146] Johnson, *Puerto Rico*, p. 151.

[147] Article 4 of P. L. 600 declared that all of the provisions of the Jones Act, as amended, would remain in effect except those eliminated by article 5, which dealt primarily with local governmental administration: García Martínez, *Puerto Rico*, p. 206. Interestingly, the constitution retained the 500-acre restriction of the Jones Act. The full text can be found in ibid., pp. 223–59.

position initially was articulated by Muñoz, but it became and still is the fundamental political position of the PPD. Ironically, Muñoz had returned to the autonomist position that his father, Muñoz Rivera, had come to support in the closing days of the Spanish empire, when all other options seemed closed.[148]

SUMMARY AND CONCLUSIONS

The emergence of the PPD as a political party able and willing to articulate the interests of the classes adversely affected by the spread of capitalism was one of the most important events of the 1940s. Under the leadership of Muñoz Marín, the PPD was able to begin a process of economic development that was able to break through the limits of the monocultural sugar economy because the party had a mass base opposed to large, particularly U.S., landed interests. The economic alterations, consciously pursued, put Puerto Rico on the path toward industrialization but also pushed the economy in the direction of greater dependence on the United States for capital, markets, and imports. Early industrialization did not have the desired or expected results. It did not lead to less unemployment, but to more. It did not result in more local ownership of capital, but in a substitution of U.S. for Puerto Rican capital. Nor did it lead to a productive structure and an economic base that would permit Puerto Ricans to make the choice of status from a position of strength; rather, it exacerbated the structural weakness of the economy. In 1951, the Puerto Rico Planning Board could still report that "the current sources of income and employment are not yet based on as firm a foundation as would be desirable."[149]

Living conditions did improve during the forties. The death rate dropped from eighteen per thousand to about ten, a rate roughly equal to that prevailing in more developed countries. The literacy rate rose to about 78 percent by the end of the decade, from 68.5 percent in 1940, and 63 percent of school-age children were in school compared to about half in 1940.[150] Yet Operation Bootstrap made it difficult for Puerto Ricans to improve their standard of living through their own efforts, since it put control over that process in the hands of U.S. firms, whose interests did not necessarily coincide with those of the majority on the island. It is likely that no one consciously intended such results from a development program that seemed so promising, but Puerto Rico's colonial relation

[148] Mathews, *Muñoz Marín*, pp. 45–46.
[149] PRPB, *Economic Development*, p. 21.
[150] Ibid., p. 14.

with the United States prevented, or at a minimum made more difficult, a more independent existence for the economy and society. The period since the early 1940s has witnessed but an intensification of the tendencies and problems that became evident at that time.

5

Growth and Misdevelopment:
The 1950s to the Present

INTRODUCTION

Between 1942 and 1952, all the institutional innovations that were to transform Puerto Rico from a rural, predominately agrarian society to an urban, manufacturing-based one were put in place. From 1952 to the mid-1980s, there were no fundamental changes of direction in development policy, only variations on the theme of industrialization dependent on U.S. markets, inputs, technology, financing, and ownership. The standard of living, and certainly the life style, of most Puerto Ricans was made dramatically different and easier as the island became little more than an extension of the U.S. economy, and while it is not meaningless to refer to the Puerto Rican economy, its distinctiveness has become blurred as a result of its nearly full integration with the mainland market, banking system, manufacturing methods, and labor, environmental, and juridical regulations. Integrated but not assimilated; *part* of but not *of* the United States, U.S. citizens by law but Puerto Ricans first—these are the tensions and contradictions that permeate society at all levels.

This chapter examines the evolution of the island's industrialization strategy from the early 1950s to the mid-1980s. Efforts to bring U.S. firms to the island dominates the story, and the government and Fomento continued their interventionist role discussed in the previous chapter. However, the local government's function as collective capitalist, entrepreneur, and social planner directly involved in the development process had come to an end with the initiation of Operation Bootstrap and its reliance on external sources of capital and entrepreneurship, except in those areas such as public utilities, where government ownership is commonplace in most capitalist economies. Despite an outward semblance of planning and the existence of a planning board and planning laws, there actually has been a surprising lack of instrumental planning for the domestic economy.[1] Fomento has done planning, of course, but of the sort

---

[1] ". . . no había ni nunca ha habido una planificación de la actividad económica" (there was not and there never has been any planning of economic activity): Curet Cuevas, *El desarrollo económico*, p. 204.

designed to get results that appealed to U.S. investors. Planning has revolved around the issue of what is necessary to attract external capital to
the island rather than around the issue of Puerto Rico's needs. This did
not happen because Fomento, Muñoz, and the PPD wished to benefit
U.S. companies at the expense of local capital or to subject the local
economy to external control, but because they believed that Puerto Rico's
needs would be met by attracting U.S. capital, which was required for
rapid growth, generation of employment, and an improved standard of
living. The two issues, in other words, collapsed into one for local policy
makers. "Fomento under Teodoro Moscoso has seen the interests of industrialists and the interests of Puerto Rico as one."[2]

There are good reasons for this conflation of what in reality are distinct
questions. They lie not in any conspiracy of assimilationist PPD leaders
but in classical and neoclassical economic theory, which has postulated
that self-interested behavior in a competitive market not only leads to
results that are socially desirable but even allows society to approach an
optimum state of well-being marked by a harmony of individual interests.
Market systems are held to convert private greed into public benefit, since
only by satisfying the desires of buyers will sellers profit. Practically the
entire corpus of orthodox economic theory is devoted to the verification
and elucidation of this result in the light of complicating factors.

As impressive as these efforts may have been, they are to great extent
unconnected with reality. The theory that the public good is best served
by private greed requires that there be perfect competition (or, in a more
recent refinement, "contestable" markets), no uncompensated external-
ties, independent individual utility functions, an optimal distribution of
wealth, and quite a number of other factors.[3] In any real economic situation, these conditions obviously cannot all be met.

Despite the striking gap between theory and reality, Operation Bootstrap from its beginning was based, at least implicitly, on the assumption
that self-interested behavior does lead to public benefit, and on the further
assumption that economic growth benefits all classes and groups—i.e.,
the "trickle-down" theory that the benefits of a growing output gradually
spread throughout the social hierarchy. These assumptions, even if not
always clearly articulated or well understood, are what gave justification
to Puerto Rico's industrialization via the market, based overwhelmingly
on self-selection by U.S. firms. As a consequence, external capital's interests have continued to shape the characteristics of the Puerto Rican
economy.

[2]Baver, "Public Policies," p. 10.
[3]Graaf lists seventeen of them: *Welfare Economics*, pp. 142–54.

ECONOMIC GROWTH AND EQUITABLE DEVELOPMENT

The orthodox models of development first put forward in the 1940s and early 1950s exerted an intellectual influence on the design and extensions of Operation Bootstrap. All of these models—whether their strategy was balanced growth, unbalanced growth, a labor surplus, or some other— suggested means by which underdeveloped countries could attempt to repeat the development that had taken place in the already developed countries by focusing on measures—fundamentally productive capital formation—to increase the rate of growth of GNP. Invariably, these recommendations called for an expansion of industrial production and a decrease in the importance of agriculture. Labor was to be transferred from traditional and backward agriculture to the modern industrial sector, since it was believed that it had been precisely this social and economic transformation that had been responsible for the success of the developed countries. One of the best-known and most influential descriptions of such a strategy was that of W. Arthur Lewis, though he emphasized the importance of agricultural transformation as well as industrial expansion.

The basic problem with these models and with their practical application in the nations that have tried to apply them was not that they did not increase the rate of economic growth and the level of GNP. Very often the results on these counts have been quite spectacular; Puerto Rico and Brazil are two especially good examples of rapid growth, but there are others as well. But what has increasingly come to be questioned is the relation between economic growth and *development* and the reliability of trickle-down as the transmission mechanism. Development is now understood to be something broader than economic growth. Though it is obvious that GNP growth can make the goals of development easier to achieve by providing the base for improving the standard of living of the poorest in society, economic growth alone has been found to be neither necessary nor sufficient for development to take place, and in some cases it actually appears to have been a hindrance to the process.[4]

Development economist Dudley Seers has suggested three criteria for determining whether development is taking place: (a) a decrease in the numbers of those in absolute poverty; (b) movement toward greater equality; and (c) a movement toward full employment for all who wish to work.[5]

[4] See Wood, "Infant Mortality Trends," which demonstrates a worsening of living conditions among the poorest sectors during Brazil's period of most rapid economic growth. The seminal work on growth and development is the econometric study by Adelman and Morris, *Economic Growth and Social Equity*, which shows that at low levels of per capita income, growth of GNP has worsened income distribution in a large number of instances. Only beyond a certain threshold of income does income distribution improve. This proposition is known as Kuznets's inverted-U hypothesis. See also Chenery et al., *Redistribution*.

[5] Seers, "Meaning of Development."

The World Bank has utilized a similar definition of development, known as "the basic needs approach."[6] Both of these approaches begin from the premise that, while the trickle-down theory of "growth first, equity later" may succeed in achieving economic growth, it often fails to meet other criteria of development. The basic needs perspective effectively turns the orthodox models on their heads by proposing that equity be accorded equal priority with economic growth. This implies a continuing need for state intervention and planning to meet the basic needs of the vast majority of the world's population, one-quarter of whom, by the World Bank's count, are in absolute poverty.[7]

Orthodox economic models had recognized the necessity for government intervention to get the growth process started, but they assumed that the market system would then take over and lead to development without significant further direction by the state. In the equity-with-growth approach, by contrast, government intervention is held to be necessary not only to launch economic growth but also to ensure that output is continuously used in ways that result in the production and distribution of goods and services that contribute to development in Seers's or the "basic needs" sense. This perspective eschews any simple faith in the automatic workings of markets, especially in an era of international oligopolies with extensive market power and price-fixing arrangements, and it assigns an important role to government actions.

The PPD program in the early 1940s was very much a forerunner of an equity-with-growth development model and was, to that extent, ahead of its time. Both social justice and economic growth had been primary goals. But the contradiction of pursuing both these goals in a colonial, capitalist economy once the relative autonomy of the war years came to an end became ever more intense, as was discussed in chapter 4. Bowing to market pressures, Operation Bootstrap represented the renunciation of the equity-with-growth strategy and its replacement by a growth-first, orthodox model of economic growth.[8] The way in which this change affected Puerto Rico's economy and society is the theme of this chapter.

VARIETIES OF ECONOMIC GROWTH

Rapid economic growth in the 1950s and 1960s became the hallmark of Operation Bootstrap, and policy makers from around the world were

[6] World Bank, *Poverty and Basic Needs*, and Streeten, *First Things First*.

[7] McNamara, *Address*, pp. 5–8. Meier, *Emerging from Poverty*, provides a balanced assessment of all the various approaches to development and suggests why orthodox economics has been incapable of meeting the challenge of helping the world's poor.

[8] Curet Cuevas, *El desarrollo económico*, p. 221.

TABLE 5.1

Gross National Product, Gross Domestic Product, and Gross Fixed Investment,
Selected Years, 1950 to 1984

	Gross National Product		Real Dollars[a] (millions)	Gross Domestic Product (millions of dollars)	Gross Fixed Investment	
	Current Dollars (millions)	Per Capita			Total (millions of dollars)	As Percent of GNP
1950	754.5	342	878.7	723.9	111.4	14.8
1960	1,676.4	716	1,473.2	1,691.9	354.9	21.2
1970	4,687.5	1,729	2,901.4	5,034.7	1,401.6	29.9
1972	5,771.0	2,045	3,231.2	6,342.6	1,761.0	30.5
1974	6,817.8	2,366	3,434.6	7,710.0	1,695.6	24.9
1976	7,555.8	2,537	3,458.4	8,996.4	1,819.0	24.1
1977	8,173.8	2,683	3,623.5	9,929.9	1,540.1	18.8
1978	8,994.0	2,903	3,817.4	11,172.4	1,744.9	19.4
1980	11,073.8	3,479	4,076.7	14,480.0	2,039.0	18.4
1982	12,626.5	3,879	3,977.5	16,414.5	1,778.6	14.1
1983[b]	12,907.7	3,953	3,891.9	16,969.3	1,636.3	12.7
1984[b]	13,993.6	4,248	4,074.1	—	1,957.7	14.0

SOURCES: Junta de Planificación, *Informe económico, 1980*, p. A-1, table 1; ibid., *1982–83* 2:A-1, table 1; GDB, *Special Economic Bulletin*, p. 6, table 1, and p. 7, table 2.

NOTE: The Junta de Planificación has been revising its accounting procedures retrospectively and many of the recent figures differ from those that were reported earlier.

[a] In 1954 prices.

[b] Preliminary figures.

brought to the island (as part of official U.S. policy under Point Four of the Truman Doctrine) to see the miracle at work. Puerto Rico went from being the "poorhouse of the Caribbean" to the "showcase of democracy," demonstrating, it was claimed, the possibilities of cooperation among developed and underdeveloped countries to the benefit of both. As table 5.1 shows, economic growth did indeed take place during Operation Bootstrap. From 1950 to 1960, GNP more than doubled, the rate of annual growth averaging 8.3 percent. From 1960 to 1970, GNP growth was even more spectacular, at an average annual rate of 10.8 percent per year, thus nearly tripling over the decade. Per capita GNP increased from $342 in 1950 (it had been $154 in 1940) to $716 in 1960 and to $3,479 in 1980. In this last year, Puerto Rico's per capita income exceeded that of all the Latin American republics except Venezuela.[9]

[9] World Bank, *World Development Report*, pp. 110–11, table 1. Venezuela's per capita GNP was $3,630. However, quite a few Caribbean countries had higher incomes than Puerto Rico.

Gross investment grew even more rapidly: 219 percent from 1950 to 1960 and another 295 percent from 1960 to 1970. The growth rate slowed down to 45.5 percent from 1970 to 1980, but that was on a much larger base. More important, gross investment as a proportion of GNP rose from 14.8 percent in 1950 to almost 31 percent in 1970 (it had been but 8 percent of GNP in 1940), though the proportion declined during the 1970s until in the early 1980s it was at a level very similar to that which had prevailed at the beginning of the industrialization program.

Table 5.1 also shows the level of real GNP (i.e., GNP adjusted for price changes). It rose 5.3 percent per year from 1950 to 1960 and 7.0 percent from 1960 to 1970; but then slowed down to 3.5 percent per year from 1970 to 1980. In total, real GNP increased 134 percent between 1940 and 1960 and a further 177 percent by 1980. There was a downturn in real GNP after 1980, the result of recession in the United States, a decline in exports, and a slowdown in federal expenditures on the island (to be discussed later). This was followed by a slight recovery in 1984, which brought aggregate real GNP back up to the 1980 level.[10]

The rapid increase in investment contributed greatly not only to the growth of GNP (total insular income) but also to the growth of gross domestic product, or GDP (the total value of output produced within Puerto Rico, regardless of its recipient). Until 1960, GNP exceeded GDP, primarily because of the payment of wages to federal employees on the island. After 1960, however, as can be seen in table 5.1, GDP exceeded GNP. This difference, as Freyre points out, "is important for a capital importing country such as Puerto Rico, because interest and dividend payments on external investment can be considered as a drainage from territorial production which does not accrue to residents of the country, although it is produced with the participation of domestic capital stock"[11]— and, it should be added, local labor.

In 1960, the difference between GNP and GDP, the "GNP/GDP gap," was equal to about 1 percent of GNP; in 1970, the gap was equal to 7.4 percent of GNP; by 1980, it had grown to 30.8 percent of GNP, and it remained near or above that level in the 1980s (table 5.2). This widening

[10] Junta de Planificación, *Informe económico, 1982–83* 1: chap. 2. There is no discussion of inflation in this chapter, not because of its absence, but because it is simply a product of inflation in the U.S. The wage earners' price index (1967 = 100) was 168.7 in 1976 and 216.6 in 1980, compared to 170.5 and 246.8 for the consumers' price index in the U.S.: Vélez Ortiz, "Rates of Inflation," p. 13. Of course, oligopolistic sellers in Puerto Rico can affect local prices, but most important are the prices that prevail on the mainland. Prices are, or have been, controlled on rice, sugar, coffee, bacalao, bread, milk, gasoline, and other products: A. Santiago, *El control de precios*, p. 31. In June 1953, the Administración, de Estabilización Económica was created to replace the Administración General de Suministros.

[11] Freyre, *External and Domestic Financing*, p. 55.

TABLE 5.2
The GNP/GDP Gap, Selected Years, 1950 to 1983

	GDP – GNP (millions of dollars)	Percentage of GNP
1950	−30.6	
1960	15.5	0.9
1970	347.2	7.4
1972	571.6	9.9
1974	892.2	13.1
1976	1,440.6	19.1
1977	1,756.1	21.5
1978	2,178.4	24.2
1980	3,406.2	30.8
1982	3,788.0	30.0
1983	4,061.6	31.5

SOURCE: Table 5.1.

gap, which there will be occasion to comment on again, is a rough measure of the volume of profits, interest, and dividends flowing out of the economy to nonresidents, primarily in the United States. (Actually, it understates the magnitude of this outflow, since it is net of the inflow of federal wages paid on the island). Table 5.2 thus shows unambiguously that an increasing share of production and income created in Puerto Rico has been appropriated by external investors and has been unavailable as income or for consumption or for local investment.

The gross fixed investment shown in table 5.1 needs to be discussed in more detail. It can be divided into two components: (a) construction, and (b) machinery and equipment. The latter category is clearly capital—the physical tools that are used in the production process in combination with labor and raw materials to produce final outputs. Construction is a more problematic category. Some construction, as for factories, is also capital, since it contributes to long-term economic growth. Other construction expenditures, such as for residential housing, have but a short-term impact on growth. It can be seen from table 5.3 that the machinery-and-equipment component of investment increased relative to total investment from 1950 to 1960, at the same time that gross investment was increasing, but that its share of total investment then began to fall. Since 1977, its share has increased, returning to its 1960 level, but total investment has not grown during that time, and indeed from 1980 to 1984, it declined in absolute terms. This suggests a potentially deleterious trend for the longer term.

TABLE 5.3
Components of Gross Investment, Selected Years, 1950 to 1984

	Construction		Machinery and Equipment	
	Total (millions of dollars)	Percent of Gross Investment	Total (millions of dollars)	Percent of Gross Investment
1950	78.7	70.6	32.6	29.3
1960	227.0	64.0	127.9	36.0
1970	988.6	70.5	413.0	29.5
1972	1,285.3	73.0	475.8	27.0
1974	1,281.9	75.6	413.6	24.4
1976	1,295.3	71.2	523.7	28.8
1977	1,003.7	65.2	536.4	34.8
1978	1,133.7	65.0	611.2	35.0
1980	1,303.1	63.9	735.9	36.1
1982	1,236.4	69.5	542.1	31.5
1983	1,033.4	63.2	602.8	36.8
1984	1,266.0	64.7	691.7	35.3

SOURCES: Same as table 5.1.

STAGES OF OPERATION BOOTSTRAP

The activities of Operation Bootstrap can be divided into two fairly distinct stages. During the first stage, which lasted from 1947 into the early 1960s, most of the firms coming from the United States were labor-intensive enterprises with relatively low capital requirements. For example, in 1949, the production of textiles and clothing—a notoriously labor-intensive industry—accounted for 13.7 percent of all manufacturing firms; in 1954, the figure was 19.5 percent, and in 1967, it was 19.9 percent.[12] They were attracted to Puerto Rico not just by tax exemption, but also by the possibility of being able to pay wages substantially below mainland rates and by the absence of such risks as political instability that are often associated with foreign operations. There was also a "push" factor: labor was in short supply in the United States.[13] Even though most managers and other officials believed that tax exemption was the key reason for moving to Puerto Rico, careful analysis has shown that low wages actually provided a larger subsidy than did the tax holiday provided by the Industrial Incentives Law. In fact, it has been estimated that if wages

[12] Merrill-Ramírez, "Operation Bootstrap," p. 87, table 1.
[13] Taylor, Industrial Tax Exemption, pp. 11, 120–21, 144.

248   CHAPTER FIVE

TABLE 5.4
Wages in Manufacturing, Puerto Rico and the United States,
Five-Year Intervals from 1950 to 1975, 1977, and 1979

| | Average Hourly Wage | | | Puerto Rico As | U.S. Minimum |
	Puerto Rico	United States	Difference	Percent of U.S.	Wage
1950	$0.42	$1.50	$1.08	28.0	$0.75
1955	0.56	1.91	1.38	29.3	1.00
1960	0.94	2.30	1.36	40.9	1.00
1965	1.26	2.64	1.38	47.7	1.25
1970	1.78	3.37	1.59	52.8	1.60
1975	2.59	4.40	1.81	58.9	2.10
1977	3.11	5.60	2.49	55.5	2.30
1979	3.58	6.54	2.96	54.7	2.90

SOURCES: USDC, *Economic Study 2:56*, table 4; PREDA, *Manufacturers Ready Reference File, 1979*, "Labor" folder.

had been 25 percent higher, they would have erased any savings from tax exemption for those firms that relocated before 1953 and tended to have a high ratio of labor costs to total costs.[14] Thus, low wage levels were the key to their profitability. This circumstance has led one observer to refer to this stage as Operation Bootstrap's "sweatshop" phase.[15]

Table 5.4 compares wages paid in Puerto Rico to those being paid on the mainland at the same time. In 1950, at the beginning of Operation Bootstrap, the average hourly wage in manufacturing in Puerto Rico was but 28 percent of the U.S. wage. By 1965, it had increased to nearly half the level in the United States, still a substantial savings from an employer's point of view but possibly a threat to the development program, if a narrowing differential tended to reduce the attractiveness of tax exemption.[16] Yet, as already noted, labor-intensive firms continued to arrive, so the higher relative wage was evidently not having the negative effect that had been feared.

It may be more significant then, that the *absolute* difference in wages between the island and the mainland has tended to *increase* since 1950, and particularly since the mid-1960s. It is this lower absolute wage level in Puerto Rico that has attracted and retained many labor-intensive producers, which is precisely the result one would expect if productivity levels were similar between the two, as they were. As long as labor-intensive firms could pay lower absolute wages in Puerto Rico than they

[14] Ibid., pp. 115–17.
[15] Merrill-Ramírez, "Operation Bootstrap," p. 22.
[16] Taylor, *Industrial Tax Exemption*, p. 13.

had to pay in the United States for equivalent work, they continued to have an incentive to produce in Puerto Rico.

Despite the absolute wage gap relative to the United States, however, Puerto Rico has been losing its comparative advantage to other low-wage countries. In 1969, the island was the largest supplier of clothing to the U.S. market; by the mid-1970s, it had slipped to fourth place. Of course, there are factors other than rising relative and absolute wage levels that explain this decline—e.g., the opening of the U.S. market as the result of the various rounds of the General Agreement on Tariffs and Trade and the tendency of international corporations to spread their operations among many countries. In any case, the apparel industry has remained the largest single employer in manufacturing in Puerto Rico, with 23 percent of total manufacturing employment in 1978 and more than 30 percent in the early 1980s, a good indication that labor-intensive production remains very important in the local economic structure.[17]

But prices in Puerto Rico were higher than in the United States,[18] so an industrialization strategy based on low-wage labor demanded a great sacrifice of Puerto Rican workers. Fomento was aware of this contradiction.[19] Pressure also was applied by island labor unions to win higher wages, and they were joined by the U.S. unions that feared a loss of jobs to the island. But, just as had been true in the 1930s, U.S. firms in Puerto Rico had nothing to gain from paying higher wages, since the bulk of their output was exported to the mainland, not sold to Puerto Rican consumers. One director of Fomento, José Madera, wrote:

> The industries attracted here by means of that [early] strategy had a common profile: Firms that needed only a modest investment (labor intensive and of a relatively low technological know-how) which produced consumer goods for unstable markets; and, moreover, industries which did not need each other, nor link themselves into a chain of economic development.[20]

The last part of this describes another important characteristic of the industries that were attracted by Fomento in the early years of Operation Bootstrap: they had few linkages or connections with the rest of the local economy. The firms were "export enclaves," largely unrelated to other

---

[17] USDC, *Economic Study* 2:270, and Junta de Planificación, *Informe económico, 1982–83* 2:II-11.

[18] Federal employees in Puerto Rico receive a supplemental cost-of-living allowance of 5 to 12.5 percent. Some have estimated the cost of living to be as much as 25 percent higher: USDC, *Economic Study* 2:689–90.

[19] PRAFE, *El desarrollo económico*, pp. 3–5.

[20] Madera, "Strategy of Development."

firms or industries in the local economy, typically as subsidiaries of a vertically integrated company headquartered in the United States. The unit located in Puerto Rico served as an assembly or production plant that imported raw or semifinished materials and reexported the finished output back to the United States. Very few inputs to the production process other than labor originated on the island, and the benefits to the island were limited to, in most cases, the wages paid. There were thus very few indirect or spinoff effects on the local economic structure, and few "satellite" firms emerged to service the enterprises. To the extent that the promoted firms were more or less integrated into supply and distribution networks in the United States, they failed to provide opportunities for supply or distribution firms to develop in Puerto Rico.

REVISION OF THE TAX INCENTIVE

Under the Industrial Incentive Act, full tax exemption was to end on June 30, 1959, to be followed by three years of partial exemption (1960, 75 percent; 1961, 50 percent; 1962, 25 percent) and then an end to the exemption altogether. As the termination approached, it became apparent that it would become increasingly difficult to convince new firms to initiate operations with these reduced tax exemptions.[21] When industrial promotion began, the idea had been to provide a few years for companies to adjust to a new location in the favorable circumstance of untaxed, above-normal profits, and then the firms were expected to become taxpaying enterprises just like any other. However, corporate decision makers in the United States and on the island perceived tax exemption quite differently.[22]

One study found that officers of 95 percent of a representative sample of forty-four firms believed tax exemption to be the key to their operations, and it was ranked an "important advantage" more often than any other factor that might have influenced a location decision. Other factors, in declining order of importance, were wage rates, efficiency of machinery and equipment, and the attitude of the community. Interestingly, the factor that was next-to-last in importance was the availability of a labor force with suitable skills. The conclusion drawn from this study was that "the new industrialists apparently do not consider tax exemption to be in the nature of a short-run subsidy."[23] One business leader commenting on tax exemption in the early 1950s said bluntly, "It should be extended, otherwise I won't be here."[24]

[21] Taylor, *Industrial Tax Exemption*, p. 22.
[22] Ibid., chap. 9.
[23] Ibid., p. 124, table 4; p. 126, table 5; and p. 130.
[24] Ibid., p. 130.

Fomento and the Commonwealth government thus faced the first real dilemma of the development strategy. Having embarked upon a path of tax exemption designed to attract firms that might create employment, generate high incomes, and encourage spinoff or satellite industries, they ended up attracting firms that were labor-intensive but that had few local linkages, firms that were therefore highly mobile and might liquidate their investments if their tax exemptions were terminated.[25] Confronted with such a possibility, the PPD-dominated legislature passed a new Industrial Incentive Act, which became effective in 1954. This law permitted a firm to receive exemption for a period of ten years after it began operations on the island, whenever that might be. This measure helped to make Puerto Rico continue to look attractive to potential investors and helped to overcome the decline in relocations which began in 1953–54, though a downturn in the U.S. economy at the time dampened investors' confidence irrespective of Puerto Rico's promotional efforts. With this action, however, the tax-exemption program shifted from being a temporary measure, as originally conceived, to being a permanent feature of the development strategy. This act essentially marks the point in time when external capital and externally owned enterprises were institutionalized as the long-term base of development.

In 1963, another Industrial Incentive Act was passed to correct some of the imbalances that had appeared after the 1954 law. One adverse consequence had been the concentration of firms in the San Juan metropolitan area (including Carolina, Cataño, and Bayamón), where more services existed, the amenities of a large city were close at hand, and most government offices were located. Almost half the new firms, accounting for more than one-third of the employment, were in this area, and two-thirds of them were in the combined urban areas of San Juan, Caguas, Ponce, and Mayagüez. This contributed to an influx of population into the cities that greatly exceeded the employment generated by the new enterprises locating there, while at the same time severely straining public services, health facilities, and the school systems. These higher social costs, moreover, could not be paid for out of additional tax revenues from the exempted corporations, and hence the growing urban population was becoming increasingly burdensome. In an attempt to remedy this, the 1963 law provided for varying periods of tax exemption depending upon where the new enterprise was to be located. In "underdeveloped indus-

[25] Ibid., p. 50, notes two cases that indicate how loosely were the criteria for granting tax exemption. In one, a needlework "factory," the one piece of equipment differentiating production from home needlework (which was ineligible for exemption) was a time clock. In the other, exemption was granted to a fishing boat on one occasion but denied on another.

trial zones" (typically in the interior), full tax exemption was possible for up to seventeen years. Location in an area of intermediate development provided for twelve years of complete exemption, and those firms choosing to operate in areas of "high industrial concentration," like the San Juan area, were to receive "only" a ten-year full tax holiday.[26] This revision in the tax law has had very limited success in bringing about decentralization, however.[27]

The 1963 law also permitted a delay of up to two years in the initiation of the exemption period, on the premise that if there were losses at the beginning of operations due to start-up problems, tax exemption would be meaningless for those years. (This provision also permitted subsidiaries of U.S. companies to include their losses in Puerto Rico on a combined income statement with the parent corporation, thus reducing their U.S. tax liability, another attraction for enterprises with high initial costs.) The length of the exemption period also could be doubled by taking 50 percent, rather than complete, exemption.[28]

THE SECOND STAGE

As early as the 1950s, but increasingly in the 1960s, an awareness grew within Fomento of the desirability of attracting capital-intensive firms requiring a semiskilled and skilled labor force.[29] Such a reorientation was believed necessary for a number of reasons. First, if wages were to increase in Puerto Rico—and this was both a goal for the sake of a higher standard of living and a need imposed by the high prices on the island—the importance of tax exemption for firms with high labor costs relative to total costs would be somewhat diminished, given the low wages that prevailed in Asia and in other countries in the Caribbean and Latin America. Capital-intensive firms, though, could afford to pay higher wages because, with their heavier use of capital, labor productivity was greater, and because, with labor costs a smaller share of total costs, increases in wages had less of an effect on profits. The attractiveness of tax exemption would thus be retained, even with increasing wage scales.

Second, it was believed that capital-intensive industries would be more resistant to the cyclical variations of the mainland economy, which tended

---

[26] Curet Cuevas, *El desarrollo económico*, pp. 133–35, table 52, and Colón de Zalduondo, *Puerto Rican Economy*, pp. 155–56.

[27] For an analysis of the effects, see Woodward, "Industrial Incentives."

[28] Baver, "Public Policies," pp. 13–14; USDC, *Economic Study* 2:74, and Curet Cuevas, *El desarrollo económico*, pp. 216–17. The 1963 law was amended a number of times to permit varying partial exemption periods and to extend the period of exemption to thirty years for firms locating on the islands of Vieques and Culebra off Puerto Rico's east coast.

[29] PRAFE, *El desarrollo económico*, pp. 3–5.

to affect subsidiaries of U.S. firms on the island more than the parent corporation in the United States.[30]

The first capital-intensive projects were in the petrochemical sector. Caribe Nitrogen, Gulf Caribbean, and Commonwealth Oil Refining Company (CORCO) were in operation by 1956. Between 1952 and 1958, new firms in this industry invested $78.4 million in Puerto Rico, equal to 27 percent of total investment in manufacturing.[31] Attracting this industry seemed to make economic sense to Fomento officials; since all energy sources were externally supplied, the construction of oil refineries would permit the capturing of at least a portion of the value added in the production process, thus contributing to local job and income creation. In actuality, however, this effect was much weaker than had been expected. In 1979, not long before the complete cessation of its refining operations in 1982, CORCO employed but 1,450 workers.

A second reason why the creation of a petrochemical sector seemed advantageous was that Venezuelan crude oil could be refined for the U.S. market, which not only was using increasing amounts of petroleum but also was relying on ever greater quantities of imported supplies. There were negative aspects to the building of the refineries, of course, primarily in terms of the costs of infrastructure and the levels of pollution and ecological damage expected—and these came to be the focus of much popular discontent—but there is no doubt that the petrochemical sector was a basic part of the second-stage strategy of Fomento and was indeed, for a time, conceived as something of a showcase.

Other capital-intensive firms were successfully promoted in the machinery, chemicals, and metal industries. Within the chemical sector, drug and pharmaceutical firms have grown especially rapidly. In 1982, chemical and related products accounted for 32.1 percent of the gross output of all industry, though they provided only 10.1 percent of employment in manufacturing, which is an indication of the capital-intensive nature of this industry. A further indication is that, in the same year, the chemical industry earned $1.9 billion in net income, equal to 35.3 percent of net manufacturing income, and of that amount, $1.6 billion, or 84 percent, was what can be called "capitalist income"—that is, the return accruing to owners and creditors of these firms as profits, interest, and dividends. Only 16 percent of net income in the chemical industry was paid to employees as wages and salaries, and it is this limited share which was retained in the Puerto Rican economy, since the capitalist income share was predominately repatriated to recipients in the United States.

[30] Ibid. See also Junta de Planificación, *Informe económico, 1980*, pp. 60–61, and Ruiz, "Impact of Economic Recession."

[31] Freyre, *External and Domestic Financing*, p. 89.

In capital-intensive industries as a whole, 75 percent of net income was paid to owners of capital, primarily external, and only 25 percent to workers. The workers' share of income in all capital-intensive industries was $947.3 million in 1982, compared to $897.2 million in all labor-intensive industries. That can hardly be regarded as incremental gain to the economy from capital-intensive promotion. In 1981, in fact, employees in labor-intensive production received total compensation that exceeded the returns to labor in capital-intensive industry.[32] Though it is true that workers were better paid, on the average, in the more capitalized firms, there were fewer of them. From 1947 to 1961, Fomento firms employed an average of 70 workers; in the late 1960s, employment per firm had declined to just 33.3 persons. In the San Juan area, Fomento firms were providing jobs to only one of every thirty-nine inhabitants in the mid-1960s. In fact, Fomento itself discovered that between 1969 and 1975, only 28.7 percent of the jobs promised by promoted firms had actually materialized, and among the highly touted petrochemical firms the percentage was ever lower.[33]

There was, however, something else expected from these capital-intensive, so-called "core" industries. Besides the jobs and incomes they might directly create, and the greater stability they were thought to bring, it was believed that (1) backward-linked spinoff effects would emerge as new firms were created to supply raw and semifinished materials, and that (2) especially in the petrochemical sector, forward linkages would develop as new firms were founded to purchase the outputs of the capital-intensive firms. What actually happened was quite different. The firms that located on the island were integrated into sourcing and distribution networks with other firms in the United States or other countries. They made no attempt to forge linkages within the island economy, nor were they motivated to do so by the government or its incentive package. As a result, they had only minor indirect employment effects. The new industrial sector thus resembled the export enclave of the earlier promotions in textiles and apparel and was not even very different from the sugar industry of the pre-1940 period.

Nevertheless, firms promoted by Fomento have dominated the manufacturing sector. In 1978, there were 2,411 enterprises operating that had been promoted by Fomento.[34] Whereas in 1960, promoted firms had provided 54 percent of all manufacturing employment, this share rose to 78 percent in 1970 and to 92 percent in 1980. Fomento firms have paid

---

[32] Junta de Planificación, *Informe económico, 1982–83* 2:II-3, II-5.

[33] Gutiérrez, *Factor Proportions*, pp. 13–14, and *San Juan Star*, March 29, 1978, p. 3.

[34] The peak number of establishments was 2,782 in 1973: *Puerto Rico Business Review* 5 (November 1980): 8–10.

slightly better wages than other firms. For example, in 1981, they paid an average of $4.55 an hour, compared to $4.11 in non-Fomento firms.[35] In 1970, Fomento firms accounted for 70 percent of all exports and 75 percent of manufacturing net income. By 1977, they were responsible for 83 percent of total exports, and in the early 1980s for more than 90 percent of net income in manufacturing.[36]

Some 84 pharmaceutical companies have been promoted, an increase from the 47 in 1972. For the pharmaceuticals, Puerto Rico has become an extremely profitable link in their worldwide operations. Besides the ability to test new products with fewer restrictions and to produce under less hampering conditions than in the United States, nearly 50 percent of their worldwide profits are earned on the island.

There also were 367 promoted firms in apparel, 177 in food processing, and 93 in petroleum and related products in the late 1970s.[37] In food processing, the tuna industry is the most important one, having displaced sugar as the leading export in that sector in 1969. In 1981, three U.S. and two Japanese firms were operating seven tuna canneries in Mayagüez and Ponce, and the Puerto Rican tuna-canning industry was supplying 40 percent of U.S. consumption. In this industry, not only the canneries but also individually owned boats are eligible for tax exemption.[38]

CHANGES IN THE ECONOMIC STRUCTURE

Table 5.5 shows how the productive structure of the economy has evolved during Operation Bootstrap. The share of GNP originating in agriculture had been more than 17 percent in 1950, but by 1960 its share had declined to less than 10 percent and by 1970 to slightly more than 3 percent. The share due to trade has remained remarkably stable, but there has been growth in services and in finance, insurance, and real estate, as would be expected from the spread of market relations and the rise in incomes, making the provision of services, which are income-elastic, more feasible and speculation more profitable. Government's contribution to GNP also has grown; if transportation and other public utilities (electricity, telephone, water, and sewage) are added to the direct contribution of government, the state's contribution to income generation appears to be second only to that of manufacturing.

[35] GDB, *Monthly Economic Indicators*, p. 10, and Junta de Planificación, *Informe económico, 1982–83* 2:II-10.
[36] PRAFE, *El desarrollo económico*, pp. 6, 11, and Junta de Planificación, *Informe económico, 1977*, p. 39.
[37] PRAFE, *Industrial Directory, 1980*, pp. 11–13, 15, 33, and *Claridad*, June 1–7, 1979.
[38] *Puerto Rico Business Review* 7 (June 1982): 2–7.

TABLE 5.5
Gross National Product by Sector, 1950, 1960, 1970, and 1980

Sector	1950		1960		1970		1980	
	Value[a]	%	Value[a]	%	Value[a]	%	Value[a]	%
Agriculture	132.1	17.5	164.0	9.8	160.9	3.4	393.9	3.6
Manufacturing	119.7	15.9	366.3	21.9	1,190.0	25.4	5,322.5	48.1
Constructing and mining	30.4	4.0	101.1	6.0	379.1	8.1	370.1	3.3
Transportation and other public utilities	61.2	8.1	155.8	9.3	439.3	9.4	1,234.8	11.2
Trade	144.3	19.1	319.1	19.0	898.3	19.2	2,277.3	20.6
Finance, insurance, and real estate	74.5	9.9	197.7	11.8	613.8	13.1	1,598.9	14.4
Services	44.7	5.9	140.9	8.4	512.2	10.9	1,316.1	11.9
Government	75.1	10.0	187.1	11.2	609.9	13.0	1,896.3	17.1
External[b]	30.6	4.1	−15.5	(0.9)	−347.2	(7.4)	−3,406.2	(30.8)
Total[c]	754.5		1,676.4		4,687.5		11,073.8	

SOURCES: Junta de Planificación, *Informe económico, 1980*, p. A-5, table 4; ibid., *1982–83* 2:A-4, table 4.

[a] Millions of dollars.

[b] Difference between income received from external sources (primarily federal wages paid in Puerto Rico) and income created in Puerto Rico but paid to external recipients (primarily payments of profits, interest, and dividends to U.S. residents). When the figure is negative, outflows exceed inflows. The percent measures the excess of GDP over GNP (or, when positive, the excess of GNP over GDP).

[c] Total value includes a category of "statistical discrepancy," not shown here, which may be positive or negative. Percentages are based on the total shown.

The growth in manufacturing output has been by far the greatest: more than 4,300 percent in absolute terms and more than tripling in relative importance.

A word of caution in interpreting manufacturing's contribution to GNP growth is in order, however. The next-to-last row of figures in table 5.5 shows a negative contribution to GNP since 1960 arising out of the payment of profits, interest, and dividends to nonresidents in excess of the inflows of income to residents from outside the local economy, and is the amount by which GNP differs from GDP (shown in table 5.2). Because it is primarily through ownership in the manufacturing sector that such income is received by nonresidents, the percentage contribution of manufacturing to GNP and local income creation is overstated in the percent-

TABLE 5.6
Total and Net Contribution to GNP from Manufacturing,
1950, 1960, 1970, 1980, and 1982

	1950	1960	1970	1980[a]	1982[a]
Total contribution of manufacturing to GNP[bc]	119.7	366.3	1,190.0	5,322.5	6,017.0
Profits and dividends paid to nonresidents[c]	14.8	75.3	408.3	3,308.2	4,131.5
(Percentage of manufacturing GNP paid to nonresidents)	(12.4)	(20.6)	(34.4)	(62.2)	(68.7)
Net contribution to GNP[c]	104.9	291.0	781.2	2,014.3	1,885.5
(Percentage of net contribution to GNP)	(13.9)	(17.4)	(16.7)	(18.2)	(14.9)

SOURCES: Freyre, *External and Domestic Financing*, p. 164, table V-8; Junta de Planificación, *Informe económico, 1980*, p. 26 and p. A-6, table 5; ibid., *1982–83* 2:VII-9 and 2:A-4, table 4; ibid., *Balanza de pagos*, p. 18.

[a] These figures do not reflect the changes in accounting procedures made by the Junta de Planificación.

[b] From table 5.5, except for 1982.

[c] Millions of dollars.

ages reported in table 5.5. However, if the payments of profits and dividends to nonresidents are subtracted from the share attributed to manufacturing, a quite different picture emerges (see table 5.6). A substantial proportion of income from manufacturing—in the 1980s, well more than half of it—has been repatriated to the mainland.[39] In 1980, though manufacturing apparently produced about 48 percent of *total* GNP, its *net* contribution was only about 18 percent—only slightly more than its contribution for the preceding twenty years. In 1982, the net contribution of manufacturing to GNP actually decreased and was once again near its 1950 level. Conversely, an increasing proportion of manufacturing's gross income has been paid to external owners: from 12.4 percent

[39] The same conclusion, though without numerical estimates, was reached in USDC, *Economic Study* 2:24 ("the manufacturing sector is not producing as much income for Puerto Rico as might be expected of it in light of its performance in terms of output"). One might not find this result so surprising, or the size of the repatriated share of income created so astounding, when it is realized that there is very likely substantial transfer pricing and other accounting devices to shift value added from the U.S. parent corporation to subsidiaries in Puerto Rico, where profits are tax-free. With the regulations in force since 1976, permitting immediate profit repatriation with minimal taxes, this effect has likely been exaggerated, though there are apparently no studies that have attempted to determine the extent of transfer pricing. See the comment in Weisskoff and Wolff, "Linkages and Leakages," p. 619, n. 21.

TABLE 5.7
Employment by Sector, Ten-Year Intervals from 1940 to 1980 and 1982

	1940		1950		1960		1970		1980		1982	
Sector	N	%	N	%	N	%	N	%	N	%	N	%
Agriculture	229	44.7	214	35.9	124	22.8	68	9.9	40	5.3	35	4.9
Manufacturing	56	10.9	55	9.2	81	14.9	132	19.2	143	19.0	134	18.6
Home needlework	45	8.8	51	8.6	10	1.8	a		a		a	
Construction	16	3.1	27	4.5	45	8.3	76	11.1	44	5.8	36	5.0
Trade	54	10.5	90	15.1	97	17.9	128	18.7	138	18.3	141	19.6
Finance, insurance, and real estate	2	0.4	3	0.5	6	1.1	13	1.9	21	2.8	21	2.9
Transportation	17	3.3	23	3.9	24	4.4	27	3.9	25	3.3	25	3.5
Communications	1	0.2	—	—	4	0.7	6	0.9	8	1.1	9	1.3
Other public utilities	2	0.4	5	0.8	8	1.5	12	1.7	14	1.8	14	1.9
Services	73	14.3	77	12.9	75	13.8	116	16.9	135	17.9	132	18.4
Public administration	13	2.5	45	7.6	62	11.4	106	15.5	184	24.4	171	23.8
Other	4	0.8	—	—	7	1.3	a		a		a	
Total	512	99.9	596	99.0	543	99.9	686	99.7	753	99.7	719	99.9

SOURCES: Junta de Planificación, *Informe económico, 1980*, p. A-27, table 24; ibid., *1982–83* 2:A-25, table 24.
NOTE: *N*'s are in thousands. Percentages are based on totals shown and do not always add up to 100 because of rounding errors and lack of exact figures for some categories in some years.
ᵃ Exact figures not available, but less than 2.

in 1950 to 34.4 percent in 1970 and 62.2 percent in 1980 and then to an extraordinary 68.7 percent in 1982, when repatriated profits equaled $4.132 billion, an increase of 9.5 percent over the $3.773 billion paid in 1981. By comparison, external income on direct investment had been $14.8 million in 1950 and $75.3 million in 1960.[40]

Table 5.7 contains further evidence on the relatively small contribution of manufacturing to the island's economy. Manufacturing's share of total employment nearly doubled from 1940 to 1980 (rising from 10.9 percent to 19 percent), a rate of increase which is closer to the rate of growth of manufacturing's *net* contribution to GNP than to its gross contribution

[40] Junta de Planificación, *Informe económico, 1982–83* 2:VII-9, and Freyre, *External and Domestic Financing*, p. 164, table V-8. Repatriated profits on direct investment was the largest category of external payments to capital, amounting to 84.1 percent of the total in 1982.

(table 5.6). The decline of agriculture, seen before in its shrinking contribution to GNP, is reflected also in the change in its share of employment, where it is now less than 5 percent. On the other hand, the expanding role of the government sector is seen in the fact that it is now the largest employer. However, the crisis of the late 1970s and early 1980s affected employment in all sectors; in 1982, total employment had fallen below the 1978 level, a decline that continued into 1983. These changes in employment will be commented on more extensively below, but it is clear from this and the preceding tables that there is now an economic structure that exhibits the characteristics of a modern social formation, in which the leading sectors in terms of income and employment are industry (even after adjustment from gross to net contribution), services, and government. This transformation from an agricultural economy was compressed into less than twenty-five years, from the late 1940s to 1970—one of the more rapid industrial revolutions.

SOURCES OF FINANCING FOR INVESTMENT

The growth of output and income since the 1940s has been partly the result of greater investment, and it is important to examine where the funds for such investment have come from. In general, a surplus of funds that is available for investment use can be generated either internally or externally. One premise upon which Operation Bootstrap was based was that the domestic surplus would be insufficient and external funds would therefore have to be mobilized to finance industrialization. Over time, as the economy grew and incomes rose, a locally generated surplus of funds was expected to become available.

However, this has not happened. The bulk of investment funds have continued to come from the United States. There has been no visible trend toward greater local financing of investment; if anything, there has developed a greater dependence on external sources (see table 5.8). In 1947, more than half of all investment funds were derived from external sources, including the U.S. federal government, external investors, and foreign banks. The proportion was lower during the early 1950s, but then, with the shift toward capital-intensive promotion as the focus of Fomento's activities, the share of external funds to the total increased, until, in the 1970s, about three-quarters of investment funds were derived from external sources, primarily from the United States. In the key sector of manufacturing, approximately 90 percent of investment funds have come from mainland firms.[41]

[41] Curet Cuevas, *El desarrollo económico*, p. 282, table 85, and USDC, *Economic Study* 2:5.

TABLE 5.8
Total and Imported Capital, Selected Years, 1947 to 1980

| | | Imported Capital[b] | |
	Total Capital Funds[a] (millions of dollars)	Amount (millions of dollars)	Percentage of Total
1947	51.6	28.8	55.8
1950	124.1	43.7	43.3
1955	236.4	96.3	40.7
1960	413.7	227.5	55.0
1965	810.0	441.3	54.5
1970	1,639.4	1,007.3	61.4
1972	1,835.9	1,310.3	71.4
1974	1,856.0	1,346.1	72.5
1976	2,104.4	1,734.9	82.4
1978	2,308.1	1,891.5	82.0
1980	3,519.5	2,607.4	74.1

SOURCES: Curet Cuevas, *El desarrollo económico*, p. 282, table 85; Junta de Planificación, *Informe económico, 1977*, p. 159; ibid., *1980*, p. 240.
[a] Total funds available in Puerto Rico (including both private and public sectors).
[b] Funds invested in Puerto Rico derived from non–Puerto Rican sources.

The sources of an internal surplus for investment consist of depreciation reserves of business enterprises (that is, funds set aside to take account of wear and tear on machinery and other capital), savings by government (budget surpluses), savings by corporations (retained earnings), and personal savings of individuals. Of these internal sources, depreciation reserves and government savings have been the most important, supplying 52.9 percent and 29.2 percent, respectively, of local investment funds between 1947 and 1972.[42] Retained earnings of business have also made a contribution, but individual savings normally have been a drain on surplus creation, since—contrary to conventional economic wisdom—consumption expenditures have risen more rapidly than incomes (see table 5.9). Net savings have exceeded income in only two years since 1947 (in 1952 by $4.4 million and in 1954 by $1.8 million). In fact, in 1977, 1978, and 1983, total consumption actually exceeded GNP. Increased

[42] Curet Cuevas, *El desarrollo económico*, p. 281. See also Freyre, *External and Domestic Financing*, chap. 4 and pp. 53–54, where Freyre calculates the "degree of self-sufficiency" as the ratio of foreign capital imports to total capital formation. Table 5.8 shows that this ratio has tended to increase since the beginning of industrial promotion and hence that the degree of self-sufficiency has declined.

TABLE 5.9
Disposable Personal Income, Total Consumption, and Personal Savings,
Selected Years, 1940 to 1983
(millions of dollars)

	Disposable Personal Income	Total Consumption	Personal Savings[a]	Net Personal Savings[b]
1940	218.2	235.6	−17.4	—
1950	637.8	662.5	−24.7	−38.0
1952	814.9	796.0	18.9	4.4
1954	931.2	911.8	19.4	1.8
1955	976.5	964.4	12.1	−9.0
1960	1,333.5	1,397.6	−64.1	−106.4
1965	2,232.9	2,197.4	35.5	−165.4
1970	3,564.8	3,746.5	−181.7	−290.2
1972	4,475.8	4,742.4	−266.6	−432.8
1974	5,582.2	5,753.3	−171.1	−347.6
1976	7,264.5	7,485.7	−221.2	—
1977	7,769.6	8,291.6	−522.0	—
1978	8,553.7	9,139.8	−586.1	—
1980	10,332.9	10,976.0	−643.1	—
1982	11,969.1	12,414.0	−444.9	—
1983	12,009.0	13,011.2	−1,002.2	—

SOURCES: Junta de Planificación, *Informe económico, 1980*, p. 425 and p.
A-1, table 1; ibid., *1982–83* 2:A-1, table 1; Colón de Zalduondo, *Puerto Rican
Economy*, p. 17, table 5.
[a] Disposable personal income less total consumption.
[b] Disposable personal income less total consumption, interest on consumer loans,
and funds sent abroad.

incomes, instead of leading to increased personal saving which could be
used for investment, have led to dissaving and the growth in personal
loans to cover current consumption expenses. Hence consumer debt rose
from $237 million in 1963 to $3,276.4 million in 1983, diverting funds
that could otherwise have been used for locally controlled productive
investment.[43]

[43] Junta de Planificación, *Informe económico, 1982–83* 2:X-11. For most years since
1947, the average propensity to consume (APC) has been close to 1; since 1970, it has
exceeded 1 in every year except 1975. The marginal propensity to consume (MPC) has
shown wide fluctuations, but in some years (most recently 1980), it too has exceeded 1,
though its instability probably indicates that it is not too reliable an indicator. Freyre, *External and Domestic Financing*, analyzed this tendency and the weakness of personal savings. He concluded that over the period from 1947 to 1963 the average propensity to save

In an exhaustive technical study, Freyre compared the dependence on external financing in Puerto Rico with that of other nations. In modern times, only the Philippines have come close to Puerto Rico's degree of external dependence, having been about 80 percent dependent. Such other countries as Italy, Denmark, Peru, Mexico, Jamaica, and Israel have shown a much lower degree of external dependence. In now developed countries such as Sweden, Canada, and the United States, external financial dependence tended to decline as production and incomes increased and industrialization expanded, which is just the opposite of Puerto Rico's experience.[44]

A high degree of external dependence brings in its wake, as Maldonado has pointed out, "such interacting problems as perpetual balance of payments deficits, overconsumption, loss of domestic control over the factors of production, and, eventually, loss of domestic control over the politico-economic structure of the economy."[45] These impacts in Puerto Rico will be considered later in the chapter.

ASPECTS OF EXTERNAL OWNERSHIP

To speak of "foreign," rather than "external," ownership and control in Puerto Rico would be somewhat of a misnomer. Since most investment funds have come from the United States and since Puerto Ricans are U.S. citizens, these funds are hardly foreign in the usual sense of the term, especially when it is added that some of them have certainly come from Puerto Ricans living on the mainland. It does not follow, however, that Puerto Rico is, for questions of capital flows, the same as any state in the United States and thus that any dichotomy between external and internal financing is meaningless. First, Puerto Rico does calculate a balance-of-payments account, just like any independent country and unlike any state. Second, and more important, Puerto Rico is not a state or even a territory of the United States. Its status is not a resolved matter, and

---

was close to zero and that "the relative constancy of personal average and marginal propensities to save during the period of reference is especially striking if we consider the extraordinary increase of personal disposable income of Puerto Rican families, which rose by $1,292.3 million or 240.7 percent during said period" (p. 120). See also Colón de Zalduondo, *Puerto Rican Economy*, pp. 13–23, for a review of some of the literature on estimating MPC and APC in Puerto Rico and comparisons of different definitions of "saving."

[44] Freyre, *External and Domestic Financing*, p. 152, table V-2, and ECLA, *Statistical Yearbook*, p. 106, table 102.

[45] Maldonado, *Financial Sector*, p. 36. See also Wasow, "Saving and Dependence," in which a formal model of differing measures of dependence is developed.

the island could become a politically sovereign entity at some future time, which is surely not the case for any state. Third, unless the Federal Relations Act which now governs relations between the United States and Puerto Rico is substantially revised, the island will not be treated exactly like a state for purposes of federal financing, laws, programs, and the like.[46] Not having full rights as U.S. citizens, the people and government of Puerto Rico must be concerned about the sources of their income and the stability of the base of their income-earning potential. Awareness of the fact of Puerto Rico's second-class status vis-à-vis the United States has become particularly acute as a result of the cuts in federal funding since 1981, which have been especially severe in their impact on the island.

Finally, and perhaps most important, the role of external financing is wrapped up with questions of power, influence, and control in the local economy. This, of course, goes back to an issue raised earlier: unless one assumes that a market system more or less automatically tends to function to the advantage of society in general, its impact is something to be investigated, probed, and evaluated, not to be taken for granted as positive or even neutral, particularly in an era of huge international corporations, many of which individually have incomes larger than Puerto Rico's. The importance of external financing is underscored by the realization that in 1978, Puerto Rico had 34.1 percent of all direct investment in Latin America, an amount equal to U.S. investment in Mexico and Brazil together, and that 42.4 percent of all profits from Latin America came from Puerto Rico.[47]

Two issues need to be separated in the ensuing discussion. One is the more or less objective measurement of the extent of external ownership and control in the local economy; the other is the judgmental question of the desirability and inevitability of externally funded investment. This section will deal with the first of these issues; the second will be taken up in a later section.

Table 5.10 presents data on several measures of the degree of external ownership in manufacturing in 1963 and 1967. It is true that, in absolute numbers, there have always been many more locally owned than externally owned firms. It is notable, however, that the proportion of externally owned firms increased during this period by about 10 percent, the number of locally owned firms declining from 1,655 to 1,502. (Even earlier, from 1954 to 1958, the number had declined from 1,718 to 1,665.)[48]

---

[46] The importance of this issue has recently been analyzed in a report by the U.S. Comptroller General, *Puerto Rico's Political Future*.

[47] Bonilla and Campos, "A Wealth of Poor," p. 140, table 2.

[48] Colón de Zalduondo, *Puerto Rican Economy*, p. 159.

TABLE 5.10
Indicators of External Ownership in Manufacturing, 1963 and 1967

	1963		1967	
Indicator	Total	Percent Due to External Ownership	Total	Percent Due to External Ownership
Number of firms	2,243	26.2	2,367	36.5
Number of employees	98,597	59.8	121,537	70.7
Wages paid (thousands)	$241,021	60.1	$371,847	70.5
Value added (thousands)	$620,815	61.4	$1,002,817	70.6
Total sales (thousands)	$1,480,379	59.5	$2,272,647	68.7
Sales in Puerto Rico (thousands)	$686,012	43.1	$1,025,983	51.0

SOURCES: Curet Cuevas, *El desarrollo económico*, p. 253, table 81. For details on locally owned industries, see Colón de Zaluondo, *Puerto Rican Economy*, pp. 176–81, tables 3–5, and pp. 190–93, tables 7 and 8.

But even that is a misleading measure, because locally owned firms tend to be much smaller than externally owned ones. In 1963, nearly three-quarters of locally owned manufacturing enterprises employed less than twenty people, while only one-quarter of externally owned manufacturing firms were that small, and these figures were virtually the same in 1967.[49] The effects of this can be seen in the other figures in table 5.10. In 1963, externally owned firms were responsible for about 60 percent of employment, wages, value added, and total sales in manufacturing; in 1967, each of those figures had increased to about 70 percent.[50] In some areas

[49] Ibid., p. 164, and p. 167, table 1. In 1961, Fomento organized a Department of Puerto Rican Industries to promote local ownership.

[50] The trends since 1967 cannot be determined precisely, because detailed data on local and external ownership are no longer reported. However, one knowledgeable economist has estimated that the external share on each of these indicators was at least 80 percent in 1972, and it has probably been no less than that in the 1980s: Curet Cuevas, *El desarrollo económico*, p. 255. In 1975, it was reported that in ten of the preceding eleven years "the Puerto Rican private sector has actually reduced its ownership of Puerto Rico's capital stock over a period

of manufacturing, external ownership has been even more marked. In the "core" industries so vigorously promoted by Fomento in the second phase of Operation Bootstrap, external ownership (by equity) in 1973 ranged from a "low" of 60 percent in petroleum products to 99.988 percent in drugs. For the entire group of core industries, which produced 57 percent of total manufacturing output by 1977, external ownership averaged 98.3 percent.[51]

Fomento's strategy of industrialization has thus clearly enlarged the role of external ownership in the manufacturing sector. External investment has not been a complement to local ownership and control, but a substitute for it, despite the fact that one goal of Operation Bootstrap was to create an environment propitious for the emergence of local capital linked to firms promoted by Fomento. The Puerto Rican capitalist class has assumed an auxiliary or even subordinate relationship to U.S. capital as small businessmen in banking, trade, insurance, and real estate.

Foreign companies also predominate in the financial field. Of fifteen mortgage companies in the late 1960s, fourteen were U.S. branch operations. Of the 225 insurance companies, 196 or 87.1 percent were externally owned (182 of them U.S.-owned), and they controlled 99.97 percent of all insurance assets at the end of 1966. In commercial banking, the two U.S. banks in operation in 1967—First National City (now Citibank) and Chase Manhattan—controlled 33.4 percent of total banking assets.[52] By 1977, the share of assets held by these two banks had increased to 40.6 percent.[53] Although external ownership in banking is not as high as in manufacturing, the global reach of Citibank and Chase Manhattan gives them greater leverage than these figures alone might suggest. Each is larger than any domestic bank on the island, and because they

---

in which that capital stock has been rising rapidly": Committee to Study Puerto Rico's Finances (Tobin Committee), *Report*, p. 25.

[51] USDC, *Economic Study* 2:6 and 2:37, table 12. The 1973 figures for external equity ownership in other industries were: petrochemicals, 99.98 percent; other chemicals, 98.3; petroleum refining, 94.6; primary metals, 89.1; fabricated metals, 99.5; machinery, 99.7; and electrical machinery, 98.9. Rates of return on direct investment in these industries are well above those in the U.S., because only about 20 percent of assets are held in physical capital; rates of returns of 15 to 20 percent on total capital (financial and physical) are thus equivalent to rates of return on direct investment in the range of 35 to 60 percent: Tobin Committee, *Report*, p. 44.

[52] Maldonado, *Financial Sector*, pp. 78–79, and p. 92, table 5.1.

[53] USDC, *Economic Study* 2:544, table 1. It is also noted (pp. 548–49) that the shift toward external banks (which after 1975 included Spanish interests as well as U.S. and Canadian interests) has increased. See PRDT, *Economy and Finances, 1976*, p. 9, and *Economy and Finances, 1978*, pp. 9, 11.

are international banks, they can move funds and assets in and out of Puerto Rico quite easily. More than 81 percent of the deposits of international corporations in financial institutions in Puerto Rico were deposited in the branches of these two banks—some $1.3 billion of the more than $1.6 billion of deposits in the late 1970s.[54]

The total gross wealth in Puerto Rico in 1974 amounted to some $22 billion. That represents the value of all tangible, reproducible assets (i.e., excluding land)—housing, capital, inventories, consumer durable goods, public works, and external financial investments owned by Puerto Ricans. Of that amount, $6.1 billion were owned by external investors, and another $6.2 billion were offset by external debt. Thus, the net worth held by island residents was $9.7 billion, or 44.1 percent of total gross wealth. The other 55.9 percent was the property of external owners, of which 27.7 percent was owned outright.[55] In 1928, as pointed out in chapter 2, the proportion of total wealth that was externally owned was 27.1 percent. The share of external ownership had more than doubled since that time period. The total wealth of the island has grown more than 3,000 percent (it had been only $650 million in 1928), but external ownership had increased even more rapidly, displacing local ownership to a substantial degree.

As was also true in 1928, a considerable proportion of the reproducible assets owned by Puerto Ricans in 1974 were not productive assets. Housing accounted for $5.1 billion of total wealth, and consumer durables (e.g., refrigerators and cars) for an additional $2.9 billion. On the other hand, external ownership has been concentrated in productive wealth like plant, machinery, equipment, buildings, and financial instruments. With the elimination of housing and consumer durables, total *productive* assets in 1974 were $14 billion, and the net holdings of island residents in such assets (i.e., after deducting external liabilities) was only $4.3 billion, or 30.7 percent.

Thus, since the late 1920s, and partly because of the growth strategy pursued by Operation Bootstrap, there has been a progressive increase in absolute and relative external ownership of the capital stock and especially of the productive wealth of Puerto Rico's economy, so that 70 percent of all productive wealth is now owned by external investors. There is no indication that anything has changed since 1974. By 1977, net di-

[54] USDC, *Economic Study* 2:561–62, and Marrero Velázquez, "Economic Development Strategy," pp. 44–45. See also NACLA, "Puerto Rico to New York."

[55] Tobin Committee, *Report*, p. 63, table X-1. See also Curet Cuevas, *El desarrollo económico*, p. 254, table 82, for a similar accounting for 1972. The calculation by the Tobin Committee of external equity as $6.1 billion may be low; for 1972, Curet Cuevas calculated it as $6.6 billion.

rect foreign investment had risen to $9.1 billion, and in 1982 it stood at $16.7 billion.[56]

IMPACT OF INTERNATIONAL FIRMS

For the administrators of Puerto Rico's economic development program, as well as for economists and a significant part of the island's population, it is investment by international firms, particularly in manufacturing, that has been responsible for rising incomes and the transition to a modern economy. The meaning and the effects of this kind of investment need to be carefully considered.

In 1978, more than 2,000 Fomento-promoted factories were in operation. Among the blue-chip corporations with plants in Puerto Rico were Westinghouse (35 plants), General Electric (20), Gulf & Western (15), Johnson and Johnson (7), Motorola (6), Squibb (5), Bell & Howell (4), Bristol-Myers (4), Du Pont (4), General Mills (3), Ralston Purina (3), RCA (3), Colgate-Palmolive (2), and Firestone, Ford, General Foods, Gillette, and R. J. Reynolds (1 each).[57] Of the international firms that have located in Puerto Rico, 80 percent are subsidiaries of a parent corporation headquartered in the United States. These subsidiaries, as the U.S. Department of Commerce has observed,

> have primarily used the island as a production point, bringing in raw materials and intermediate goods while shipping the output directly to their mainland parent companies for distribution. . . . Corporate investment and production decisions, materials supply, and product distribution systems are almost entirely related to policies, practices, and financial, and tax considerations of mainland parent corporations with little influence from Puerto Rican economic forces.[58]

Marx was the first to consider in detail the "circuit of capital" of capitalist production.[59] Figure 5.1 extends his analysis to the situation in which this circuit is not only interrupted by the time necessary for production, as Marx recognized, but is also separated in space. In the figure, the production process is shown as being initiated within the U.S. economy by the purchase, using finance capital M, of raw material C, means of production (MP_u), and labor (L_u). Typically, from this phase of production P_1 comes a partially transformed output C' with a value, as yet unrealized, greater than M. C' is shipped by the company to its Puerto

[56] Junta de Planificación, *Informe económico, 1977*, p. 124, and ibid., *1982–83* 2:IV-30.
[57] PRIDCO, *Annual Report, 1942–1982*, p. 17.
[58] USDC, *Economic Study* 1:21 and 2:7.
[59] Marx, *Capital* 2:chaps. 1–4; see also Palloix, *La internacionalización de capital*.

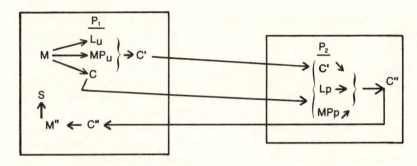

United States   Puerto Rico

KEY: M = money or finance capital
        C = commodity
        L_u = labor, U.S.
        MP_u = means of production, U.S.
        L_p = labor, Puerto Rico
        MP_u = means of production, Puerto Rico
        S = surplus

Figure 5.1 Circuit of Capital for U.S. Firms with Subsidiaries in Puerto Rico

Rican subsidiary for assembly and/or further production. There, the raw material or semiprocessed product is combined with Puerto Rican labor L_p, and perhaps some local means of production MP_p, to constitute the Puerto Rican phase of production P_2. The Puerto Rican subsidiary then reexports its product C'' back to the United States, where it is sold for a value M''. The surplus S ($= M'' - M$) from the sale of the final product represents the profit, which accrues to the parent company.[60] The entire production process is thus completed and reproduced at the international level between the United States and Puerto Rico, but ultimate control over it resides with the international firm headquartered in the United States.

The location of the P_2 portion of the production process in Puerto Rico, however, is not fundamental to the circuit of capital, as it would be for a critical raw material like bauxite, but is based on the international firm's profit considerations. That part of the production process might just as easily be located, or relocated, elsewhere without any effect on production, since it is basically labor power alone which Puerto Rico contributes. Many apparel firms, for example, have in fact closed their Puerto

[60] The tax-exemption laws in Puerto Rico have obscured this last step in the process to some extent, but this is less true now, under section 936 of the Internal Revenue Code (to be discussed below).

Rican plants when they were able to find financial advantages, less risk to supplies, or lower wages elsewhere in the Caribbean or in East Asia.

It can thus be argued that the growing incomes and GNP that were noted earlier in this chapter are less the result of the growth of the productive structure and productive power of the Puerto Rican economy than of the transfer of income within the circuit of capital of international firms. The linking of Puerto Rico into this circuit is not intrinsic to the production process, but rather is contingent on the goals of the international corporations, the investment climate in Puerto Rico, the tax laws, the wage rates, and so on. The predictions of doom every time legislation is introduced into Congress that might change a portion of the tax code affecting Puerto Rico underscores the transitory nature of much of the investment on the island.[61]

There are several sorts of evidence with which this interpretation of the production process and its impact on Puerto Rico's productive structure can be tested. The first of these is the extent of backward linkages within the local economy. Backward linkages are the use of local raw materials and intermediate goods as inputs to the production process. The greater the ratio of imported inputs to total inputs, the fewer are the backward linkages in the economy. In the absence of a measure of total inputs, GDP can serve as a proxy measure. Table 5.11 shows that backward linkages have been decreasing: the ratio of imported inputs to GDP grew from 24.5 percent in 1950 to 44.4 percent in 1980. There has been a decline in the ratio since then, but it remains above its 1950 level. Moreover, at least some of the recent increase in backward linkages is due to interfirm transfers and sales among the Puerto Rican subsidiaries of international corporations. Unfortunately, a more detailed and disaggregated investigation of this subject is not possible from existing published statistics. On the whole, however, it seems reasonable to say that the decrease in backward linkages since 1950 supports the interpretation of the production process made above.

A second kind of evidence can be obtained from an examination of forward linkages—that is, the extent to which firms in Puerto Rico sell their products to other firms on the island. This can be measured as the ratio of interindustry sales to the total value of shipments of industries in Puerto Rico. From 1963 to 1972, this ratio increased slightly, from 23.1 to 24.7 percent. For some industries, such as paper, chemicals, rubber and plastics, and fabricated metals, the expansion in forward linkages was substantial. For others, they have long been neglible. For example, only 0.9 percent of pharmaceutical production in 1977 was sold in the

[61] For a more complete analysis of the circuit of capital, see Dietz, "Export-Enclave Economies."

TABLE 5.11
Extent of Backward Linkages,
1950, 1963, and 1972 to 1983

	Value of Imported Inputs As a Percentage of GNP
1950	24.5
1963	29.4
1972	28.4
1973	28.4
1974	35.3
1975	40.8
1976	39.1
1977	40.1
1978	38.3
1979	39.0
1980	44.4
1981	40.4
1982	36.1
1983	34.6

SOURCES: USDC, *Economic Study* 2:89;
Junta de Planificación, *Informe económico, 1980*, p. A-1, table 1, and p. A-17,
table 16; ibid., *1982–83* 2:A-1, table
A-1, and p. A-16, table 16.

local market, and the value of sales in that year was less in absolute and
relative terms than in 1967. In the textile industry, only twenty of the
seventy-seven producers sold any significant portion of their output locally, and of these six were locally owned. (Only five of them bought a
significant part of their intermediate inputs from local sources, and three
of these were local firms.)[62] Some of these interindustry sales are, of
course, only between branches of international firms, as noted above, and
are ultimately exported by the purchasing enterprise after being transformed further, so that they are not forward linkages at all. In any case,
the evidence from forward linkages is more ambiguous than that from
backward linkages.

It is worth noting that a study of the Puerto Rican economy made by
the U.S. Department of Commerce concluded that the potential for both
forward and backward linkages was limited and that "the industrial process in Puerto Rico is not vertically integrated, despite the tremendous

[62] USDC, *Economic Study* 2:143, table 5, and 2:89, table 2.

TABLE 5.12
Import and Export Dependence,
Selected Years, 1950 to 1983

	Import Dependence[a]	Export Dependence[b]
1950	.48	.34
1960	.54	.37
1970	.50	.35
1972	.49	.32
1974	.55	.44
1976	.58	.38
1978	.57	.44
1980	.57	.49
1981	.58	.52
1982	.52	.55
1983	.50	.52

SOURCES: Junta de Planificación, *Informe económico, 1980*, p. 154; p. A-1, table 1; and p. A-16, table 15; ibid., *1982–83* 2:A-15, table 15.
[a] Ratio of value of merchandise imports to GDP.
[b] Ratio of value of merchandise exports to GDP.

increase in industrial output over the last 30 years."[63] In general, the industries promoted by Fomento have formed export enclaves unarticulated with other industries, and in this respect they have been little different from the sugar production of the first forty years of the century. The manufacturing firms attracted by Fomento do differ in one crucial way, however: they not only export their final product, as did the sugar companies; they also import the intermediate products, as well as the physical capital, necessary to make it.

A third kind of evidence with which to evaluate the impact of the international corporations is the degree of dependency of the Puerto Rican economy on external economies. Table 5.12 shows that the ratio of merchandise imports—i.e., all imports, not merely industrial imports—to GDP has tended to increase during the period of industrialization until, in the late 1970s, nearly 60 cents of every $1 of gross income was being used to pay for imported goods, primarily from the United States. This import-dependency ratio, however, declined slightly in 1982 and 1983. The trend of export dependence has been somewhat less regular, but has shown a tendency to rise during the late 1970s and into the 1980s; in 1983, mer-

[63] Ibid. 2:90.

chandise exports equaled 52 percent of local production. Naturally the more that locally produced goods are exported, the more income needs to be spent on imported goods, leading Gordon Lewis to comment that Puerto Rico is compelled "to produce what it does not consume, and consume what it does not produce."[64] The tendency toward capital-intensive promotion and the networking of international firms have exacerbated the weakness of the island's industrial structure. Very little import substitution has taken place in the food industry, for example. Import substitution has been most visible in industries such as machinery and chemicals, which, however, are producing for the international, not the local, market.[65]

Particularly revealing is the perverse productive-consumption pattern which emerged in some sectors due to the nature of the export/import patterns. In 1948, 80 percent of local textile demand was met by imports. By 1963, this had risen to 87 percent, despite the expansion of the textile industry as a result of Fomento's activities. Meanwhile, 72 percent of textile output was exported in 1948, and 91 percent in 1963. Weisskoff and Wolff refer to this pattern as the "criss-cross" effect: Imports of a particular product expand as a proportion of total supply at the same time that exports of that product from the island increase, though the goods leaving are often quite different from, and typically of higher quality than, those entering the Puerto Rican market. They point out that 100 percent of leather goods were imported in both 1948 and 1963 despite the introduction of a leather-goods (basically a shoe) industry in the intervening period.[66] Interestingly, the criss-cross effect appeared in the basic consumption good industries which in other countries have been prime areas for import substitution.

Since much of what Puerto Rico produces is only part of the circuit of capital of international firms, doubts must be raised about the efficacy of its productive structure and the organization of its manufacturing sector to provide a foundation for self-sustained growth and a secure base from which to create future income. It also raises doubts about the effectiveness of the strategy of dependence on export-oriented external capital as

[64]Lewis, *Puerto Rican Revolution*, p. 53. The average income elasticity of imports for 1950–77 was 1.14, meaning that imports in general were relatively elastic (i.e., superior) goods: USDC, *Economic Study* 1:107, table 9.

[65]C. Santiago, "Import Substitution."

[66]Weisskoff and Wolff, "Development and Trade Dependence," pp. 474–75. Fomento itself was aware of the criss-cross effect: "The textile plants sold almost all their production in the United States, while the clothing factories imported the greatest part of their fabrics from the United States." It was suggested that this lack of integration was what motivated the decision to shift to capital-intensive promotion: PRAFE, *El desarrollo económico*, pp. 2–3.

an engine of growth. External capital dependence has created a situation in which an important segment of the economy is controlled from abroad and is unintegrated with the local economic structure. Even where linkages appear to have emerged, it is unclear as to how meaningful they are, given the pervasive presence of the international corporations in buying and selling within the local manufacturing sector. This would hardly seem to be an examplar of a successful or stable model of development.

EMPLOYMENT AND UNEMPLOYMENT

It had long been recognized that agriculture alone could not provide the base for long-term economic progress, in view of the declining market for sugar, the limited external demand for the island's coffee, and the drastic reduction in outlets for Puerto Rican tobacco. Certainly part of the decision to encourage greater industrialization had been based on a desire to repeat the success of the now developed countries, but it is also true that dependence on agricultural exports could not have been a viable strategy when the natural market for such exports, given the colonial ties, was the United States. The United States was on the way to becoming the world's largest producer and exporter of food products. For certain crops, like tropical and citrus fruits there would still have been an external market for Puerto Rico's output, but it would not have been large enough to absorb the labor force or to provide sufficiently high incomes to enough people, especially given the lower productivity in that sector.

A further consideration which motivated the shift away from agricultural production was that the demand for it does not tend to grow as rapidly as that for manufactured goods, due to the differences in income elasticities and the consequences of Engels' Law.[67] If revenue from the sale of farm products had been relied on to pay for imported manufactured goods, the strategy would have turned against the island as the demand for agrarian exports, with their relatively low income elasticities, lagged behind that for manufactured imports, with their higher income elasticities, making it more and more difficult to maintain, let alone improve, the standard of living, as the purchasing power of exports declined relative to the demand for imported goods.[68] This problem is one that has plagued other Latin American countries and has been fundamental to the

[67] Engels' Law holds that the demand for food products increases as income increases, but not as rapidly (in technical terms, the income elasticity of demand is positive but less than 1), while the demand for manufactured goods tends to increase faster than increases in income (i.e., the income elasticity for manufactured goods is greater than 1).

[68] This imbalance, which is said to adversely affect the terms of trade, is one cornerstone of the structuralist analyses of Latin American underdevelopment: see Love, "Raúl Prebisch."

balance-of-payments difficulties that many of them have faced, and it has contributed to the growth of external debt which, in the 1980s, became the leading international financial problem. In short, the turn to industrialization rested on sound economic reasoning, whose intellectual tradition in Latin America lay in the work of the structuralist economists and the UN Economic Commission for Latin America (ECLA). The colonial context and the inability of the island to protect its agriculture or to easily penetrate other markets lent the bias against agriculture additional weight.

The flaw in the development program, however, was the degree to which it extended the otherwise sound premise that agriculture was too fragile a base for economic development. From the assertion that industrialization was required because agriculture *alone* could not provide an adequate economic base, a program was forged that functioned as if agriculture could be ignored altogether and industrialization, at nearly any cost, was the exclusive goal. Yet, the choice need not have been either agriculture *or* industry; it could have been a mix of agriculture *and* industry, and of industry *in* agriculture, along with selective manufacturing.

The initial step away from agriculture toward manufacturing began, as was seen in chapter 4, during the phase of state capitalism in the 1940s, but it was soon decided that a strategy of state capitalist development was too expensive and would not create a sufficient number of jobs for the growing labor force. The subsequent shift to external capital promotion was virtually total, and there was little effort to anticipate what its total impact would be. Faith in the workings of the market system prevailed over a full analysis of, or even caution about, the possible effects of external investment on employment. The failure of the industrialization strategy to reduce unemployment must certainly be counted as one of the major weaknesses of the Puerto Rican model. High unemployment has been perhaps the most enduring problem of the Puerto Rican economy, and development by invitation has not solved it.

Table 5.13 presents basic information on the labor force. It shows, first, that after 1950 the number of participants in the labor force declined, and it did not reach its 1950 level again until about 1965. The labor force participation rate reached its postwar maximum in 1951 at 55.5 percent and its minimum of 41 percent in 1983. This general decline indicates that the willingness of workers to enter the labor market began to decline at precisely the same time that the industrialization program, which had been implemented to provide jobs and reduce unemployment, began to take off and as industrial promotions by Fomento speeded up.

A second pattern to be observed in table 5.13 is that the rate of unemployment, after falling during the 1960s and dropping to its post–

TABLE 5.13
Labor Force, Participation Rate, and Unemployment,
Selected Years, 1940 to 1983

	Potential Labor Force[a]	Actual Labor Force	Participation Rate (percent)	Unemployed	
				Thousands	Percent of Labor Force
1940	1,154	602	52.2	90	15.0
1950	1,289	684	53.1	88	12.9
1953	1,268	646	50.9	96	14.9
1955	1,300	637	49.0	97	15.3
1958	1,350	637	47.2	82	12.8
1960	1,379	625	45.4	83	13.3
1963	1,454	643	44.2	82	12.8
1965	1,526	681	44.6	76	11.2
1968	1,639	739	45.1	86	11.6
1970	1,718	765	44.5	79	10.3
1972	1,853	837	45.1	100	12.0
1974	1,992	884	44.4	109	12.3
1976	2,138	890	41.6	172	19.4
1978	2,146	961	44.8	180	18.8
1980	2,093	907	43.3	154	17.0
1982	2,192	918	41.8	199	21.7
1983	2,235	918	41.0	215	23.4

SOURCES: Junta de Planificación, *Informe económico, 1980*, p. A-26, table 23; ibid., *1982–83* 2:A-24, table 23; and ibid., *Serie histórica del empleo*, p. 1, table 1.

[a] Thousands of noninstitutionalized persons 14 years of age and over until 1976, 16 and over after that.

World War II minimum of 10.3 percent in 1970, has increased steeply from then until now, reaching its recorded peak of 23.4 percent in 1983. The post–Vietnam War recession, exacerbated by the oil crises of 1974 and 1979–80, played a role in this increase, but it is not the entire explanation.

Puerto Rico's historical unemployment statistics are, in fact, more consistent with those of an underdeveloped country than with those of a developed one or with those of other economies at an equivalent income level, and they are exceedingly high by the standards of developed capitalist countries. In the late 1970s, unemployment was at levels seen in the United States only during the depths of the Great Depression. Even the lower unemployment rates of the late 1950s and 1960s were due

primarily to increased migration and lower labor-force participation rates
during that period, particularly among male workers of prime labor-force
participation age.[69]

Unlike the case in other countries, the unemployment rate for women
has generally been lower than that for men, in all age brackets. In some
years, the difference has been substantial. In 1960, the male unemployment rate was 14.1 percent and 11.3 percent for women; in 1965, the
respective rates were 12.5 and 7.6; in 1970, 11.0 and 9.0; and in 1979,
19.8 and 12.9.[70] Given the employment problems faced by women workers in general as members of a secondary, segmented labor market with
limited employment alternatives, their labor-force participation rate has
been lower than for males, as is "normal" in other countries as well.
Through the 1960s, the participation rate averaged 69.3 percent for males
but only 23.5 percent for females; in the seventies, the respective percentages were 63.3 and 26.6.[71] Thus, the measured unemployment rate
for female workers may have been reduced by disguised unemployment,
as relatively fewer women have entered the labor force because work was
difficult to find. On the other hand, the female participation rate (except
for teenagers and women over 65) has been increasing, while the rates
for men in prime working-age groups have been declining. This suggests
that either there has been a substitution of female for male labor, reducing
female unemployment rates, or the "additional worker" effect has come
into play, as unemployment among male heads of families has forced
more women into the workplace, much as happened in the pre-1940 period, when women entered the needlework industry especially (see chapter 3).[72]

It also needs to be noted that the official definition of an unemployed
person is a member of the labor force who is not working *at all*. At any
point in time, however, there are many people who are working, but for
fewer hours than they would like. Such part-time workers who would
take a full-time position if it were available are referred to as "underemployed." In 1953, 38 percent of all employed workers worked less

[69] Junta de Planificación, *Serie histórica del empleo*, p. 16, table 13. Puerto Rico's labor-
force participation rate is lower than that in other Latin American countries. However, with
the exception of the Dominican Republic, all countries in Latin America show declining
rates of participation, perhaps in these countries more so than in Puerto Rico as a result of
increased school attendance: ECLA, *Statistical Yearbook*, pp. 14–15, table 12.

[70] Junta de Planificación, *Serie histórica del empleo*, pp. 2–3, tables 2 and 3, and pp.
11–12, tables 8 and 9.

[71] Ibid.

[72] C. Santiago, " 'Discouraged-Worker' Effect," p. 5; Holbik and Swan, *Industrialization and Employment*, pp. 56–60. See also C. Santiago, "Labor Force Participation." On
women workers, their occupations, and their incomes, see Presser, "Labor Force Status of
Puerto Rican Women."

than thirty-five hours a week; in 1960, it was 33 percent; in 1970, 24 percent; in 1974, 37 percent; and in 1977, 23 percent.[73] If 90 percent of these persons voluntarily preferred part-time work and only 10 percent were underemployed (a very conservative estimate), then the combined rate of unemployment and underemployment, or the *underutilization* rate, in 1953 would have been 18.6 percent; in 1960, 16.6 percent; in 1970, 12.7 percent; in 1974, 16.0; and in 1977, 22.3 percent.[74]

The profile of the unemployed is very similar to that found in the United States, with the exception of the lower rate of unemployment for women. The young are more likely to be unemployed than older workers; those with less than twelve years of education have a higher rate of unemployment than high-school graduates; white-collar workers have lower rates of unemployment than do blue-collar workers; and so on. However, these characteristics cannot explain the high rates of unemployment, as some have suggested. The growth of the labor force has been most rapid among those aged 25 to 44, not among teens; the proportion of the population 18 to 24 years of age attending college has grown from 1.4 percent in the 1940 school year and 4.7 percent in 1950 to 29.9 percent in the 1978 school year; and workers classified as white collar have been the fastest-growing category of workers, increasing 20.8 percent between 1973 and 1978 while the number of blue-collar workers was increasing by just 4.9 percent and the number of agricultural workers remained constant.[75]

A study done for the Government Development Bank suggested that the "natural rate of unemployment—i.e., the rate of unemployment below which it is difficult to reach and toward which the economy tends to gravitate—is higher in Puerto Rico than in the U.S. and other countries for which evidence exists."[76] The authors of this study speculate that the higher "natural" rate of unemployment may be in part a result of the

[73] Marrero Velázquez, "Economic Development Strategy," p. 12, table 7 (drawn from data of the Puerto Rico Department of Labor and Human Resources).

[74] Official data of the Puerto Rican government count as "underemployed" only self-employed persons (principally subsistence farmers) who wish to work more, regardless of the hours actually worked. For 1966, the Department of Labor reported 83,000 underemployed workers, which was almost equal to the total number of unemployed; the underutilization was thus almost double the unemployment rate (23.3 percent rather than 11.7 percent): Gutiérrez, *Factor Proportions*, pp. 8–9, and Junta de Planificación, *Serie histórica del empleo*, p. 1. See also USDC, *Economic Study* 2:598, which estimates that underemployment rates have averaged about 10 percent of the labor force, in which case the underutilization rate since 1950 was in the range of 20 to 34 percent.

[75] Junta de Planificación, *Serie histórica del empleo*, p. 1, and *Estadísticas sociales*, pp. 21, 64, 68.

[76] Piore and Montiel, "Youth Unemployment," pp. 17–19. The study suggests that there were "weaknesses" inherent in the development model that caused a movement away from this natural rate in the 1970s (ibid., pp. 26–29).

types of industries that have located on the island. For example, the textile and garment industries tend to be unstable and to generate high unemployment rates (in the United States as well as on the island). To the extent that this is true, it amounts to a reproach of the development strategy, since the industrial structure, or at least an important part of it, is the outcome of Fomento's efforts—and the authors suggest that one effect has been to increase Puerto Ricans' "tolerance of unemployment."[77]

To be fair, it should be pointed out that unemployment rates in underdeveloped and developing countries may not be measuring the same thing as in developed nations. In developing countries, wage labor may not be necessary to the extent that it is in developed countries, because of different goals and lower levels of "needs" among persons who still retain the ideology, consumption and leisure patterns, behavioral characteristics, and expectations characteristic of other modes of production or of a less developed capitalist social formation. A higher "natural" rate of unemployment might be expected to be manifested in these circumstances until the behavorial, cultural, and ideological values of wage workers became more widespread. In that case, however, unemployment ought to diminish, unless the rate of rural-urban migration increases too rapidly. No such diminution in unemployment has been visible in Puerto Rico; in fact, just the opposite has occurred, and the pace of rural-urban migration has not been such as to be able to account for it.

Interestingly, when a Puerto Rican worker is unemployed, it is for only a relatively short duration. About 50 percent of those unemployed between 1950 and 1964 were out of work for less than five weeks and 30 percent for five to fourteen weeks; the remainder were out of a job for more than fourteen weeks. In 1977–78, 43.3 percent were unemployed for less than five weeks and 21.7 percent for fifteen weeks or more; in 1978–79, the respective figures were 46.2 and 18.7 percent.[78] Apparently, then, there is movement in and out of the ranks of the unemployed during the year for a substantial part of the population.

It also seems likely that there is a substantial number of discouraged workers in the economy—that is, workers who have decided they will be unable to find employment and hence have stopped looking (and are therefore not counted as being in the labor force or as being unemployed). This may partly explain the low rate of labor-force participation. On the other hand, some persons officially counted as unemployed are involved in the "underground," parallel, or informal economy (as street vendors, other self-employed persons, or even criminals), and in this sense

[77] Ibid., p. 1.

[78] Torres de Romero, *El desempleo*, pp. 73–74, table 17; Junta de Planificación, *Serie histórica del empleo*, p. 38, table 32; and USDC, *Economic Study* 2:596–97.

might be regarded as "employed" (though in low-productivity, low-income activities). Still, the labor-force participation rate in Puerto Rico must be regarded as "unusually low." In 1972, "seventy-three percent of the people who could be working but had no job, had never had a job," compared with 10 percent in the United States, and more than a third of those aged 16 to 24 were neither in school nor working.[79]

It has been argued that the high unemployment rates are the result of the federal minimum-wage legislation, which is alleged to have raised wages above the level justified by worker productivity, so that employers could not afford to hire as many workers. Almost since the beginning of its application to Puerto Rico in 1938, the Fair Labor Standards Act had permitted industries on the island to petition for a lower wage standard than that specified in federal law. Special industry committees determined the appropriate minimum wage for "hardship" cases, and nearly all industries in Puerto Rico fell into that category. However, in 1977, Congress decided—with support from pro-statehood forces and unions—that Puerto Rico's minimum-wage level was to be brought up to the prevailing level in the United States by January 1, 1981. This was to be accomplished by a gradual process, which differed among industries depending upon how far they fell short of the ultimate wage goal at the time the legislation went into effect. Since 1981, then, Puerto Rico and the United States have had the same minimum wage.[80] This step has undoubtedly contributed to closing the gap between mainland and island wages that was seen in table 5.4.

The authors of the Government Development Bank study that was cited previously believe not only that "it is extremely difficult to identify an empirical link between rising wage costs on the Island and [the] rise in the level of unemployment in recent years,"[81] but even that the argument that lower wages would reduce unemployment is no longer valid, because the development program itself has changed workers' values and expectations. Many workers have had working experience in the United States, and virtually all families have some indirect knowledge of mainland jobs and wages. They have become unwilling to accept less pay for a job requiring the same skills as one performed on the mainland simply because it is performed on the island.

[79]Tobin Committee, *Report*, p. 23; Marrero Velázquez, "Economic Development Strategy," p. 4.

[80]There are exceptions, where subminimum wages are still permitted, typically in agriculture, agriculture-related, or apparel industries: USDC, *Economic Study* 2:639–42, table 5. See Junta de Planificación, *Informe económico, 1980*, p. 72, n. 1, for the timetable and wage increases mandated by the law.

[81]Piore and Montiel, "Youth Unemployment," p. 12.

In this sense, wage setting institutions appear to express more basic social forces making for wage equalization. And while congressional action might affect the precise timing of the wage increase, the longrun trend should not be attributed to it.[82]

The authors point out that the wage gap was closing, anyway (see table 5.4). In short, it is the wage structure prevailing in the United States that affects the labor force in Puerto Rico, not the wage structure prevailing on the island, and a reduction in unemployment and an increase in labor-force participation will require not a further decrease in wages in Puerto Rico but an *increase* in wages to levels comparable to those prevailing on the mainland.

Marginal productivity theory would explain the low wages on the island by the lower productivity of Puerto Rican workers. In 1972, however, the value added per dollar of wages paid was $4.03 in Puerto Rico, compared to $3.36 in the United States. Thus, $1 spent on wages in Puerto Rico returned 1.19 times the value in output as a dollar spent on wages in the United States. By 1977, Puerto Rican workers were creating an average of $5.58 of value added per dollar of wages, compared to $3.72 for U.S. workers, a ratio of 1.5:1. Furthermore, absenteeism among Puerto Rican workers is 9 percent less than on the mainland, and labor turnover is lower as well.[83]

Another attempt to account for the higher unemployment levels is Gutiérrez's econometric study of the substitutability of labor for capital. He found that Fomento-promoted firms tended to be more capital-intensive than similar enterprises in the southern United States, because Fomento's activities had been devoted to driving the opportunity cost of capital down by enhancing its profitability through tax exemption. In other words, the cost of capital was being subsidized, and firms have thus had relatively little incentive to create more jobs. Hence, Gutiérrez argues, the unemployment problem in inextricably a part of the nature of the development strategy itself, especially in its second phase, focused on capital-intensive industry.[84]

The adverse impact on employment from the promotion of capital-intensive firms can be illustrated by the changes in the capital-output

[82]Ibid., p. 13; on pp. 13–16 is a discussion of the way in which the social expectations of parents for their children affect what is perceived as an "acceptable" wage.
[83]PREDA, *Labor Force*, pp. 16–18.
[84]Gutiérrez, *Factor Proportions*, p. 54. Gutiérrez recognizes that the capital intensity of firms also might be explained by the transfer of plants similar to those in the U.S. to the island, rather than to the lower cost of capital and any margin-calculating decisions made by firms locating in Puerto Rico, though this hypothesis is not tested.

(K/Y) ratio, which measures the value of capital used to produce $1 of output. This increased from an average of 2.50 over the period from 1947 to 1963 to 2.55 between 1963 and 1973 and 3.01 between 1973 and 1977. Even more revealing, for new capital introduced during this last period, the K/Y ratio was 7.96, compared to a ratio of 3.28 for new capital introduced during the preceding decade, which means that less and less employment was being generated as output rose.[85]

Reviewing all the evidence, it is difficult to escape the conclusion that the persistence of high unemployment has been a result of the development strategy itself. No doubt the economic recession of the 1970s hit Puerto Rico particularly hard, because of the extreme openness of the economy and its consequent vulnerability to external shock. But this very openness has been at the heart of the overall development strategy, which has stressed external investment and "export-platform industrialization," to the neglect of agricultural production for local use, and which has attempted to use the "special relation" with the United States to speed the growth process. Thus, external crises cannot be separated from the framework of the development model itself and used to explain away its failure. As Gutiérrez concluded, "Industrial growth, based on modern techniques and given a degree of 'rational' calculation on the part of investors in a labor surplus economy, will be unable to create the necessary jobs to reduce the rate of unemployment to 'tolerable' levels.' "[86] In other words, development programs like Puerto Rico's appear to be destined to fail by their inherent structure.

Puerto Rico's development dilemma is also intimately connected to its colonial relation with the United States, which has delimited in large measure the development possibilities and the acceptable strategies for growth, though these always have been wider than what Operation Bootstrap has institutionalized. When world economic activity is on the upswing, this dependence has paid off, at least in terms of GNP growth. However, since the development process has been dependent, conditional, and externally articulated, its vitality has resided in forces largely outside the power of the island to affect. Economic crisis as well as economic progress can only be passively accepted, and Operation Bootstrap has done nothing to alleviate this problem or to strengthen the base of the economy in such a way that employment on the island, rather than unemployment or migration, could be a choice for more Puerto Ricans.

[85] USDC, *Economic Study* 1:97–98. Curet Cuevas, *El desarrollo económico*, p. 230, table 79, provides estimates of incremental K/Y ratios from 1948 to 1972.
[86] Gutiérrez, *Factor Proportions*, p. 83.

THE ECONOMICS OF MIGRATION

The demographic shift from rural to urban areas that took place between 1940 and 1950 (see table 4.5 and the accompanying discussion)
continued into the following decades. Between 1960 and 1970, the urban
population grew 51.6 percent, while the rural population actually declined 13.3 percent. By 1970, nearly 60 percent of the population was
living in urban areas, the first time that urban dwellers outnumbered rural
inhabitants.[87]

The rise in emigration from Puerto Rico during the twentieth century
has already been noted (see table 4.6 and the accompanying discussion).
Previously, it will be recalled, Spanish colonial policy had been to try to
halt emigration, since landowners faced a labor shortage. However, with
the transfer to U.S. control, the whole issue of labor supply and population began to be seen from a different perspective, and overpopulation
seemed to be the problem. The emphasis shifted from discouraging emigration to fostering it, on the ground that there was now an "excessive"
number of Puerto Ricans. In Governor Allen's first report in 1901, the
first of the civilian government, for example, it was made clear that the
policy of the United States, if not to actively foster emigration, was to
do nothing to block it either: "Porto Rico has plenty of laborers and poor
people generally."[88] This was to become a recurring theme in official
studies: there were believed to be both too many people and too few
resources on the island, and emigration to the United States or other areas
was necessary if long-term progress was to be achieved.[89] The island's
own policy makers seemed to share this view. The 1934 Chardón Plan
included a proposal to encourage emigration "to under-populated regions
of tropical countries similar to Puerto Rico."[90] Many other studies have
reiterated this concern over "excess population."[91]

The U.S. Department of Commerce study, the most extensive and detailed one covering recent economic and social development, quoted with
apparent approval a 1977 study by the Puerto Rican government:

We have evidently exceeded the population level that can be adequately attended to in Puerto Rico, not only in economic terms, but in

[87] U.S. Bureau of the Census, *1970 Census of Population*, tables 1 and 2.
[88] See CENEP, *La migración*, p. 11.
[89] CENEP, *Labor Migration*, esp. chap. 1, and Maldonado-Denis, *Emigration Dialectic*,
chaps. 2 and 3, provide sketches of various studies, and their conclusions, with this perspective.
[90] PRPC, *Report*, pp. 6–7.
[91] See Curet Cuevas, *El desarrollo económico*, pp. 6, 383, and Perloff, *Puerto Rico's
Economic Future*, chaps. 1 and 12.

social, physical, and human terms as well. The projected growth in population and economic activity surpasses the absorption capacity of the Puerto Rican economy and geographical extension, and it is incompatible with the goal of maintaining and improving the quality of life.[92]

"Overpopulation" is of course a matter of the number of people relative to the ability of an economic structure to employ those needing to work. Marx wrote in *Capital* of the tendency of the capitalist mode of production to require relatively less labor as more and more capital is accumulated.

. . . [I]t is capitalistic accumulation itself that constantly produces, and produces in the direct ratio of its own energy and extent, a relatively redundant population of labourers, i.e., a population of greater extent than suffices for the average needs of the self-expansion of capital, and therefore a surplus-population. . . . The labouring population therefore produces, along with the accumulation of capital produced by it, the means by which itself is made relatively superfluous, is turned into a relative surplus-population; and it does this to an always increasing extent. This is the law of population peculiar to the capitalist mode of production. . . [93]

That is, the extension of capitalist relations tends to establish a condition in which the economic structure cannot make use of all those who wish and need to work. Migration and emigration in Puerto Rico are like all migrations created by capitalist development: labor goes to where capital requires employment and it leaves those areas where it is not needed, the intensity of this flow being greater where capitalist relations of production are most advanced and lesser where they are weak.

Table 5.14 presents a historical series on birth and death rates and the natural rate of population growth, which is the difference between birth and death rates. For comparison, the natural rate of population growth for the United States is also shown. From these figures, it can be seen that the birth rate has tended to decline slowly, the death rate has decreased much more rapidly, especially since 1940, and the natural rate of population growth has been rising since the turn of the century (since 1970 it has dropped to approximately its pre–twentieth century level, though of course at much lower birth and death rates).[94] In comparison

[92] USDC, *Economic Study* 2:692.

[93] Marx, *Capital* 1:630–32. CENEP, *Labor Migration*, chap. 2, is an excellent, short discussion of the Marxist approach to population and migration. For a full discussion, see Giménez, "Population and Capitalism."

[94] One important factor in Puerto Rico's declining birth rate is the sterilization of a third or more of women of child-bearing age, many involuntarily: Mass, "Puerto Rico," and Presser, *Sterilization*.

TABLE 5.14
Birth and Death Rates and Natural Rate of Population Growth, 1897–99 to 1982
(per 1,000 population)

	Birth Rate, Puerto Rico	Death Rate, Puerto Rico	Natural Rate of Growth	
			Puerto Rico	United States
1897–99	45.7	31.4	14.3	15.1
1899–1910	40.5	25.3	15.2	15.4
1910–20	40.4	24.0	16.4	14.7
1920–30	39.3	22.1	17.2	10.0
1930–35	39.0	20.1	18.9	8.6
1935–40	40.2	19.2	21.0	8.6
1940	39.0	18.2	20.8	8.6
1950	39.5	10.5	29.0	14.5
1960	32.5	6.7	25.8	14.2
1970	25.3	6.6	18.7	8.9
1975	25.0	6.6	18.4	5.8
1980	24.2	6.6	17.6	7.1
1982	21.8	6.5	15.3	7.4

SOURCES: Perloff, *Puerto Rico's Economic Future*, p. 197, table 70; Junta de Planificación, *Informe económico, 1980*, p. A-25, table 22; ibid., *1982–83* 2: A-23, table 22; U.S. Bureau of the Census, *Historical Statistics*, pp. 49, 59; ibid., *Statistical Abstract*, pp. 64, 75.

with the rest of Latin America, Puerto Rico's natural rate of growth has been quite low; only Cuba and Argentina have had lower rates. In 1975–80, Cuba's was 13.2 (birth rate of 19.5 and death rate of 6.3), and Argentina's was 12.5 (birth rate of 21.4 and death rate of 8.9). Many other Latin-American countries have had higher rates of both births and deaths during the same period—e.g., the Dominican Republic, 36.7 and 9.1; Brazil, 36.0 and 7.8; Mexico, 41.7 and 7.6; and Jamaica, 30.7 and 6.6.[95]

Until the 1970s, the real rate of population growth in Puerto Rico was less than the natural rate, because of emigration. As can be seen from table 5.15, out-migration was at its peak in the 1950s; during that decade, a net of 460,826 persons left the island, dramatically more than the 145,010 emigrants of the 1940s. The total movement of persons was, of course, much larger, since some Puerto Ricans returned to the island while others were beginning or renewing their lives on the mainland. What is striking, though, is that the pace of emigration quickened precisely during the

[95] ECLA, *Statistical Yearbook*, p. 9, table 7. See also U.S. Bureau of the Census, *World Population*, p. 268, table 31.

TABLE 5.15
Migration to and from Puerto Rico,
Selected Years, 1950 to 1983

Year (ending June 30)	Arrivals	Departures	Net Out-Migration
1950	136,572	170,727	34,155
1953	230,307	304,910	76,603
1955	284,309	315,491	31,182
1957	391,372	439,656	48,284
1960	643,014	666,756	23,742
1963	925,868	930,666	4,798
1965	1,254,338	1,265,096	10,758
1967	1,594,735	1,628,909	34,174
1970	2,032,628	2,076,710	44,082
1972	2,347,483	2,306,399	−41,084
1974	2,575,900	2,539,783	−36,117
1976	2,354,880	2,316,122	−38,758
1978	2,538,671	2,558,953	20,282
1980	—	—	16,101
1982	—	—	33,297
1983	—	—	44,433

SOURCES: U.S. Commission on Civil Rights, *Puerto Ricans in the Continental U.S.*, pp. 26–27, table 8; Junta de Planificación, *Estadísticas sociales*, p. 3; ibid., *Informe económico, 1980*, p. 290; ibid., *1982–83* 2:XIII-3.

NOTE: There are unexplained discrepancies in the figures of the Junta de Planificación. The figures also include non–Puerto Ricans, but their significance in the net figures is small.

"take-off" period of the PPD's industrialization program. In the 1960s, the pace of emigration slowed somewhat, but it still remained, on balance, in the direction of the United States: 144,724 persons left the island, but that was less than one-third of the number who had left in the preceding decade. In some years of the 1970s, the flow was reversed. (from 1970 to 1980, net immigration amounted to 158,513 persons), giving rise to concern that the "safety valve" of emigration might not be working any more.[96] But in the last years of the decade, net emigration resumed, and soon it was again as high as it had been in the 1950s. This outflow, combined with a relatively low natural growth rate, has kept the real rate of growth of Puerto Rico's population quite low in comparison

[96] See Bonilla and Colón, "Return Migration," and Torruellas and Vázquez, *Los puertorriqueños que regresaron.*

TABLE 5.16
Population and Natural and Real Rates
of Population Growth,
Selected Years, 1950 to 1983

	Population (thousands)	Rate of Population Growth[a]	
		Natural	Real
1950	2,200	2.9	1.7
1960	2,340	2.6	0.6
1970	2,710	1.9	1.2
1972	2,835	1.9	3.2
1974	2,878	1.8	2.7
1976	2,982	1.8	3.0
1978	3,100	1.9	1.2
1980	3,184	1.8	1.8
1982	3,261	1.5	0.5
1983	3,265	1.5	0.1

SOURCES: Table 5.14; Junta de Planificación, *Informe económico, 1980*, p. A-25, table 22; ibid., *1982–83* 2: XIII-1 and p. A-23, table 22; ibid., *Estadísticas sociales*, p. 2.

[a] Percent per year.

with the rest of Latin America and with the world as a whole (see table 5.16).[97]

It is sobering to realize that between 1950 and 1970, the total net emigration from Puerto Rico was about 605,550 persons, a figure equivalent to 27.4 percent of the 1950 population. This represents a costly drain of human resources (or "human capital," as it is sometimes, perhaps inappropriately, called). Emigrants had received training and education on the island, the costs of which were borne by island residents; their productivity, however, was transferred to the U.S. economy.[98] Such outflows of resources do not appear in balance-of-payments accounts. Yet

[97] The real rate of population growth in Latin America was 2.6 percent annually between 1950 and 1955, 2.8 percent between 1960 and 1965, and 2.4 percent between 1975 and 1979. World population grew 1.9 percent annually between 1950 and 1955, 2.0 percent between 1955 and 1960, 2.1 percent between 1965 and 1970, and 1.7 percent between 1975 and 1979: U.S. Bureau of the Census, *World Population*, p. 24, table 2.

[98] Vidal Vázquez, "Political Economy," pp. 7, 24–29, calculates that the cost of social investment and lost income due to emigration for the period 1940 to 1970 was more than $60 billion, an amount greater than the total GNP from 1950 to 1970.

it was the outward flow of labor resources until 1969 which kept the real rate of population growth below the natural rate, as shown in table 5.16.

Puerto Rico's growing population has resulted in a relatively high population density: in 1940, it was 546.1 persons per square mile; in 1950, it was 643.1; in 1960, 684.0; 1970, 792.2; and in 1980, 930.7.[99] Many observers have argued that it is this high density which explains the high levels of unemployment and the lower living standards than those in the United States. However, the majority of Puerto Ricans in the United States—817,712 of the 1,391,463 in 1970 (58.8 percent)—live in New York City, which had a population density in that year of 26,343 persons per square mile.[100] While it is true that Puerto Ricans tend to be poorer and to have higher levels of unemployment than other groups in the city,[101] no one has suggested that this is due to New York City's high population density or to an imbalance between people and resources. For manufacturing and service economies like Puerto Rico's, unlike the case for agricultural economies, population size and density are relatively unimportant.[102] Moreover, if the figures for the densely populated San Juan metropolitan area are removed from the totals, the density of the rest of the island is substantially reduced. The population of this area (all or part of the municipios of San Juan, Bayamón, Carolina, Guaynabo, Trujillo Alto, Cataño, and Toa Baja) in 1970 was 894,631, and its total area was 216 square miles (yielding a density of 4,142 persons per square mile). Putting that population and area aside, the population density for the rest of the island in 1970 would be 567.1 persons per square mile, nearly 30 percent less than the figure which includes San Juan.[103]

Without doubt, emigration has helped to keep unemployment down. During the 1950s, 70 percent of those who left the island were between

[99] The 1940 figure is from Perloff, *Puerto Rico's Economic Future*, p. 193, table 69. For other years, the population figures shown in table 5.16 were used, together with the fact that Puerto Rico's land area is 3,421 square miles: U.S. Bureau of the Census, *1970 Census of Population*, pp. 16–17, table 7.

[100] U.S. Commission on Civil Rights, *Puerto Ricans*, p. 24, table 7, and USDC, *Economic Study* 2:418.

[101] For details on the conditions of Puerto Ricans in the U.S., see CENEP, *Labor Migration*. Also relevant and interesting is Levine, *Benjy López*.

[102] Perloff, *Puerto Rico's Economic Future*, p. 193, table 69, provides a comparison of Puerto Rico's population density with that of states in the U.S. and of various countries. England, the Netherlands, and Belgium (which have manufacturing-based economies) were more densely populated than Puerto Rico. The states of Rhode Island and New Jersey had higher population densities than Puerto Rico, and New York state had about the same.

[103] U.S. Bureau of the Census, *1970 Census of Population*, pp. 16–17, table 7, and pp. 18–26, table 8. The San Juan urbanized area had a population of 820,442. However, since area estimates are available only for entire municipios, total population figures for each municipio have been used, so the estimate in the text is a slight underestimate.

TABLE 5.17
Estimated Impact on Unemployment Rates of Lower Emigration

	Adjusted Number of Unemployed (thousands)[a]	Adjusted Unemployment (percentage)	Reduction in Unemployment Due to Emigration (percentage points)	Estimated Unemployment at 1950 Participation Rate (percentage)
1950	115	16.2	3.3	16.2
1960	179	24.8	11.5	26.5
1970	196	22.2	11.9	24.1
1980	261	24.0	7.0	25.4

SOURCES: See tables 5.13 and 5.15.

[a] Assuming an unchanged labor-force participation rate with fewer emigrants; one-half the actual amount of net emigration each year, beginning in 1940; and 100 percent unemployment among hypothetical nonmigrants.

the ages of 15 and 39 and hence were potential members of the labor force.[104] This percentage was double that of persons in that age group residing on the island. If emigration had not been so easy, because of the absence of legal barriers to entry into the United States, the relatively inexpensive air fares, and the existence of a large Puerto Rican community in New York City that eased the cultural transition, unemployment since the beginning of Operation Bootstrap certainly would have been greater. Table 5.17 presents estimates of what the rate of unemployment would have been if net emigration had been only half as large. For 1960 and 1970, after two and three decades of out-migration, unemployment was more than 11 percentage points lower than it would have been otherwise—and that leaves out of account the unemployment among the additional Puerto Ricans who would have been born on the island. The 1980 adjusted unemployment figure, on the other hand, was only seven percentage points above the actual rate, reflecting the impact on unemployment of returning migrants.

EXTERNAL TRADE

The shift to a manufacturing economy has done nothing to alter Puerto Rico's long-standing dependence on external trade. In fact, Fomento's success at industrial promotion has augmented that dependence, for three reasons: (1) The promotion concentrated on attracting export-oriented firms,

[104] See José L. Vázquez Calzada, "Demographic Aspects of Migration," in CENEP, *Labor Migration*, pp. 228–29. This study provides useful comparisons between migrants and the island population as a whole.

TABLE 5.18
External Trade and Trade Dependence,
Selected Years, 1950 to 1982

	Value of Merchandise Exports (millions of dollars)	Coefficient of Export Dependence[a]	Value of Merchandise Imports (millions of dollars)	Coefficient of Import Dependence[b]	Percentage of Exports to U.S.	Percentage of Imports from U.S.
1950	244	.32	350	.46	96.8	92.3
1955	372	.33	580	.51	95.9	—
1960	629	.38	906	.54	94.4	83.1
1965	997	.36	1,504	.54	91.4	—
1970	1,751	.37	2,510	.54	88.7	76.8
1972	2,003	.35	3,081	.53	88.3	73.0
1974	3,386	.50	4,279	.63	85.1	62.8
1976	3,413	.45	5,223	.69	84.2	62.4
1978	4,880	.54	6,316	.70	85.2	59.7
1980	7,140	.64	8,189	.74	84.6	59.4
1982	9,053	.72	8,524	.68	89.0	64.1

SOURCES: Junta de Planificación, *Informe económico, 1976*, p. A-1, table 1, and p. A-13, able 13; ibid., *1980*, p. A-1, table 1, p. A-16, table 15, pp. 156–57, 168; ibid., *1982–83* ?:A-15, table 15, and p. VI-14; USDC, *Economic Study* 1:107, table 10; Merrill-Ramírez, 'Operation Bootstrap,'' p. 32.
[a] Value of exports as a ratio to GNP.
[b] Value of imports as a ratio to GNP.

on the assumption that the local market was too small to permit the economies of scale necessary for efficient and profitable production. (2) As already noted, the vertically integrated structure of the companies that have located on the island has prevented any substantial growth of domestic linkages with supplying firms. (3) The push to industrialization was accomplished at the expense of agriculture and so brought about a greater need for imports of foodstuffs.

The results are shown in table 5.18.

Both exports and imports as a percent of GNP (i.e., of total income) have tended to increase. In 1950, a little less than half of total income was spent on imports; by 1980, that figure had risen until about 74 cents of every dollar of gross income was being used to purchase imported goods. Over the same period, the value of GNP exported increased from 32 percent to 64 percent, and the figure rose further to 72 percent in 1982. The import dependence means that the domestic income multiplier is quite small. The U.S. Department of Commerce estimated it at 1.4, an indication that spending on subsequent turnovers after the initial expenditure has its greatest effect in the United States, not in the local economy. This represents a decline in the value of the multiplier from 2.3 in 1948 and 1.9 in 1963.[105]

The overall degree of external dependence is extremely high. In 1976, for example, the total value of exports and imports exceeded total gross national product; the coefficient of external trade in that year was 1.14—that is, total trade exceeded GNP by 14 percent. In 1980, this coefficient reached 1.38, and in 1982, it was 1.40. In 1975, by comparison, the United States had a trade coefficient of .14; Jamaica, .75; the Netherlands, .91; and West Germany, .41. For Latin America as a whole in 1960, the coefficient was .21; in 1978, it was .19.[106]

Table 5.18 suggests that dependence on the United States as an export market has eased somewhat, declining from almost 97 percent in 1950 to about 85 percent in 1980 (though rising again in 1982). But since the bulk of exports are controlled by international firms with production located on the island—for example, in recent years chemical and drug exports alone have amounted to more than 40 percent of all exports[107]—this small reduction does not mean much. What is significant is that not only the ultimate destination of exports, but also the location of effective control over them resides in the United States. If more exports have gone to foreign markets other than the United States, it is only as a result of the particular industrial profile that has been created and the decisions of the international firms, most of them headquartered in the United States but distributing their output worldwide.

The decline in import dependence on the U.S. market shown in table 5.18 is somewhat illusionary. It is largely due to the rising price of oil. All the oil used in Puerto Rico is imported, most of it from non-U.S. sources. Between 1970 and 1973, the proportion of chemicals and related products (including oil) in total foreign imports averaged 35 percent; this figure rose to 66 percent over the next four years, and hence non-U.S. imports as a share of total imports also rose. Between 1967 and 1973,

---

[105] USDC, *Economic Study* 1:14; Weisskoff and Wolff, "Development and Trade Dependence," p. 473, n. 12, and p. 476, table 3.

[106] Junta de Planificación, *Informe económico, 1976*, p. 94, and ECLA, *Statistical Yearbook*, p. 55, table 48. The figures given here are in relation to GDP (see table 5.12 for the ratios to GDP for Puerto Rico). The island's dependence was also very high for imports and exports considered separately. In 1978, the Latin American country with the highest degree of import dependence was El Salvador, with a coefficient of .36 of GDP; the highest degree of export dependence was in Panama, whose exports equaled 38 percent of GDP; and the country with the lowest import dependence was Argentina, whose coefficient was .06: ECLA, *Statistical Yearbook*, p. 55, table 48.

[107] Junta de Planificación, *Informe económico, 1982–83* 2:VI-16.

TABLE 5.19

Composition of Imports, Five-Year Intervals from 1950 to 1980 and 1982

	Value of Total Imports	Durables		Food		Other Nondurables		Capital and Intermediate Goods	
		Value	Percent	Value	Percent	Value	Percent	Value	Percent
1950	350.3	22.4	6.4	89.3	25.5	61.5	17.6	177.1	50.6
1955	580.3	49.5	8.5	127.1	21.9	95.4	16.4	308.3	53.1
1960	906.0	79.7	8.8	156.8	17.3	129.0	14.2	540.5	59.7
1965	1,504.3	167.1	11.1	200.0	13.3	169.1	11.2	968.1	64.4
1970	2,509.9	267.8	10.7	306.8	12.2	276.1	11.0	1,659.2	66.1
1975	5,006.9	344.3	6.9	786.9	15.7	482.1	9.6	3,393.5	67.8
1980	8,189.2	701.3	8.6	1,041.4	12.7	686.9	8.4	5,759.6	70.3
1982	8,523.8	686.4	8.1	1,137.1	13.3	775.9	9.1	5,924.4	69.5

SOURCES: Junta de Planificación, *Informe económico, 1976*, p. A-22, table 22; ibid., *1980*, p. A-17, table 16; ibid., *1982–83* 2:A-16, table 16.

NOTE: All values in millions of dollars.

Puerto Rico's imports from the OPEC countries rose from $113.0 million to $229.9 million, an increase of 103 percent—but in the course of just the next year, these imports had jumped to $938.9 million, an increase of 308 percent.[108] For the other goods Puerto Rico imports, the United States remains the primary source, its dependence on that market having declined only slightly. In 1978, Puerto Rico was the seventh largest customer for U.S. goods and was the largest per capita importer.[109]

It is useful to disaggregate the import figures in order to see more precisely how import dependence has been affected by more than thirty years of industrial promotion. Table 5.19 details the breakdown of imports by category since 1950. Capital and intermediate inputs (which include raw materials) have grown more rapidly than all imports, as is reflected in their increasing relative share of the total, though some of this increase is attributable to the rising price of oil. Consumer nondurable imports, particularly food, have tended to decrease as a share of total imports, though in absolute value food imports increased more than 1,000

[108] Merrill-Ramírez, "Operation Bootstrap," pp. 55–56, and USDC, *Economic Study* 1:102, table 3, and 1:57.

[109] Bonilla and Campos, "A Wealth of Poor," p. 146. In 1976–77, Puerto Rico had been the fifth largest customer; by 1979, the island economy had slipped to eighth position, behind Canada, Japan, West Germany, the United Kingdom, Mexico, the Netherlands, and France: PREDA, *Manufacturers Ready Reference File, 1977* and ibid., *1979* (New York: EDA).

percent between 1950 and 1980. Imports of durable goods have grown more than 3,000 percent in absolute terms, though in relative terms they have fluctuated a good deal.

The fact that food imports have decreased as a proportion of total imports does not mean that there is now less dependence on imported food supplies. As was discussed earlier (see chapter 2), what is significant is the proportion of imported food in total food supplies. In the period from 1947 to 1951, 71 percent of all food was imported; this increased to 73 percent in 1961–66 and to 77 percent in 1966–71. While food dependence has declined somewhat in recent years, due to increased local dairy, poultry, and meat production, the U.S. Department of Commerce study determined that between 60 and 70 percent of aggregate food needs were still being met externally in the mid-1970s.[110]

In the case of certain specific goods, import dependence is total or nearly so. Rice, for example, a staple of the diet, was until very recently virtually all imported, primarily from California. There is now a government-sponsored effort to expand rice production; it has had difficulties in getting started, but "benefit-cost studies show that rice grown in Puerto Rico can compete favorably."[111] In no food product is Puerto Rico now self-sufficient. There was self-sufficiency in fresh fruits until the early 1970s, but that has since changed. In many traditional food crops—starchy vegetables like plantains, bananas, and sweet potatoes—local production has dropped off dramatically, so that now 30 to 35 percent of total demand is met by imports. Garden vegetables have declined just as precipitously, from 70 percent self-sufficiency in 1961 to less than 40 percent in 1976. On the other hand, Puerto Rico had achieved 90 percent self-sufficiency in dairy products by the late 1970s.[112]

Much of the dependence on food is for processed products sold in supermarkets or in the ubiquitous *colmados*, small neighborhood grocery stores. A demand for convenience foods has been stimulated by advertising, which of course promotes imported products rather than traditional,

[110] C. Santiago "Import Substitution," p. 39, table 7, and USDC, *Economic Study* 1:24. Santiago did find that there was some import substitution taking place. The share of imports to total supplies available for consumption fell from 75 percent in 1947–61 to 66 percent in 1961–71, though after 1956–61, import substitution virtually halted (at the time that Fomento shifted to promotion of capital-intensive industries). He found no import substitution, and thus greater import dependence, for food and related products, tobacco, and wood and furniture, the usual cases of horizontal (or "easy") import substitution in other countries. There was import substitution for chemicals, machinery and metals, and textiles and apparel, examples of vertical (or "difficult") import substitution, which is reflective of the type of industry promoted rather than any real capital deepening in the local economy.
[111] USDC, *Economic Study* 2:295–96. This program will be discussed further below.
[112] Ibid., pp. 293–94.

locally produced goods, making it even more difficult for local farmers to market their output and compete with mainland suppliers. The result of high-visibility advertising, of a considerable number of consumers who have lived in the United States and have absorbed mainland consumption patterns, and of a manufacturing sector oriented toward an external market is the high ratio of imports to local consumption over a wide range of goods in addition to food. Whereas in 1960 nearly all the beer consumed on the island was produced on it, 53 percent of it was imported in 1972.[113] It is very likely that for many durable goods—cars, certainly—Puerto Rico will never be, and probably should not try to be, self-sufficient. In 1977, 88 percent of durable goods were imported. But for many other goods, a more rational policy of import substitution could be implemented. Agricultural especially is an area in which the absence of planning and the over-attention directed to manufacturing has led to an unnecessary waste of the island's resources and potential.

BALANCE OF PAYMENTS

Although Puerto Rico calculates a balance-of-payments account, it cannot experience a balance-of-payments crisis of the kind that has plagued so many developing nations in the 1970s and 1980s. It has no independent currency whose value is affected by movements of capital or whose quantity can be controlled. Imbalances can and do exist, of course, but they are different in cause and implications.

In 1970, Puerto Rico's balance on trade and services was −$1,276 million, meaning that Puerto Rico paid that much more to the external sector (mostly the United States) than it received.[114] Of this amount, $759 million or 59.5 percent arose out of a deficit in the balance of trade; another $538 million or 42.2 percent represented the net outflow of payments to investors. (These two figures add up to more than 100 percent principally because expenditures by visitors to Puerto Rico exceeded those by Puerto Ricans in the exterior, leading to a net inflow in that account.) By 1975, the deficit on trade and services had grown to −$3,109 million, with 57.8 percent coming from the deficit in the balance of trade and 40.1 percent from the net outflow of payments on investments. In 1980, the trade and services deficit rose to −$4,641 million, but the balance-of-trade deficit that year was equal to only 22.6 percent of the imbalance, while external income repatriation amounted to 78.5 percent. In 1982, the trade and services deficit fell to −$3,451 million; the bal-

---

[113] Curet Cuevas, *El desarrollo económico*, p. 250.

[114] The data in this and the next two paragraphs are from Junta de Planificación, *Informe económico, 1982–83*, p. A-15, table 15.

ance of trade actually showed a surplus that year of $529 million, but this was overwhelmed by the repatriation of investment income to U.S. owners totaling $4,912 million, or a net outflow equal to 118.3 percent of the deficit.

These deficits have been balanced by two key inflows: transfers from the federal government and new investment from external sources. In 1970, federal transfers (net of return payments, chiefly for Social Security and federal pensions) "financed" 25.8 percent of the trade and services deficit and net increases in investments financed 84.8 percent. In 1975, the respective figures were 39.4 percent and 71.8 percent; in 1980, 67.4 percent and 65.3 percent; and in 1982, 92.4 percent and 26.7 percent. These statistics indicate the growing importance of federal transfers (discussed in more detail below) in making possible the outflow of profits, interest, and dividends to external investors. Net federal transfers increased from $329 million in 1970 to $3,189 million in 1982, an 869 percent increase, slightly more than the 728 percent increase in external income repatriated over the same period. Without these transfers, Puerto Rico, in order to make up for the deficit on its trade and services would have had either to increase the level of external borrowing or to reduce imports of consumption goods. The latter would obviously have severely reduced living standards on the island, the more so given the major role that food imports played. Thus, in effect federal transfers have fundamentally contributed to the "success" of the industrialization strategy and to the rising standard of living on the island.

The inflow of new investment also has helped to cover the trade and services deficit in the short run, but unlike federal transfers it increases the deficit over the long term, as more factor income and GDP must be paid to external investors. In 1970, one-third of export income was used to service payments to external investors. By 1980, this external income servicing ratio had risen to 58 percent. In other words, in 1980 there was a circulation of spending from the United States to Puerto Rico and back to the United States again of nearly 60 percent of Puerto Rico's export income that was being used not to pay for imports of goods but to finance the outflow on externally held investments.

A further implication of these figures is that the standard of living and purchasing power of the Puerto Rican population are highly precarious. Reductions in federal transfers unmatched by reductions in outflows of investment income could abruptly cause a deterioration. The industrialization strategy has been implemented not on a firm productive footing but on a fragile financial basis that is vulnerable to decisions about the amount of federal spending made in Washington.

The Marginalization of Agriculture

Contrary to the labor-surplus models upon which the industrialization program drew and which anticipate productivity growth in agriculture, Puerto Rico's development program set agriculture adrift. It would be wrong, however, to attribute the need for food imports which followed agriculture's decline to the industrialization strategy alone. Since before the beginnings of U.S. control, Puerto Rico's economic structure has not been capable of meeting all the island's food needs. Even when the economy was primarily agricultural, production was externally oriented. Sugar, tobacco, and coffee were produced for export and the best land was turned over to these crops, leaving the cultivation of domestic food crops to relatively small plots of land of marginal productivity. It has thus been the development of a particular structure of capitalism, together with the external orientation and control of the system of production, that has laid the foundation for an enduring disequilibrium between local food supplies and demand. Operation Bootstrap, the penetration of mainland advertising, and the demonstration effect of well-stocked supermarkets have exacerbated the problem.

Between 1950 and 1970, agricultural output grew at less than 1 percent a year, and since the population was increasing at a higher rate, per capita agricultural output fell. Between 1960 and 1970, the growth rate of agricultural output was actually negative, -1.9 percent. Only since 1970 has there been growth in the agrarian sector equal to the overall growth of GNP (see table 5.5). In terms of employment, however, there has been a nearly continuous decrease in the number of agricultural workers, from 214,000 in 1950 to 40,000 in 1980 (see table 5.7). The area under cultivation has also declined steadily, from 740,000 cuerdas in 1940 to 719,000 cuerdas in 1959 and a steep drop to 362,642 cuerdas in 1969, a decrease of nearly 50 percent in just one decade.[115] By the 1970s, the collapse of agriculture could no longer be ignored.

Some efforts have been made, if not to revitalize agriculture, at least to improve its performance. In 1973, the Sugar Corporation was created to oversee the operation of the five government-owned centrals and the one refinery. This step did little to halt the decline of the sugar industry, which has continued to be beset by problems of crop disease, obsolete technology, poor choice of crop varieties, and mismanagement. Sugar production was 454,998 tons on 188,775 cuerdas in 1970; 298,960 tons on 127,078 cuerdas in 1975; 174,708 tons on 85,003 cuerdas in 1980;

[115] Curet Cuevas, *El desarrollo económico*, p. 145, table 58.

and 111,948 tons of sugar on only 55,016 cuerdas in 1982. Because of the drop in sugar production, 80 percent of the molasses for the rum industry, which produces the largest-selling hard liquor in the U.S. market, must now be imported. The number of centrals in operation also declined, from 36 in 1948 to 29 in 1960 and only 11 in 1974.[116] Throughout the entire period since the beginning of Operation Bootstrap, the yield of sugar per ton of cane or per cuerda has declined.[117] As a result of lower production, the government has closed most of its centrals.

The commonwealth government has now turned to a strategy of the pre-1940 era in its effort to revive the sugar industry. Sugar lands owned by the Sugar Corporation are being rented to colonos who, by the 1982–83 season, were cultivating 87 percent of the cuerdas planted in cane. They are paid a guaranteed price, but whether this experiment will be beneficial or not will not be known for some time.[118]

Another step was the creation in 1977 of the Agricultural Development Administration (Administración de Fomento y Desarrollo Agrícola de Puerto Rico), the first time such an agency has existed since the ineffective Agricultural Development Company was created in 1945, lasting only until 1947. Part of the purpose of this new agency is to encourage the production of crops appropriate to Puerto Rico by demonstrations of their commercial viability and by offering incentives, which amounted to $42.3 million in 1981. Since 1982, farms of up to 200 cuerdas have been eligible for property-tax exemption for various periods of time for the production of those crops that the agency wishes to promote.[119]

This program appears to have met with some success, since the value of some of the promoted crops, like starchy and other vegetables and fruits, rose 30 percent from 1977 to 1980.[120] The one crop that has not responded to the incentives has been tobacco, which in 1980 was being produced on only slightly more than 2,000 cuerdas, compared to 37,000 in 1950–51 and an average of 5,000 during the 1970s. The fastest-growing outputs in the agricultural sector have been milk, which increased its share of the value of total agricultural production from 12.2 percent in 1950 to 31.0 percent in 1982; meat, from 10.5 to 20.6 percent; and coffee, from 4.2 to 9.9 percent. Sugar and molasses, however, as already

[116] Junta de Planificación, *Informe económico, 1977*, pp. 22–25; ibid., *1980*, pp. 37–40; ibid., *1982–83* 2:I-7; and Cruz Baez, "Puerto Rico's Agriculture," p. 6.

[117] Junta de Planificación, *Informe económico, 1982–83* 2:I-7.

[118] Junta de Planificación, *Informe económico, 1982–83* 2:I-8.

[119] Fruit farms are eligible for twenty-five years of exemption; coffee farms, fifteen; and tobacco, rice, and vegetable farms, ten: ibid., *1977*, p. 34; ibid., *1982–83* 2:I-2.

[120] Ibid., *1977*, p. 28, and ibid., *1980*, p. 45.

noted, have declined precipitously, from 51.8 percent of total agricultural value to 4.7 percent during the same period.[121]

The increased awareness by those in power that agriculture cannot be neglected without further imperiling the economic structure has not resulted in any noticeable increase in the total amount of cultivated land: In 1976, some 350,000 cuerdas were in production, less than half the area that was in production in 1959.[122] However, agricultural productivity and the value of agricultural output have increased during the 1970s, and if a rice-growing plan begun in 1981 is ultimately successful—there is now also a rice-processing plant in operation in Arecibo, and Puerto Rican rice is on the shelves of the island's stores—there is some hope that the dependence on imported food and agricultural products can be reduced.

One of the most difficult problems has been to persuade the large Puerto Rican retail food distributors to buy from local producers. At present, they buy in bulk from mainland distributors and ship packaged and fresh food daily to the island via air freight. Without easier access to consumers through supermarkets, local agriculture faces an uphill struggle.[123] The multiplier effect from local agricultural production on income and employment is greater than for any other sector in the economy, because of the predominance of local ownership—compelling evidence of the importance of the agricultural sector and, by inference, of the need for expanded local ownership in other sectors as well.[124]

THE ROLE OF FEDERAL FUNDS

A University of Puerto Rico economist has said, "Puerto Rico is living today under a mirage of economic affluence."[125] Federal expenditures in, and federal transfer payments to, the island have been the key to sustaining this illusion. In 1950, at the beginning of Operation Bootstrap, transfer payments from the federal and Puerto Rican governments accounted for 12 percent of personal income; by 1970, they had increased to 20 percent and by 1980 to 30 percent, where they remain. (By comparison, transfer payments in the United States amounted to about 14 or 15 per-

[121] Ibid., *1982–83* 2:I-1.

[122] USDC, *Economic Study* 2:303, table 7. The figures in this table are in acres; they may be slightly high.

[123] Cruz Baez, "Puerto Rico's Agriculture," pp. 24–26.

[124] Hill, "Preliminary Assessment," pp. 1–2. See also Vicente-Chandler, "Potencial y problemas básicos," for a general plan for agricultural recovery and an argument for greater self-sufficiency in a world divided by politics and class.

[125] J. Santiago, "Puerto Rican Economy," p. 30.

cent of personal income in the early 1980s.) Of these transfers to individuals, federal transfers—primarily social security and food assistance—have constituted between 75 and 80 percent of the total.[126]

In 1982, total government transfers to individuals were \$3.7 billion, of which \$2.9 billion represented transfers from the federal government. These federal transfers were the equivalent of nearly \$900 per person, and it is certain that without them there would have been a decrease in the average standard of living. Though per capita transfers in the United States are larger in dollar amounts, their relative importance is greater in Puerto Rico because of its lower income level.[127] In fact, transfer payments have permitted an increase in disposable personal income in every year since 1970, even in years in which total GNP fell. As well, real disposable income has been prevented from declining, so that even when the local economy has suffered decreases in production, the purchasing power of per capita income has continued to grow every year.[128] Puerto Rico may be the only place in the world where this phenomenon can be observed.

The transfers of income do not stimulate production in Puerto Rico, however. Given the openness of the economy, they quickly leak from the local spending stream to boost aggregate demand in the United States. They do help, though, to keep spending higher than it would be in their absence, and in the case of federal food assistance, they have been fundamental to the ability of the economy to continue functioning while other aggregate statistics, such as those on unemployment, suggest economic collapse. One author, in fact, has written that these transfers have "institutionalized unemployment."[129]

Federal food assistance has been an important component of the federal transfer program since the mid-1970s. Food-stamp legislation was extended to Puerto Rico in 1971, but it was not until 1974 that *cupones* were in use. In their very first year, food stamps were "a major source of income for two-thirds of the families" on the island.[130] Food-stamp transfers amounted to \$388.4 million in 1975, rising to \$754.8 million in 1976 and to \$879.0 million in 1978. They dropped to \$812.1 million in 1980, but rose again during the recession of the following years. The proportion of the population receiving stamps grew from 27.8 percent in

[126] Junta de Planificación, *Informe económico, 1982–83* 2:IX-1, IX-2, IX-4, and ibid., *1980*, p. 426.

[127] Ibid., *1982–83* 2:XII-1, and Merrill-Ramírez, "Puerto Rico," p. 12. Indiana had the lowest per capita federal transfers of any state in 1978—viz., \$1,322.

[128] Junta de Planificación, *Informe económico, 1982–83* 2:A-1, table 1.

[129] Merrill-Ramírez, "Puerto Rico," p. 12.

[130] Tobin Committee, *Report*, p. 66.

1975 to 58.4 percent in 1980, though 70 to 80 percent of the population was eligible to receive them by virtue of their low incomes.[131] Before food stamps were introduced, 30 percent of families had incomes of $60 per month or less; after 1975, less than 1 percent of families had incomes that low. Families with incomes of more than $200 a month rose from 20 percent of all families to more than 60 percent. For the average family in 1978, food stamps added $125 of monthly income, effectively doubling its spending power.[132]

On July 1, 1982, the food stamp program became the Programa de Asistencia Nutricional (PAN—the acronym means "bread" in Spanish), under the new block-grant distribution system initiated by the Reagan administration. Now, checks rather than cupons are distributed to participants, thus permitting them to spend the money on whatever they please.[133] With the PAN, food assistance declined to $775 million in 1983, down 13.5 percent from the $895.9 million distributed in 1982, as recipients were cut from the program with the decreases in the Reagan administration budget.[134]

However, besides constituting a substantial injection of money into the economy, food assistance contributed to the collapse of local agriculture, because the cupones made it so easy to buy imported food rather than to produce. Local agriculture's contribution to food consumption declined from 55.2 percent in 1950 to 38.8 percent in 1960, to an average of 17.2 percent in 1971–75, and to 13.3 percent in 1975–80. This decline was reflected in a decline in the proportion of their income that farms received from farming. In 1974, half of all farms derived 25 percent or less of total income from farming; in 1978, nearly two-thirds of farms fell into this category.[135] Increased local agricultural production was thus rendered unnecessary as consumers enjoyed an illusionary "food-stamp prosperity." In 1979, for example, 32.7 percent of all food consumption was

[131] Weisskoff, "Crops vs. Coupons," p. 136, and pp. 148–49, table 6-1; and Junta de Planificación, *Informe económico, 1982–83* 2:A-19, table 19.

[132] Merrill-Ramírez, "Puerto Rico," pp. 21–22 and table 9. In 1978, Puerto Rico was receiving twice as much in food stamps as California, though it had but one-eighth the population: *Washington Post,* August 20, 1978.

[133] Payment in cash rather than coupons will, as simple indifference-curve analysis can demonstrate, make most consumers better off (or at least no worse off) in their own individual utility-maximizing calculus. Whether or not nutrition is enhanced by cash distribution is a question that is more difficult to answer. One bit of evidence is that most checks are cashed in food stores, but that is hardly meaningful in terms of how the money is spent. Only further study will reveal the full impact of this change. See Hill, "Nutritional Assistance Program," for an initial, but superficial, evaluation of the program's impact.

[134] Junta de Planificación, *Informe económico, 1982–83* 2:XII-10.

[135] Weisskoff, "Crops vs. Coupons," p. 154, table 6-3, and p. 170, table 6-8.

financed by food stamps, leaving more cash income to be used for other purposes.[136]

The commonwealth government itself has also become a large "consumer" of federal money. In 1970, federal grants of $142.2 million provided 17.3 percent of recurrent revenues. In 1975, the share attributable to federal transfers had increased to 23.1 percent, and in 1980 to 27.0 percent. Other federal grants are received by particular agencies and departments, since under many programs (though not all) Puerto Rico is treated as a state for federal funding purposes. The largest recipients of these program funds are the commonwealth departments of Education, Social Services, and Health, and the Unemployment Insurance Fund. Municipalities also receive substantial amounts of federal funds—$1 billion or more a year since 1978.[137] Additionally, the U.S. Department of Defense and other federal agencies make expenditures on the island in the course of their operations. The federal government does not just pay, however. It receives payments for social security, retirement plans, and other contributions, which amounted to nearly $1 billion in 1982 and 1983.[138] Nevertheless, in 1976, net transfers from and expenditures by the federal government amounted to 28.9 percent ($2,182.9 million) of Puerto Rico's GNP and to 28.1 percent in 1982.[139]

From the beginning, Fomento's policies depended upon special treatment from Washington, including tax exemptions and loopholes, selective minimum-wage exemption, transfer payments, and direct funding. The policy of the past, however, and the underlying political and social consensus forged by Muñoz Marín and the PPD around Operation Bootstrap, are increasingly threatened by collapse. New policies have been proposed, as will be seen in the next section, but nothing fundamental is being done to alter the productive base of the economy in such a way as to create an internal dynamic of growth that, if not completely autonomous, at least has some local character.

New Industrial Investment Incentives

From its inception, Operation Bootstrap has been based on subsidizing the cost of capital investment by means of tax exemptions. On top of the exemption from U.S. corporate income taxes that was granted to firms operating in Puerto Rico, the commonwealth government added exemp-

[136] Ibid., pp. 137, 153, and Merrill-Ramírez, "Puerto Rico," table 8.
[137] Junta de Planificación, *Informe económico, 1982–1983* 2: chaps. 8 and 12, and Tobin Committee, *Report*, p. 32, table V-1.
[138] Junta de Planificación, *Informe económico, 1982–1983* 2:XII-16.
[139] Ibid., p. XII-1; Dietz, "Imperialism and Underdevelopment," p. 28.

tions to qualifying corporations from the local corporate income tax, the income tax on dividends distributed to individuals, municipal taxes, license fees, and the property tax, and it also provided a variety of subsidies on rent and labor costs (see chapter 4). U.S. corporations could completely avoid taxes on their operations in Puerto Rico unless they repatriated profits to the parent corporation. Only at the end of the exemption period could they remit profits tax-free to the parent company, the purpose of this provision being to encourage reinvestment of profits in Puerto Rico. But that is not what occurred.

It turned out that profits earned in Puerto Rico exceeded the willingness of U.S. companies to reinvest on the island. They chose instead to hold their money in unproductive bonds or to send the money to other U.S. possessions, where they could more easily manipulate its use. There was a further adverse outcome:

> Almost every firm elected to accumulate its profits until the end of the tax exemption grant and then liquidate its subsidiary company into the parent corporation and send home all the profits free of any taxes in Puerto Rico or the United States.[140]

Thus, the tax laws effectively encouraged and rewarded "footloose" companies. The need for revision was apparent.

Section 936 of the 1976 Federal Tax Reform Act replaced the former 931 provisions. This section permits U.S. subsidiaries operating in Puerto Rico (and other "possessions") to remit their profits to the parent corporation at any time without paying federal corporate income tax. Their sole obligation, imposed by the Puerto Rican government, is to pay a "tollgate" tax to the commonwealth on any dividends paid to the parent. This tax was set at a maximum of 10 percent of remitted earnings, but it could be reduced to less than 4 percent if not all earnings are returned and if the remainder is invested in so-called section 2(j) assets, which include commonwealth bonds and certain kinds of bank deposits. In addition to preventing U.S. corporations from using profits earned in Puerto Rico in other countries to escape U.S. taxes, it was hoped that this legislation would have at least three beneficial effects in Puerto Rico: an expansion of productive investment on the island; a reduction in the frequency of plant liquidations at the end of the tax-exempt period, by per-

[140] *Industrial Newsletter* (PREDA) 17 (1976): 1. Such liquidation and profit remittance was permitted under section 332 of the U.S. Internal Revenue Code and section 4 of the 1963 Puerto Rico Industrial Incentive Act. If a corporation elected to repatriate profits before the exemption ended, it paid a tax of 15 percent to Puerto Rico and the 48 percent corporate rate in the U.S., though the amount paid in Puerto Rico was treated as a foreign tax credit.

mitting immediate repatriation of profits with only a small penalty; and an increase in the commonwealth government's revenues through the toll-gate tax.

The tollgate tax of 10 percent on repatriated earnings can be reduced to 5 percent (and effectively to 3.97 percent if the 3-percent investment tax credit is used) by placing at least 50 percent of earnings for five years in section 2(j) investments and remitting the remaining 50 percent to the parent corporation over a five-year period. By doing so, the 50 percent invested in financial obligations in Puerto Rico becomes tax-free. If a business is totally liquidated, the tollgate tax is still reduced to 4 percent if the section 2(j) investments had been made.[141]

In 1978, there was further development in tax legislation. Under a new Industrial Incentive Act, full tax exemption for newly locating companies was ended. Although the law provides complete exemption from municipal license fees over the life of the exemption, it sets out a declining schedule of exemption for property and income taxes, as follows:

Years 1 - 5 : 90% exemption

Years 6 -10 : 75% exemption

Years 11-15 : 65% exemption

Years 16-20 : 55% exemption

Years 21-25 : 50% exemption

Ten-year partial exemptions based on the above schedule were available in high development zones (zone I); fifteen years in areas of intermediate development (II); twenty years in zones of low development (III); and twenty-five years for firms locating on the islands of Vieques and Culebra (zone IV), with the possibility of a ten-year extension at reduced rates of exemption (from 35 to 50 percent). Furthermore, exemption was granted not only to the thirty-two industries specified in the earlier incentive legislation but also to tourist hotels and export-oriented service industries like advertising, computer services, catalog sales, and so on, legislation which has permitted even large retailers like Sears Roebuck to receive exemption.

There was a compelling reason for an end to total tax exemption. In 1973, almost one-quarter of industrial operations were exempt from taxes. This rose to more than a half by 1976, and it was expected that it would be three-quarters by 1980, as some 1,700 of the approximately 2,500 industrial plants would be operating free of any tax obligation to the island.[142]

---

[141] *Puerto Rico Business Review*, special supplement, July–August 1980. The first $100,000 of income is exempted from taxes for all firms.

[142] *San Juan Star*, February 3, 1978.

The end of total tax exemption has not visibly deterred most corporations, and there is good reason for that. Profits have remained high for external investors despite the economic crisis affecting the rest of society. In 1982–83, the section 936 corporations had profits equal to 98.6 percent of their capital. Firms in the pharmaceutical industry had profits equal to 246 percent of their capital.[143] The results of the 936 legislation and the 1978 tax revision have been less than anticipated, however. The rate of productive investment rose 14.5 percent in 1976 but only 7 percent in 1980.[144] Profits have not found their way into productive uses in the usual economic sense of expanding the capital and productive base of the economy but instead have continued to be invested in financial assets. In 1979, certificates of deposits held by 936 corporations amounted to nearly $3 billion, equal to 34 percent of all bank deposits.[145] By March 1983, these funds had increased to $5.9 billion, or 37 percent of all bank deposits. Such large deposits, created to reduce the tollgate tax obligation, required new legislation to redefine the qualifying investments. Instead of just plant and equipment and other specified capital investments, 936 funds can now be used by banks with such deposits to finance residential construction, thus reducing the cost of mortgage loans and subsidizing housing costs. Such loans do not increase the productive base of the economy, but the change has nevertheless been important since it permits a greater volume of 936 funds to find profitable outlets (and hence permits corporations to more easily take advantage of the 936 tax savings) while creating a new local use for these funds.[146] It must be reiterated, however, that this amounts to a further short-run subsidy of the costs of consumption for Puerto Ricans, a policy that has been a cornerstone of the development model from the beginning but which has not contributed to the expansion of the productive base of the economy.

These legislative initiatives have done little to boost investment, output, or employment, as a glance back at the tables of this chapter will confirm. It has been argued, though, that the economic crisis of the late 1970s and early 1980s inhibited new investment and that when "normal" times return and the prospects for renewed export growth improve, the potential positive impact of the new laws will become a reality. There would appear to be little foundation for such expectations. The existing tax laws reinforce U.S. branch plant production and profit extraction as the base of the economic structure. The alteration in the law which has

[143] Economistas de CEREP, *La crisis económica*, p. 2.
[144] Escobar, "936 Market," p. 5.
[145] Mier, "936 Funds," pp. 10–11.
[146] Sarmiento, "Use of 936 Funds," pp. 2–3. The 936 legislation was revised in 1982 to close certain loopholes: *Puerto Rico Business Review*, special supplements, April and September 1982.

permitted 936 funds to be used by banks for residential construction is also consistent with the historical thrust of Operation Bootstrap in its efforts to provide attractive incentives to external investors.

The commonwealth government continues to attract support for its development policy, however, by spreading the gains of income growth through subsidized housing, health care, transportation, and other public utilities. This has been made possible only by the presence of the 936 funds and the transfers from the federal government, not by anything within the local economy. If the externally generated funds decline or disappear, as they can as a result of changes in the tax and spending laws of the federal government, the social costs to Puerto Rico would be very high. The threat during 1985 to remove section 936 from the U.S. tax code created a profound crisis in the commonwealth government, which has argued that it would result in a depression in Puerto Rico.[147]

POLITICAL CHANGES

From 1940 to 1968, the PPD dominated island politics. Muñoz Marín was governor from the first election in 1948 until he voluntarily declined to run again in 1964 (though he was then elected as a senator). During this period, the party had no real opposition, though members of the Independence and Statehood parties were able to be elected as representatives and senators as a consequence of article III, section 7 of the new constitution, requiring minority-party representation when any one party won more than two-thirds of the votes in either chamber. Still, the reality was a virtually one-party political system, as Muñoz himself often lamented. The weak Socialist party actually disbanded prior to the 1956 elections, recommending to its members that they join the PPD.[148]

Attempts by PPD leaders to "culminate" and "perfect" the commonwealth status were rebuffed by Congress, and increasingly, as in the thirties, status became an issue again. For PPD supporters, the status of an "associated state" has the character of an agreement with the United States based upon mutuality. However, the reactions of the United States to PPD initiatives have led to extreme pessimism as to whether the United States shares this view. The response of Congress to proposals to renegotiate or clarify the terms and articles of association (particularly the rejection of the Fernós-Murray Bill in 1959) has created despair among the leaders of the PPD. To many members of Congress, however, as well as to supporters of independence and statehood on the island, the PPD has seemed to want a relation with the United States which combines the

---

[147] *Puerto Rico Business Review* 10 (July 1985) and special supplement of April 1985.

[148] Bayrón Toro, *Elecciones y partidos políticos*, p. 224.

benefits and powers that would come with being both a state and an independent nation while incurring neither the costs nor the responsibilities of either status. It was perhaps these contradictions in the PPD's position (to be discussed further below) that allowed the Statehood party to receive 32 percent of the votes in the 1960 election, a substantial gain over its showing in the previous election. The PPD, still supporting commonwealth status, received 58 percent.[149]

On July 23, 1967, a plebiscite was held to permit Puerto Ricans to express their status preference, with the hope of finally settling the question. The Estado Libre Asociado, or commonwealth, status received 60.4 percent of the vote; statehood, 39.0 percent; and independence, 0.6 percent. However, judging by the number of registered voters in 1964, abstention amounted to nearly 30 percent. Supporters of independence and statehood, believing the vote illegitimate, stayed away from the polls.[150] The results, then, while pleasing to PPD supporters, hardly amounted to a mandate for commonwealth status. The plebiscite thus did little to resolve the issue, after all.

Political divisions within the autonomist ranks in 1968 led to the election of Luis Ferré, a millionaire industrialist whose family had purchased the government corporations at the end of the state-capitalist experiment in the late 1940s, as the first pro-statehood governor. Ferré was a member of a new statehood party, the New Progressive Party (Partido Nuevo Progresista, or PNP), which captured the governorship but not a legislative majority. The PPD was back in power again from 1973 to 1977, but in 1976 and, very narrowly, in 1980, the gubernatorial post was returned to the PNP in the person of Carlos Romero Barceló, grandson of Antonio Barceló.[151] Though, as seen above, some changes in the details of the economic model (in particular, partial tax exemption) were initiated under Romero Barceló, its fundamentals went unchanged.

In 1984, former governor Rafael Hernández Colón of the PPD was returned to office. Prior to the elections, the statehood forces had divided into two parties (the new one being the Party of Puerto Rican Renewal— Partido de Renovación Puertorriqueña, led by former San Juan mayor Hernán Padilla), in a historical inversion of the split among the autonomists before the 1968 elections. The 1984 elections revealed, too, what may be the beginnings of a resurgence of the independence vote, partly the result of the crisis within the major parties but also perhaps one of the fruits of the unification which the independence forces have been striving for since a split in the Socialist party in 1982. Rubén Berríos,

[149] Ibid., p. 231, and Bayrón Toro, *Las elecciones de 1980*, pp. 4–5, 23–24.
[150] Bayrón Toro, *Elecciones y partidos políticos*, pp. 239, 245–46.
[151] Ibid., *Las elecciones de 1980*, pp. 32–33.

president of the Independence party, was elected to the Senate with one of the biggest at-large votes on record. Independence supporters are probably more influential than their small percentage of the vote (3.6 percent in 1984) might suggest, particularly in culture, the law, education, and other critical areas. In any event, the slightly higher pro-independence vote in 1984 reflects a growing dissatisfaction with the traditional economic model and with the solutions to Puerto Rico's social, economic, and political problems that continue to be proposed by the two centrist parties.

But the major political division remains that between the PNP and the PPD, between statehood and autonomous association. Ironically, the increasing strength of the statehood forces has been at least partly a consequence of the Operation Bootstrap development project launched by the PPD. The rapid transition from a rural, agrarian economy to a manufacturing and service economy undercut the PPD's traditional électoral base. Workers in the factories and in the banks and other support institutions of a modern economy, as well as the vast numbers of the idle and unemployed, have found in the PNP their "natural" protector. To many such voters, the PPD must seem to favor a return to the untrammeled exploitation of the past, as it requests exemption from the federal minimum wage, from environmental protection laws, and from a wide variety of other legislation protective of workers' rights.

Constrained by an economic model whose success depended upon Puerto Rico's remaining poor relative to the mainland, the PPD has been forced to take positions that are difficult to defend, and this has opened political space for the opposition. For example, while the PPD was arguing for exemption from the federal minimum wage, the PNP led the fight for its application; while the PNP advocates equal application of all federal spending and other programs to Puerto Rico, the PPD asks for selective exclusion, which commonwealth status permits and, in some cases, requires; and while the PNP charges that commonwealth status retains "vestiges of colonialism" and is undignified, the leaders of the PPD try to defend it, even though some of them believe it needs to be changed. Thus, the demographic and occupational transformations initiated by the PPD's economic program have created the base for the rise of the PNP, which, in many ways, has appropriated the populist mantle of the PPD.

The period since the mid-1970s has been one of the most politically tragic in forty years.[152] The details are too far removed from the subject

[152] The killings of independentistas Arnaldo Darío Rosado and Carlos Soto Arriví by the police at Cerro Maravilla on July 25, 1978, has resulted in charges of official assassination and of a high-level cover-up. Arrests of police and former officials of the Romero Barceló government have been made. There have been other unfortunate incidents—like the destruc-

of this study to warrant detailed description, but in many ways the events had roots very similar to those which precipitated the collapse of the thirties: continued economic stagnation and the unresolved issue of the island's status vis-à-vis the United States.

Another major item of political importance has been the now annual appearance of representatives of several of Puerto Rico's political parties—not including the PPD—before the UN Decolonization Committee, asking that Puerto Rico again be considered a colony of the United States, as it had been prior to the creation of the commonwealth status. This has focused international attention on the island, putting renewed pressure on policy makers to resolve the status issue. Whatever the ultimate decision, it is bound to have an impact on the economic conditions and possibilities.[153]

CONCLUSIONS

Since the 1940s, the Puerto Rican economy has exhibited dramatic growth in total output and income. Puerto Rico has left underdevelopment behind and has entered the ranks of the developing and industrialized nations, at least as measured by the level of per capita income and the size of the manufacturing sector in comparison to the rest of the world. Improvement in many social indicators has been quite marked, suggesting that this transformation has not just been in terms of overall economic growth, but that development has succeeded in meeting at least a significant part of the island's basic needs.

There are many examples of such improvement. The number of persons per physician decreased from 1,130 in 1960 to 534 in 1980, which is about the same as in the United States and better than the average for all industrial economies. Life expectancy has increased from 46 years in 1940 to 69 in 1960 and 73 in 1980, equal to that in societies with much

---

tion of the squatter community, Villa Sin Miedo, by the armed forces of the government—that are reminders of some of the worst periods of rule by U.S. colonial governors, but now it is Puerto Ricans repressing Puerto Ricans.

[153] For an excellent overview of recent political divisions and crises in Puerto Rico's parties, see Carr, *Puerto Rico*, esp. part 2. For the new party realignments, see R. Anderson, "Party System." For a useful discussion of the international dimension and Puerto Rico at the UN, see Carr, *Puerto Rico*, chap. 14, and Robert Pastor, "Puerto Rico as an International Issue: A Motive for a Movement," in Bloomfield, *Puerto Rico*, pp. 99–136. García-Passalacqua's recent book, *Puerto Rico*, is also valuable for its analysis of current policy options, and in many other ways as well. See also GAO, *Insular Policy*, for a discussion of possible future status options and a set of conclusions that have caused considerable controversy. (I am indebted to Juan M. García-Passalacqua for bringing this document to my attention and for invaluable conversations about it.)

higher levels of income. (Life expectancy in Venezuela, the only country in Latin America with a larger per capita GNP than Puerto Rico, is 67 years.) In 1974, 79.1 percent of families owned their homes (though only 16 percent could qualify to buy a house in 1970); more than 70 percent of dwellings had indoor toilets, 99.2 percent had television sets, and 94.4 percent had a refrigerator, though only 29 percent had a telephone.[154] The literacy rate rose from 68.5 percent in 1940 to 83 percent in 1960 and to 91.3 percent in 1976 (though this is below the literacy rate of the advanced capitalist countries and of most socialist nations, including Cuba).[155] Income distribution seemed to show a tendency to worsen until the mid-1960s, but the evidence since then, and even for that period, is inclusive.[156] There can be no question, then, that the Puerto Rican model of development has provided real material gains to the great majority of Puerto Ricans since the 1940s. While incomes and the standard of living remain well below those of the United States, to which Puerto Rico must be compared because of the relationship between them, they are well above almost every country in Latin America.

These social gains have come out of a complex model of economic and social development and control. The components of this model have been: (1) Industrial tax exemption and other incentives designed to attract mainland capital producing primarily for export (Operation Bootstrap). (2) Increases in public-sector employment. (3) Transfers by the federal government to individuals and the commonwealth government. (4) Expansion of public debt to finance social welfare programs and employment generation. (5) Unimpeded migration of surplus workers to the mainland. The five components of the model are interrelated, but the last four have been necessitated by the failure of the first, which is the fundamental part of the model, to provide for an adequate expansion of output, income, and employment within a viable economic structure. It should be added that these five components have functioned in a unique way within the "special"—i.e., colonial—relation that governs Puerto Rico. The model cannot readily be used in other countries, because components (3) and (5) would not be operative elsewhere.

[154] Jiménez de Ramírez, "Estudio de las condiciones de vida," pp. 40, 47–48, 54.

[155] Junta de Planificación, *Estadísticas sociales*, pp. 9–10, 13–14; *Puerto Rico Business Review*, special supplement, May 1984, p. 4, table 2; and World Bank, *World Development Report*, pp. 110–11, table 1, and pp. 152–53, table 22. In 1977, per pupil expenditure on education was $694, compared to $1,740 for the U.S. and $900 for Arkansas: Bonilla and Campos, "A Wealth of Poor," p. 163.

[156] Weisskoff, "Income Distribution," p. 210, table 10-1. In 1953, the Gini coefficient (a measure of the degree of equality of distribution, which ranges from 0, for perfect equality, to 1, for perfect inequality) was .428, but it rose to .471 in 1963: Maldonado, "Economic Costs and Benefits," tables 2 and 3, and Cao García, "Distribución del ingreso."

State expenditures in Puerto Rico, whether by the federal or the commonwealth government, are not typical Keynesian-type outlays that stimulate the local economy, increase GNP, and drive production to the full-employment level. Given the openness of the economy and the small domestic multiplier, spending has a greater impact on production in the United States than in Puerto Rico. Large state expenditures do lead to more consumer spending, which has made Plaza las Américas the busiest and most profitable shopping mall in the western hemisphere. These demand-side expenditures alone, however, cannot generate an integrated productive structure. Puerto Rico in the 1980s, as much as in the 1930s, suffers from a structurally disarticulated economy. Local demand is articulated to an external supply source; local supply is articulated to an external demand source. More federal spending without constructive measures to promote linkages between local supply and local demand simply perpetuates this structural defect.

Though industrial incentives in various forms have been seen as the key forces behind the "success" of Puerto Rico's development experience, they have succeeded only in perpetuating this structure of disarticulated production that has required federal and commonwealth government spending and the subsidization of housing, food, and public utilities at a level unique among capitalist market economies. The Puerto Rican economy and society could not have continued to function if the development program had consisted of Operation Bootstrap alone. As a development strategy in the wider sense of the term, it has been a failure. Operation Bootstrap provided neither adequate incomes nor sufficient employment. It has forced hundreds of thousands of workers and their families to migrate to the mainland to fill some of the lowest-paid positions there and to occupy some of the worst slums, worse even than the living conditions most left behind. Only through expanded state welfare expenditures and through migration has the economic crisis been prevented from deteriorating into chaos.

Operation Bootstrap, then, is a monument not to economic progress but to the costs and dangers inherent in a development program based upon capital-intensive, foreign-owned, vertically integrated, and export-oriented corporate expansion. This experiment has been carried out more fully in Puerto Rico than in any other country in the world, and the island's experience should serve as a lesson for other nations in what *not* to do. Yet, the Caribbean Basin Initiative (CBI), enacted by Congress in 1983, encourages other Caribbean nations to emulate the Puerto Rican strategy. Puerto Rico's initial objections to the CBI resulted in changes designed to minimize damage to its economy, and since then a new concept of "twin plants" has been advanced as a means by which Puerto

Rico can take advantage of the local-content provisions of the CBI.[157] An evaluation of the impact of the CBI on Puerto Rico and the region as a whole must await further analysis and the passage of time. But judging from what has happened in Puerto Rico since 1947, what is most likely to happen is an increase in the structural dependence of the countries involved on the U.S. and on external investment and a movement away from an internal growth dynamic. In this respect, the future is not bright. Economic growth may occur for some, as in Puerto Rico in the past, but the price to be paid is high: an inappropriate and locally disarticulated structure of production.

[157] Under this concept, a Puerto Rican subsidiary of a U.S. company sets up complementary ("twin") production facilities elsewhere in the Caribbean. The Puerto Rican subsidiary is responsible for skilled and high-technology work, while the "twin" plant carries out that part of the production process requiring less skill, thus enabling the company to take advantage of the lower wages available in other areas of the Caribbean. This strategy is an integral part of Fomento's and the commonwealth's efforts to link the continuation of 936 tax exemption (which benefits primarily corporations locating on the island and has been recently subjected to renewed criticism in Washington) to the future of the CBI, a potentially important component of U.S. economic and political policy in the Caribbean region. For background and details on the twin-plant concept, see *Puerto Rico Business Review* 9 (January–February 1984) and 10 (July 1985 and August–September 1985).

Bibliography

Adelman, Irma, and Cynthia Taft Morris. *Economic Growth and Social Equity in Developing Countries*. Stanford, Calif.: Stanford University Press, 1973.

Albizu Campos, Laura de. *Albizu Campos y la independencia de Puerto Rico*. New York: n. p., 1961.

Albizu Campos, Pedro. *La conciencia nacional puertorriqueña*. Edited by Manuel Maldonado-Denis. Mexico City: Siglo XXI, 1974.

————. *Obras escogidas, 1923–1936*. Vol. 1. San Juan: Jelofe, 1975.

Amin, Samir. *Accumulation on a World Scale*. New York: Monthly Review, 1974.

Anderson, Robert. "The Party System: Change or Stagnation." In Heine, *Time for Decision*, pp. 3–25.

Anderson, William S., ed. *Ballentine's Law Dictionary*. 3rd ed. San Francisco: Bancroft-Witney, 1969.

Andic, Fuat M. "Income of Wage Earner Families and Economic Development, 1941–1953." *Caribbean Studies* 2 (January 1963): 14–27.

Andreu Iglesias, Cesar, ed. *Memorias de Bernardo Vega*. Río Piedras: Huracán, 1977.

Azize, Yamila. *Luchas de la mujer en Puerto Rico, 1878–1919*. San Juan: Litografía Metropolitana, 1979.

Ballesteros, Paulino A. "External Capital in Puerto Rico's Industrial Development." Ph.D. diss., University of Illinois, 1959.

Baralt, Guillermo A. *Esclavos rebeldes: Conspiraciones y sublevaciones de esclavos en Puerto Rico, 1795–1873*. Río Piedras: Huracán, 1981.

Barton, H. C., Jr. *Puerto Rico Family Incomes*. San Juan: Puerto Rico Planning Board, 1953.

Baver, Sherrie L. "Public Policies and the Private Sector: The Case of Industrial Incentives in Puerto Rico." Paper presented at the annual meeting of the Latin American Studies Association, Bloomington, Ind., October 1980.

Bayrón Toro, Fernando. *Las elecciones de 1980*. Mayagüez: Isla, 1982.

————. *Elecciones y partidos políticos en Puerto Rico, 1809–1976*. Mayagüez: Isla, 1976.

Berbusse, Edward J. *The United States in Puerto Rico, 1891–1900*. Chapel Hill: University of North Carolina Press, 1966.

Bergad, Laird W. "Agrarian History of Puerto Rico, 1870–1930." *Latin American Research Review* 13, no. 3 (1978): 66–94.

————. "Coffee and Rural Proletarianization in Puerto Rico, 1840–1898." *Journal of Latin American Studies* 15 (May 1983): 83–100.

————. *Coffee and the Growth of Agrarian Capitalism in Nineteenth-Century Puerto Rico*. Princeton: Princeton University Press, 1983.

———. "Toward Puerto Rico's Grito de Lares: Coffee, Social Stratification, and Class Conflict." *Hispanic American Historical Review* 60 (November 1980): 617–42.

Bhaduri, Amit. "A Study in Agricultural Backwardness under Semi-Feudalism." *Economic Journal* 83 (March 1973): 120–37.

Bhana, Surendra. *The United States and the Development of the Puerto Rican Status Question, 1936–1968.* Lawrence: University Press of Kansas, 1975.

Bird, Esteban A. *Report on the Sugar Industry in Relation to the Social and Economic System of Puerto Rico.* Senate Document No. 1. San Juan: Bureau of Supplies, Printing, and Transportation, 1941.

Black, Henry C., et al. *Black's Law Dictionary.* 5th ed. St. Paul, Minn.: West, 1979.

Block, Fred. "Beyond Relative Autonomy: State Managers as Historical Subjects." In *The Socialist Register, 1980,* edited by Ralph Miliband and John Saville, pp. 227–42. London: Merlin, 1980.

Bloomfield, Richard J., ed. *Puerto Rico: The Search for a National Policy.* Boulder, Colo.: Westview, 1985.

Boggs, Carl. *Gramsci's Marxism.* London: Pluto, 1976.

Boletín Histórico de Puerto Rico. *Boletín histórico de Puerto Rico (BHPR).* 14 vols. San Juan, 1914–27.

Bonilla, Frank, and Ricardo Campos. "A Wealth of Poor: Puerto Ricans in the New International Order." *Daedalus* 110 (Spring 1981): 133–76.

Bonilla, Frank, and Hector Colón. "Puerto Rican Return Migration in the '70s." *Migration Today* 7 (April 1979): 7–12.

Booth, David. "André Gunder Frank: An Introduction and Appreciation." In *Beyond the Sociology of Development,* edited by Ivar Oxaal, Tony Barnett, and David Booth, pp. 50–85. London: Routledge and Kegan Paul, 1975.

Boserup, E. *The Condition of Agricultural Growth: The Economics of Agrarian Change under Population Pressure.* Chicago: Aldine, 1965.

Brau, Salvador, "Las clases jornaleras de Puerto Rico." In Brau, *Ensayos,* pp. 9–73.

———. *La colonización de Puerto Rico.* 1907. Reprint. San Juan: Instituto de Cultura Puertorriqueña, 1966.

———. *Ensayos: Disquisiciones sociológicas.* Río Piedras: Edil, 1972.

———. *Historia de Puerto Rico.* 1904. Reprint. Río Piedras: Edil, 1978.

Buitrago Ortiz, Carlos. *Los orígenes históricos de la sociedad precapitalista en Puerto Rico.* Río Piedras: Huracán, 1976.

Calero, Heidie. "Intent and Outcome of Local 936 Regulations." *Puerto Rico Business Review* 9 (September 1984): 3–8.

Cao García, Ramón J. "Distribución del ingreso en Puerto Rico: Unos comentarios y un nuevo análisis." *Revista de ciencias sociales* 21 (September-December 1979): 321–59.

Carr, Raymond. *Puerto Rico: A Colonial Experiment.* New York: New York University Press and Vintage Books, 1984.

Centro de Estudios Puertorriqueños (CENEP). *Documentos de la migración puertorriqueña, 1879–1901.* No. 1. New York: CENEP, 1977.

————. *Taller de migración*. New York: CENEP, 1975.

————. History Task Force. *Labor Migration under Capitalism: The Puerto Rican Experience*. New York: Monthly Review, 1979.

————. *Sources for the Study of Puerto Rican Migration, 1879–1930*. New York: CENEP, 1982.

Chase, Stuart. *"Operation Bootstrap" in Puerto Rico*. Pamphlet no. 75. Washington, D.C.: National Planning Association, 1951.

Chenery, Hollis, et al. *Redistribution with Growth*. New York: Oxford University Press, 1974.

Clark, Truman R. *Puerto Rico and the United States, 1917–1933*. Pittsburgh: University of Pittsburgh Press, 1975.

Clark, Victor S., et al. *Porto Rico and Its Problems*. Washington, D.C.: Brookings Institution, 1930.

Cohen, Sanford. "Puerto Rico's Development Paradox." *Growth and Change* 1 (July 1970): 3–7.

Colón de Zalduondo, Baltazara. *The Growing Puerto Rican Economy*. New York: Gordon, 1977.

Colton, George R. *Report of the Governor of Porto Rico, 1910*. Washington, D.C.: Government Printing Office, 1910.

Committee to Study Puerto Rico's Finances (Tobin Committee). *Report to the Governor*. December 11, 1975.

Connell-Smith, Gordon. *The United States and Latin America*. London: Heinemann, 1974.

Cordero, Rafael de J. *El progreso económico de Puerto Rico en los ultimos 50 años*. San Juan: Editorial del Departamento de Instrucción, 1952.

Córdova, Pedro Tomás de. *Memorias geográfica, histórica, económica, y estadística de la isla de Puerto Rico*. 6 vols. 1831–33. Reprint. San Juan: Instituto de Cultura Puertorriqueña, 1968.

Costello, Paul. "Capitalism, the State, and Crises." *Theoretical Review*, no. 20 (January-February 1981): 3–10.

Crist, Raymond E. "Sugar Cane and Coffee in Puerto Rico." *American Journal of Economics and Sociology* 7 (January, April, July 1948): 173–84, 321–37, 469–74.

Cruz Baez, Angel D. "Puerto Rico's Agriculture from 1950 to 1976: Trends and Perspectives (Notes for Further Study)." Paper presented at the Woodrow Wilson International Center for Scholars, Washington, D.C., April 1980.

Cruz Monclova, Lidio. *Historia de Puerto Rico (siglo XIX)*. 6 vols. Río Piedras: Editorial Universitaria, 1952–64.

Cubano Iguina, Astrid T. "Economía y sociedad en Arecibo en el siglo XIX: Los grandes productores y la inmigración de comerciantes." In *Inmigración y clases sociales*, edited by Francisco Scarano, pp. 67–124. Río Piedras: Huracán, 1981.

Cueva, Agustín. *El desarrollo del capitalismo in América Latina*. Mexico City: Siglo XXI, 1977.

Curet, José. *De la esclavitud a la abolición*. Working Papers 7. San Juan: Centro de la Realidad Puertorriqueña, 1979.

Curet Cuevas, Eliézer. *El desarrollo económico de Puerto Rico, 1940–1972.* Hato Rey: Management Aid Center, 1976.

Dalton, George, ed. *Primitive, Archaic, and Modern Economies: Essays of Karl Polyani.* Boston: Beacon, 1971.

Descartes, Sol L. *Basic Statistics on Puerto Rico.* Washington, D.C.: Office of Puerto Rico, 1946.

Díaz Hernández, Luis E. *Castañer: Una hacienda cafetalera en Puerto Rico, 1868–1930.* Ponce: Academia de Artes, Historia, y Arqueología de Puerto Rico, 1981.

Díaz Soler, Luis. *Historia de la esclavitud negra en Puerto Rico, 1493–1890.* Río Piedras: Editorial Universitaria, 1970.

Dietz, James L. "Delusions of Development." *Revista/Review Interamericana* 11 (Winter 1981-82): 472–75.

————. "Export-Enclave Economies, International Corporations, and Development." *Journal of Economic Issues* 19 (June 1985): 513–22.

————. "La falacia de desarrollo." *Pensamiento crítico* 5 (August-September 1982): 11–16.

————. "Imperialism and Underdevelopment: A Theoretical Perspective and a Case Study of Puerto Rico." *Review of Radical Political Economics* 11 (Winter 1979): 16–32.

————. "Puerto Rico in the 1970s and 1980s: Crisis of the Development Model." *Journal of Economic Issues* 16 (June 1982): 479–506.

————. "Puerto Rico's New History." *Latin American Research Review* 19 no. 1 (1984): 210–22.

————. "Stuck on Status: New Ideas about an Old Problem." *Caribbean Review* 14 (Summer 1985): 34–37, 46–47.

Diffie, Baily W., and Justine W. Diffie. *Porto Rico: A Broken Pledge.* New York: Vanguard, 1931.

Dobb, Maurice. *Studies in the Development of Capitalism.* New York: International, 1947.

Dowd, Douglas. *The Twisted Dream.* Cambridge, Mass.: Winthrop, 1977.

Duncan, Kenneth, and Ian Rutledge. *Land and Labour in Latin America.* Cambridge: Cambridge University Press, 1977.

Economic Commission for Latin America (ECLA). *Statistical Yearbook for Latin America, 1979.* New York: United Nations, 1981.

Economistas de Centro de Estudios de la Realidad Puertorriqueña. *La crisis económica de Puerto Rico.* Avances para discusión, no. 7. Río Piedras: CEREP, 1984.

Edel, Matthew D. "Land Reform in Puerto Rico." *Caribbean Studies* (October 1962): 26–60, and 2 (January 1963): 28–50.

Elliott, John E. *Comparative Economic Systems.* Englewood, N.J.: Prentice-Hall, 1973.

Elliott, J. H. *Imperial Spain, 1469–1716.* New York: St. Martin's, 1964.

Escobar, Manuel. "The 936 Market: Risk, Inflation, and Fixed Investment in Puerto Rico." *Puerto Rico Business Review* 6 (September 1981): 4–9.

Fernández Méndez, Eugenio. *Desarrollo histórico de la sociedad puertorriqueña*. San Juan: Instituto de Cultura Puertorriqueña, 1959.

———. *Historia cultural de Puerto Rico*. San Juan: Rodadero, 1964.

Figueroa, Loida. *Breve historia de Puerto Rico*. 2 vols. Río Piedras: Edil, 1977.

Fite, Gilbert C., and Jim E. Reese. *An Economic History of the United States*. 3rd ed. Boston: Houghton Mifflin, 1973.

Flinter, George D. *An Account of the Present State of the Island of Puerto Rico*. London: Longman, 1834.

Foner, Philip S. *The Spanish-Cuban-American War and the Birth of American Imperialism*. 2 vols. New York: Monthly Review, 1972.

Frank, André Gunder. *Capitalism and Underdevelopment in Latin America*. New York: Monthly Review, 1967.

———. "The Development of Underdevelopment." In Frank, *Latin America*, pp. 3–17.

———. *Latin America: Underdevelopment or Revolution*. New York: Monthly Review, 1969.

Freyre, Jorge F. *External and Domestic Financing in the Economic Development of Puerto Rico*. Río Piedras: University of Puerto Rico Press, 1969.

Furtado, Celso. *Economic Development in Latin America*. 2nd ed. London: Cambridge University Press, 1976.

Galeano, Eduardo. *Open Veins of Latin America*. New York: Monthly Review, 1973.

Galvin, Miles. "The Early Development of the Organized Labor Movement in Puerto Rico." *Latin American Perspectives* 3 (Summer 1976): 17–35.

———. *The Organized Labor Movement in Puerto Rico*. Rutherford, N.J.: Fairleigh Dickinson University Press, 1979.

García, Gervasio L., and A. G. Quintero Rivera. *Desafío y solidaridad: Breve historia del movimiento obrero puertorriqueño*. Río Piedras: Huracán, 1982.

García Martínez, Alfonso L. *Puerto Rico: Leyes fundamentales*. Río Piedras: Edil, 1978.

García Passalacqua, Juan M. "Luis Muñoz Marín: Visión y tragedia." *El nuevo día Sunday Magazine*, February 15, 1981, pp. 12–14.

———. *Puerto Rico: Freedom and Equality at Issue*. New York: Praeger, 1984.

Gayer, A. D., Paul T. Homan, and Earle K. Jones. *The Sugar Economy of Puerto Rico*. New York: Columbia University Press, 1938.

Gerschenkron, Alexander. *Economic Backwardness in Historical Perspective*. Cambridge: Harvard University Press, 1962.

Giménez, Martha E. "Population and Capitalism." *Latin American Perspectives* 4 (Fall 1977): 5–40.

Golding, Morton J. *A Short History of Puerto Rico*. New York: New American, 1973.

Gómez Acevedo, Labor. *Organización y reglamentación del trabajo en el Puerto Rico del siglo XIX*. San Juan: Instituto de Cultura Puertorriqueña, 1970.

González, Antonio. *La economía política de Puerto Rico*. San Juan: Editorial Cordillera, 1967.

González, José Luis. *El país de cuatro pisos y otros ensayos.* Río Piedras: Huracán, 1980.

Goodsell, Charles T. *Administration of a Revolution: Executive Reform in Puerto Rico under Governor Tugwell, 1941–46.* Cambridge: Harvard University Press, 1965.

Gould, Lyman J. *La Ley Foraker: Raíces de la política colonial de los Estados Unidos.* Río Piedras: UPR, 1969.

Gould, Maurice M., and Lincoln W. Higgie. *The Money of Puerto Rico.* Racine, Wis.: Whitman, 1962.

Government Accounting Office (GAO). *Issues Affecting U.S. Territory and Insular Policy.* Washington, D.C.: GAO, 1985. Rept. no. GAO/NSIAD-85-44.

Government Development Bank for Puerto Rico (GDB). *Special Economic Bulletin: The Economy of Puerto Rico.* December 1984.

———. *Monthly Economic Indicators.* November 1984.

Graaf, J. de V. *Theoretical Welfare Economics.* Cambridge: Cambridge University Press, 1967.

Gutiérrez, Elías R. *Factor Proportions, Technology Transmission, and Unemployment in Puerto Rico.* Río Piedras: Editorial Universitaria, 1977.

Hamilton, E. J. *American Treasure and the Price Revolution in Spain, 1501–1650.* Cambridge: Harvard University Press, 1934.

Hanson, Alice C., and Manuel A. Pérez. *Incomes and Expenditures of Wage Earners in Puerto Rico.* Bulletin no. 1. Puerto Rican Department of Labor, May 1, 1947.

Hanson, Earl Parker. *Transformation: The Story of Modern Puerto Rico.* New York: Simon and Schuster, 1955.

Heine, Jorge, ed. *Time for Decision: The United States and Puerto Rico.* Landham, Md.: North-South, 1983.

Herrero, José A. *La mitología del azúcar: Un ensayo en [la] historia económica de Puerto Rico, 1900–1970.* Working Paper no. 5. Río Piedras: Centro de Estudios de la Realidad Puertorriqueña, 1971.

Hill, Marianne T. "The Nutritional Assistance Program in Puerto Rico: Present Impact and Proposed Changes." *Puerto Rico Business Review* 7 (July-August 1982): 3–13.

———. "A Preliminary Assessment of the Economic Situation of Puerto Rico's Agriculture." *Puerto Rico Business Review* 8 (May 1983): special supplement.

Hobsbawm, E. J. *The Age of Revolution, 1789–1848.* New York: World, 1962.

Holbik, Karel, and Philip L. Swan. *Industrialization and Employment in Puerto Rico, 1950–1972.* Studies in Latin American Business, no. 16. Austin: Bureau of Business Research, University of Texas, 1975.

Hunt, William H. *Second Annual Report of the Governor of Porto Rico.* Washington, D.C.: Government Printing Office, 1902.

———. *Third Annual Report of the Governor of Porto Rico.* Washington, D.C.: Government Printing Office, 1903.

Hunter, Robert J. *Puerto Rico: A Survey of Historical, Economic, and Political*

Affairs. Report prepared for the House Committee on Interior and Insular Affairs. 86th Cong., 1st sess., 1959.

Jaffe, A. J. *People, Jobs, and Economic Development*. Glencoe, Ill.: Free Press, 1959.

Jessop, Bob. "Recent Theories of the Capitalist State." *Cambridge Journal of Economics* 1 (December 1977): 353–73.

Jiménez de Ramírez, Iris. "Estudio de las condiciones de vida de las familias de Puerto Rico y su relación con algunos factores socioeconómicos." Master's thesis, University of Puerto Rico, 1974.

Jiménez de Wagenheim, Olga. *Puerto Rico's Revolt for Independence: Grito de Lares*. Boulder, Colo.: Westview, 1985.

Johnson, Roberta Ann. *Puerto Rico: Commonwealth or Colony?* New York: Praeger, 1980.

Junta de Planificación. *Balanza de pagos, 1975*. San Juan: Junta de Planificación, 1976.

———. *Compendio de estadísticas sociales, 1979*. San Juan: Junta de Planificación, 1979.

———. *Informe económico al gobernador, 1976*. San Juan: Junta de Planificación, 1977.

———. *Informe económico al gobernador, 1980*. San Juan: Junta de Planificación, 1981.

———. *Informe económico al Gobernador, 1982–83*. 2 vols. San Juan: Junta de Planificación, 1984.

———. *Serie histórica del empleo, de desempleo, y grupo trabajador en Puerto Rico, 1979*. San Juan: Junta de Planificación, 1979.

Kloosterboer, W. *Involuntary Labour since the Abolition of Slavery*. 1960. Reprint. Westport, Conn.: Greenwood, 1976.

Koenig, Nathan. *A Comprehensive Agricultural Program for Puerto Rico*. Washington, D.C.: Government Printing Office, 1953.

Lenin, V. I. *Imperialism: The Highest Stage of Capitalism*. 1916. Reprint. New York: International, 1939.

Levine, Barry J. *Benjy López: A Picaresque Tale of Emigration and Return*. New York: Basic, 1980.

Lewis, Gordon K. *Notes on the Puerto Rican Revolution*. New York: Monthly Review, 1974.

———. *Puerto Rico: Freedom and Power in the Caribbean*. New York: Monthly Review, 1963.

Lewis, W. Arthur. "Economic Development with Unlimited Supplies of Labour." *Manchester School of Economic and Social Studies* 22 (May 1954): 139–91.

Lidin, Harold J. *History of the Puerto Rican Independence Movement, 19th Century*. Vol. 1. Maplewood, N.J.: Waterfront, 1981.

López, Adalberto. "The Beginnings of Colonization: Puerto Rico, 1493–1800." In López and Petras, *Puerto Rico*, pp. 12–41.

———. "Socio-Politico Developments in a Colonial Context: Puerto Rico in the Nineteenth Century." In López and Petras, *Puerto Rico*, pp. 42–86.

López, Adalberto, and James Petras, eds. *Puerto Rico and Puerto Ricans*. Cambridge, Mass.: Schenkman, 1974.

Love, Joseph. "Raúl Prebisch and the Origins of Unequal Exchange." *Latin American Research Review* 15, no. 3 (1980): 45–72.

Luque de Sánchez, María Dolores. *La ocupación norteamericana y la ley Foraker: La opinion pública puertorriqueña, 1898–1904*. Río Piedras: Editorial Universitaria, 1980.

McCreery, David. "Debt Servitude in Rural Guatemala, 1876–1936." *Hispanic American Historical Review* 63 (November 1983): 735–59.

McNamara, Robert S. *Address to the Board of Governors*. Washington, D.C.: World Bank, 1976.

Madera, José R. "The Strategy of Development." *Industrial Newsletter* (Puerto Rico Economic Development Administration) 22 (1982): 1–2.

Maldonado, Rita M. "The Economic Costs and Benefits of Puerto Rico's Political Alternatives." *Southern Economic Journal* 41 (October 1974): 267–82.

———. *The Role of the Financial Sector in the Economic Development of Puerto Rico*. Washington, D.C.: Federal Deposit Insurance Corporation, 1970.

Maldonado-Denis, Manuel. *The Emigration Dialectic: Puerto Rico and the USA*. New York: International, 1980.

———. *Hacia una interpretación marxista de la historia de Puerto Rico y otros ensayos*. Río Piedras: Editorial Antillana, 1977.

———. "Prospects for Latin American Nationalism: The Case of Puerto Rico." *Latin American Perspectives* 3 (Summer 1976): 36–45.

———. *Puerto Rico: A Socio-Historic Interpretation*. New York: Vintage, 1972.

Mann, Arthur T. "Economic Development, Income Distribution, and Real Income Levels: Puerto Rico, 1953–1977." *Economic Development and Cultural Change* 33 (April 1985): 485–502.

Marrero Velázquez, Wanda I. "The Economic Development Strategy and Unemployment in Puerto Rico." Master's thesis, University of Texas, 1981.

Marx, Karl. *Capital*. 3 vols. New York: International, 1967.

———. *The Eighteenth Brumaire of Louis Bonaparte*. New York: International, 1963.

Mass, Bonnie. "Puerto Rico: A Case Study of Population Control." *Latin American Perspectives* 14 (Winter 1977): 66–81.

Mathews, Thomas. *Luis Muñoz Marín*. New York: American R.D.M., 1967.

———. "The Political Background to Industrialization." In *El desarrollo socio-económico de Puerto Rico*, edited by Ronald Duncan, pp. 5–17. San Germán: Universidad Interamericana de Puerto Rico, 1979.

———. *Puerto Rican Politics and the New Deal*. Gainesville: University of Florida Press, 1960.

Mattos Cintrón, Wilfredo. *La política y lo político en Puerto Rico*. Mexico City: Era, 1980.

Meier, Gerald M. *Emerging from Poverty: The Economics That Really Matters*. New York: Oxford University Press, 1984.

Merrill-Ramírez, María. "Operation Bootstrap: A Critical Analysis of the Puerto Rican Development Program." Master's thesis, University of Texas, 1979.

————. "Puerto Rico: Economic Miracle or Welfare State?" Paper presented at the annual meeting of the Western Social Science Association, Denver, April 1982.

Mier, Mariano. "The 936 Funds: A View from the Banking Sector." *Puerto Rico Business Review*, Special Supplement, October 1982, pp. 10–12.

Mintz, Sidney W. *Caribbean Transformations*. Chicago: Aldine, 1974.

————. "Foreword." In *Sugar and Society in the Caribbean*, edited by Ramiro Guerra y Sánchez, pp. xi–xliv. New Haven: Yale University Press, 1964.

————. "Labor and Sugar in Puerto Rico and Jamaica, 1800–1850." *Comparative Studies in Society and History* 1 (March 1959): 273–81.

————. "A Note on the Definition of Peasantries." *Journal of Peasant Studies* 1 (1973): 91–106.

————. "The Rural Proletariat and the Problem of Rural Proletarian Consciousness." *Journal of Peasant Studies* 1 (April 1974): 291–325.

————. "The So-Called World System: Local Initiative and Local Response." *Dialectical Anthropology* 2 (November 1977): 253–70.

————. *Worker in the Cane: A Puerto Rican Life History*. 1960. Reprint. New York: W. W. Norton, 1974.

Miranda Quintero, Carmen. *On the Development of the Puerto Rican People*. New York, [1970?].

Montalvo, Roberto. *External Investment in Puerto Rico: The Role of the Government Development Bank for Puerto Rico*. San Juan: Government Development Bank, 1958.

Morales Carrión, Arturo. *Albores históricos del capitalismo en Puerto Rico*. Río Piedras: Editorial Universitaria, 1972.

————. *Puerto Rico and the Non-Hispanic Caribbean*. Río Piedras: University of Puerto Rico Press, 1952.

Moscoso, Francisco. "Chiefdom and Encomienda in Puerto Rico: The Development of Tribal Society and the Spanish Colonization to 1530." In *The Puerto Ricans*, edited by Adalberto López, pp. 3–24. Cambridge, Mass.: Schenkman, 1980.

Moscoso, Teodoro. "Orígen y desarrollo de la 'Operación Manos a la Obra.'" In Navas Dávila, *Cambio y desarrollo*, pp. 161–69.

Mundie, John. "The Role of the Government Development Bank in Puerto Rico's Economic Program." Ph.D. diss., University of Texas, 1960.

Muñoz Marín, Luis. *Memorias, 1898–1940*. San Juan: Universidad Interamericana de Puerto Rico, 1982.

————. "Muñoz Marín recapítula desarrollo del pensamiento político sobre el status." Speech delivered at Barranquitas, Puerto Rico, July 17, 1951.

Naipaul, V. S. *The Loss of El Dorado*. New York: Alfred A. Knopf, 1969.

Natal, Carmelo Rosario. *Exodo puertorriqueño: Las emigraciones al Caribe y Hawaii, 1900–1915*. San Juan, 1983.

Navas Dávila, Gerardo, ed. *Cambio y desarrollo en Puerto Rico: La transformación del Partido Popular Democrático*. Río Piedras: Editorial Universitaria, 1980.

———. *La dialéctica del desarrollo nacional: El caso de Puerto Rico.* Río Piedras: Editorial Universitaria, 1978.

Negrón de Montilla, Aida. *Americanization, Puerto Rico, and the Public School System, 1900–1930.* Río Piedras: Editorial Universitaria, 1975.

Negrón-Portillo, Mariano. *El autonomismo puertorriqueño: Su transformación ideológica, 1895–1914.* Río Piedras: Huracán, 1981.

North American Congress on Latin America (NACLA). "Puerto Ricans on Contract." *NACLA Report on the Americas* 11 (November-December 1977): 18–28.

———. "Puerto Rico: The End of Autonomy." *NACLA Report on the Americas* 5 (March-April 1981): entire issue.

———. "Puerto Rico to New York: The Profit Shuttle." *NACLA's Latin America and Empire Report* 10 (April 1976): 11–13.

———. *Yanqui Dollar.* Berkeley, Calif.: NACLA, 1971.

Ortiz, Altagracio. *Eighteenth-Century Reforms in the Caribbean: Miguel de Muesas, Governor of Puerto Rico, 1769–76.* Rutherford, N.J.: Fairleigh Dickinson Press, 1983.

Pagán, Bolívar. *Historia de los partidos políticos puertorriqueños.* 2 vols. San Juan: Campos, 1972.

Palloix, Christian. *La internacionalización del capital.* Madrid: H. Blume, 1978.

———. "The Internationalization of Capital and the Circuit of Social Capital." In *International Firms and Modern Imperialism,* edited by Hugo Radice, pp. 63–88. Baltimore, Md: Penguin, 1975.

Pantojas-García, Emilio. "Estrategias de desarrollo y contradicciones ideológicas en Puerto Rico, 1940–1978." *Revista de ciencias sociales* 21 (March-June 1979): 73–117.

Pedreira, Antonio S. *El año terrible del 87.* Río Piedras: Edil, 1968.

Peoples Press. *Puerto Rico: The Flame of Resistance.* San Francisco: Peoples, 1979.

Perloff, Harvey. *Puerto Rico's Economic Future.* Chicago: University of Chicago Press, 1950.

Picó, Fernando. *Amargo café: Los pequeños y medianos caficultores de Utuado en la segunda mitad del siglo XIX.* Río Piedras: Huracán, 1981.

———. "Deshumanización del trabajo, cosificación de la naturaleza: Los comienzos del café en el Utuado del siglo XIX." In *Inmigración y clases sociales,* edited by Francisco A. Scarano, pp. 187–206. Río Piedras: Huracán, 1981.

———. *Libertad y servidumbre en el Puerto Rico del siglo XIX.* Río Piedras: Huracán, 1979.

Picó, Rafael. *The Geography of Puerto Rico.* Chicago: Aldine, 1974.

Piore, Michael J., and Peter Montiel. "Youth Unemployment and Economic Development Strategy in Puerto Rico." Paper prepared for the Government Development Bank, July 1978.

Poulantzas, Nicos. *Political Power and Social Classes.* London: New Left, 1973.

———. *State, Power, Socialism.* London: New Left, 1978.

Presser, Harriet B. "Changes in the Labor Force Status of Puerto Rican Women."

Paper presented at the annual meeting of the Caribbean Studies Association, Charlotte Amalie, St. Thomas, V.I., May 1981.

————. *Sterilization and Fertility Decline in Puerto Rico.* Berkeley, Calif.: Institute of International Studies, 1973.

Puerto Rico. Administración de Fomento Económico (PRAFE). *El desarrollo económico de Puerto Rico durante los ultimos veinte años.* San Juan: Fomento, 1971.

————. *Puerto Rico Official Industrial Directory, 1980.* 12th ed. San Juan: Witcom, 1980.

Puerto Rico. Department of Agriculture and Commerce (PRDAC). *Annual Book on Statistics, 1934–35.* San Juan, 1935.

————. *Annual Book on Statistics, 1935–36.* San Juan, 1936.

————. *Annual Book on Statistics of Puerto Rico, 1943–44.* San Juan, 1944.

Puerto Rico. Department of Labor (PRDL). *Annual Report, 1936–37.* San Juan: Bureau of Supplies, Printing, and Transportation, 1937.

Puerto Rico. Department of the Treasury (PRDT). *Economy and Finances, 1976.* San Juan: General Services Administration, 1977.

————. *Economy and Finances, 1978.* San Juan: General Services Administration, 1979.

Puerto Rico. Economic Development Administration (PREDA). *New Manufacturing Firms.* San Juan: Economic Development Administration, 1953.

————. *A Profile of the Labor Force in Puerto Rico, November 1983.* San Juan: Economic Development Administration, 1983.

————. Industrial Development Company (PRIDCO). *Annual Report 1942–1982.* San Juan: Economic Development Administration, 1982.

Puerto Rico. Planning Board (PRPB). *Economic Development of Puerto Rico, 1940–1950, 1951–1960.* San Juan, 1951.

Puerto Rico. Puerto Rican Policy Commission (PRPC). *Report of the Puerto Rican Policy Commission* (Chardón Report). June 14, 1934.

Quintero Rivera, Angel G. "Background to the Emergence of Imperialist Capitalism in Puerto Rico." In López and Petras, *Puerto Rico*, pp. 87–117.

————. "La base social de la transformación ideológica del Partido Popular en la década del '40." In Navas Dávila, *Cambio y desarrollo*, pp. 35–119.

————. *Conflictos de clase y política en Puerto Rico.* Río Piedras: Huracán, 1976.

————. "El desarrollo de clases sociales y los conflictos políticos en Puerto Rico." In *Problemas de desigualidad social en Puerto Rico*, edited by Rafael L. Ramírez, Barry B. Levine, and Carlos Buitrago Ortiz, pp. 31–75. Río Piedras: Librería Internacional, 1972.

————. "Socialist and Cigarmaker: Artisans' Proletarianization in the Making of the Puerto Rican Working Class." *Latin American Perspectives* 10 (Spring-Summer 1983): 19–38.

————. *Workers' Struggles in Puerto Rico.* New York: Monthly Review, 1976.

Raffucci de García, Carmen I. *El gobierno civil y la ley Foraker.* Río Piedras: Editorial Universitaria, 1981.

Ramos Mattei, Andrés A. *La hacienda azucarera: Su crecimiento y crisis en*

Puerto Rico (siglo XIX). San Juan: Centro de Estudios de la Realidad Puertorriqueña, 1981.

————. "La importación de trabajadores contratados para la industria azucarera puertorriqueña, 1860–80." in *Inmigración y clases sociales*, edited by Francisco A. Scarano, pp. 125–41. Rio Píedras: Huracán, 1981.

————. "Las inversiones norteamericanas en Puerto Rico y la ley Foraker, 1898–1900." *Caribbean Studies* 14 (October 1974): 53–69.

————. "El liberto en el régimen de trabajo azucarero de Puerto Rico, 1870–1880. In *Azúcar y esclavitud*, edited by Andrés A. Ramos Mattei, pp. 91–124. Río Piedras: Universidad de Puerto Rico, 1982.

Rivera Quintero, Marcia. "Educational Policy and Female Labor, 1898–1930." In Závala and Rodríguez, *Intellectual Roots*, pp. 349–53.

Robertson, Ross M., and Gary M. Walton. *History of the American Economy*. New York: Harcourt Brace Jovanovich, 1979.

Rodríguez, Alma I. "Inversión, reinversión, y empleo en las empresas promovidas por Fomento, 1954–1958." Master's thesis, University of Puerto Rico, 1960.

Rodríguez, Artemio P. *A Report on Wages and Working Hours in Various Industries and on the Cost of Living, in the Island of Puerto Rico, during the Year 1933*. San Juan: Bureau of Supplies, Printing, and Transportation, 1934.

Roosevelt, Theodore. "Colonial Policies of the United States." In López and Petras. *Puerto Rico*, pp. 164–74.

Rosario, José C. *The Development of the Puerto Rican Jíbaro and His Present Attitude towards Society*. Monographs of the University of Puerto Rico, ser. C (Social Sciences), no. 1. Río Piedras: University of Puerto Rico, 1935.

Ross, David. *The Long Uphill Path: A Historical Study of Puerto Rico's Program of Economic Development*. San Juan: Edil, 1969.

Ruiz, Angel L. "The Impact of Economic Recession on the Puerto Rican Economy: An Input-Output Approach." *Caribbean Studies* 16 (October 1976–January 1977): 125–48.

Ruiz Belvis, Segundo, José Julián Acosta, and Francisco Mariano Quiñones. *Proyecto para la abolición de la esclavitud en Puerto Rico*. 1867. Reprint. Río Piedras: Edil, 1978.

Sahlins, Marshall. *Stone Age Economics*. Chicago: Aldine, 1972.

Saldaña, Jorge E. *El café en Puerto Rico*. San Juan: Real Hermanos, 1935.

Sánchez Dergan, Joselo. "La industria azucarera operada por el gobierno de Puerto Rico." Master's thesis, University of Puerto Rico, 1975.

Sánchez Tarniella, Andrés. *La economía de Puerto Rico*. 5th ed. Río Piedras: Bayoán, 1973.

Santana Rabell, Leonardo. *Planificación y política durante la administración de Luis Muñoz Marín: Un análisis crítico*. Santurce, P.R.: Análisis, 1984.

Santiago, Ana. "El control de precios en Puerto Rico." Master's thesis, University of Puerto Rico, 1963.

Santiago, Carlos E. "How Significant Is the 'Discouraged-Worker' Effect in Puerto Rico?" *Puerto Rico Business Review* 6 (July-August 1981): 3–10.

————. "Human Resources and Economic Growth in Puerto Rico." *Wayne Economic Papers*, no. 124. Detroit: Wayne State University, 1981.

————. "Import Substitution in Puerto Rico: An Empirical Study." Master's thesis, University of Puerto Rico, 1975.

————. "Male-Female Labor Force Participation and Rapid Industrialization." Detroit: Wayne State University, 1982. Photocopy.

Santiago, Jaime. "The Puerto Rican Economy: A Big Challenge Ahead." Paper presented at the Woodrow Wilson International Center for Scholars, Washington, D.C., April 1980.

Santiago, K. Antonio. "La concentración y la centralización de la propiedad en Puerto Rico, 1898–1929." *Homines* 8 (January 1984): 129–56.

Sarmiento, Manuel F. "Treasury Department Update on the Use of 936 Funds." *Puerto Rico Business Review* 8 (October 1983): 2–4.

Scarano, Francisco A. "Azúcar y esclavitud en Puerto Rico: La formación de haciendas en Ponce, 1815–1849." In *Azúcar y esclavitud*, edited by Andrés A. Ramos Mattei, pp. 13–52. Río Piedras: Universidad de Puerto Rico, 1982.

————. "Sugar and Slavery in Puerto Rico: The Municipality of Ponce, 1815–1849." Ph.D. diss., Columbia University, 1978.

Scitovsky, Tibor. *The Joyless Economy*. New York: Oxford University Press, 1976.

Seers, Dudley, "The Meaning of Development." *International Development Review* 11 (December 1969): 2–6.

Senior, Clarence. *Santiago Iglesias*. Hato Rey: Interamerican University Press, 1972.

Serralles, Jorge J. *Farm Prices and Price Relationships of Sugar Cane in Puerto Rico from 1910 to 1945*. Bulletin no. 71. Río Piedras: Agriculture Experiment Station, University of Puerto Rico, 1947.

Silén, Juan Angel. *Apuntes para la historia del movimiento obrero puertorriqueño*. Río Piedras: Cultural, 1978.

————. *Historia de la nación puertorriqueña*. Río Piedras: Edil, 1973.

————. *Pedro Albizu Campos*. Río Piedras: Editorial Antillana, 1976.

————. *We, the Puerto Rican People*. New York: Monthly Review, 1971.

Silvestrini [de Pacheco], Blanca G. "La mujer puertorriqueña y el movimiento obrero en la década de 1930." In *La mujer en la sociedad puertorriqueña*, edited by Edna Acosta-Belén, pp. 67–90. Río Piedras: Huracán, 1980.

————. *Los trabajadores puertorriqueños y el Partido Socialista, 1932–1940*. Río Piedras: Editorial Universitaria, 1979.

Smith, Dudley. *Puerto Rico's Trade with Continental United States*. Washington, D.C.: Association of Sugar Producers of Puerto Rico, [1937?].

————. *Some Standards for Measuring Puerto Rico's Economic and Social Progress*. Washington, D.C.: Association of Sugar Producers of Puerto Rico, 1937.

Smith, Dudley, and William Requa. *Puerto Rico Sugar Facts*. Washington, D.C.: Association of Sugar Producers of Puerto Rico, 1939.

Stahl, John E. "Economic Development through Land Reform in Puerto Rico."
Ph.D. diss., Iowa State University, 1966.

Stead, William H. *Fomento: The Economic Development of Puerto Rico*. Washington, D.C.: National Planning Association, 1958.

Stein, Stanley J., and Barbara H. Stein. *The Colonial Heritage of Latin America*.
New York: Oxford University Press, 1970.

Steiner, Stan. *The Islands*. New York: Harper and Row, 1974.

Steward, Julian, et al. *The People of Puerto Rico*. Urbana: University of Illinois
Press, 1956.

Streeten, Paul. *First Things First*. New York: Oxford University Press, 1981.

Stubbs, Jean. *Tobacco on the Periphery: A Case Study in Cuban Labour History,
1860–1958*. Cambridge: Cambridge University Press, 1985.

Suarez Díaz, Ada. *El Doctor Ramón Emeterio Betances y la abolición de la
esclavitud*. San Juan: Instituto de Cultura Puertorriqueña, 1980.

Taller de Formación Política. *¡Huelga en la caña!* Río Piedras: Huracán, 1982.

Taylor, Milton C. *Industrial Tax Exemption in Puerto Rico*. Madison: University
of Wisconsin Press, 1957.

Thurow, Lester. *The Zero-Sum Society*. New York: Penguin, 1981.

Torres de Romero, Conchita. *El desempleo en Puerto Rico y sus principales
cambios estructurales, 1950 a 1964*. Río Piedras: Editorial Universitaria,
1966.

Torruellas, Luz M., and José L. Vázquez. *Los puertorriqueños que regrasaron:
Un análisis de su participación laboral*. Río Piedras: Centro de Investigaciones Sociales, 1982.

Tuchman, Barbara. *The Proud Tower*. New York: Macmillan, 1966.

Tugwell, Rexford Guy. *Puerto Rican Public Papers*. San Juan: Service Office of
the Government of Puerto Rico, 1945.

———. *The Stricken Land*. Garden City, N.Y.: Doubleday, 1947.

U.S. Bureau of the Census. *Historical Statistics of the United States*. Washington, D.C.: Government Printing Office, 1975.

———. *1980 Census of Population and Housing* (Advance Reports). January
1982.

———. *1970 Census of Population*. Vol. 1, *Characteristics of the Population*,
part 53, *Puerto Rico*. Washington, D.C.: Government Printing Office, 1973.

———. *1977 Economic Census of Outlying Areas, Puerto Rico, Manufactures*.
Washington, D.C.: Government Printing Office, 1980.

———. *Statistical Abstract of the United States, 1984*. Washington, D.C.: Government Printing Office, 1983.

———. *World Population, 1979*. Washington, D.C.: Government Printing Office, 1980.

U.S. Commission on Civil Rights. *Puerto Ricans in the Continental United States:
An Uncertain Future*. Washington, D.C., 1976.

U.S. Comptroller General (USCG). *Puerto Rico's Political Future: A Divisive
Issue with Many Dimensions*. Report to the Congress of the U.S., March 2,
1981.

U.S. Congress. House. Committee on Ways and Means. *Tax Reform Act of 1976*. 94th Cong., 1st sess., 1975. H. Rept. 94-658.

U.S. Department of Commerce (USDC). *Economic Study of Puerto Rico*. 2 vols. Washington, D.C.: Government Printing Office, 1979.

U.S. Department of Labor (USDL). *Labor Conditions in Porto Rico*. Washington, D.C.: Government Printing Office, 1919.

U.S. Department of War (USDW). *Census of Porto Rico, 1899*. Washington, D.C.: Government Printing Office, 1900.

Vélez Ortiz, Benito. "Methodology and Problems in Computing and Comparing the Rates of Inflation in Puerto Rico and the U.S. Mainland." *Puerto Rico Business Review* 6 (September 1981): 9–13.

Vicente-Chandler, José. "Potencial y problemas básicos en la producción de alimentos en Puerto Rico." Mayagüez: Estación Experimental Agrícola, Universidad de Puerto Rico, 1974.

Vidal Vázquez, Julio. "A Political Economy of Puerto Rico: Underdevelopment, Negative Growth, and Human Capital, 1950–1970." Albany: State University of New York, 1980. Photocopy.

Villar Roces, Mario. *Puerto Rico y su reforma agraria*. Río Piedras: Edil, 1968.

Wagenheim, Kal. *The Puerto Ricans: A Documentary History*. Garden City, N.Y.: Anchor, 1973.

Wallerstein, Immanuel. *The Modern World System*. New York: Academic, 1974.

Wasow, Bernard. "Saving and Dependence with Externally Financed Growth." *Review of Economics and Statistics* 61 (February 1970): 150–54.

Weaver, Frederick Stirton. "Capitalist Development, Empire, and Latin American Underdevelopment: An Interpretative Essay on Historical Change." *Latin American Perspectives* 3 (Fall 1976): 17–53.

Weisskoff, Richard. "Crops vs. Coupons: Food Stamps and Agricultural Development in Puerto Rico." In Heine, *Time for Decision*, pp. 135–81.

———. "Income Distribution and Export Promotion in Puerto Rico." In *Advances in Input-Output Analysis*, edited by K. Polenske and J. Skolka, pp. 205–28. New York: Ballinger, 1976.

Weisskoff, Richard, and Edward Wolff. "Development and Trade Dependence: The Case of Puerto Rico, 1948–1963." *Review of Economics and Statistics* 57 (November 1975): 470–77.

———. "Linkages and Leakages: Industrial Tracking in an Enclave Economy." *Economic Development and Cultural Change* 25 (July 1977): 607–28.

Wessman, James W. "The Demographic Structure of Slavery in Puerto Rico: Some Aspects of Agrarian Capitalism in the Late Nineteenth Century." *Journal of Latin American Studies* 12 (November 1980): 271–89.

———. "Is There a Plantation Mode of Reproduction? Comparative Evidence from Puerto Rico and Cuba." 1977. Photocopy.

———. "The Sugar Cane Hacienda in the Agrarian Structure of Southwestern Puerto Rico in 1902." *Revista/Review Interamericana* 8 (Spring 1978): 99–115.

———. "Theory of Value, Labor Process, and Price Formation: A Study of a

Puerto Rican Sugarcane Hacienda.'' *American Ethnologist* 7 (August 1980): 479–92.

———. ''Towards a Marxist Demography: A Comparison of Puerto Rican Landowners, Peasants, and Rural Proletarians.'' *Dialectical Anthropology* 2 (August 1977): 223–33.

Wolf, Eric. ''San José: Subcultures of a 'Traditional' Coffee Municipality.'' In Steward et al., *People of Puerto Rico*, pp. 171–264.

Wood, Charles H. ''Infant Mortality Trends and Capitalist Development in Brazil: The Case of São Paulo and Belo Horizonte.'' *Latin American Perspectives* 4 (Fall 1977): 56–65.

Woodward, Robert S. ''Intra-Island Industrial Incentives in Puerto Rico.'' *Review of Regional Studies* 4 (Spring 1974): 50–61.

World Bank. *Poverty and Basic Needs*. Washington, D.C.: World Bank, 1980.

———. *World Development Report, 1979*. Washington, D.C.: World Bank, 1979.

———. *World Development Report, 1982*. New York: Oxford University Press, 1982.

Závala, Iris M., and Rafael Rodríguez, eds. *The Intellectual Roots of Independence: An Anthology of Puerto Rican Political Essays*. New York: Monthly Review, 1980.

Index

LIBRARY OF CONGRESS CATALOGING-IN-PUBLICATION DATA

Dietz, James L., 1947–
Economic history of Puerto Rico.

Bibliography: p.
Includes index.
1. Puerto Rico—Economic conditions.   2. Puerto Rico—Commerce—History.
3. Investments—Puerto Rico—History.   4. Capitalism—Puerto Rico—History.
5. Puerto Rico—History.   I. Title.

HC154.5.D54 1986   330.97295   86-12313
ISBN 0-691-07716-9 (alk. paper)   ISBN 0-691-02248-8 (pbk.)